LIFE ™

Volume 9

Created by
Keiko Suenobu

TOKYOPOP®

HAMBURG // LONDON // LOS ANGELES // TOKYO

LIFE Volume 9
Created by Keiko Suenobu

Translation - Michelle Kobayashi
English Adaptaion - Darcy Lockman
Copy Editor - Shannon Watters
Retouch and Lettering - Star Print Brokers
Graphic Designer - James Lee
Production Artist - Lauren O'Connell

Editor - Stephanie Duchin
Digital Imaging Manager - Chris Buford
Pre-Production Supervisor - Lucas Rivera
Production Manager - Elisabeth Brizzi
Managing Editor - Vy Nguyen
Creative Director - Anne Marie Horne
Editor-in-Chief - Rob Tokar
Publisher - Mike Kiley
President and C.O.O. - John Parker
C.E.O. and Chief Creative Officer - Stu Levy

A  Manga

TOKYOPOP Inc.
5900 Wilshire Blvd. Suite 2000
Los Angeles, CA 90036

E-mail: info@TOKYOPOP.com
Come visit us online at www.TOKYOPOP.com

ISBN: 978-1-59816-196-0

First TOKYOPOP printing: June 2008
10 9 8 7 6 5 4 3 2 1
Printed in the USA

ラ
イ
フ

Life

9

CONTENTS

ライフ

9

Life

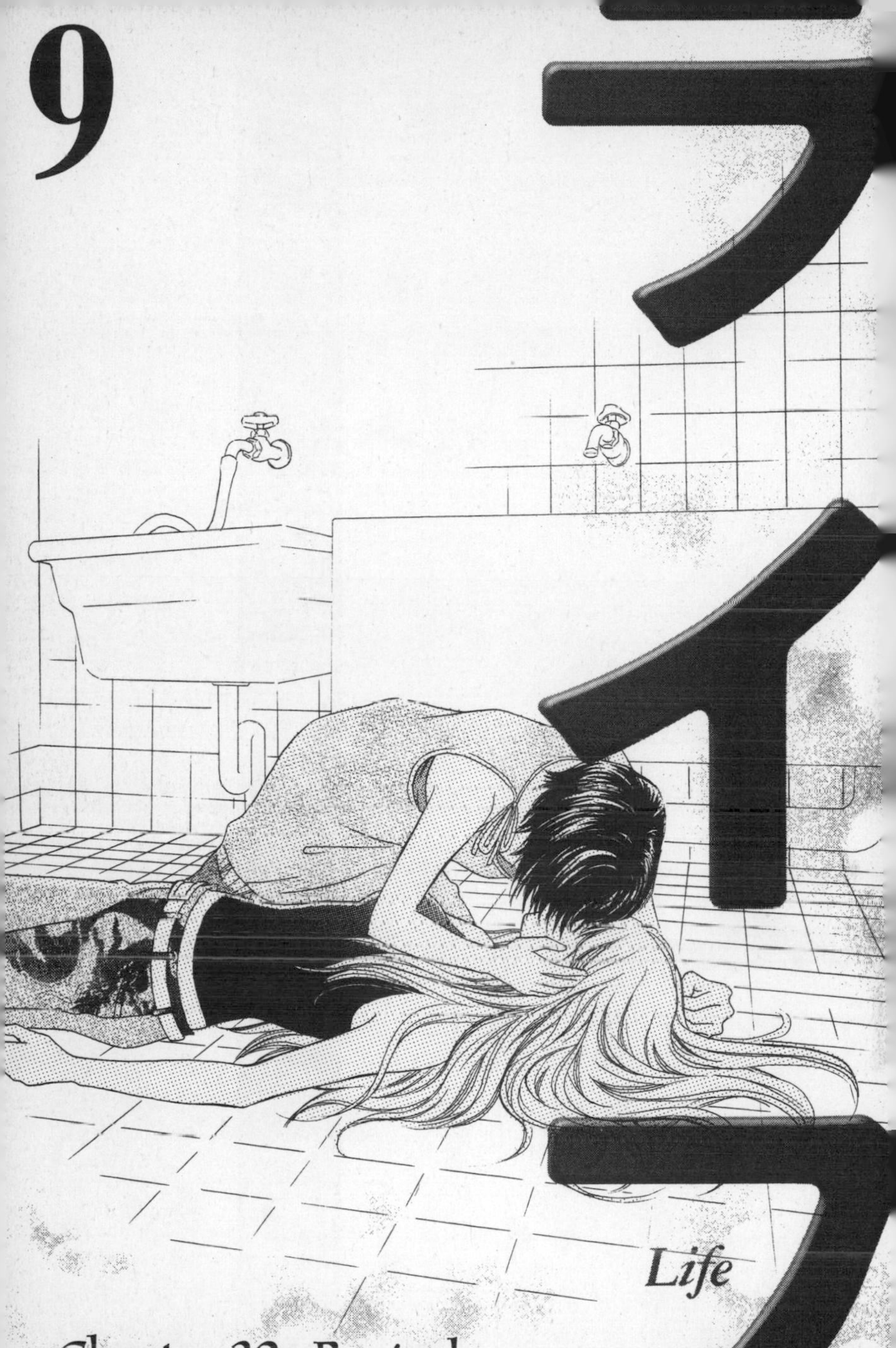
9
ライフ
Life

Chapter 32: Revival

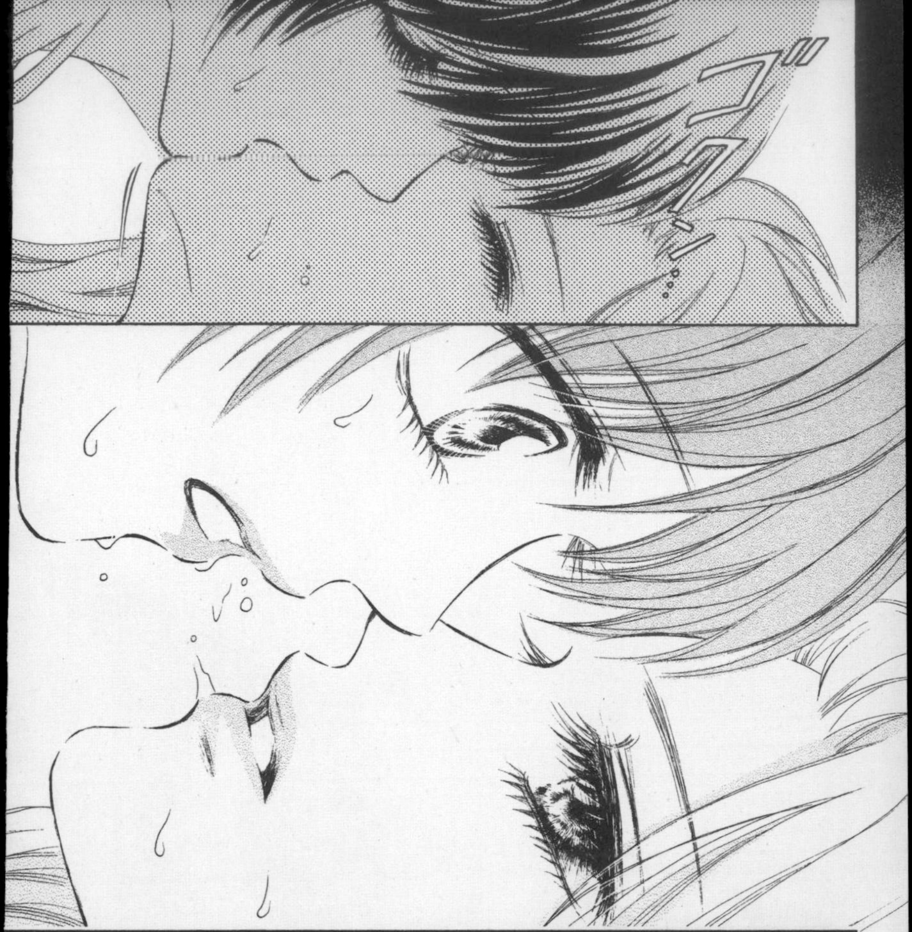

The real story of life

ライフ *Life*

The Story So Far

Ayumu is a troubled girl who deals with pain and loneliness by cutting herself. After Manami--her only friend at her new school--became convinced that Ayumu was trying to steal her evil boyfriend Katsumi, the girls in Manami's clique began to torture her at every opportunity. Things got both better and worse for Ayumu when she befriended Miki, another school outcast. Miki understood Ayumu's pain, and gave her a wristband to cover her scars. Ayumu decided she had to begin standing up to her tormentors. In her efforts, she soon had help from Sonoda, a boy in her class who could no longer stand watching her be abused. Ayumu was overjoyed to have another friend. Manami, however, was not pleased with this development. So she convinced the delinquent Akira to kidnap Ayumu. When Miki went to search for her friend, she, too, fell victim to Akira. Confined in a room together, the friends resolve to make it out alive.

Akira Karino

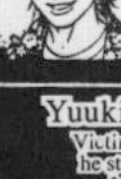

Juvenile delinquent who's infatuated by Manami. At Manami's request, he and his gang attacked and then kidnapped Ayumu and Miki.

Katsumi Sako

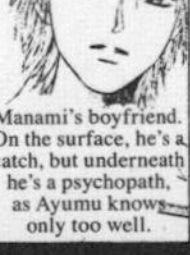

Manami's boyfriend. On the surface, he's a catch, but underneath he's a psychopath, as Ayumu knows only too well.

Manami Anzai

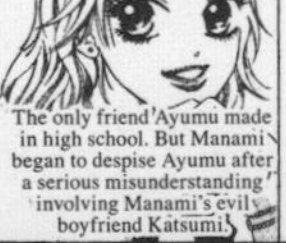

The only friend Ayumu made in high school. But Manami began to despise Ayumu after a serious misunderstanding involving Manami's evil boyfriend Katsumi.

Miki Hatori

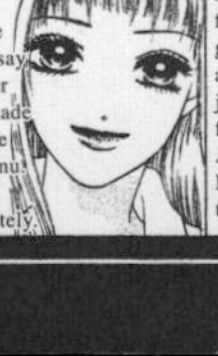

Because she has a part-time job waitressing at a strip club, the girls at school say she's a slut. Her kindness has made her a secret role model for Ayumu. She supports Ayumu completely.

Ayumu Shiiba

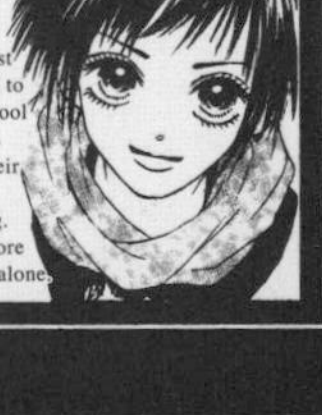

A 10th grader in high school. Her brainy best friend Shi-chan failed to get in to the same school as her, and Shi-chan's jealousy destroyed their friendship. After that, Ayumu started cutting. Nothing scares her more than being hated and alone.

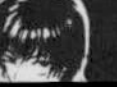

Yuuki Sonoda

Victimized by Akira in junior high, he stepped in to save Ayumu from

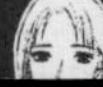

Toda

Homeroom Instructor

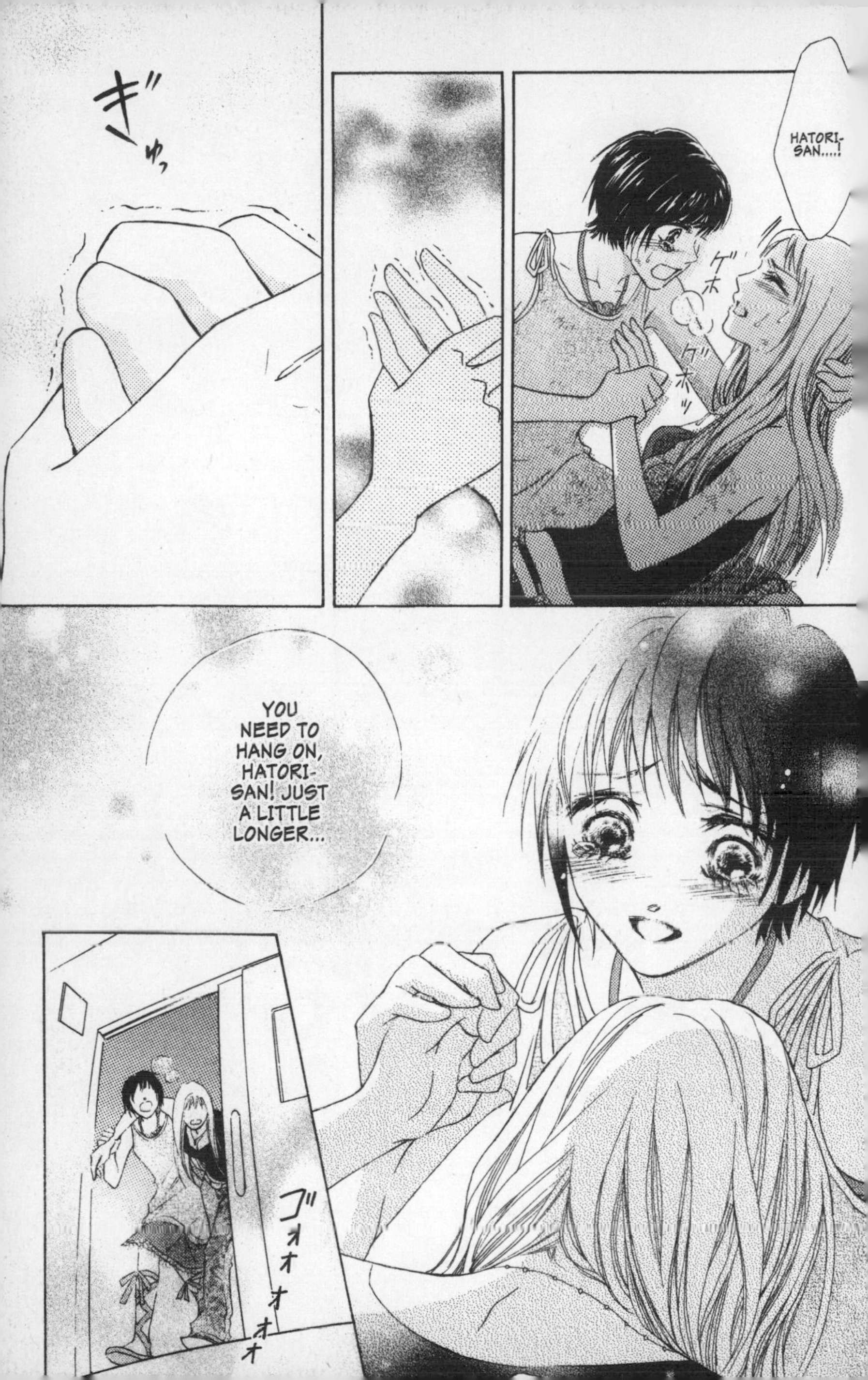
HATORI-SAN....!
ゲホ
ゲホッ
ぎゅっ
YOU NEED TO HANG ON, HATORI-SAN! JUST A LITTLE LONGER...
ゴォオオオ

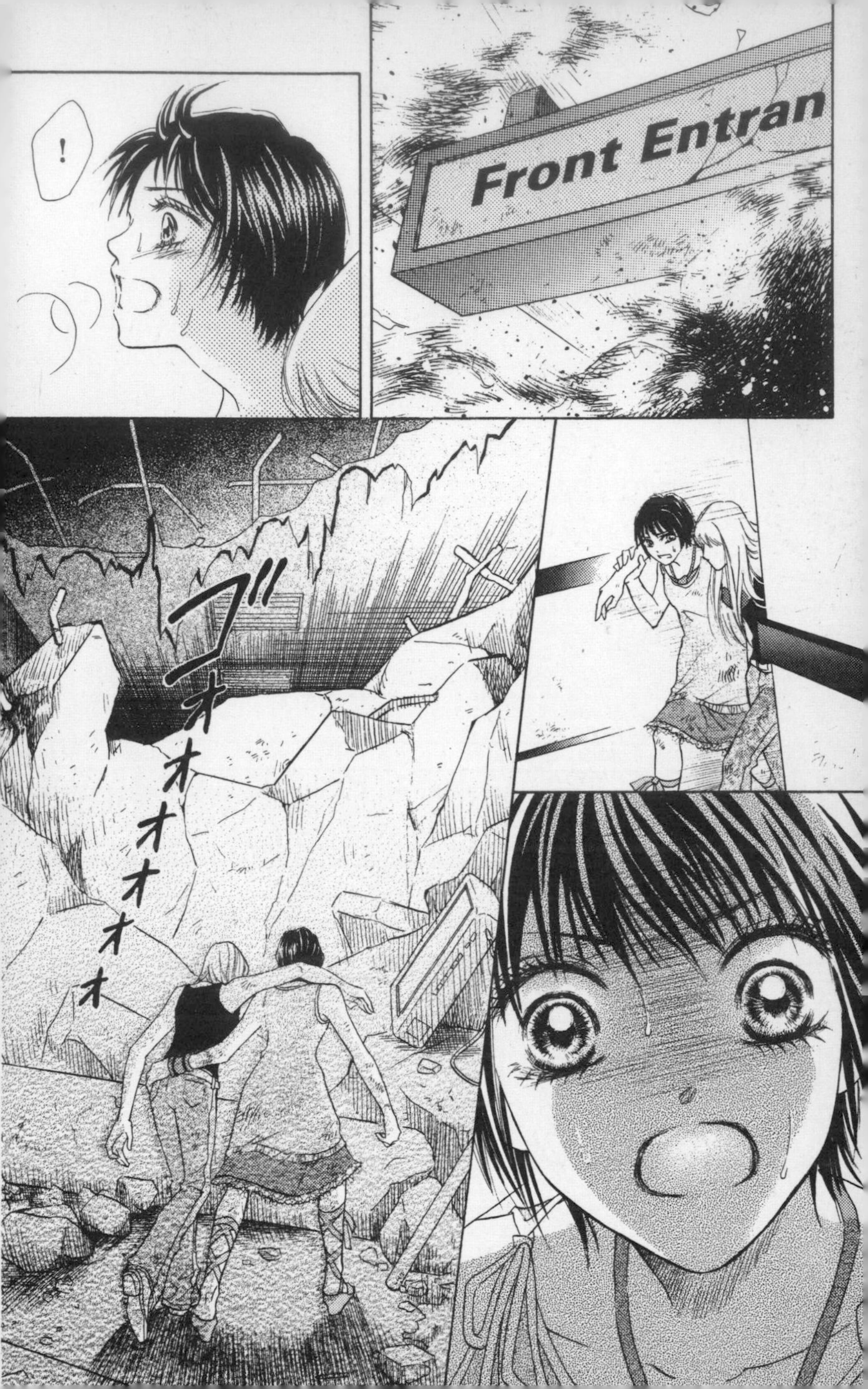
Front Entran
!
ゴオオオオオオ

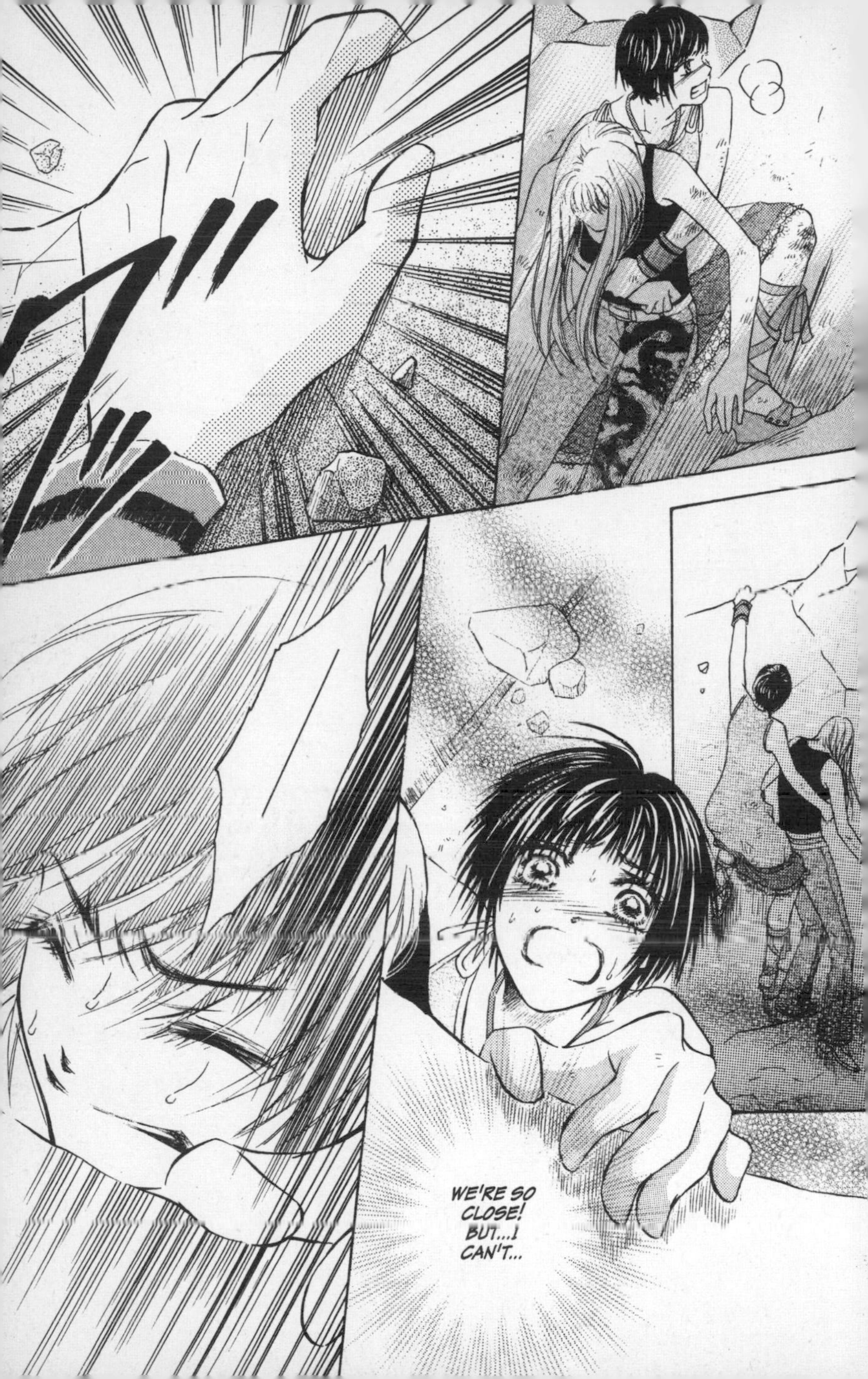
WE'RE SO CLOSE! BUT...I CAN'T...

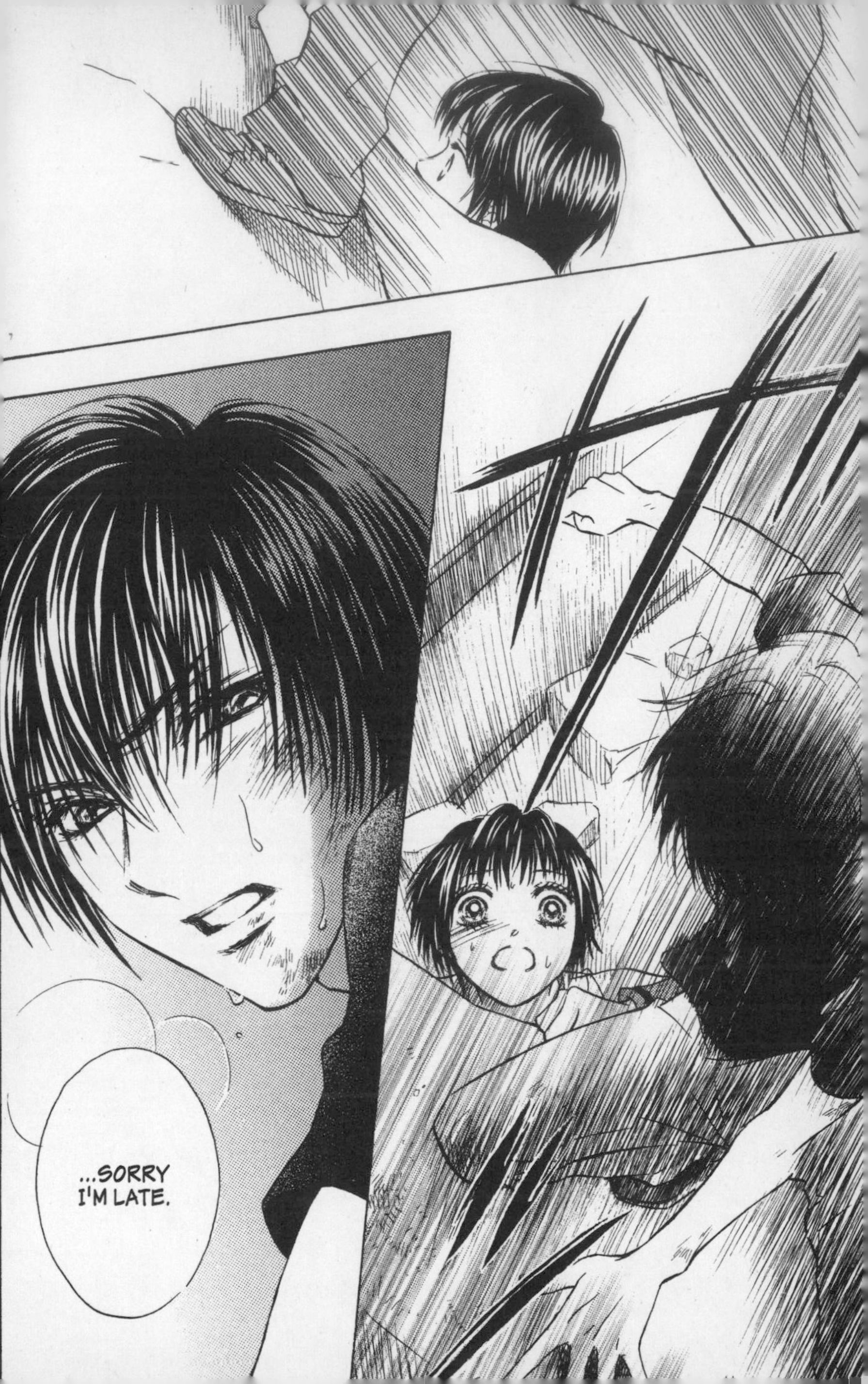
...SORRY I'M LATE.

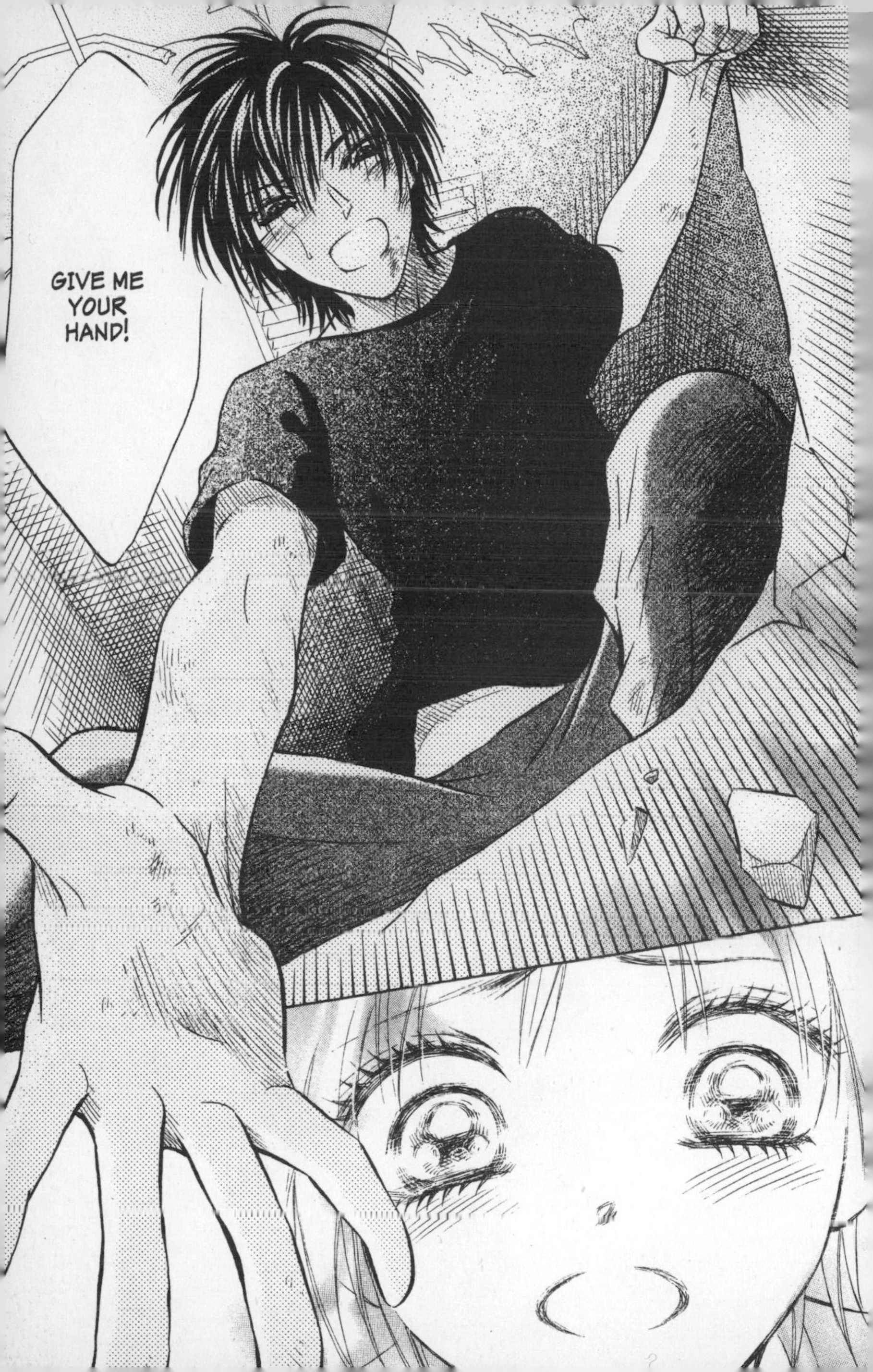
GIVE ME YOUR HAND!

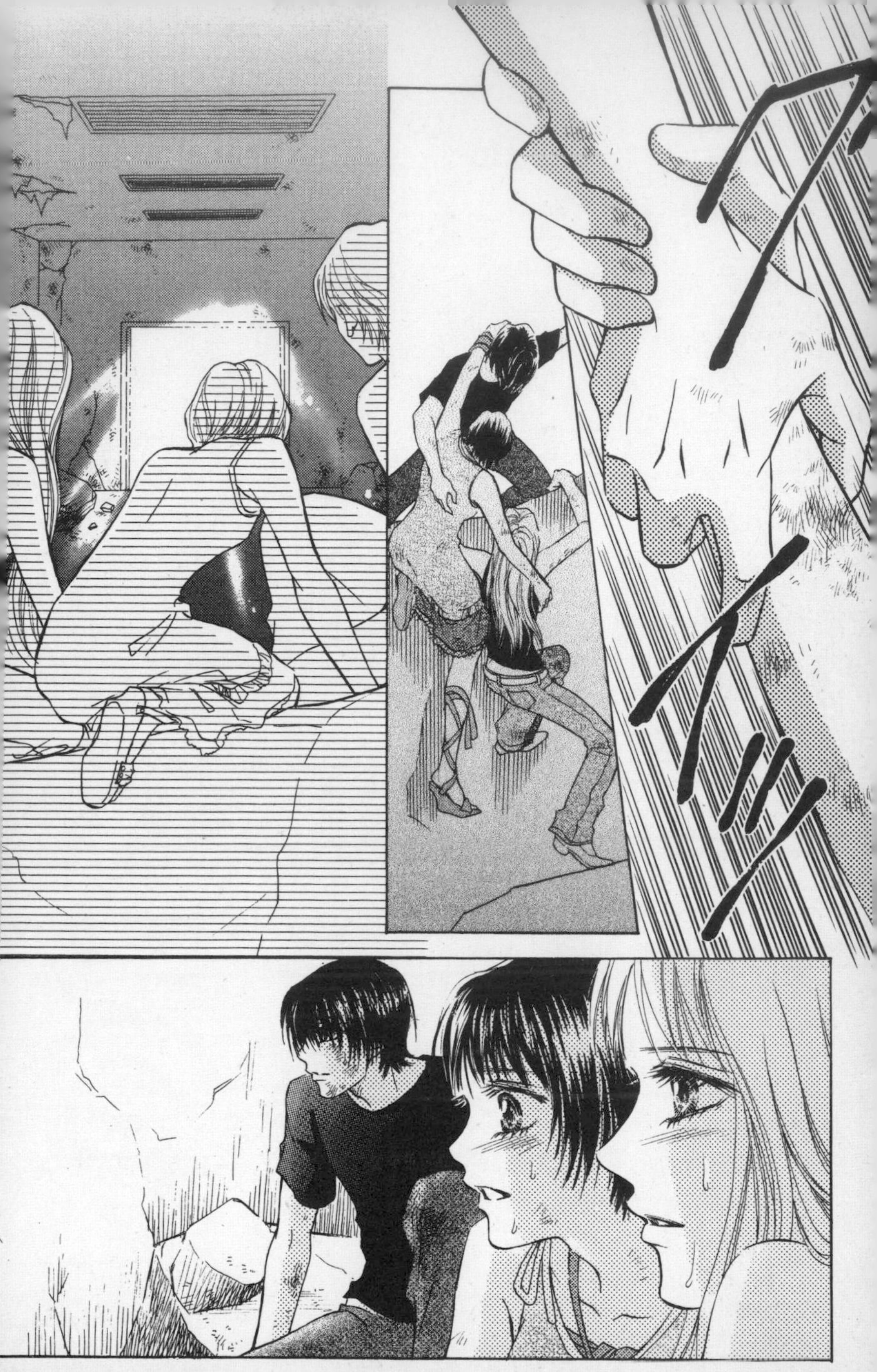

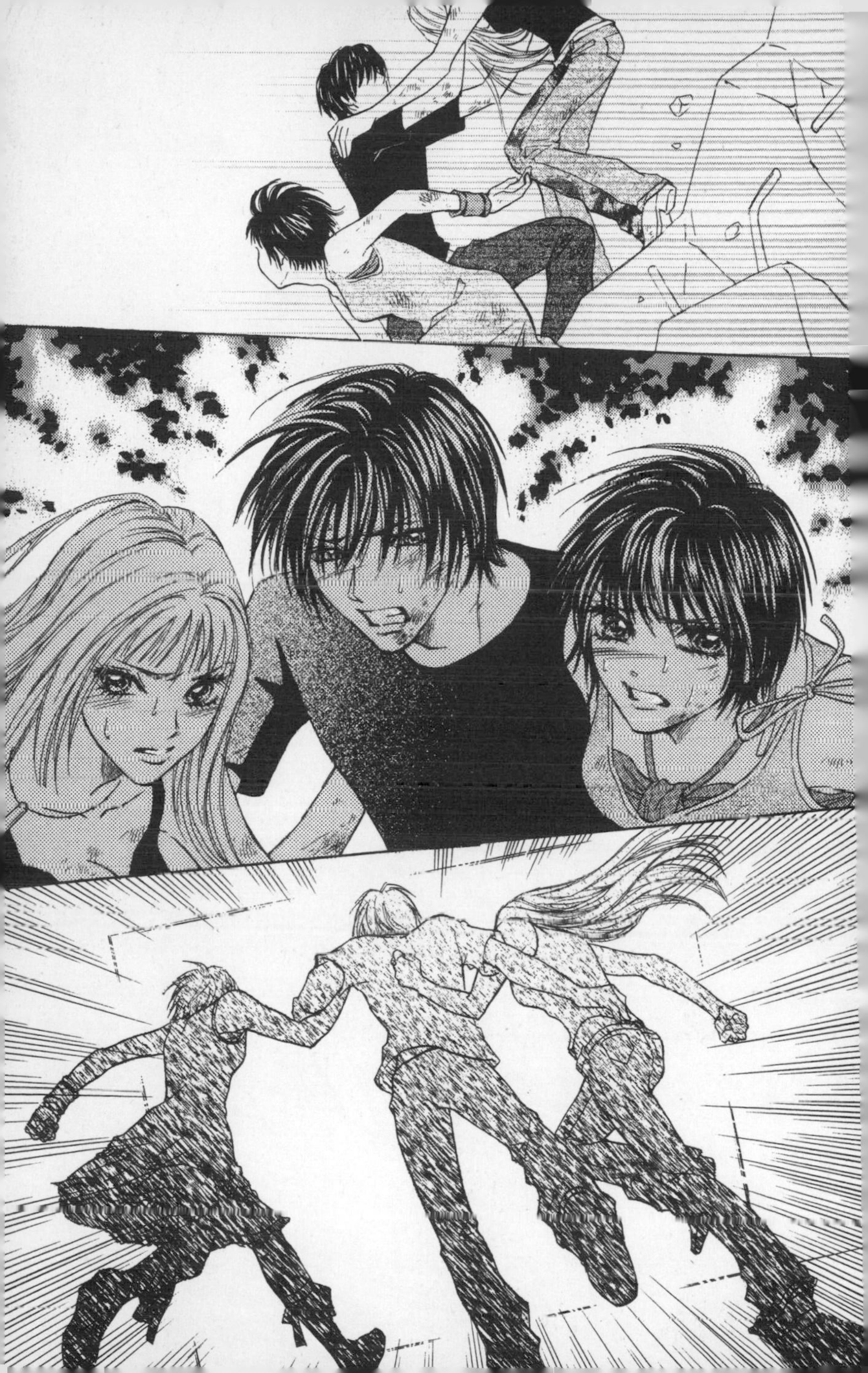

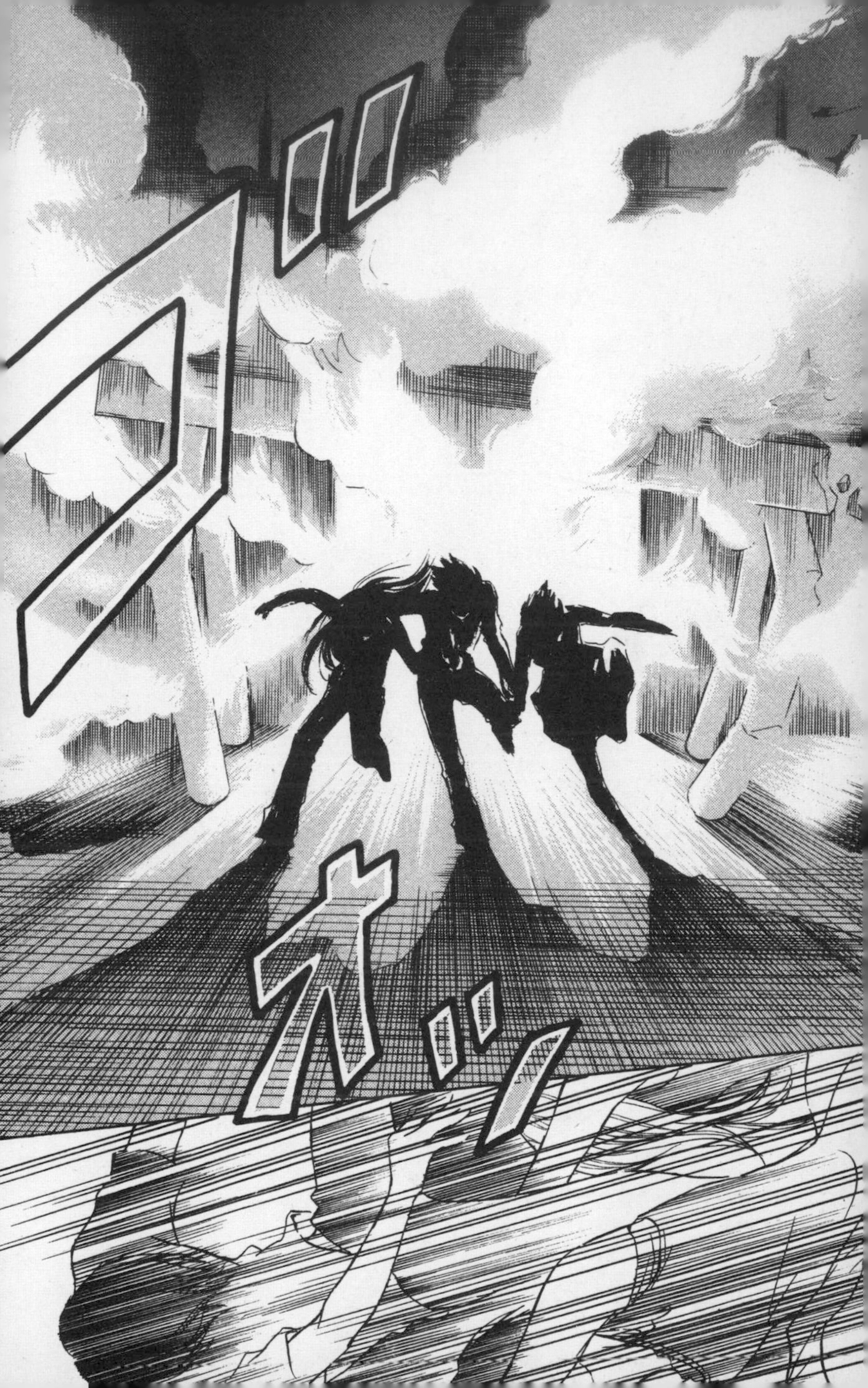
グ
オ゛

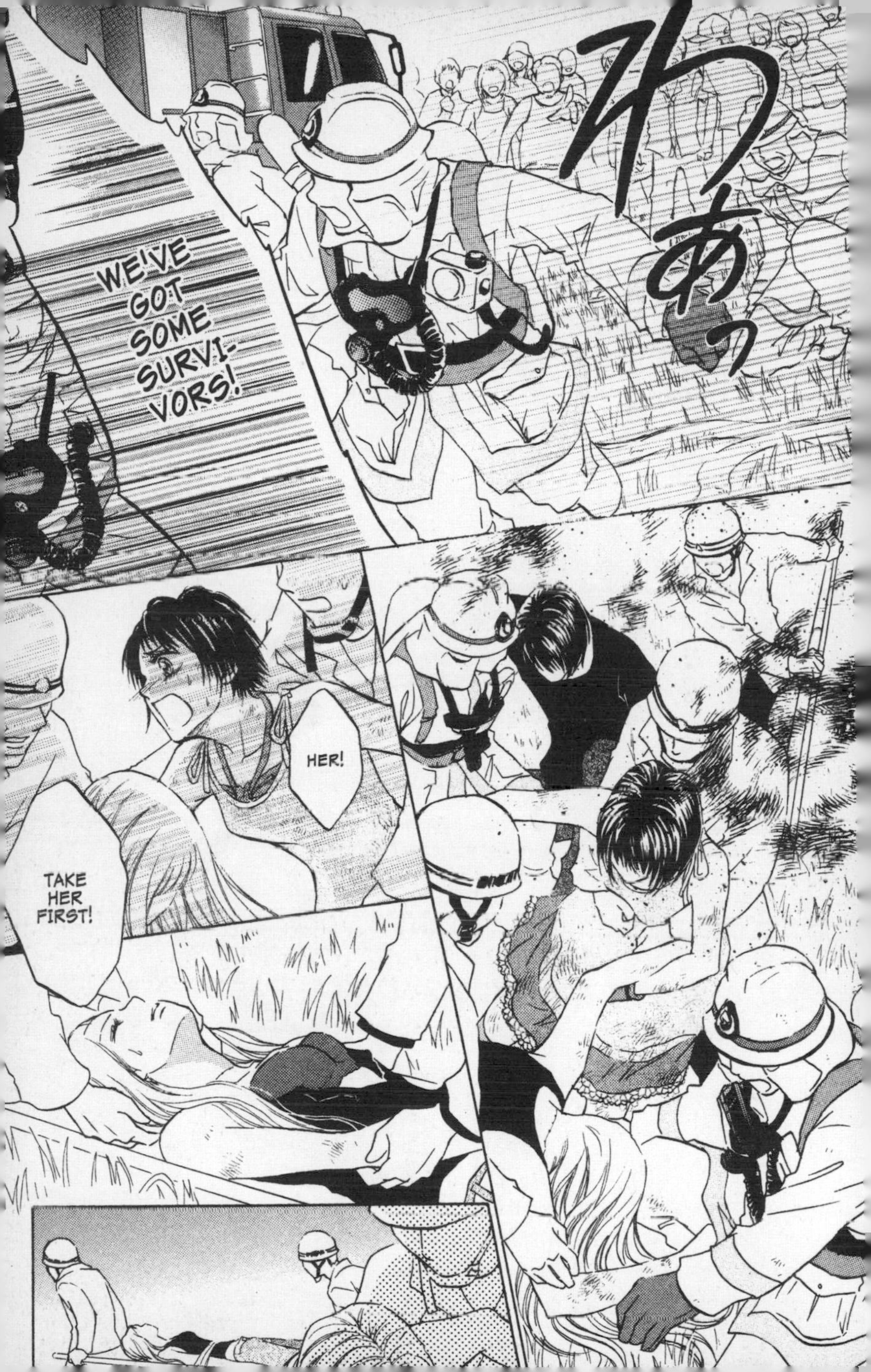
わあっ
WE'VE GOT SOME SURVIVORS!
HER!
TAKE HER FIRST!

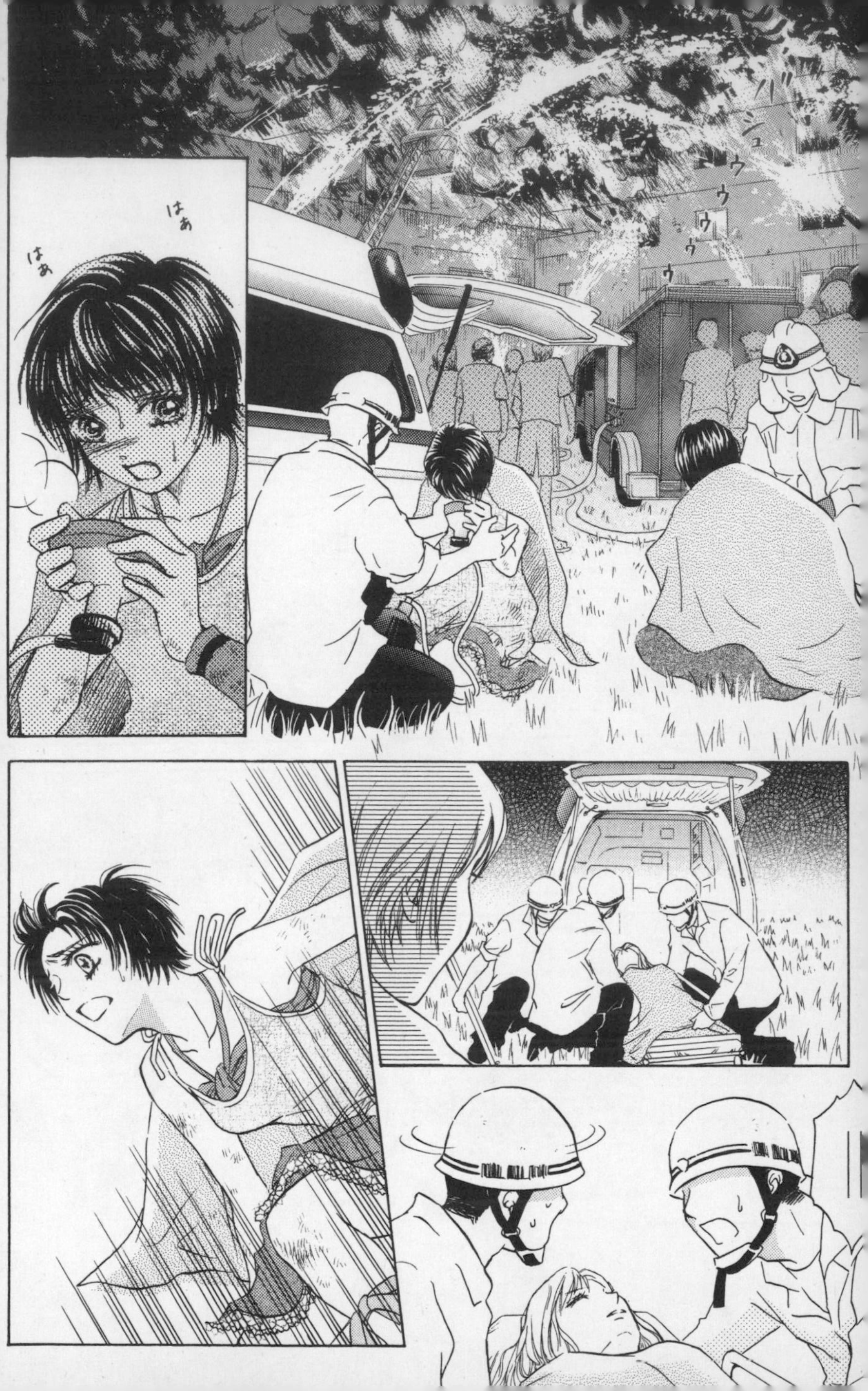
バシュウウウウウ
はぁ
はぁ

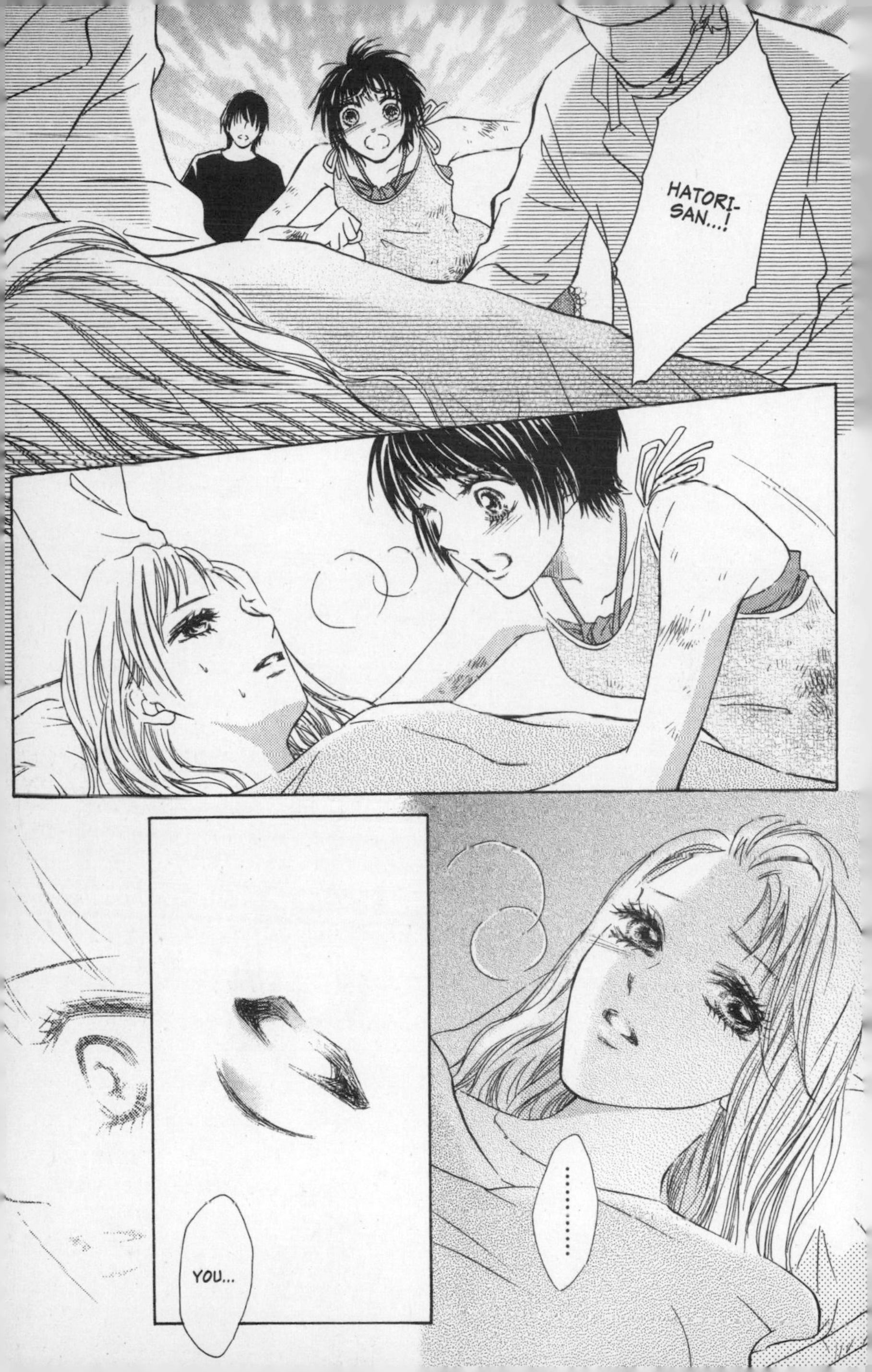
HATORI-SAN...!
......
YOU...

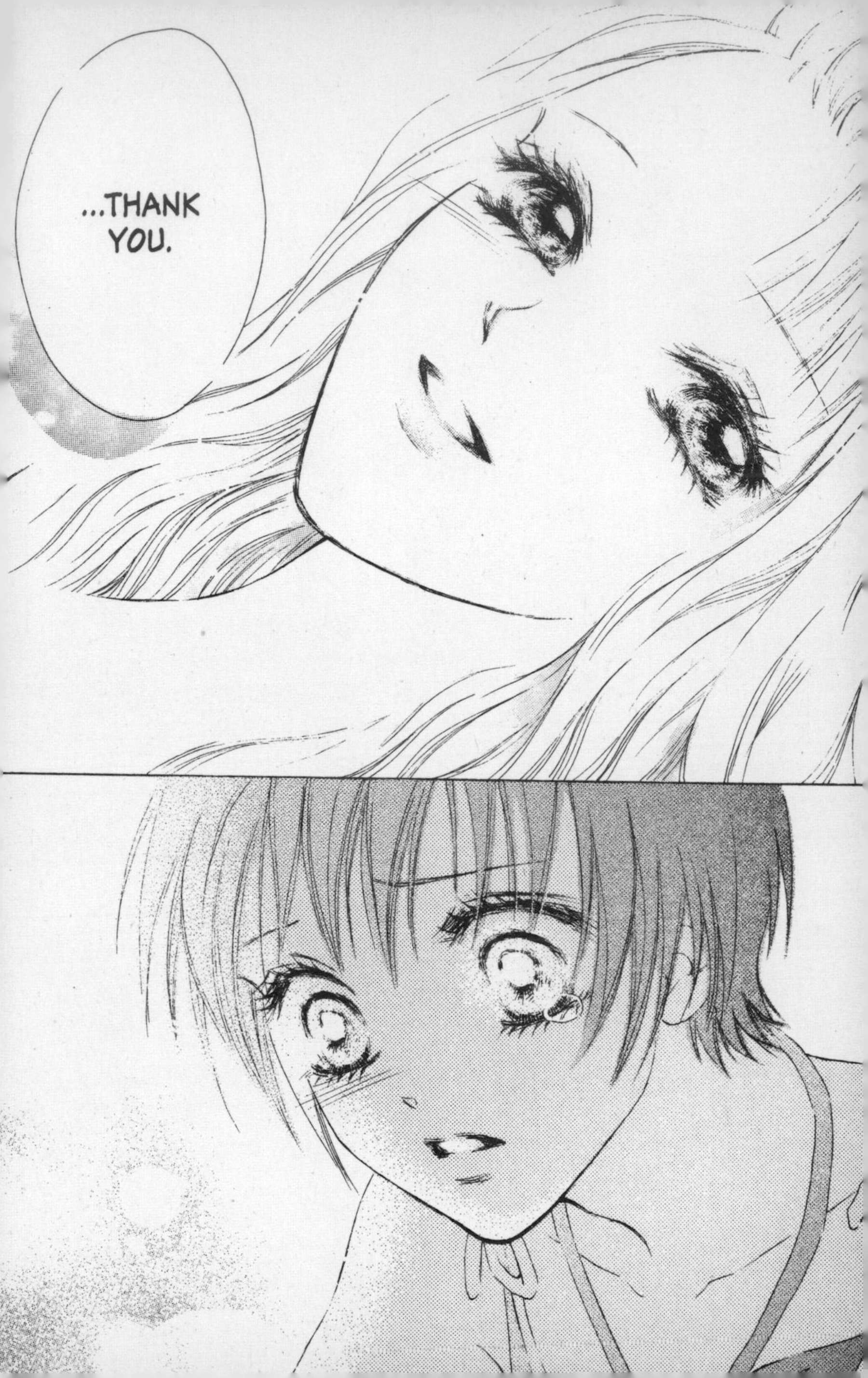
...THANK YOU.

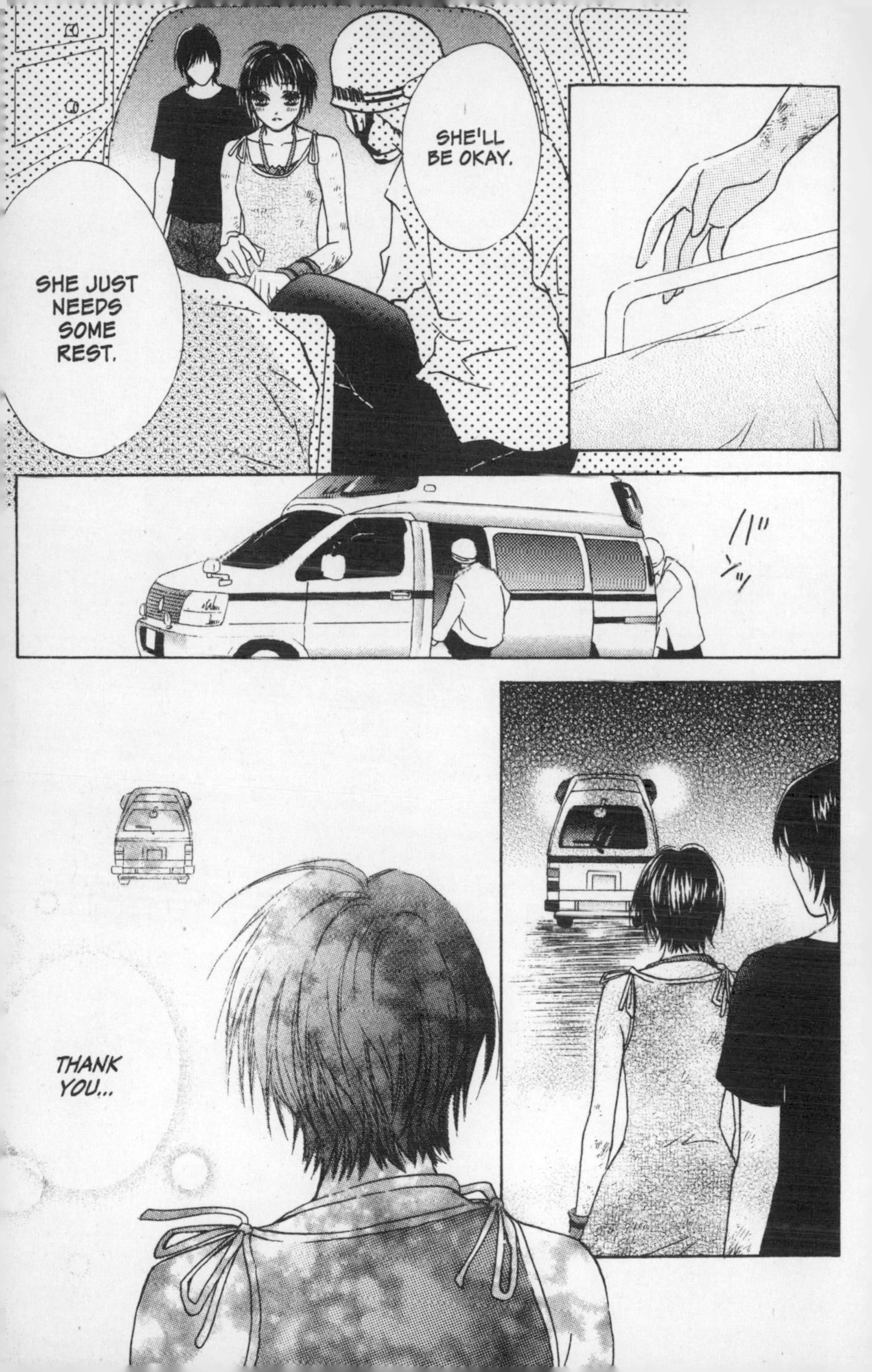
SHE'LL BE OKAY.
SHE JUST NEEDS SOME REST.
THANK YOU...

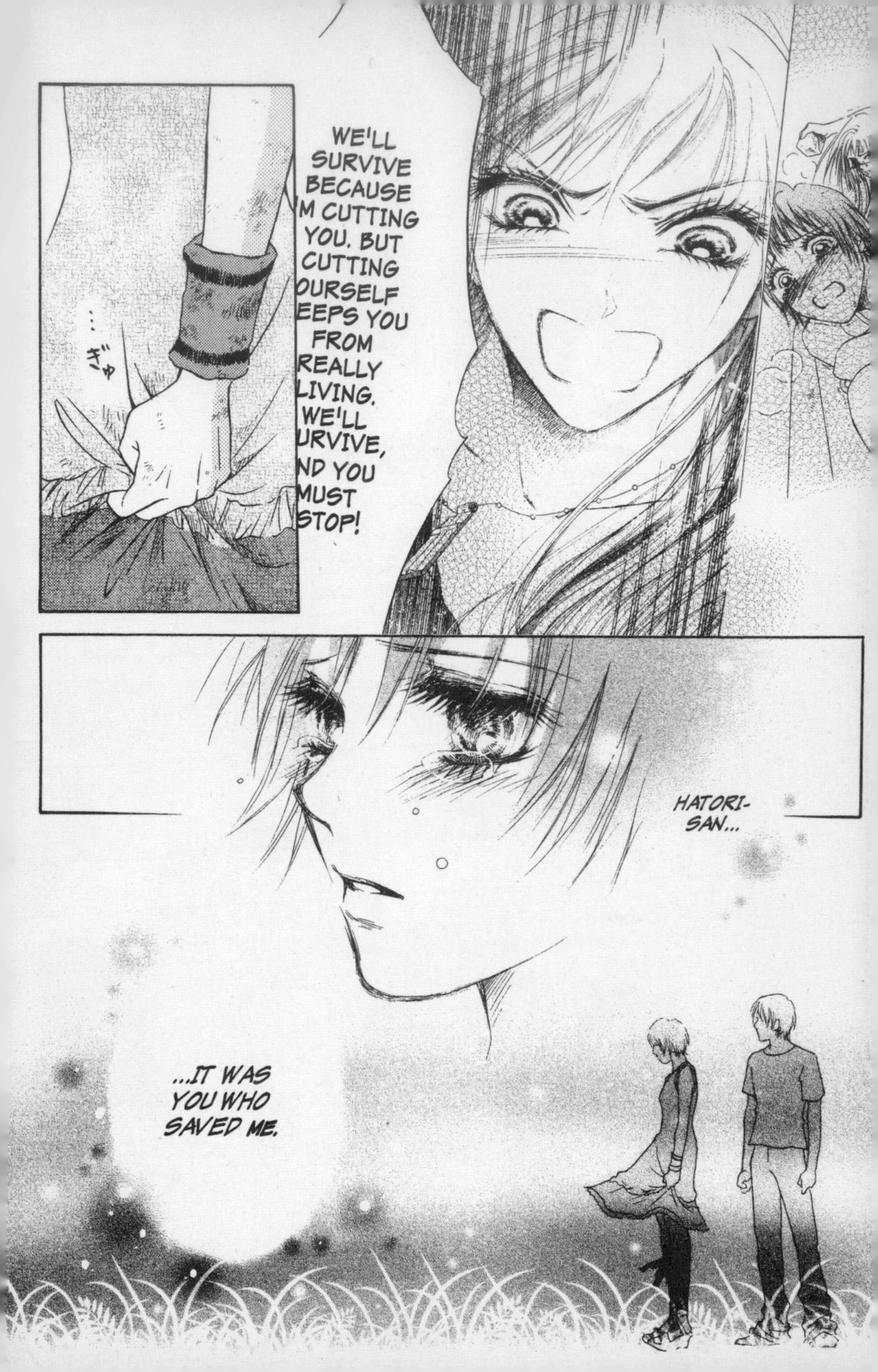
WE'LL SURVIVE BECAUSE M CUTTING YOU. BUT CUTTING OURSELF EEPS YOU FROM REALLY LIVING. WE'LL URVIVE, ND YOU MUST STOP!
…ぎゅ
HATORI-SAN...
...IT WAS YOU WHO SAVED ME.

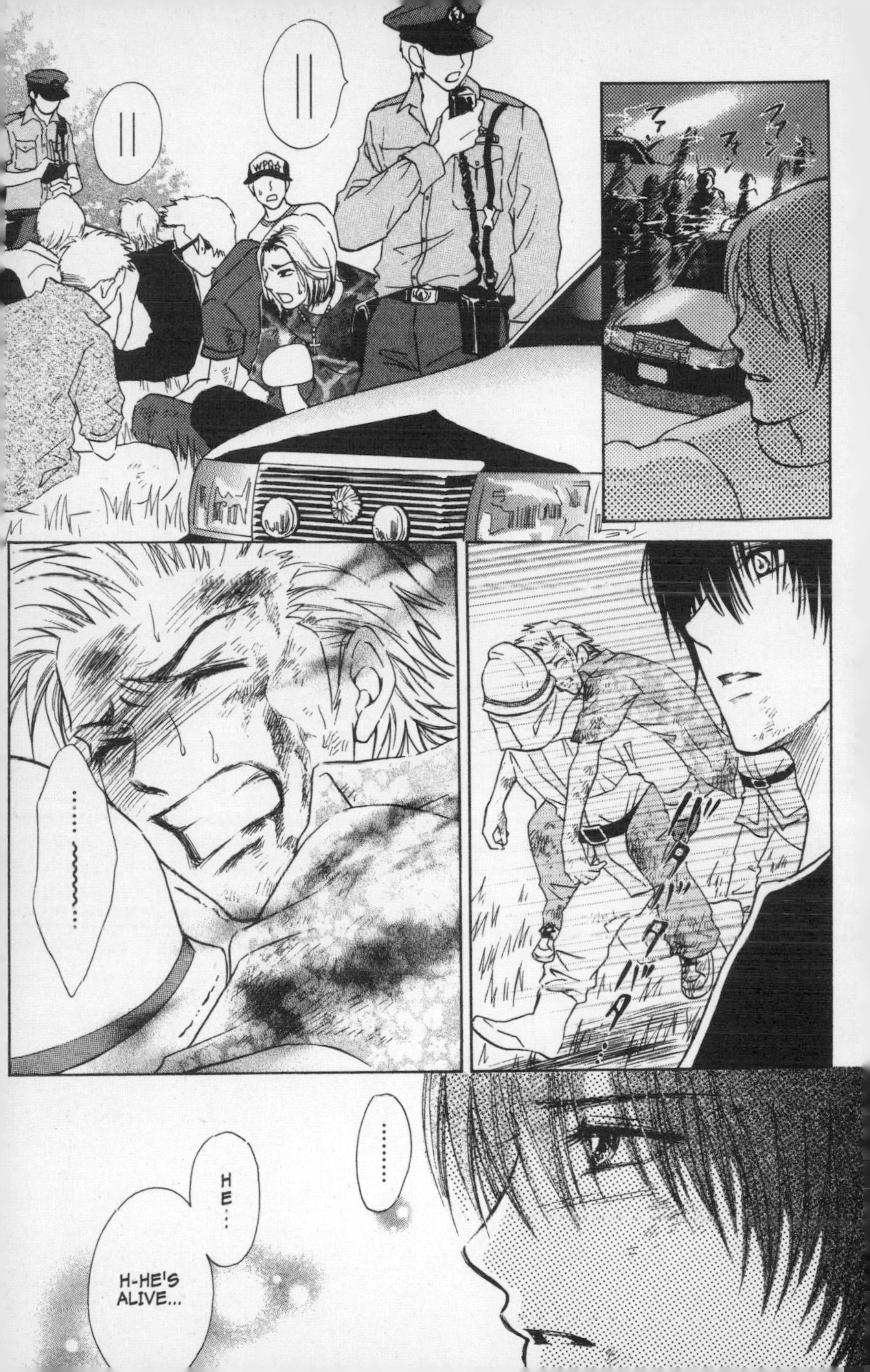
ファン
ファン
ファン
!!
!!
バタバタ…
......~~~......
......
HE...
H-HE'S ALIVE...

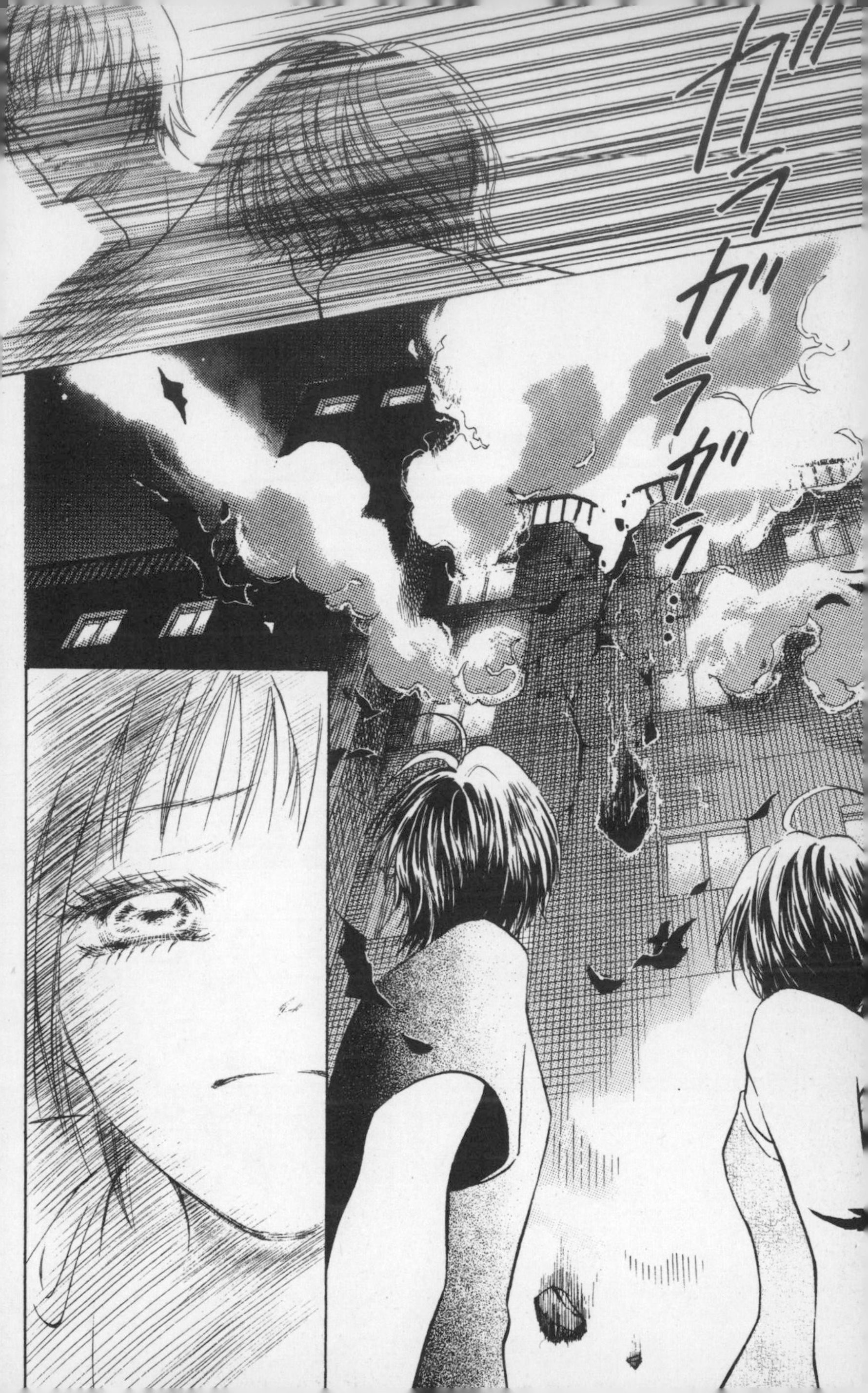
ガラガラガラガラ…

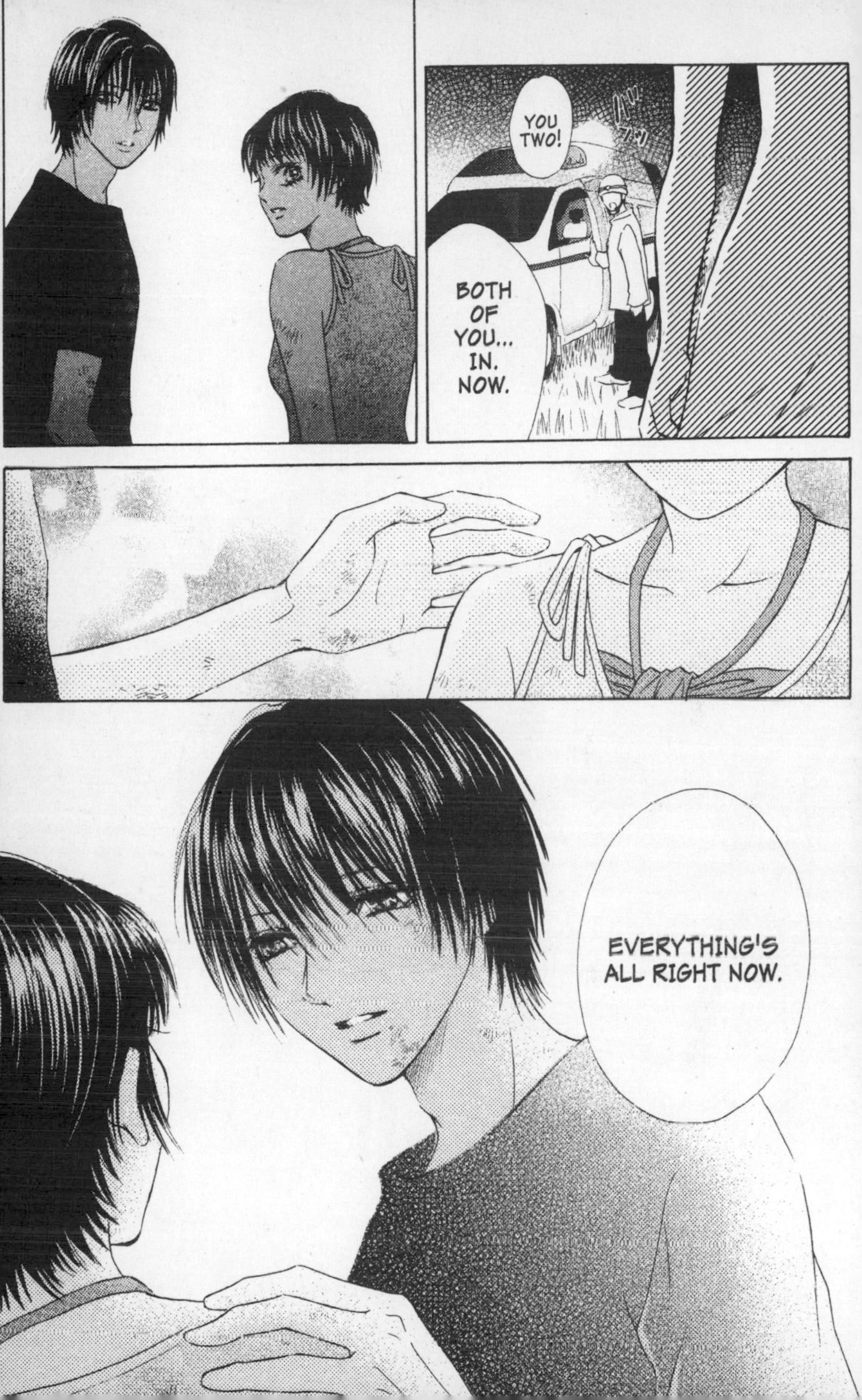
YOU TWO!
BOTH OF YOU... IN. NOW.
EVERYTHING'S ALL RIGHT NOW.

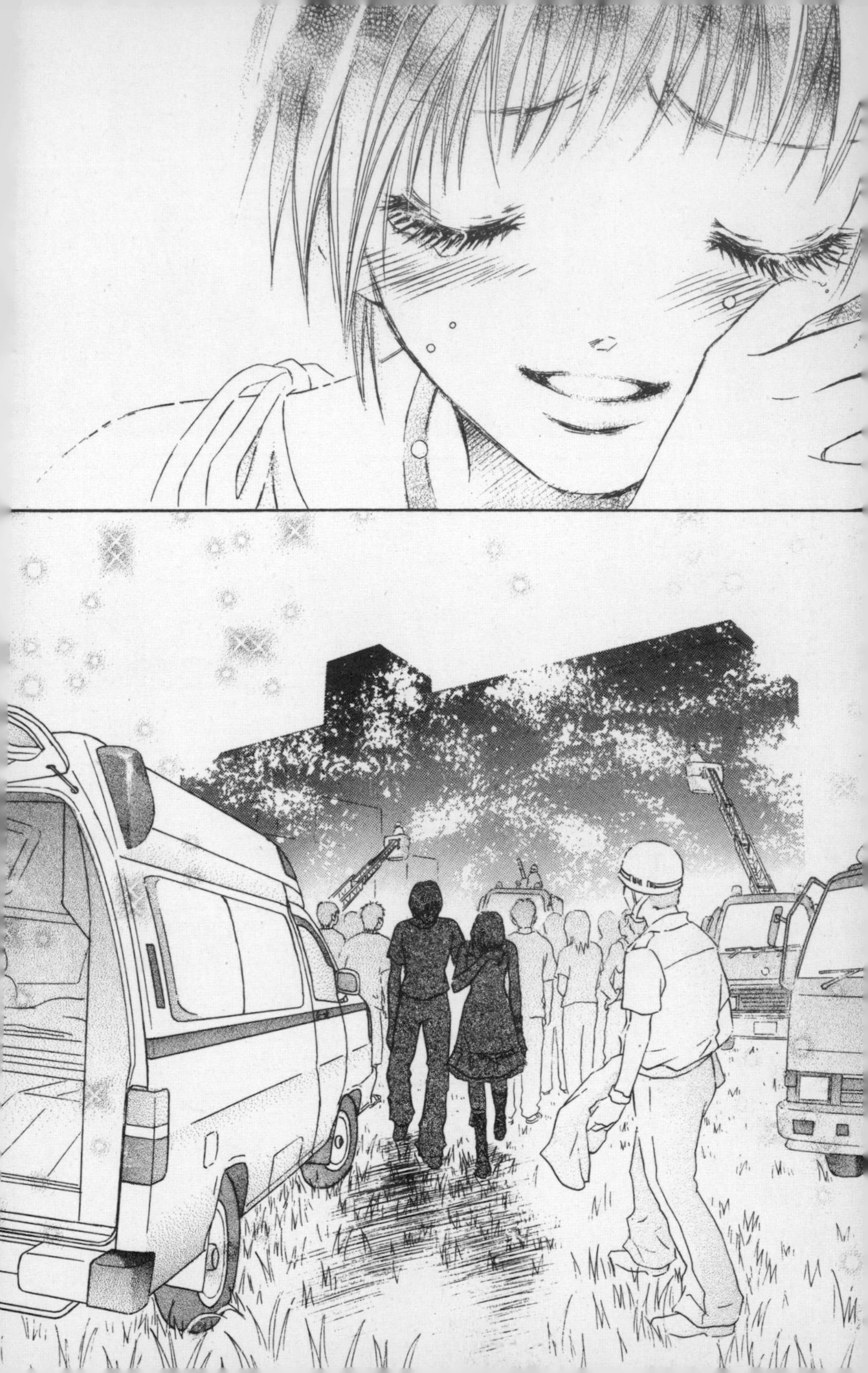

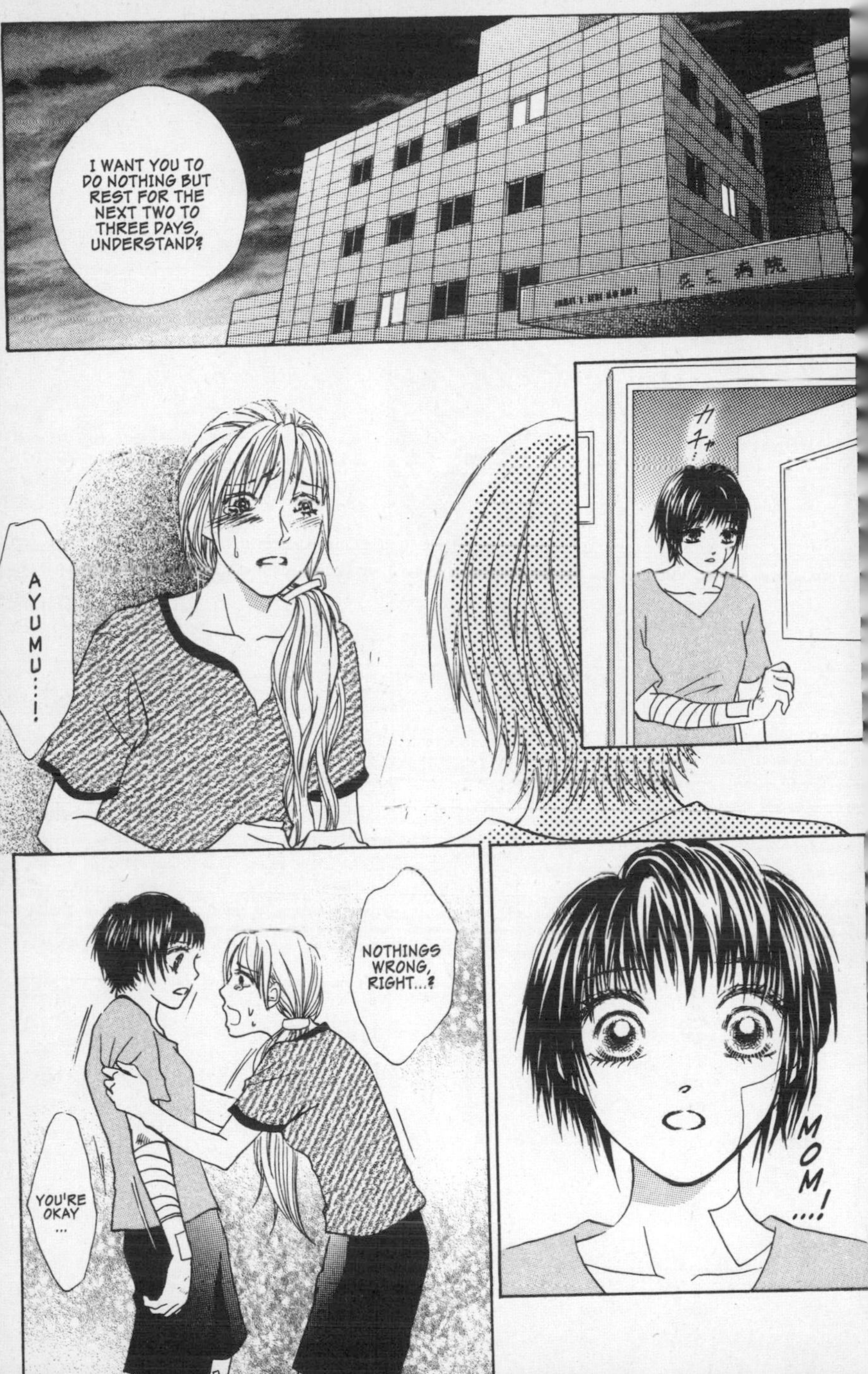
I WANT YOU TO DO NOTHING BUT REST FOR THE NEXT TWO TO THREE DAYS, UNDERSTAND?
カチャ
AYUMU...!
MOM...!
NOTHINGS WRONG, RIGHT...?
YOU'RE OKAY ...

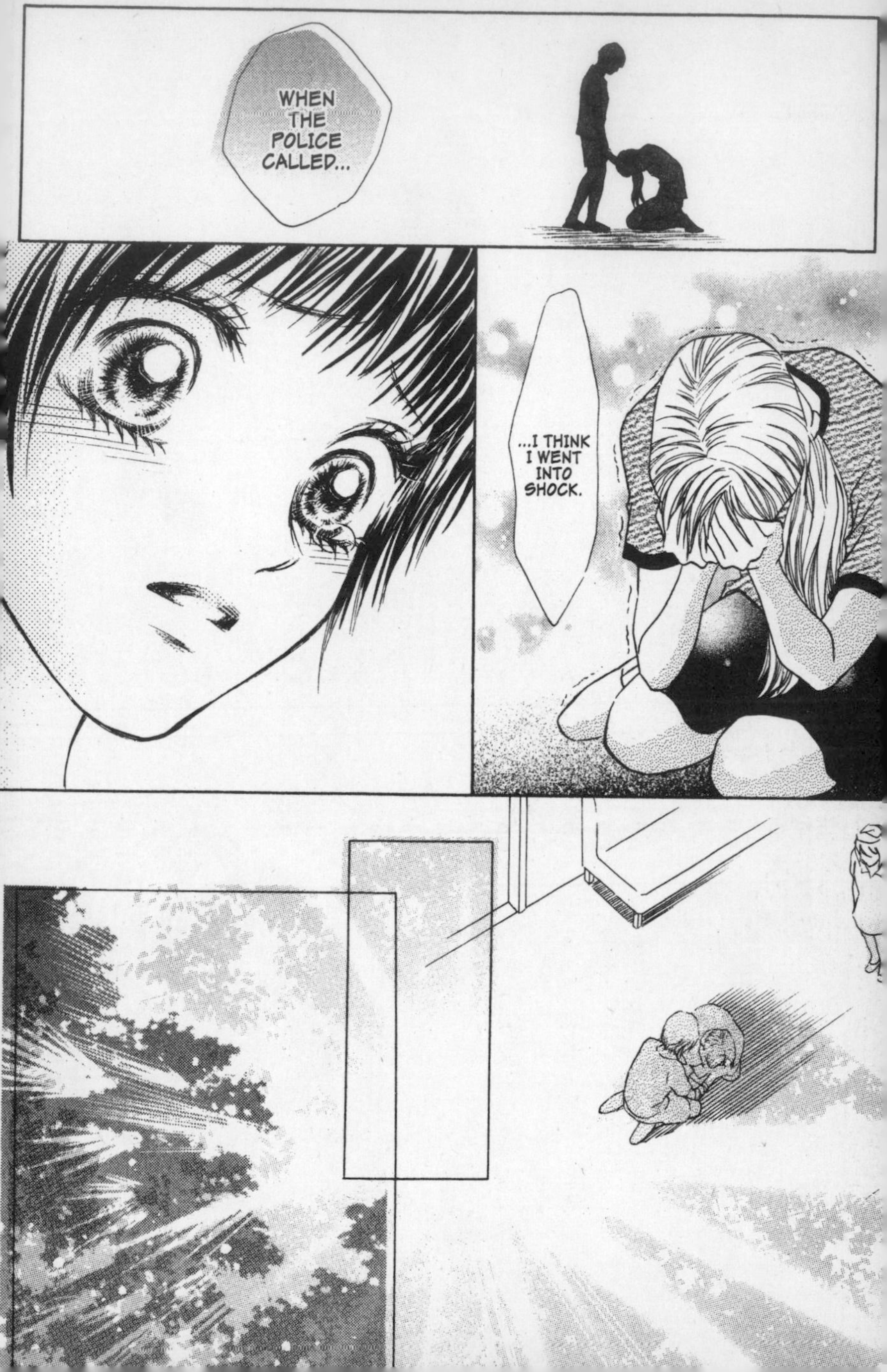
WHEN THE POLICE CALLED...
...I THINK I WENT INTO SHOCK.

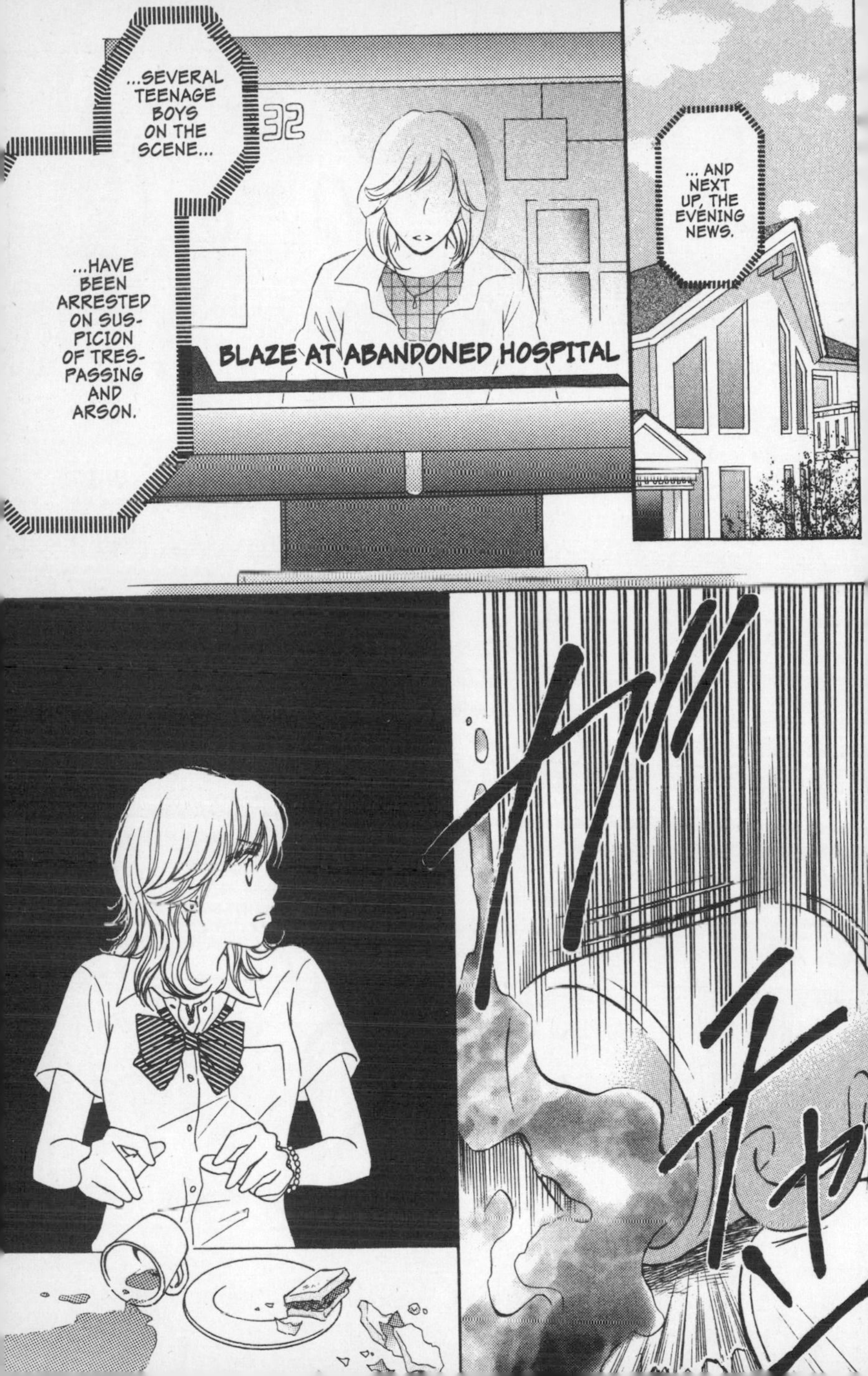
... AND NEXT UP, THE EVENING NEWS.
...SEVERAL TEENAGE BOYS ON THE SCENE...
BLAZE AT ABANDONED HOSPITAL
...HAVE BEEN ARRESTED ON SUSPICION OF TRESPASSING AND ARSON.

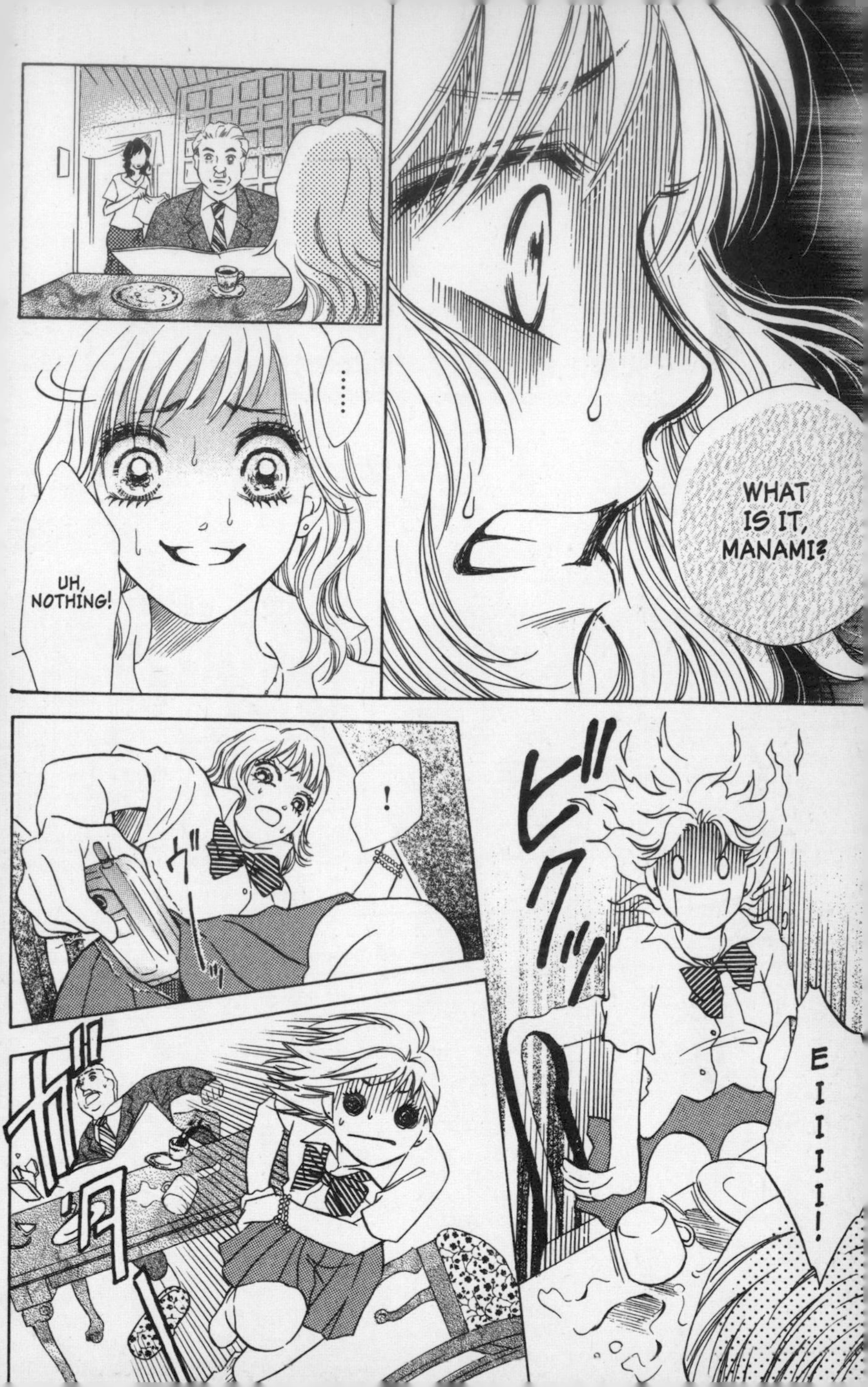
WHAT IS IT, MANAMI?
……
UH, NOTHING!
ビクッ
EIIIII!
!
ヴー

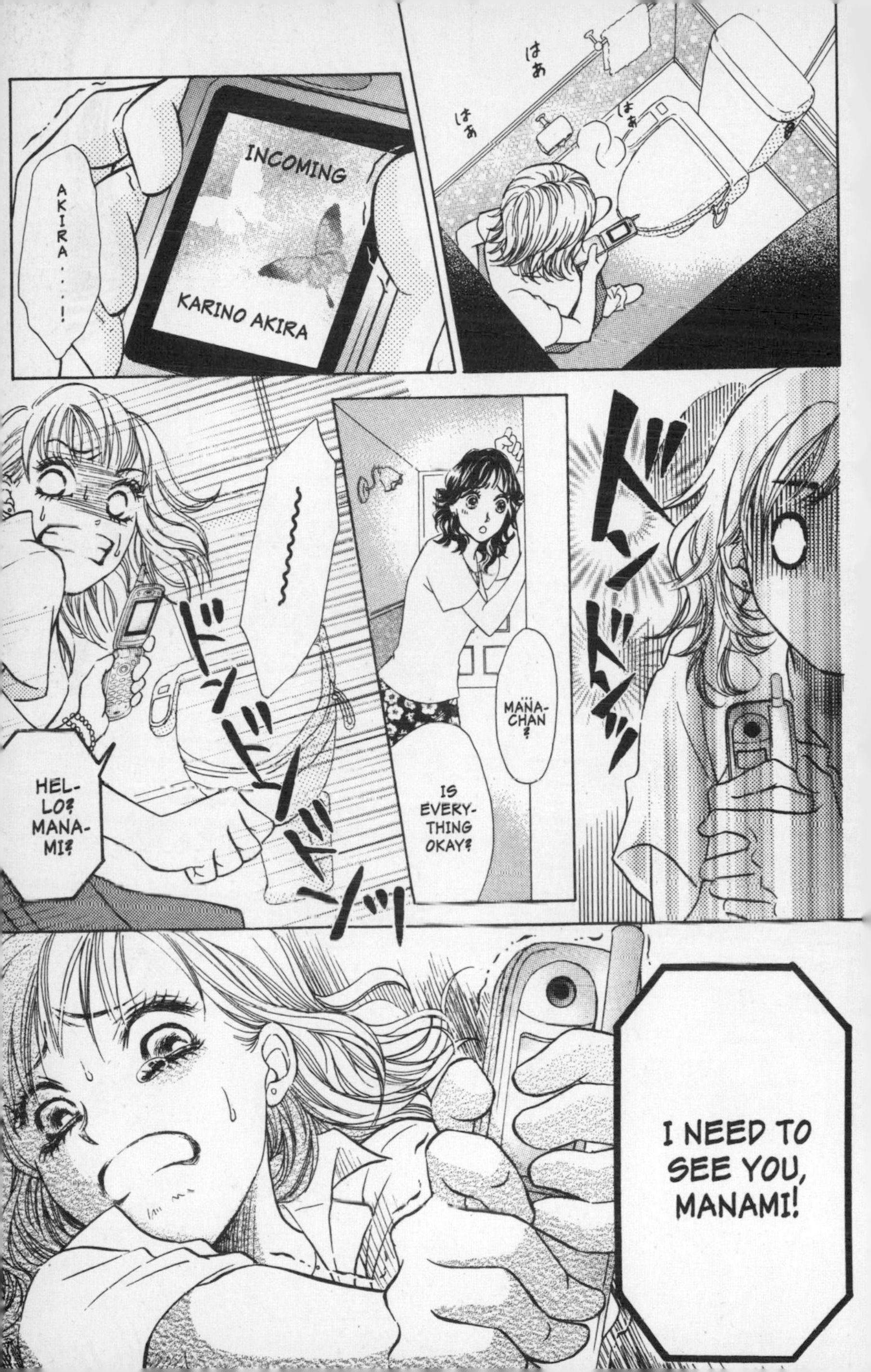

はあ
はあ
はあ
INCOMING
KARINO AKIRA
AKIRA...!
MÄNA-CHAN?
IS EVERYTHING OKAY?
HEL-LO? MANAMI?
I NEED TO SEE YOU, MANAMI!

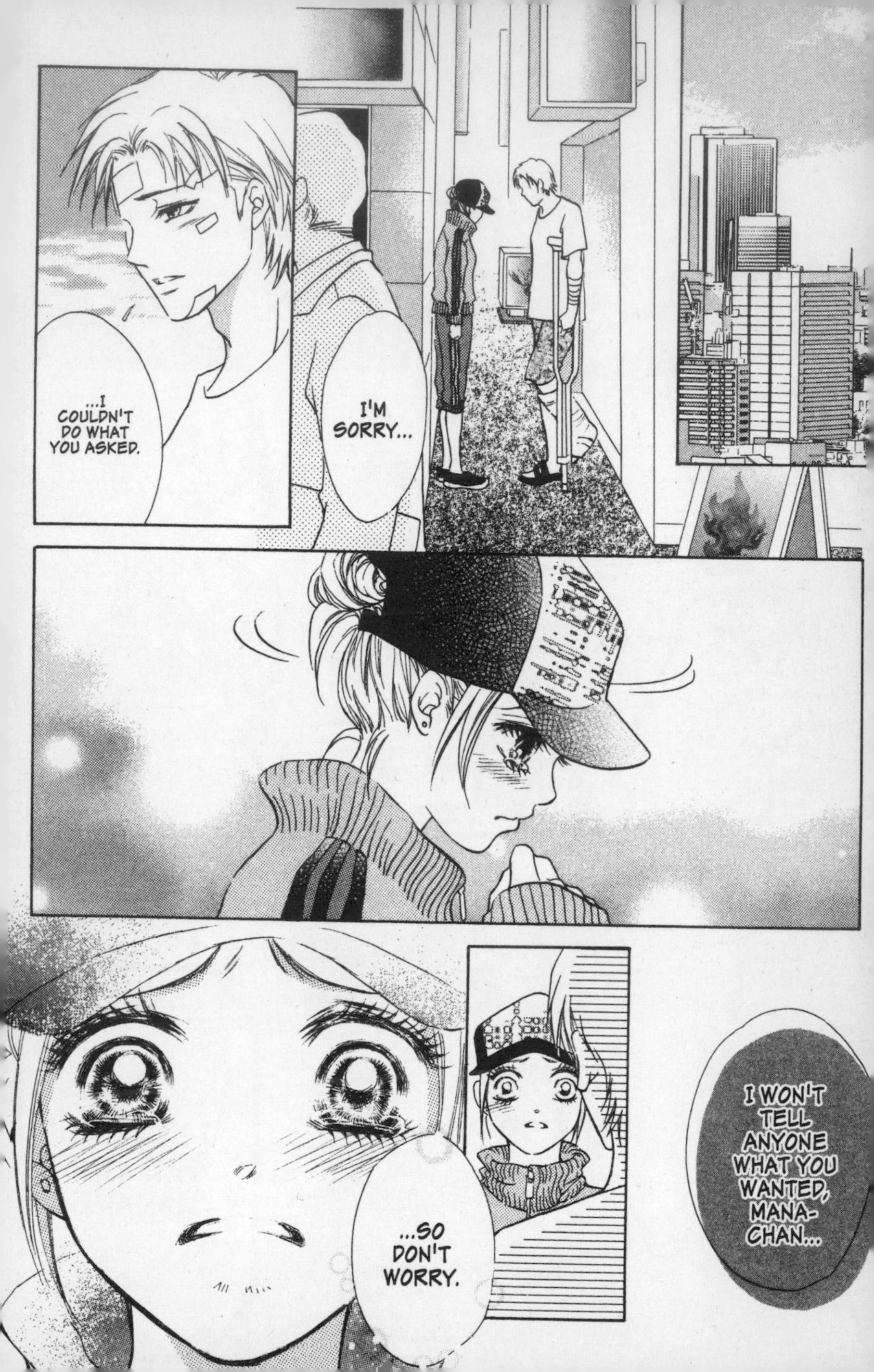
I'M SORRY...
...I COULDN'T DO WHAT YOU ASKED.
I WON'T TELL ANYONE WHAT YOU WANTED, MANA-CHAN...
...SO DON'T WORRY.

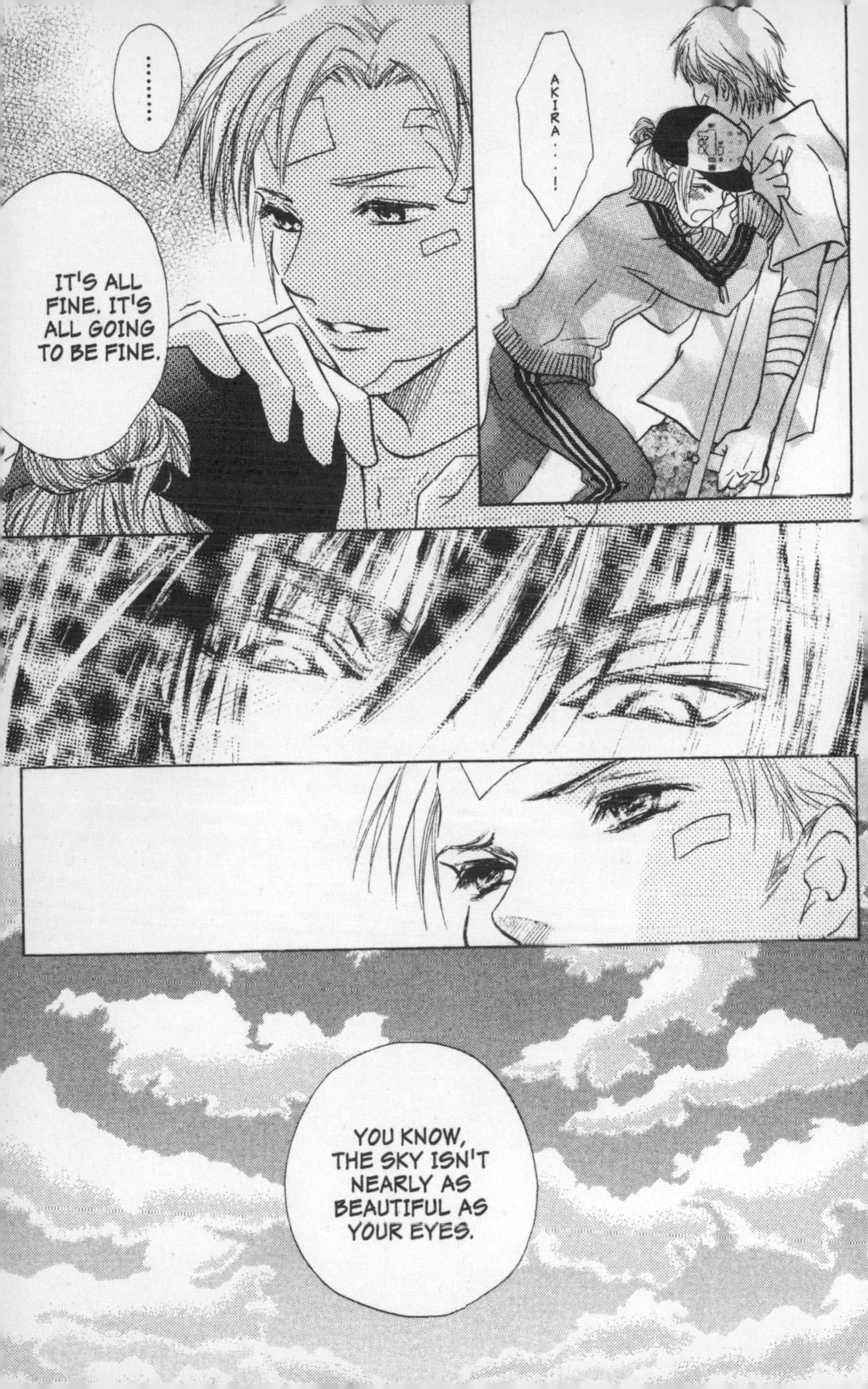
AKIRA....!
....
IT'S ALL FINE. IT'S ALL GOING TO BE FINE.
YOU KNOW, THE SKY ISN'T NEARLY AS BEAUTIFUL AS YOUR EYES.

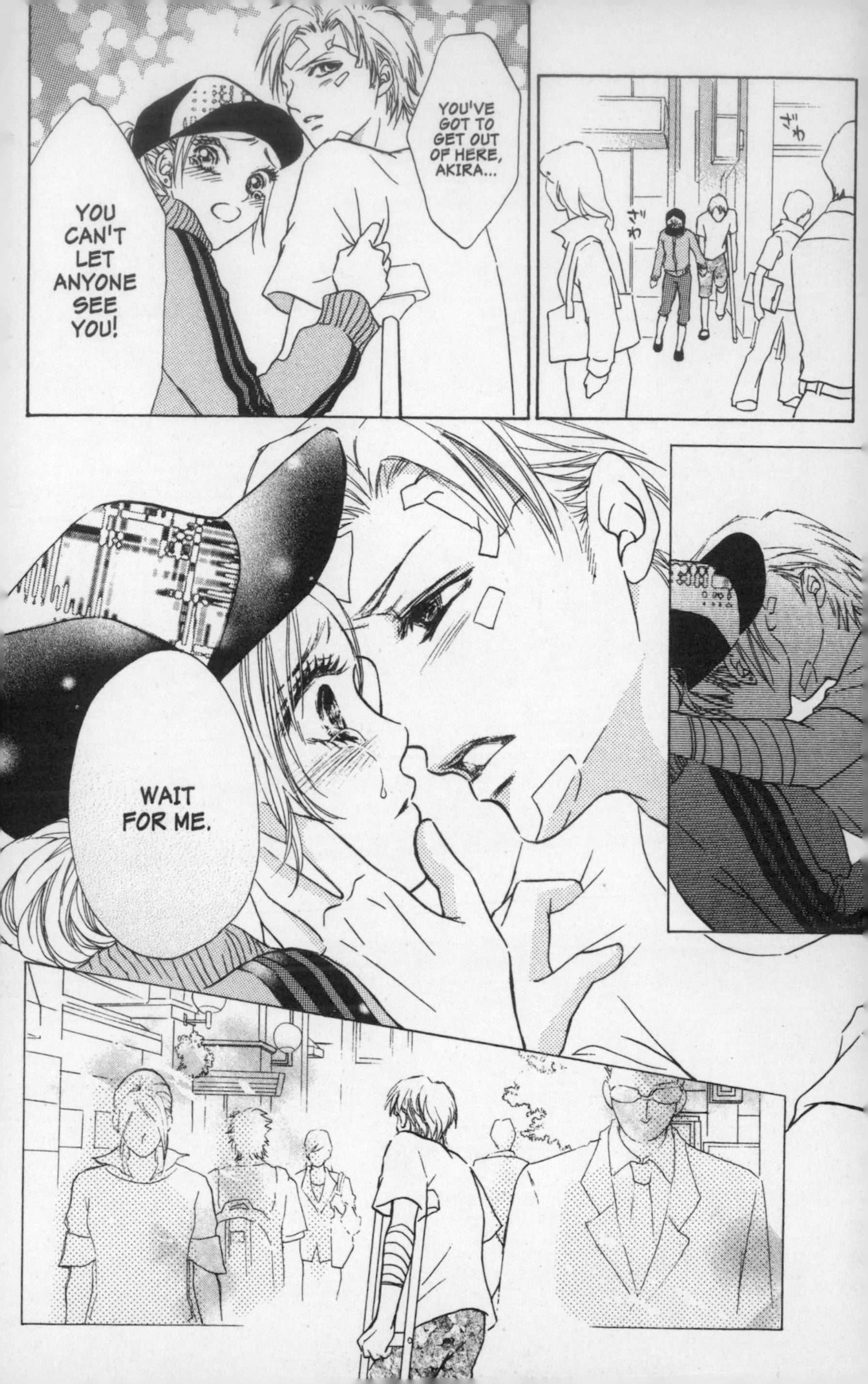
ざわ
ざわ
YOU'VE GOT TO GET OUT OF HERE, AKIRA...
YOU CAN'T LET ANYONE SEE YOU!
WAIT FOR ME.

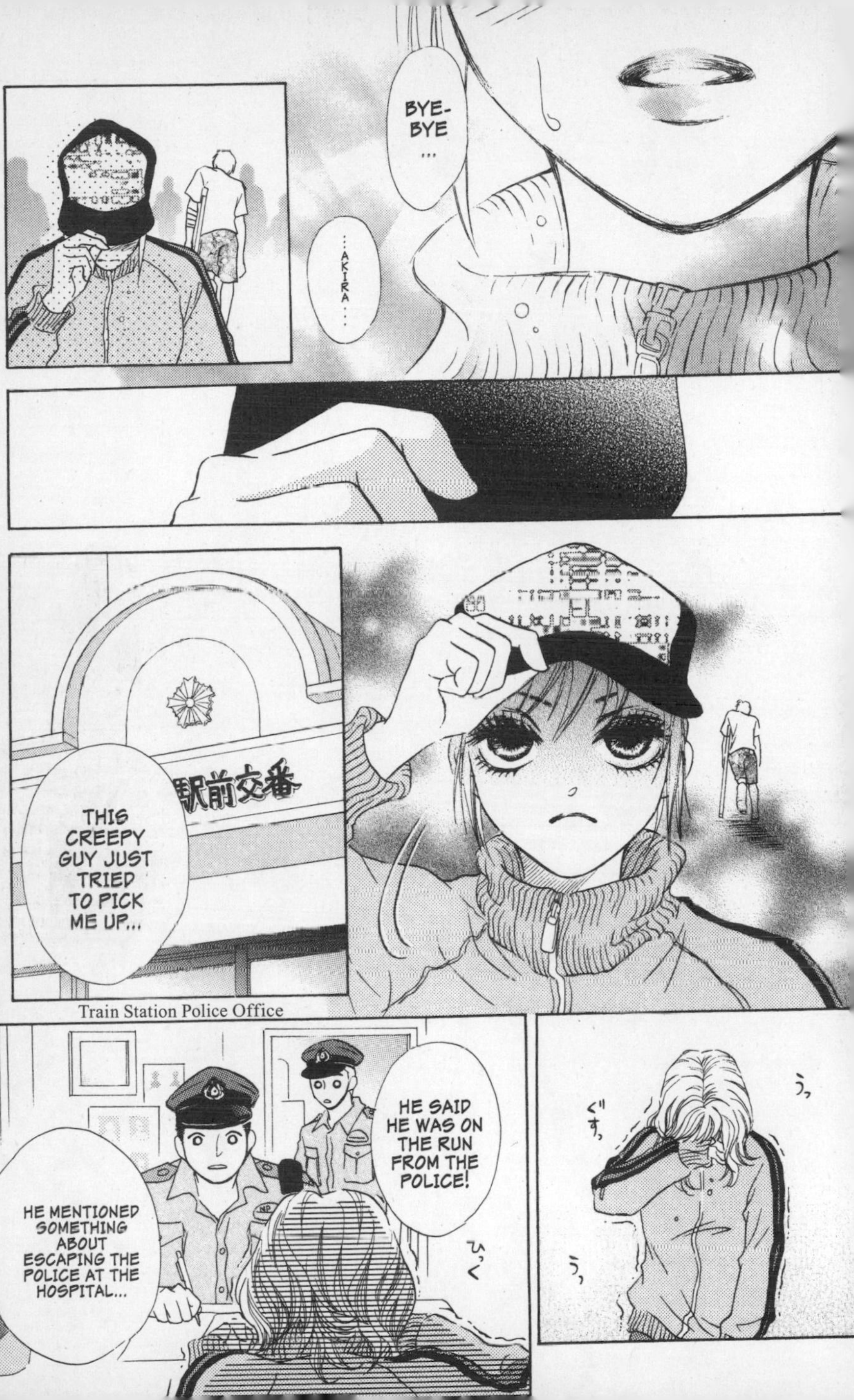
BYE-BYE...
...AKIRA...
THIS CREEPY GUY JUST TRIED TO PICK ME UP...
駅前交番
Train Station Police Office
うっ
ぐすっ
うっ
HE SAID HE WAS ON THE RUN FROM THE POLICE!
ひっく
HE MENTIONED SOMETHING ABOUT ESCAPING THE POLICE AT THE HOSPITAL...

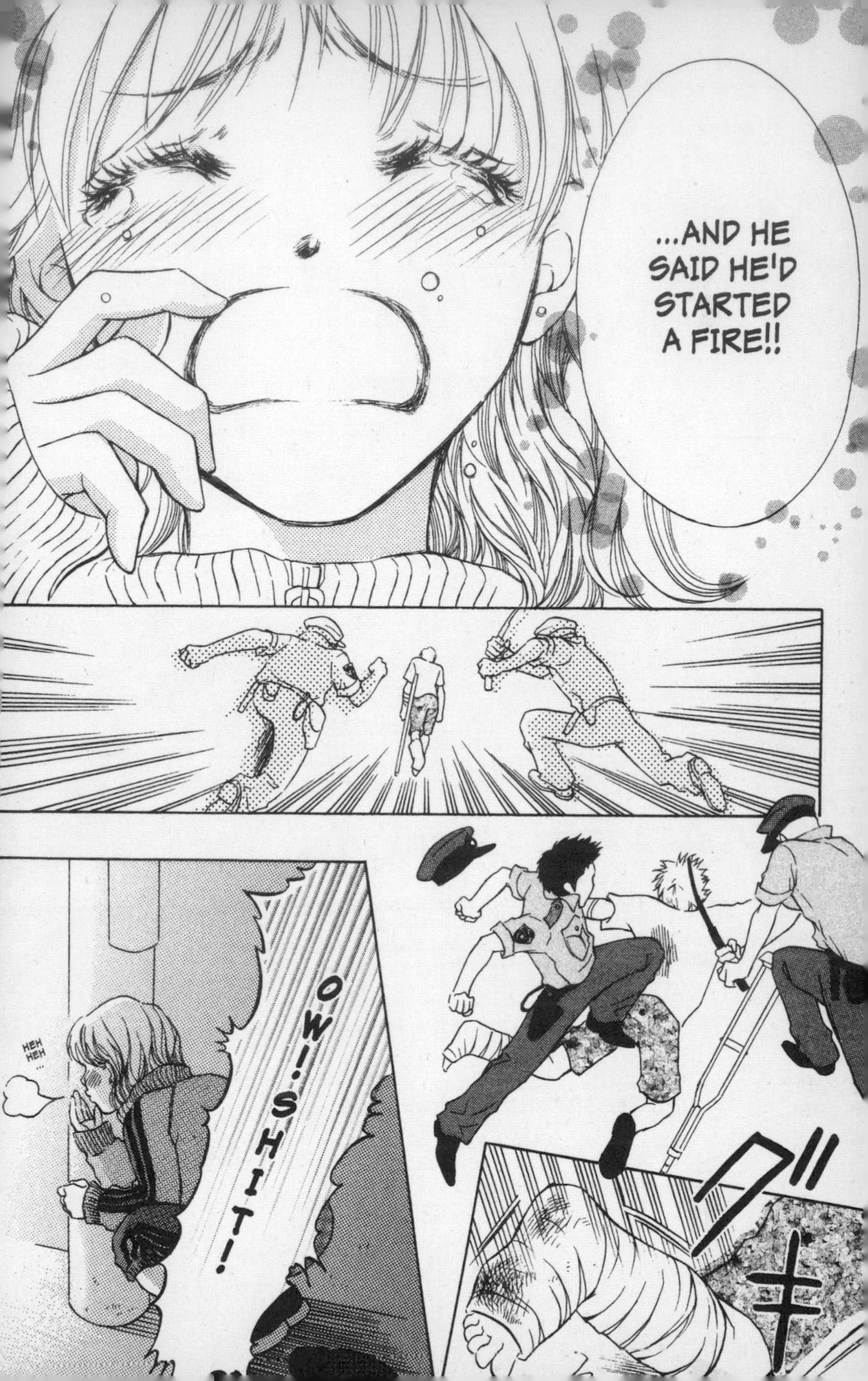
...AND HE SAID HE'D STARTED A FIRE!!
OW!! SHIT!!
HEH HEH ...

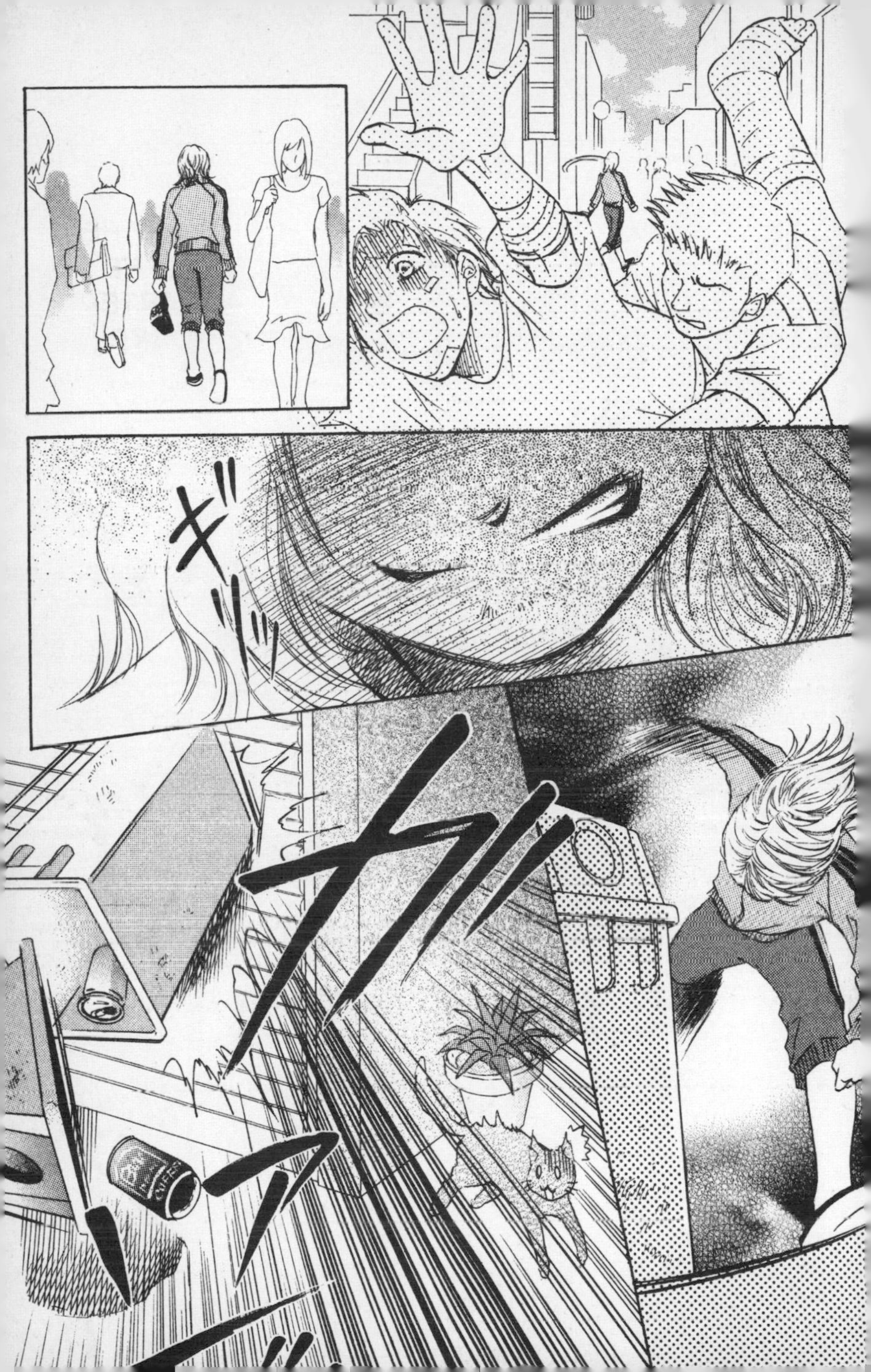
ギリッ

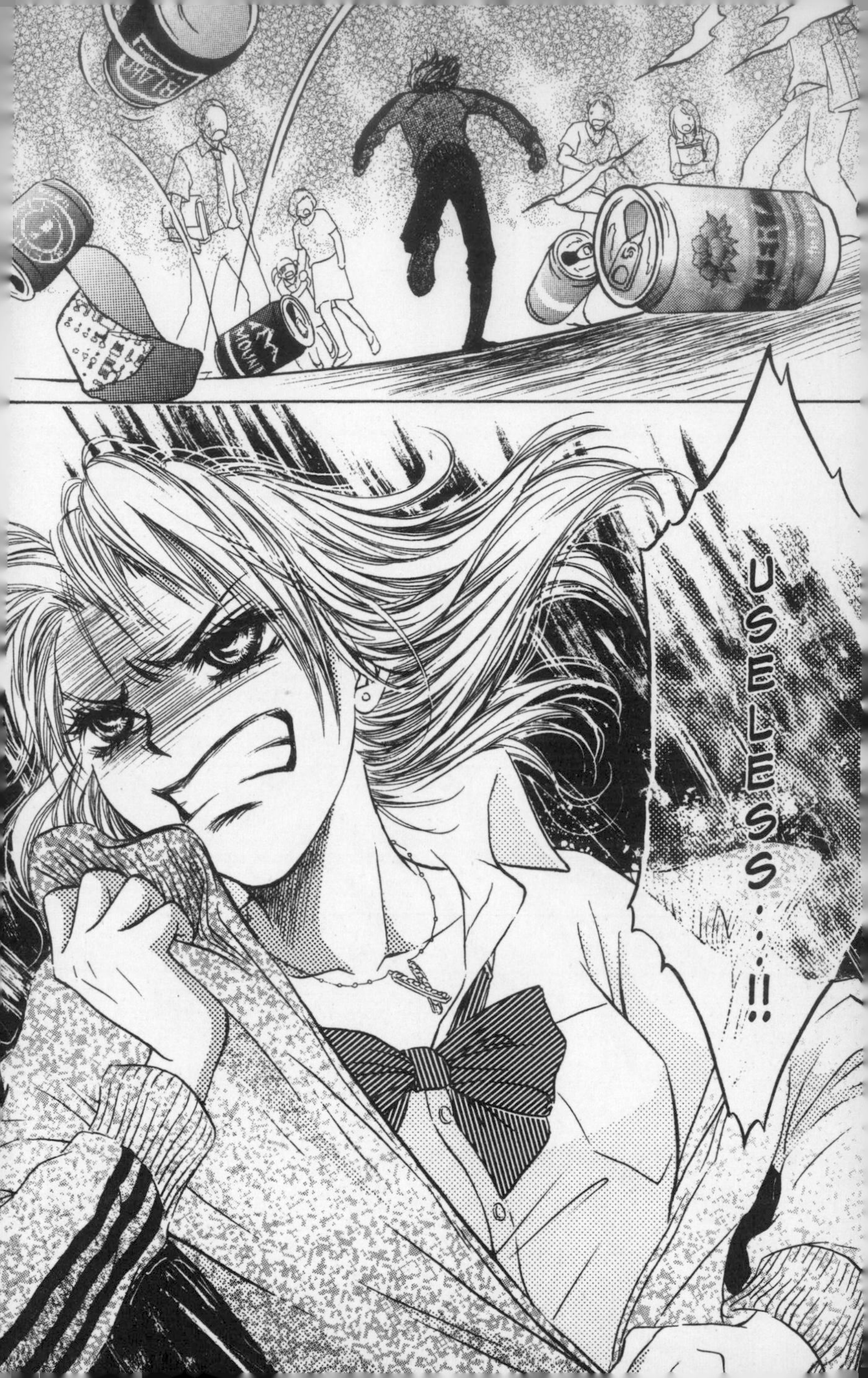
USELESS......!!

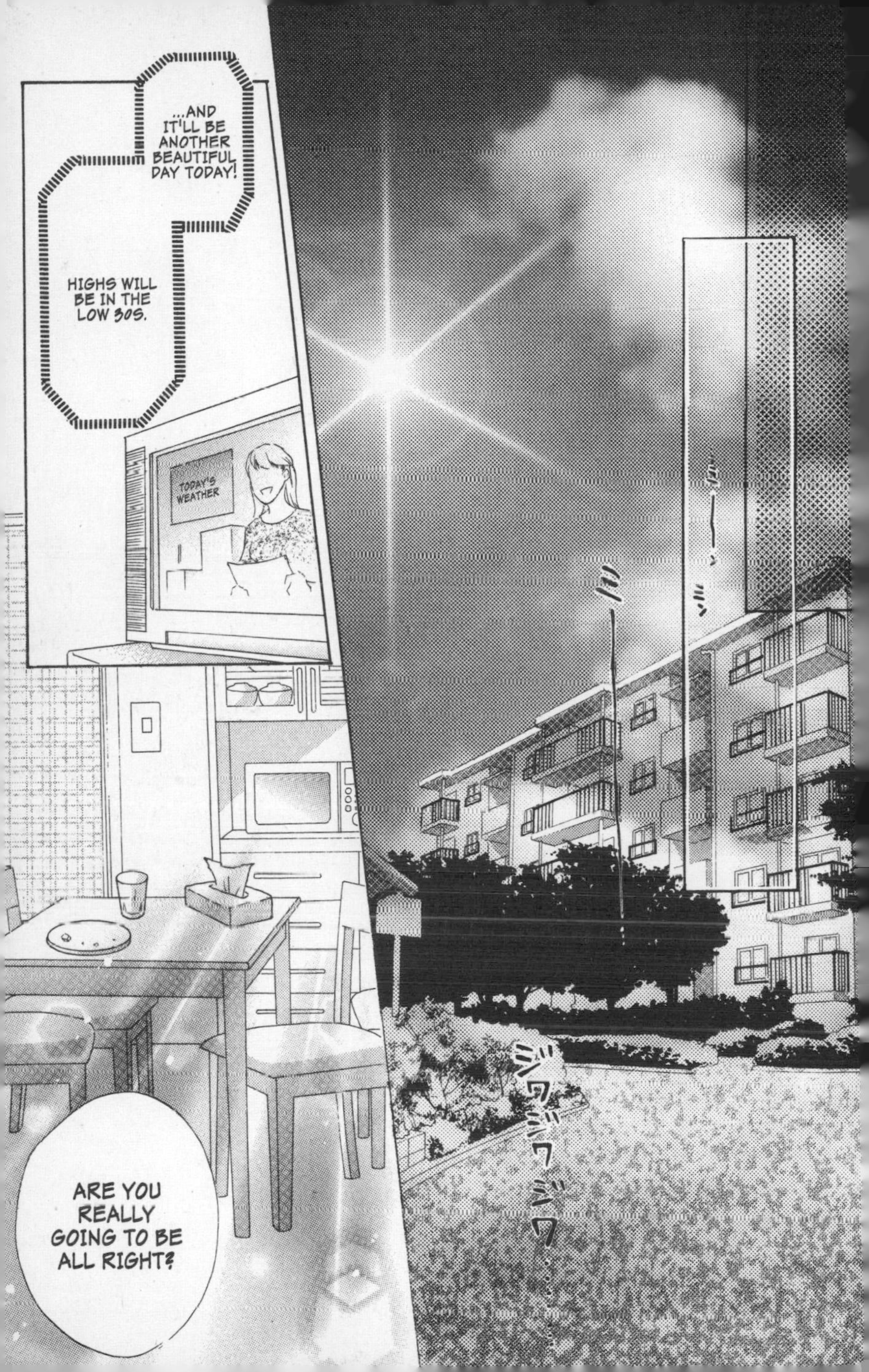
ジワジワジワ……
...AND IT'LL BE ANOTHER BEAUTIFUL DAY TODAY!
HIGHS WILL BE IN THE LOW 30S.
TODAY'S WEATHER
ARE YOU REALLY GOING TO BE ALL RIGHT?

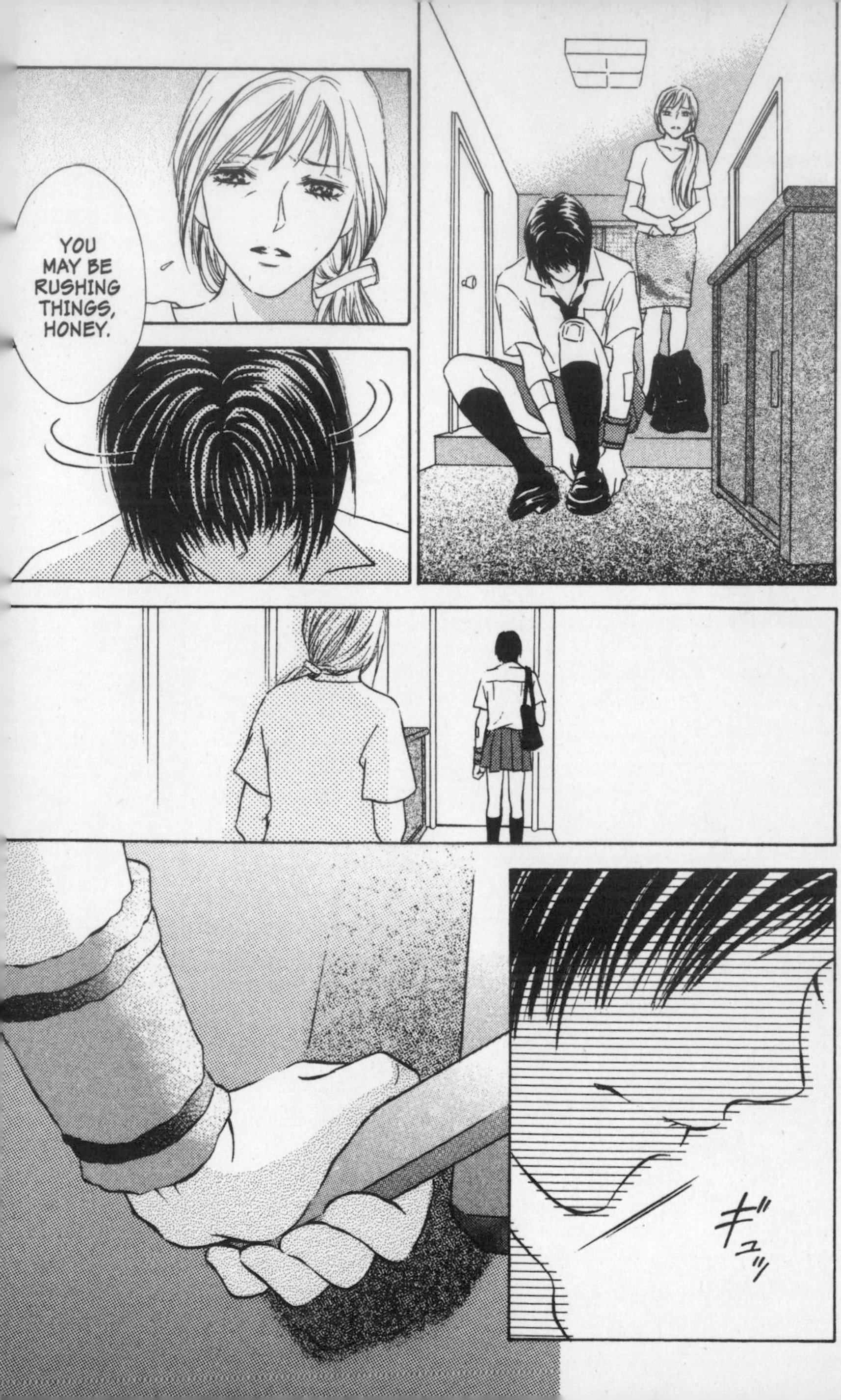
YOU MAY BE RUSHING THINGS, HONEY.
ギュッ

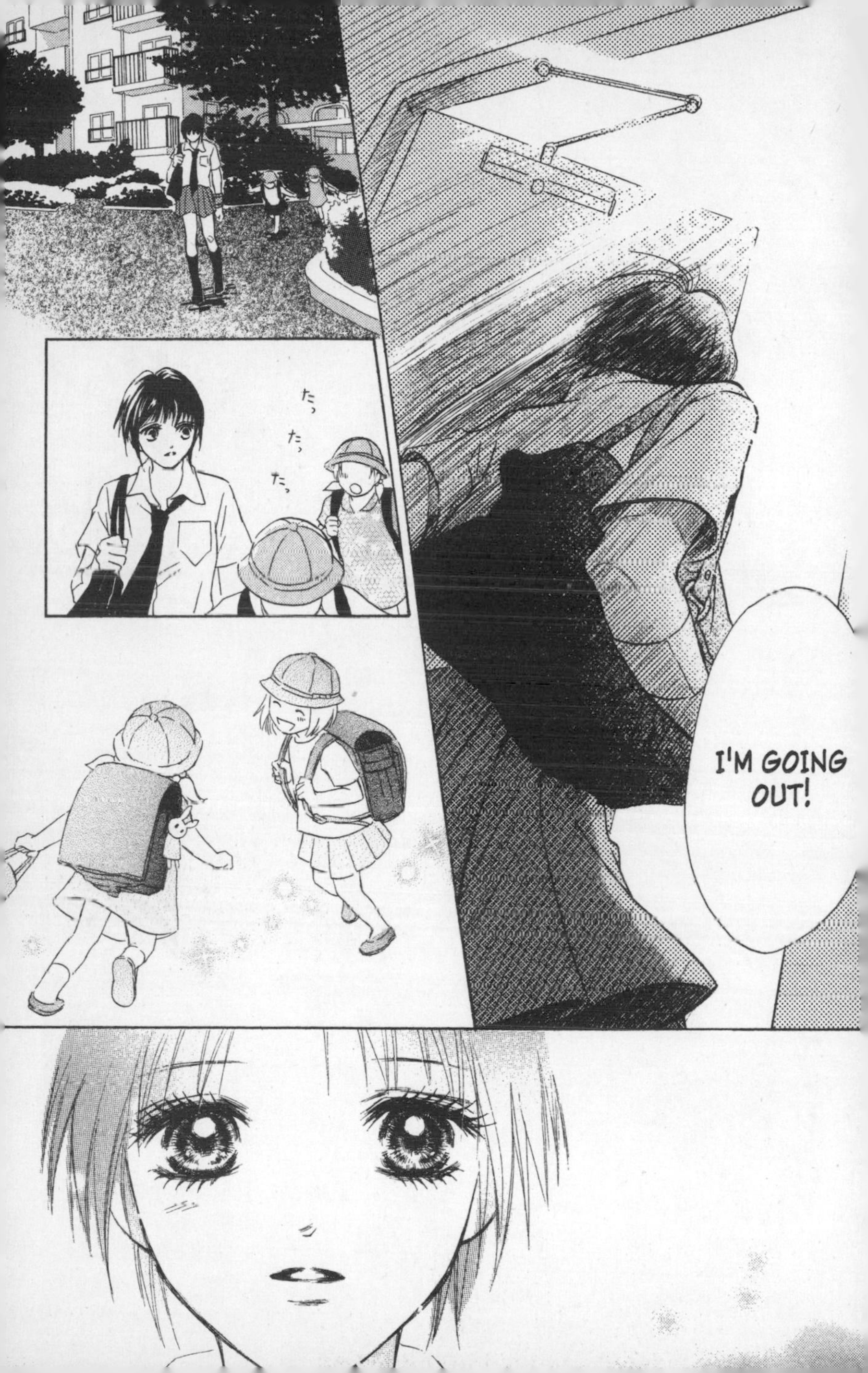
I'M GOING OUT!
たっ
たっ
たっ

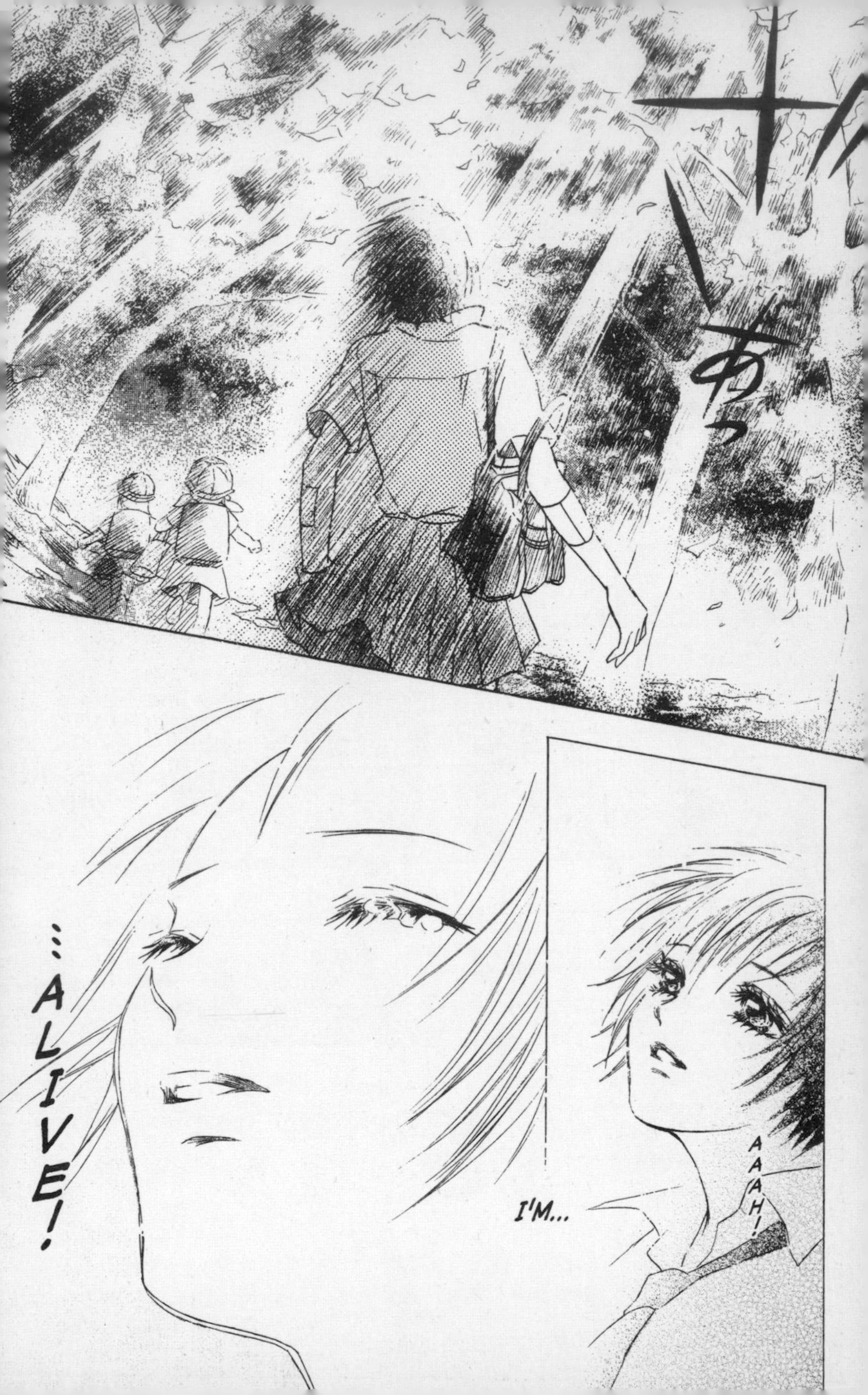

あっ
AAAH!
I'M...
...ALIVE!

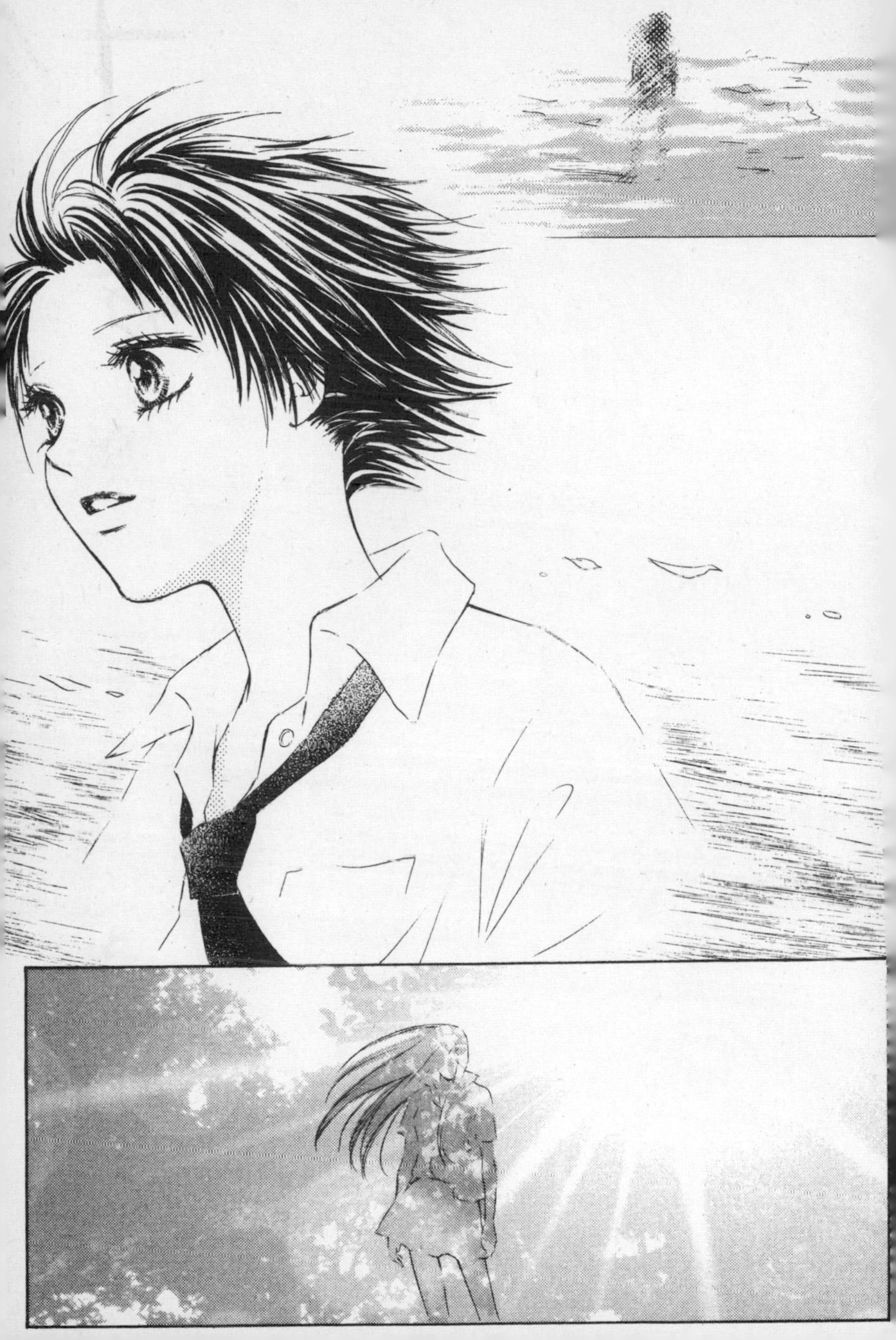

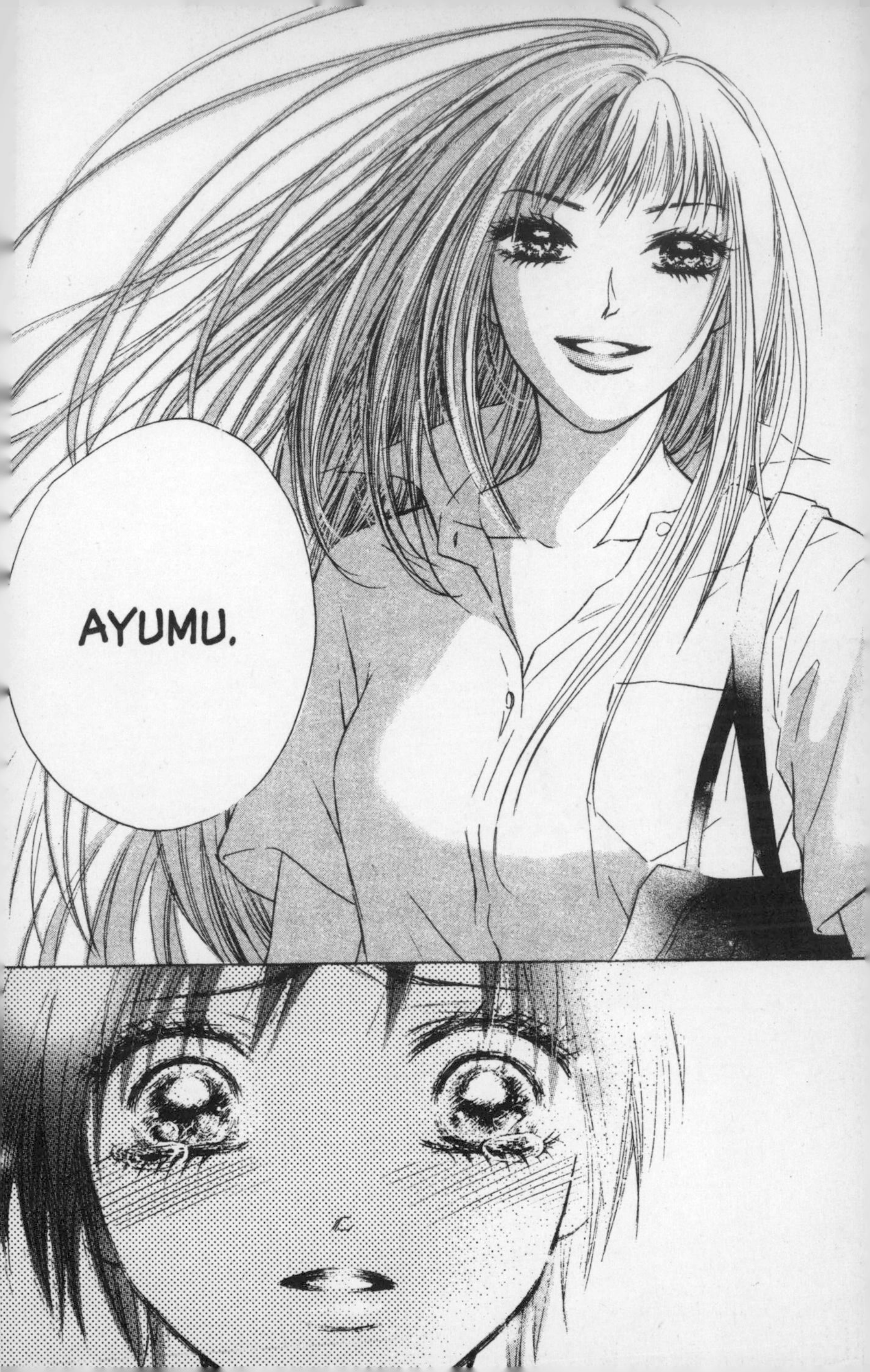
AYUMU.

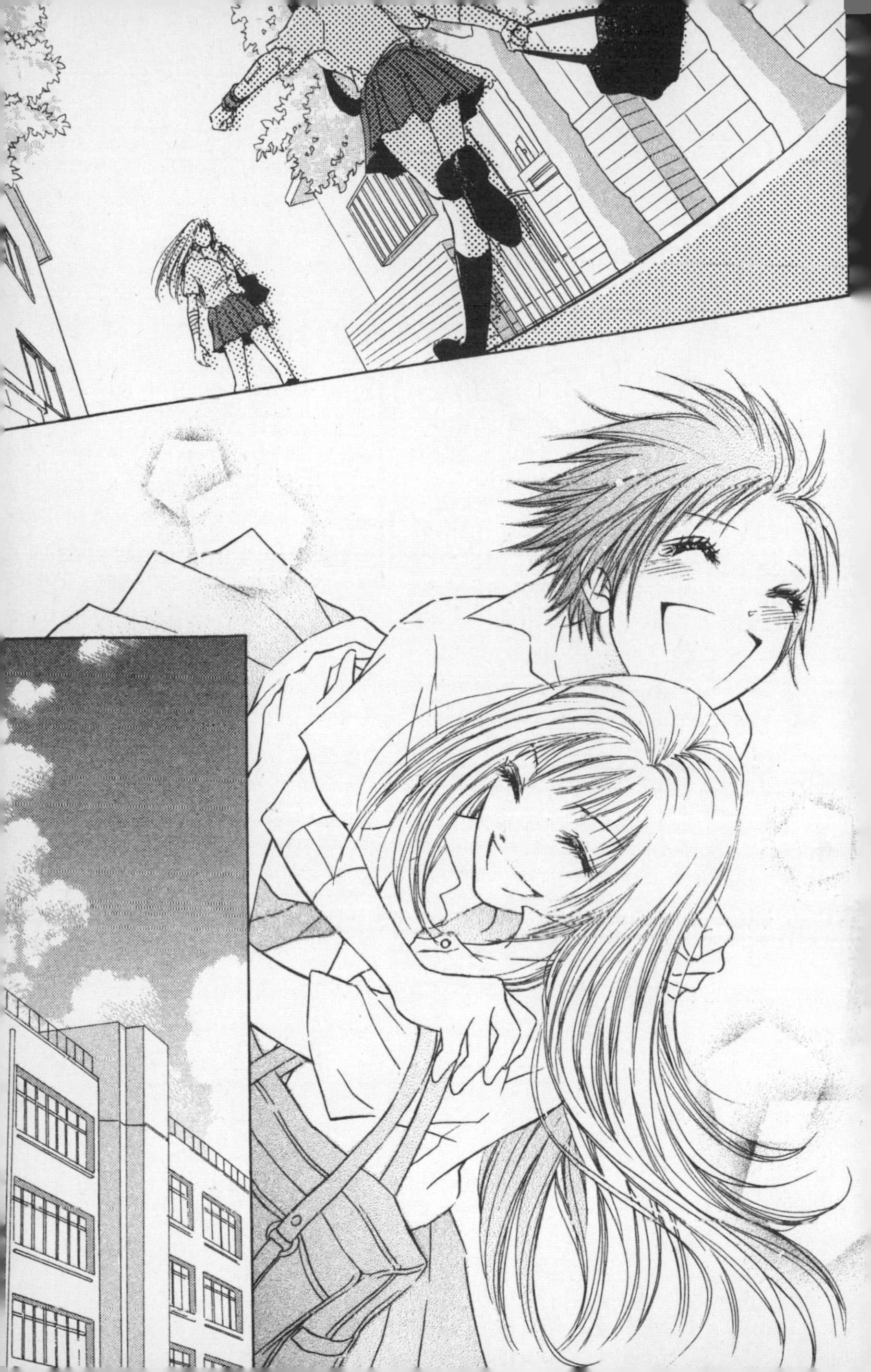

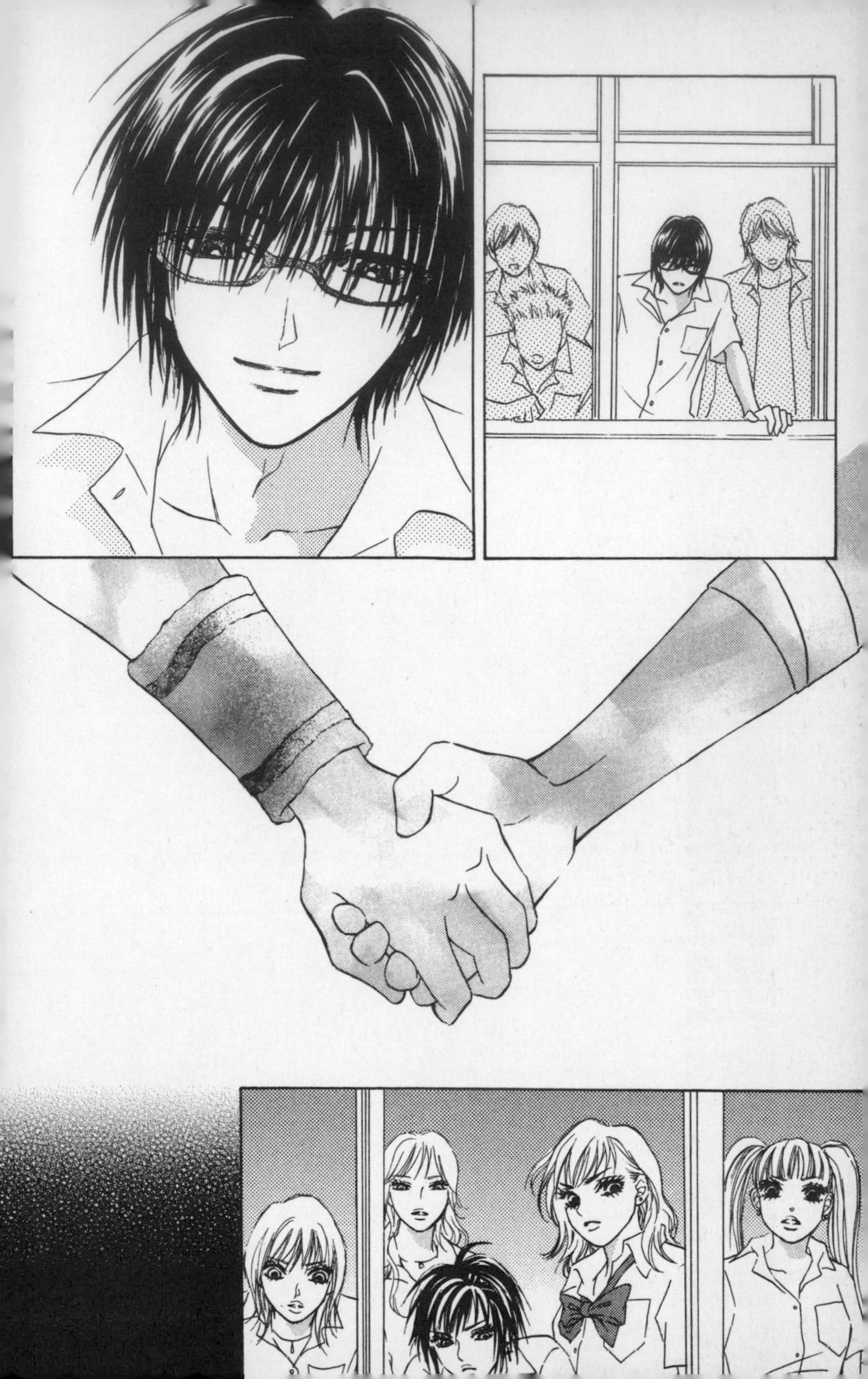

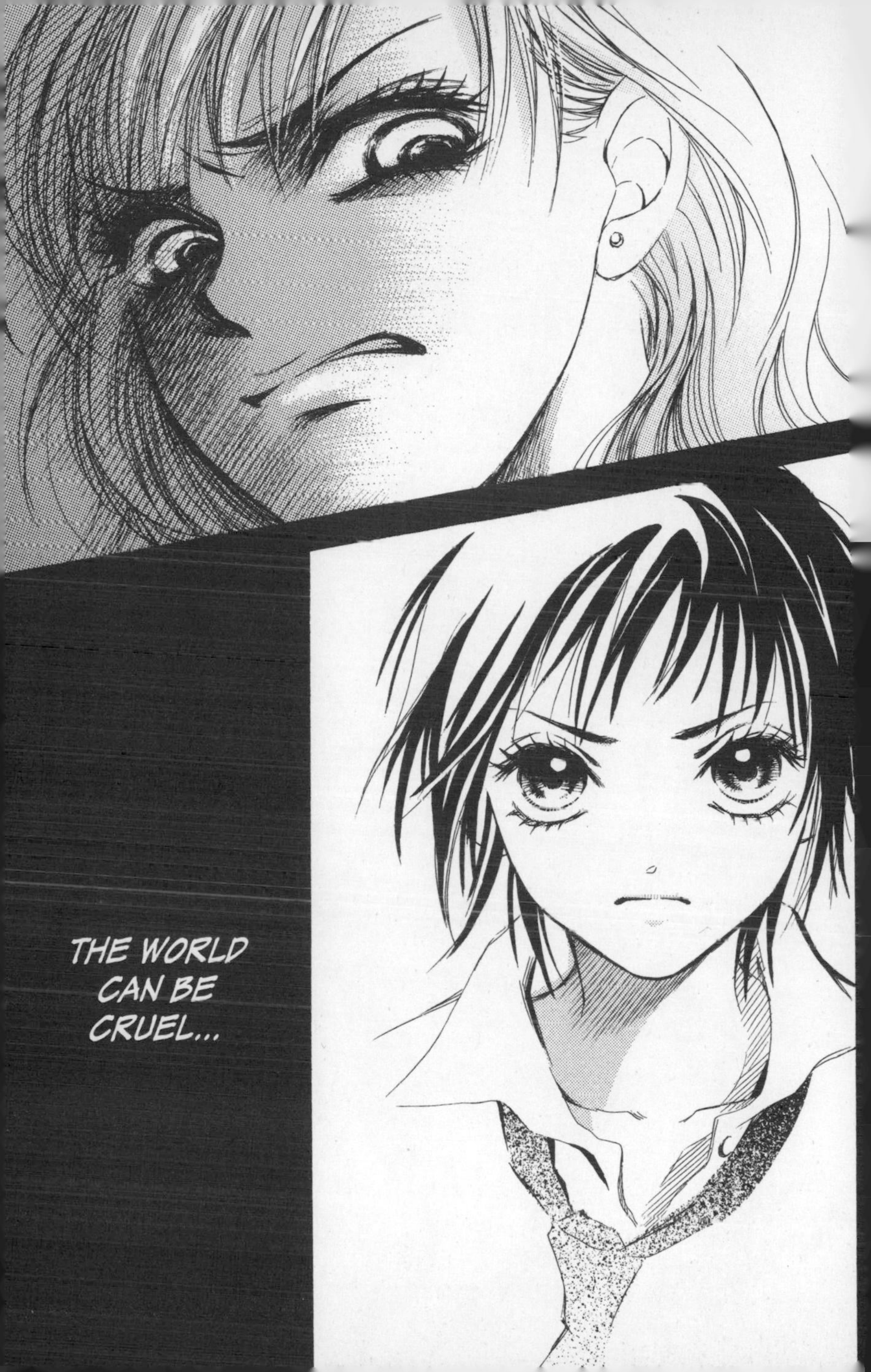
THE WORLD
CAN BE
CRUEL...

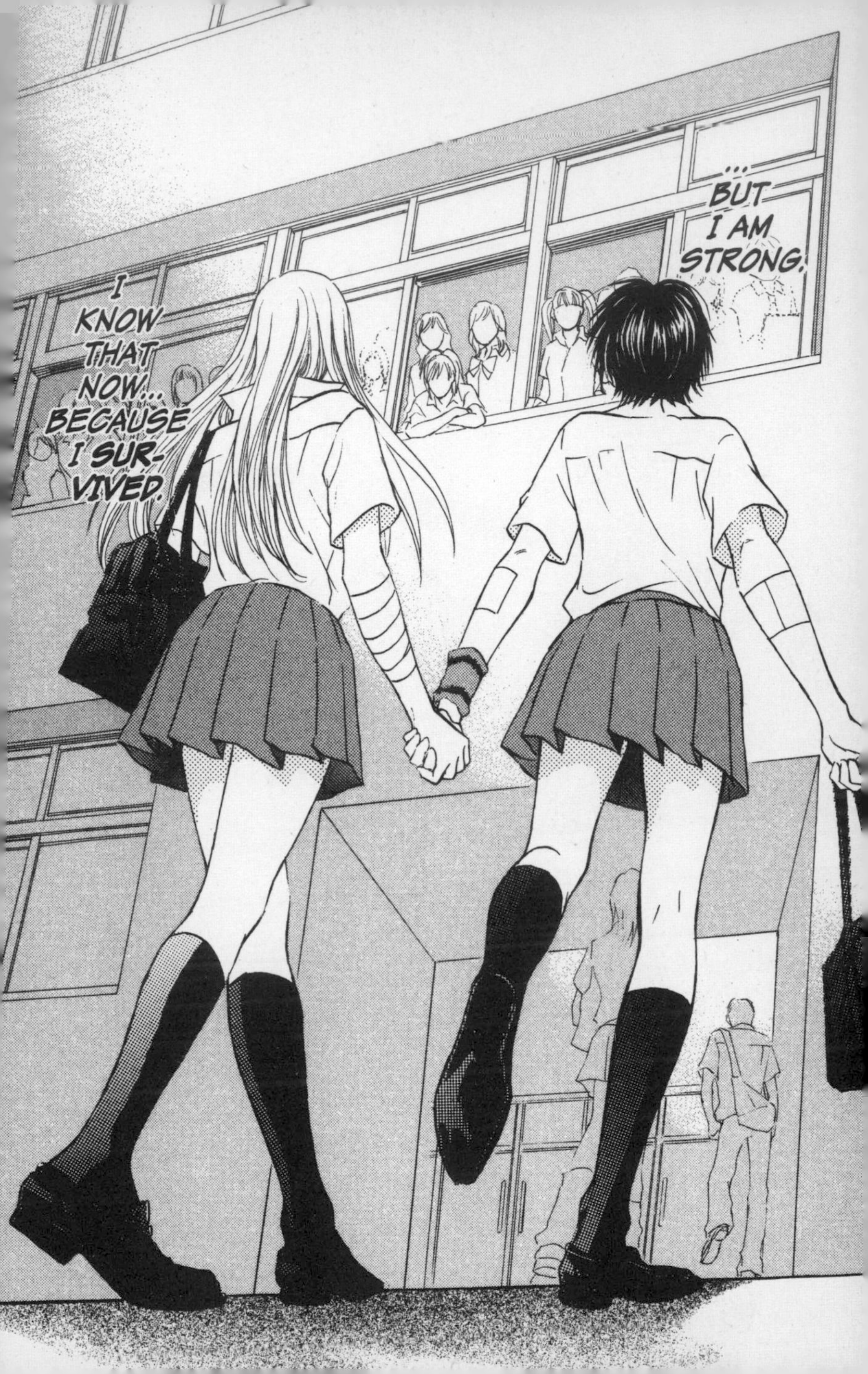
...BUT I AM STRONG.
I KNOW THAT NOW... BECAUSE I SUR-VIVED.

Chapter 33: Black Curtain

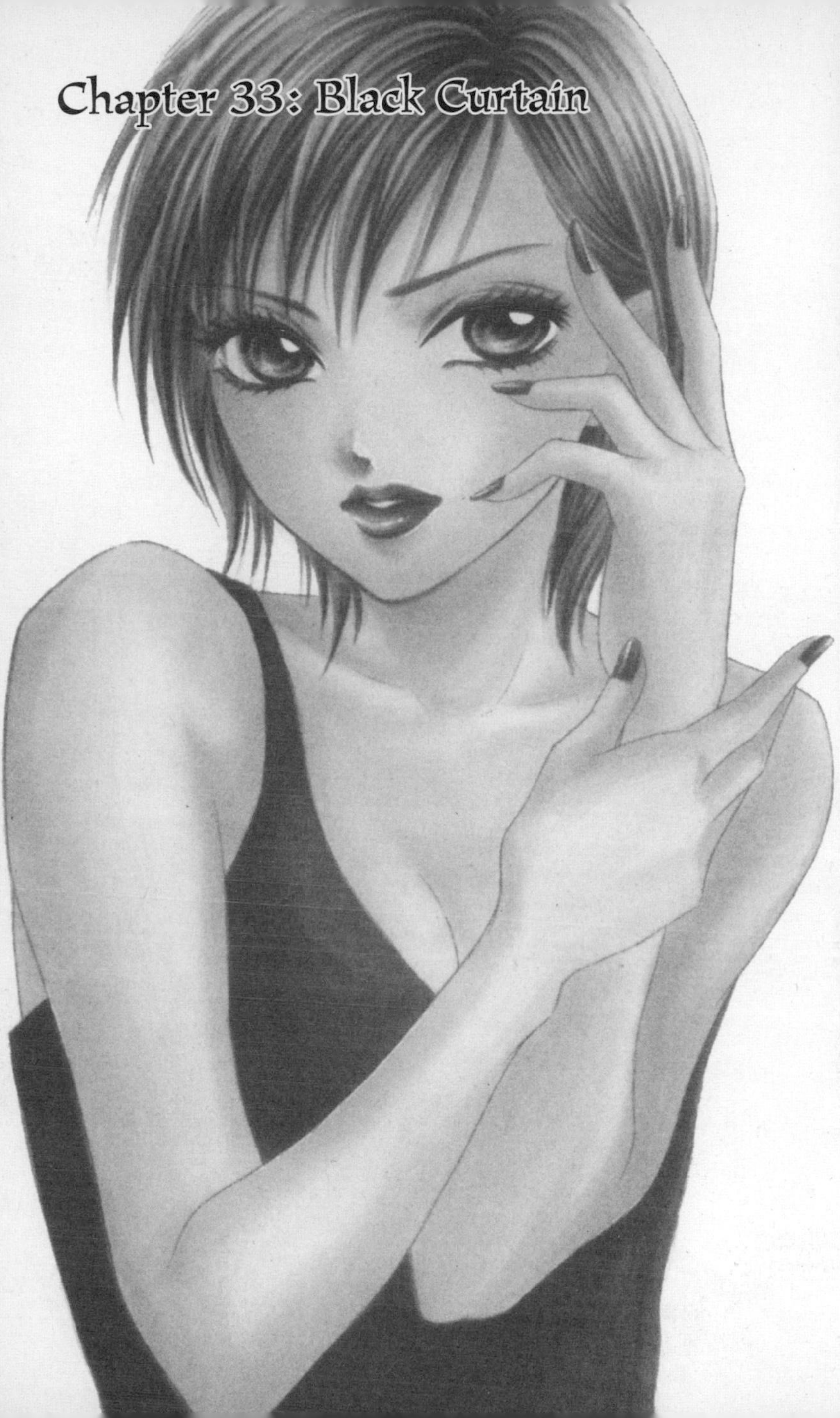

ライフ
Life

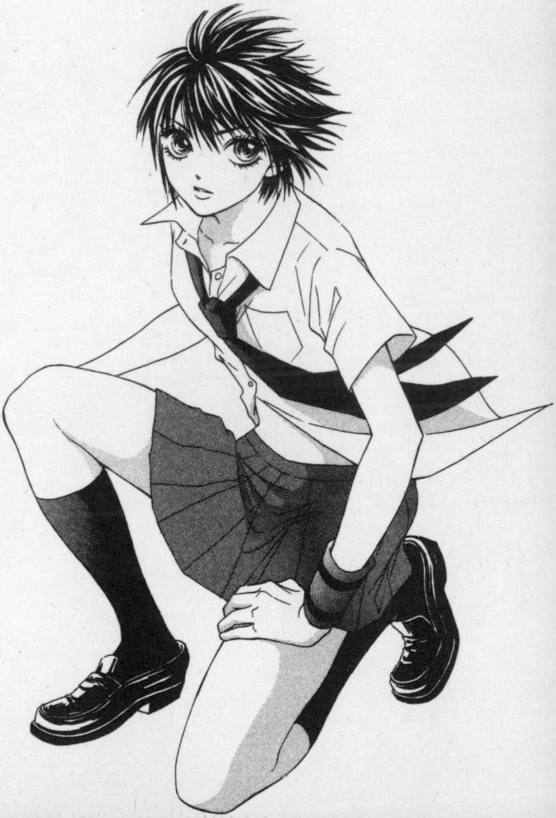

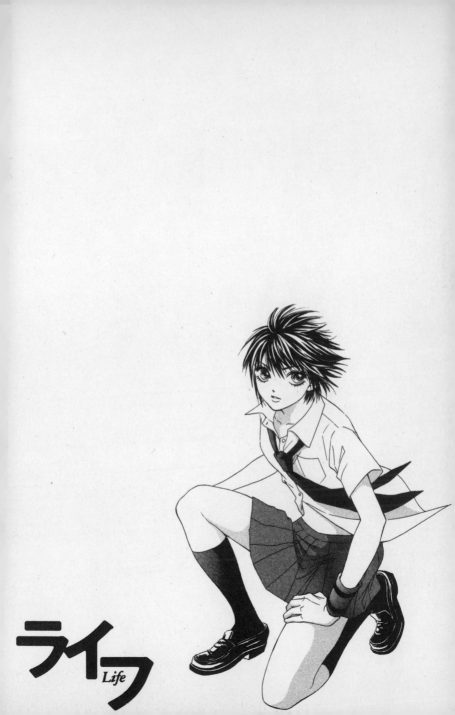

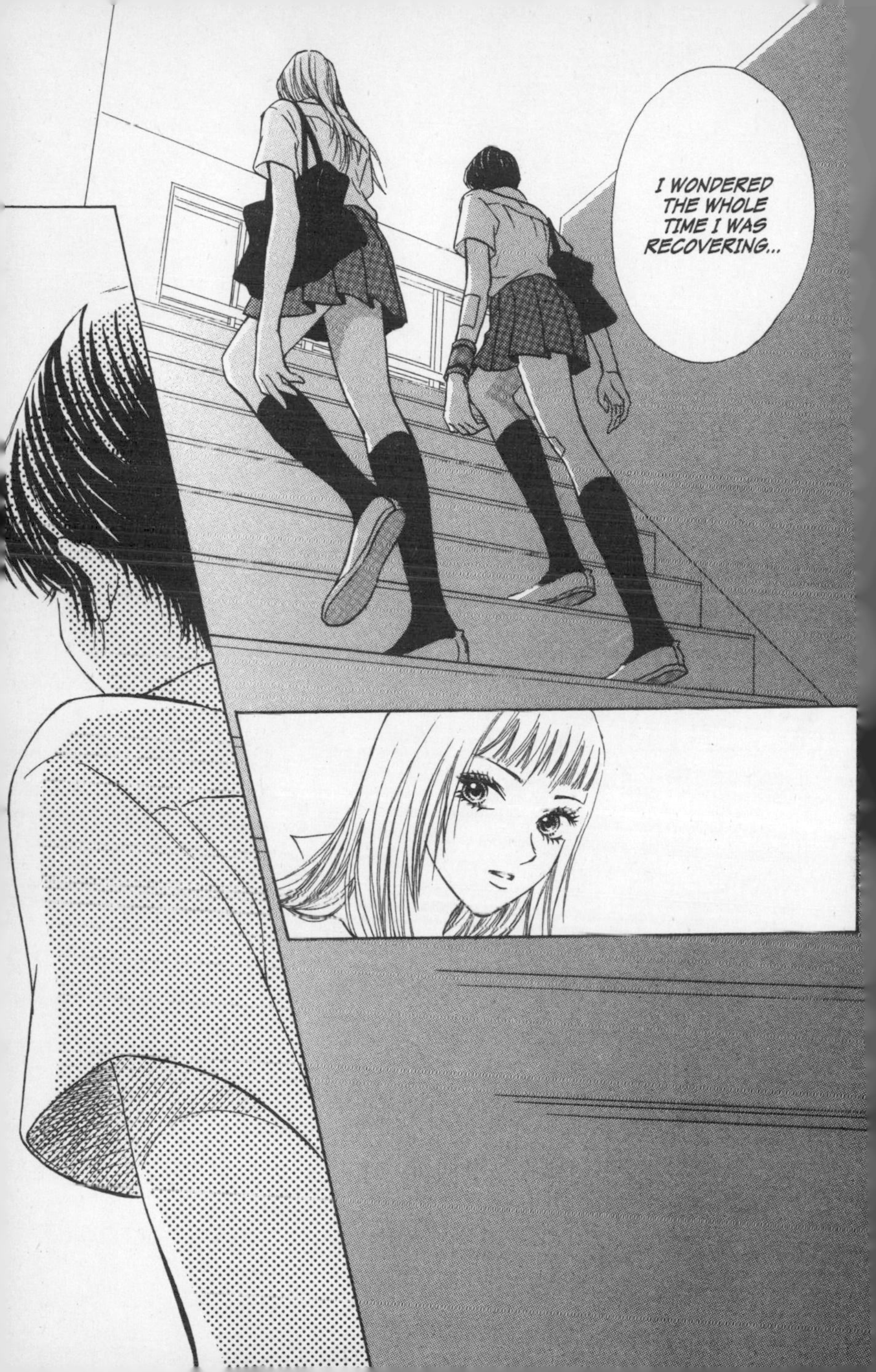
I WONDERED THE WHOLE TIME I WAS RECOVERING...

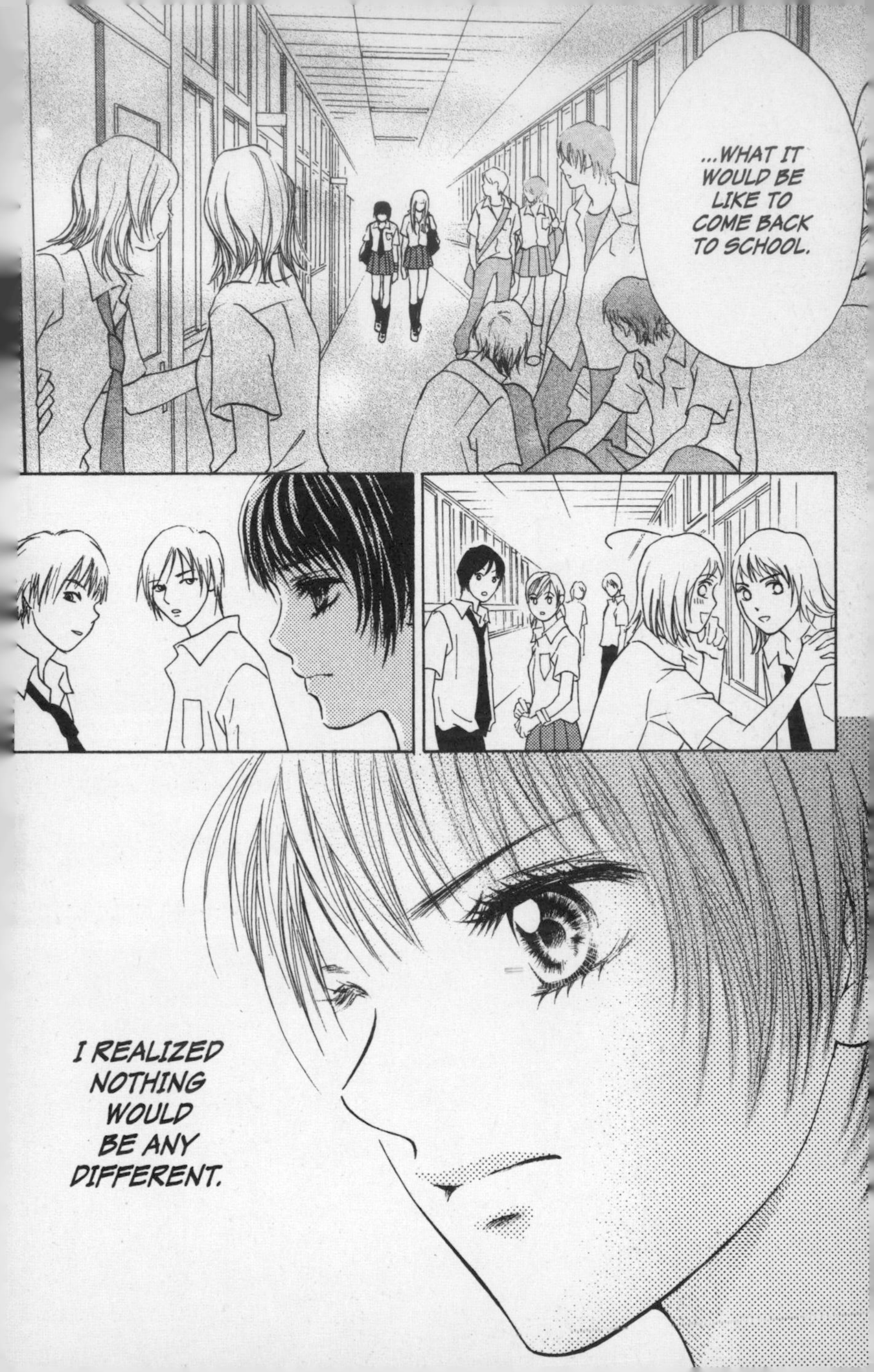
...WHAT IT WOULD BE LIKE TO COME BACK TO SCHOOL.
I REALIZED NOTHING WOULD BE ANY DIFFERENT.

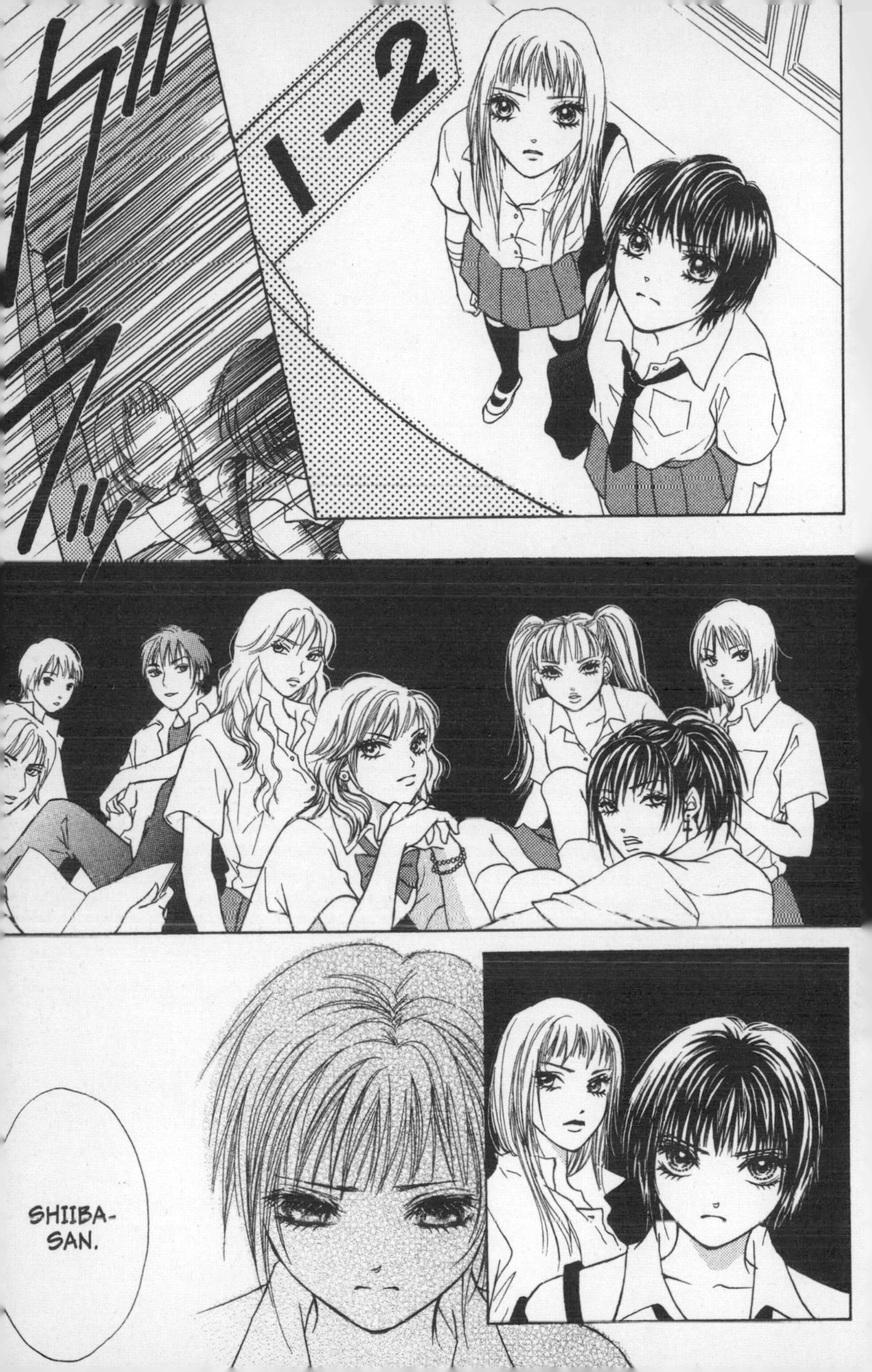
1-2
SHIIBA-SAN.

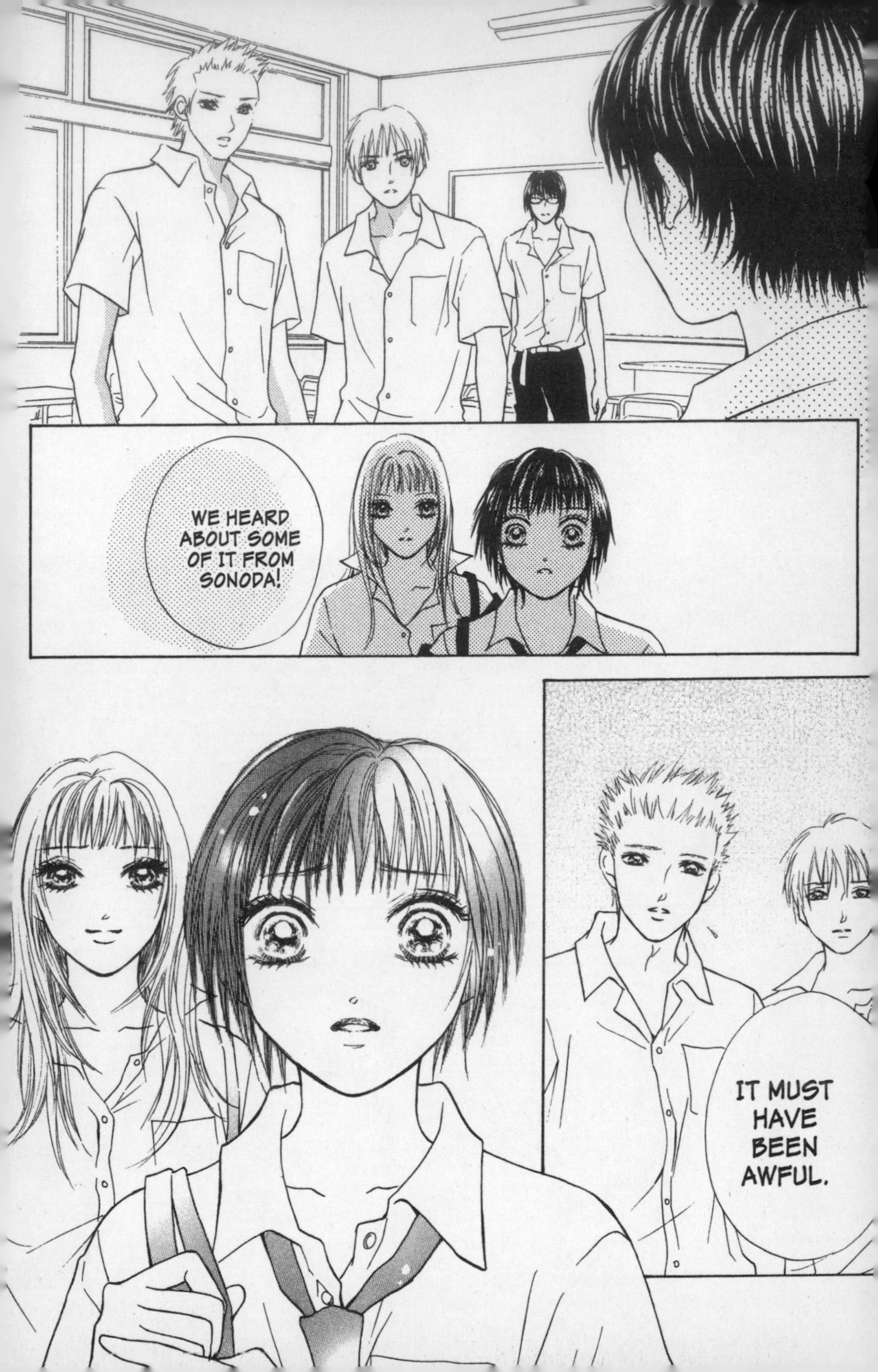
WE HEARD ABOUT SOME OF IT FROM SONODA!
IT MUST HAVE BEEN AWFUL.

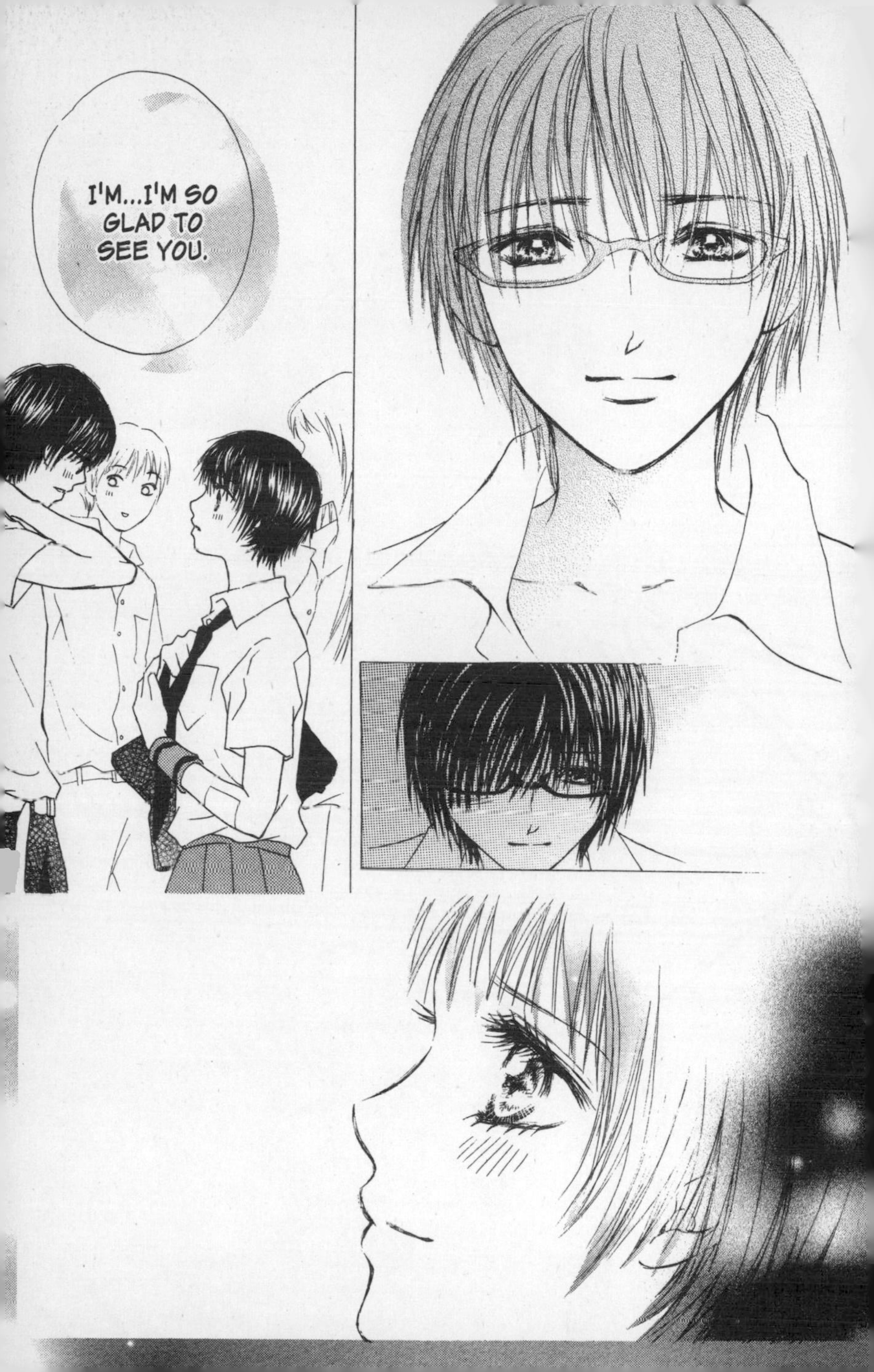
I'M...I'M SO GLAD TO SEE YOU.

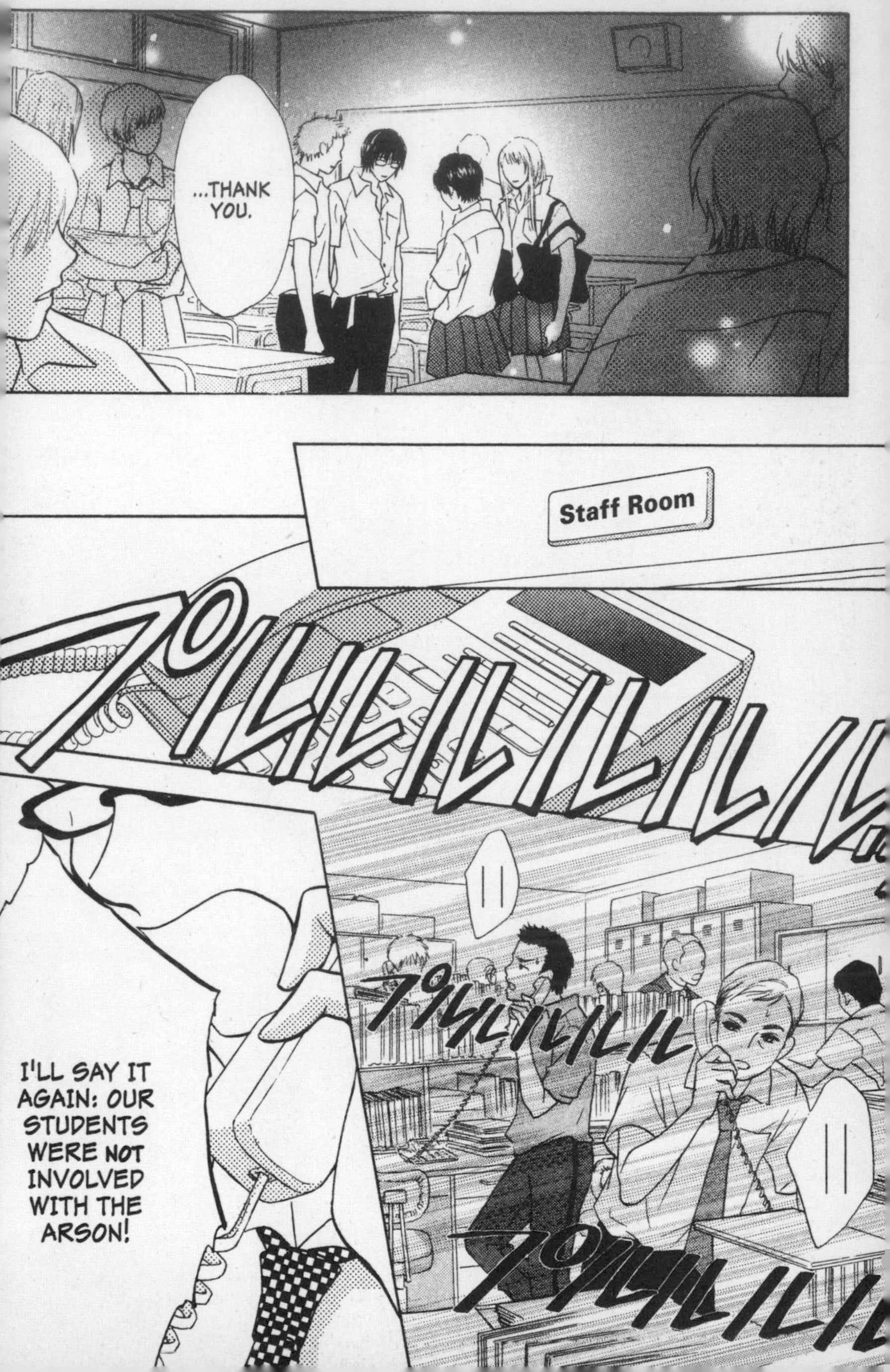
...THANK YOU.
Staff Room
I'LL SAY IT AGAIN: OUR STUDENTS WERE NOT INVOLVED WITH THE ARSON!

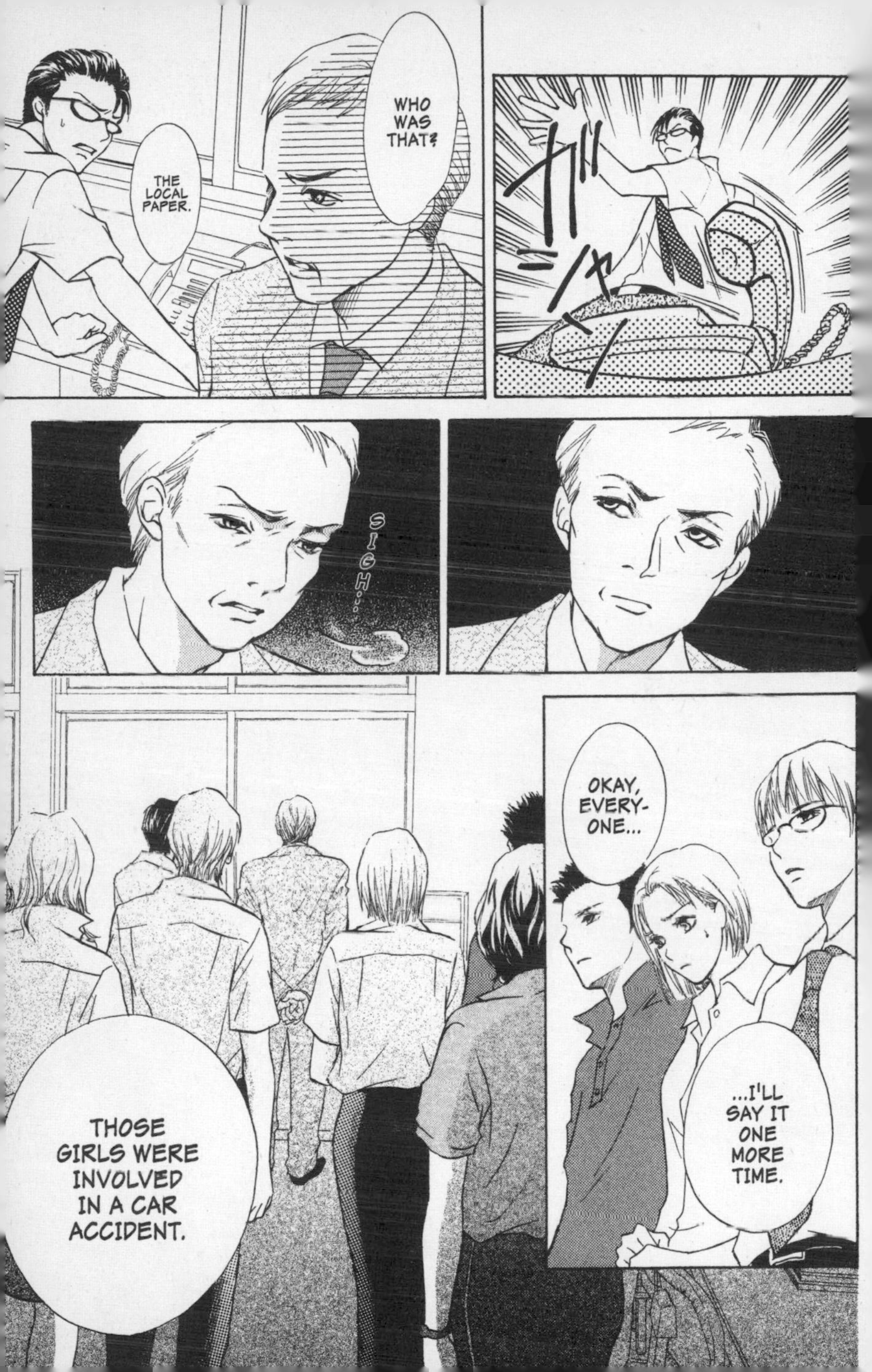
WHO WAS THAT?
THE LOCAL PAPER.
SIGH...
OKAY, EVERY-ONE...
...I'LL SAY IT ONE MORE TIME.
THOSE GIRLS WERE INVOLVED IN A CAR ACCIDENT.

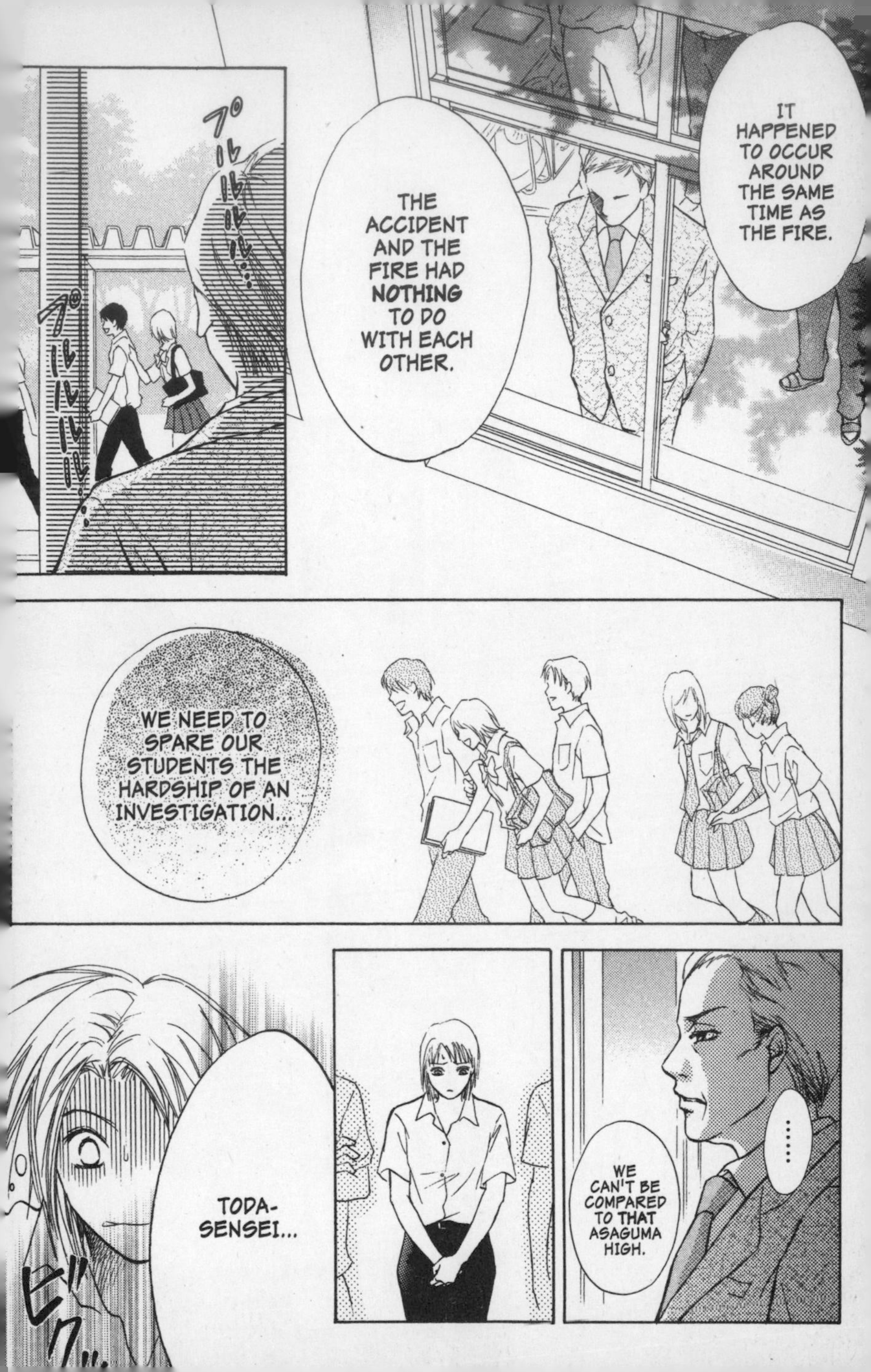
IT HAPPENED TO OCCUR AROUND THE SAME TIME AS THE FIRE.
THE ACCIDENT AND THE FIRE HAD NOTHING TO DO WITH EACH OTHER.
WE NEED TO SPARE OUR STUDENTS THE HARDSHIP OF AN INVESTIGATION...
......
WE CAN'T BE COMPARED TO THAT ASAGUMA HIGH.
TODA-SENSEI...

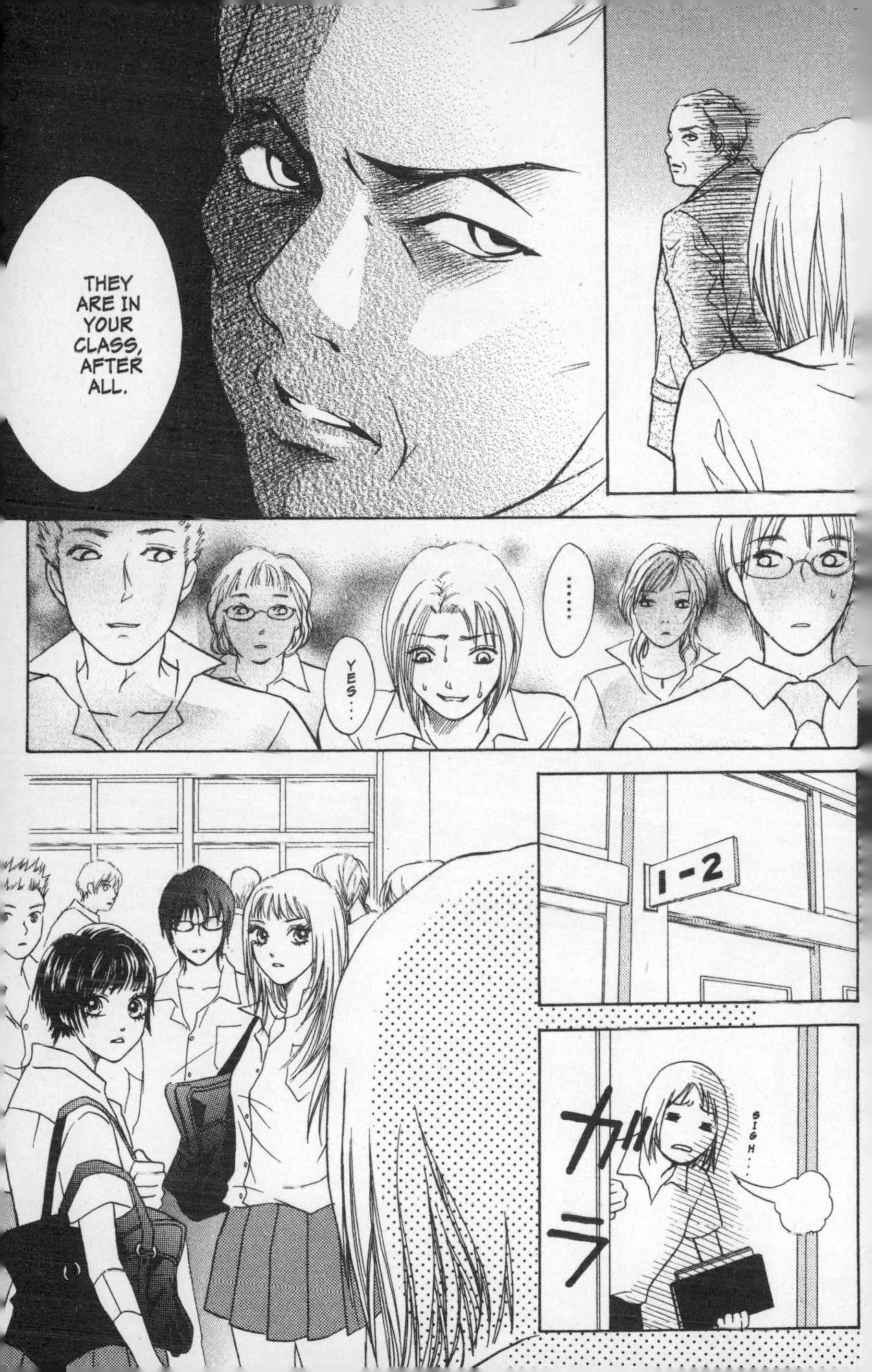
THEY ARE IN YOUR CLASS, AFTER ALL.
......
YES...
1-2
ガラ
SIGH...

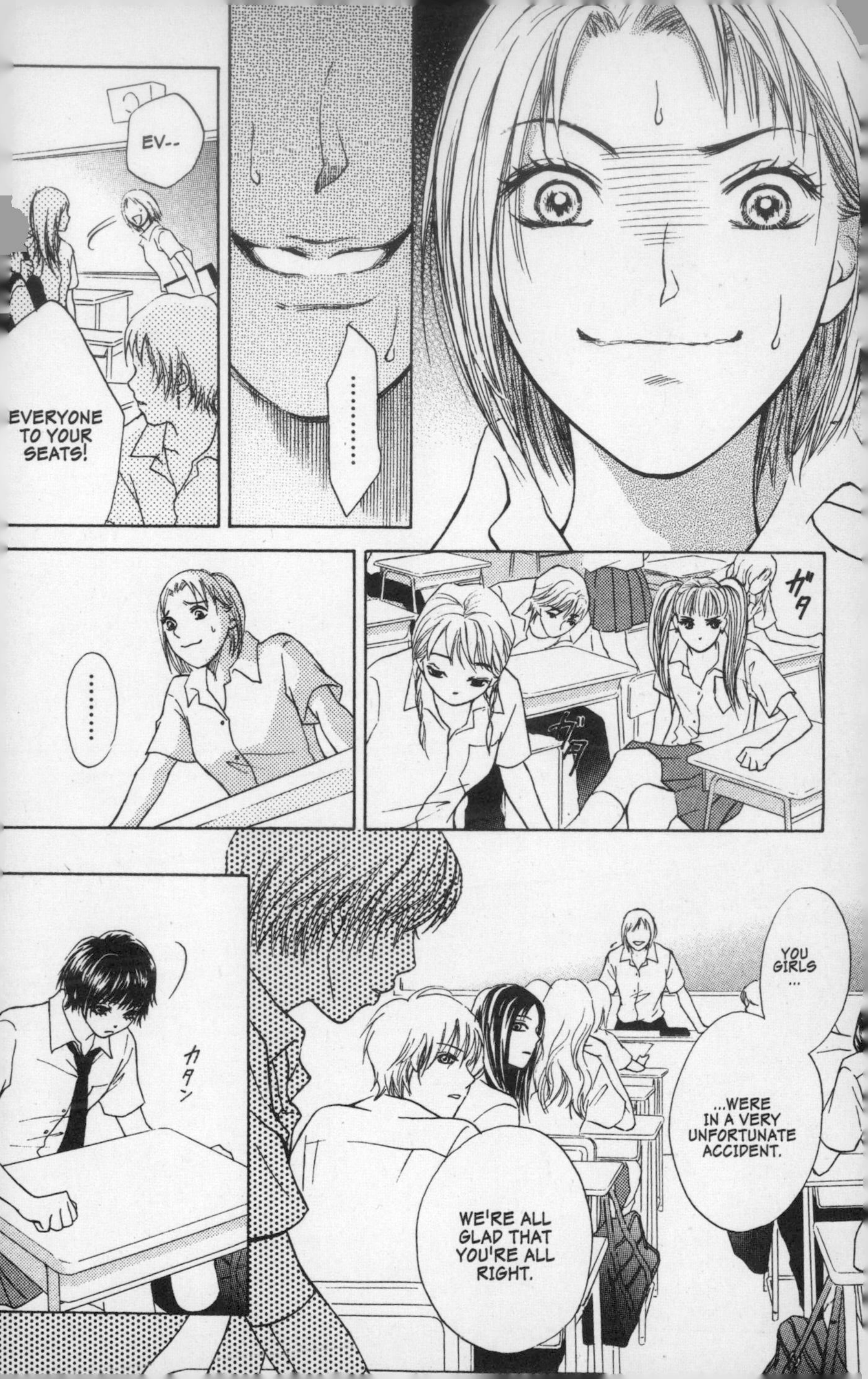
......
EV--
EVERYONE TO YOUR SEATS!
ガタ
ガタ
......
YOU GIRLS ...
...WERE IN A VERY UNFORTUNATE ACCIDENT.
WE'RE ALL GLAD THAT YOU'RE ALL RIGHT.
カタン

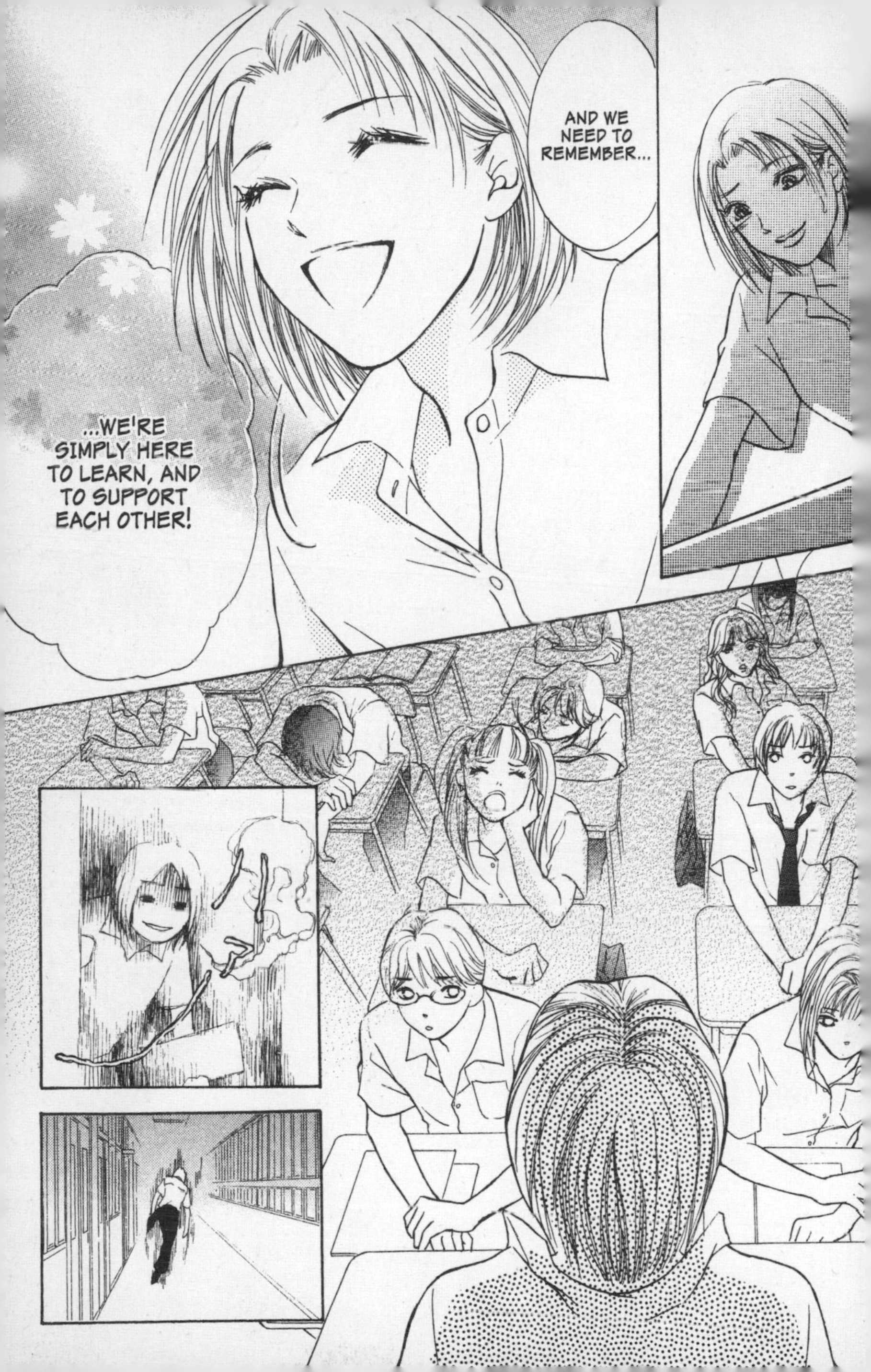
AND WE NEED TO REMEMBER...
...WE'RE SIMPLY HERE TO LEARN, AND TO SUPPORT EACH OTHER!

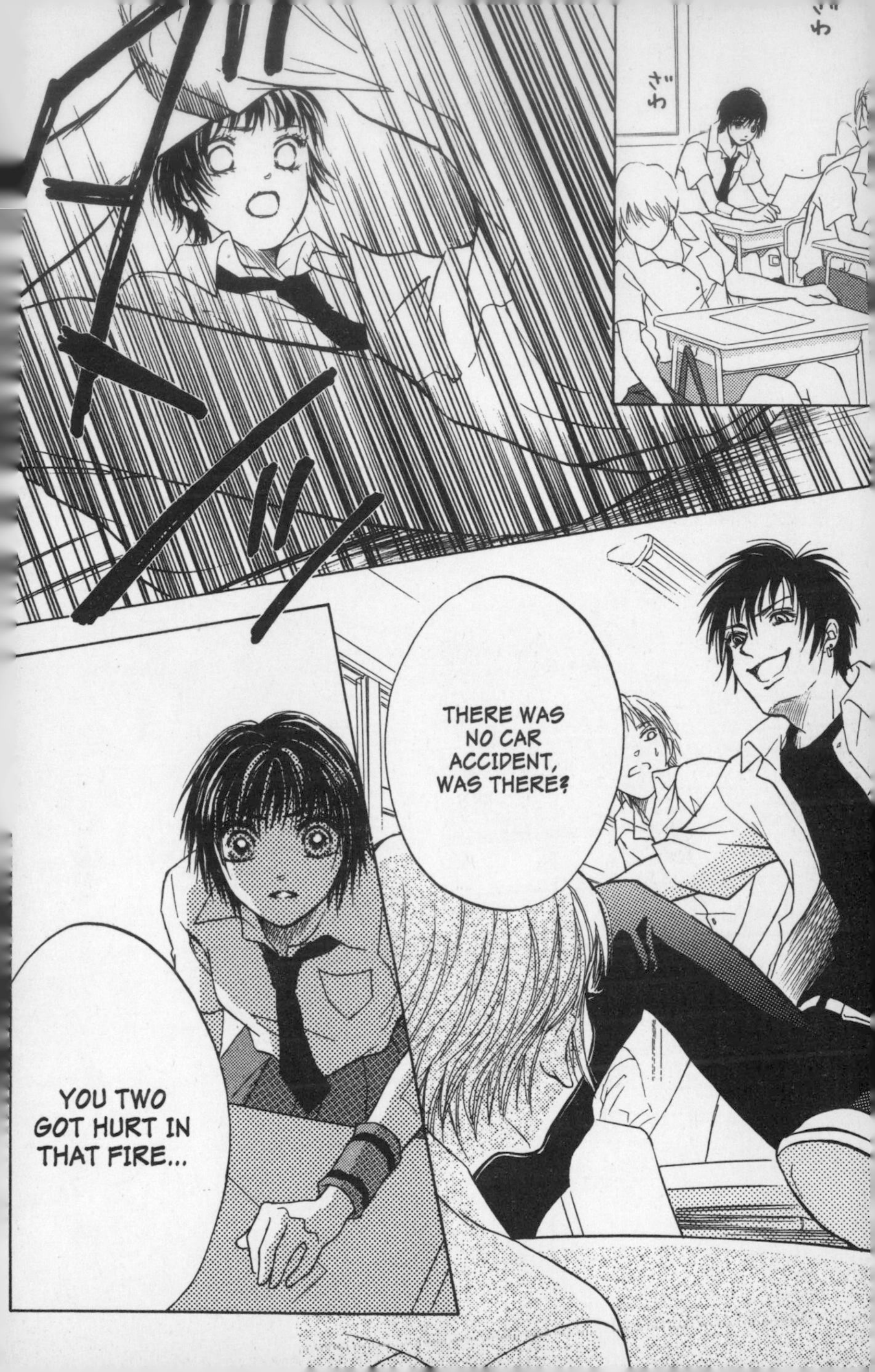
ざわ
ざわ
THERE WAS NO CAR ACCIDENT, WAS THERE?
YOU TWO GOT HURT IN THAT FIRE...

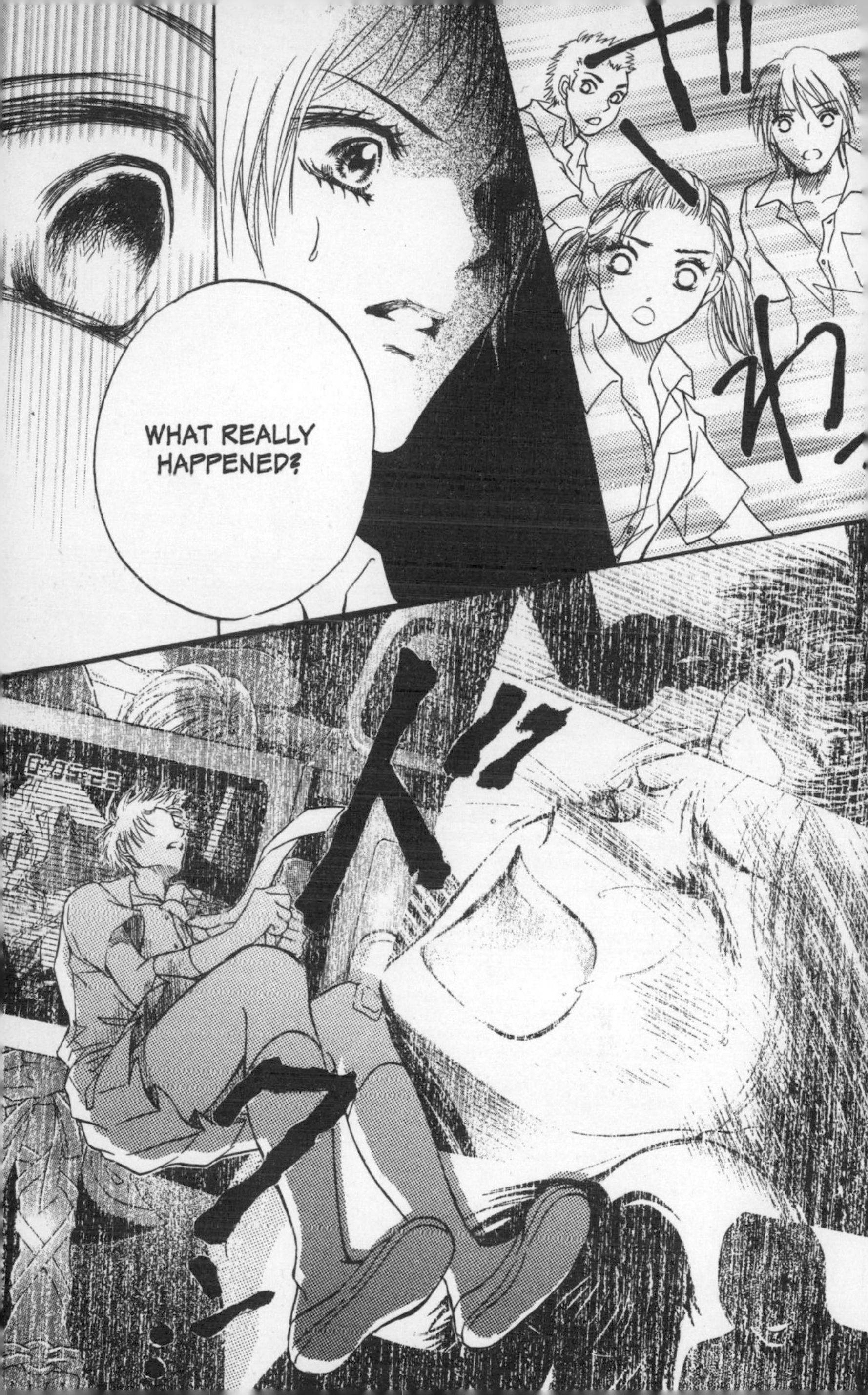
WHAT REALLY HAPPENED?

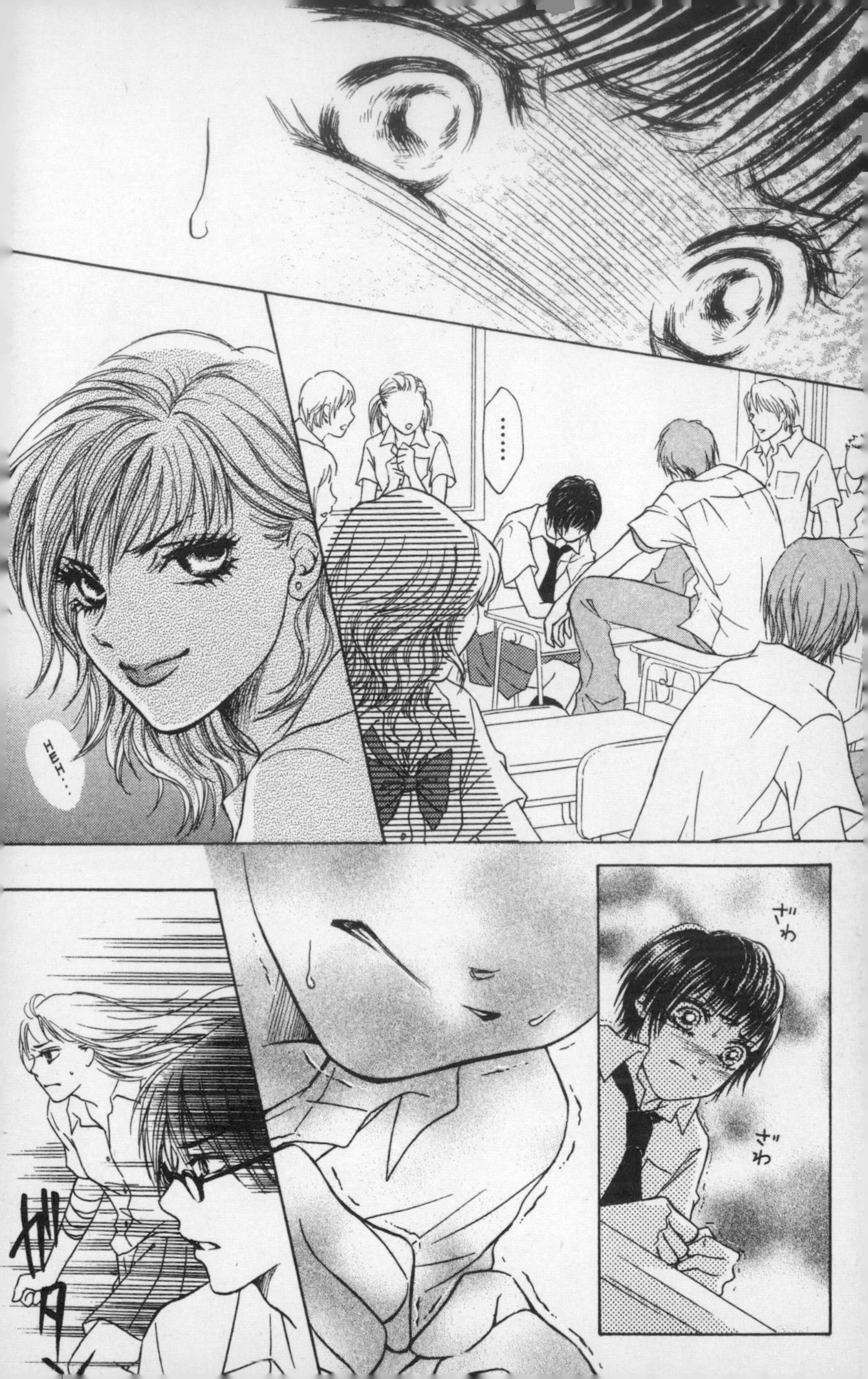
......
HEH...
ざわ
ざわ
ガタ

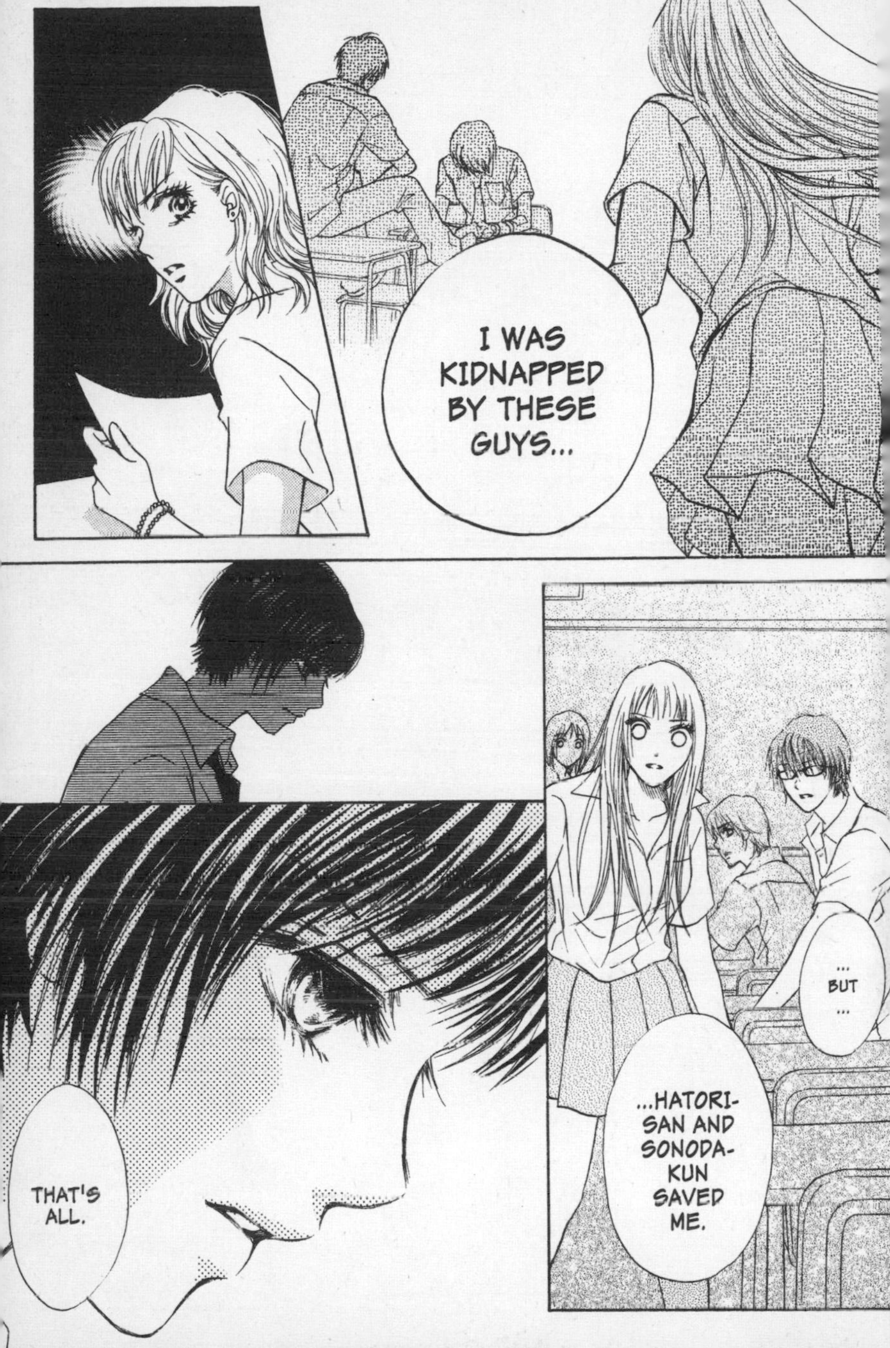
I WAS KIDNAPPED BY THESE GUYS...
...BUT...
...HATORI-SAN AND SONODA-KUN SAVED ME.
THAT'S ALL.

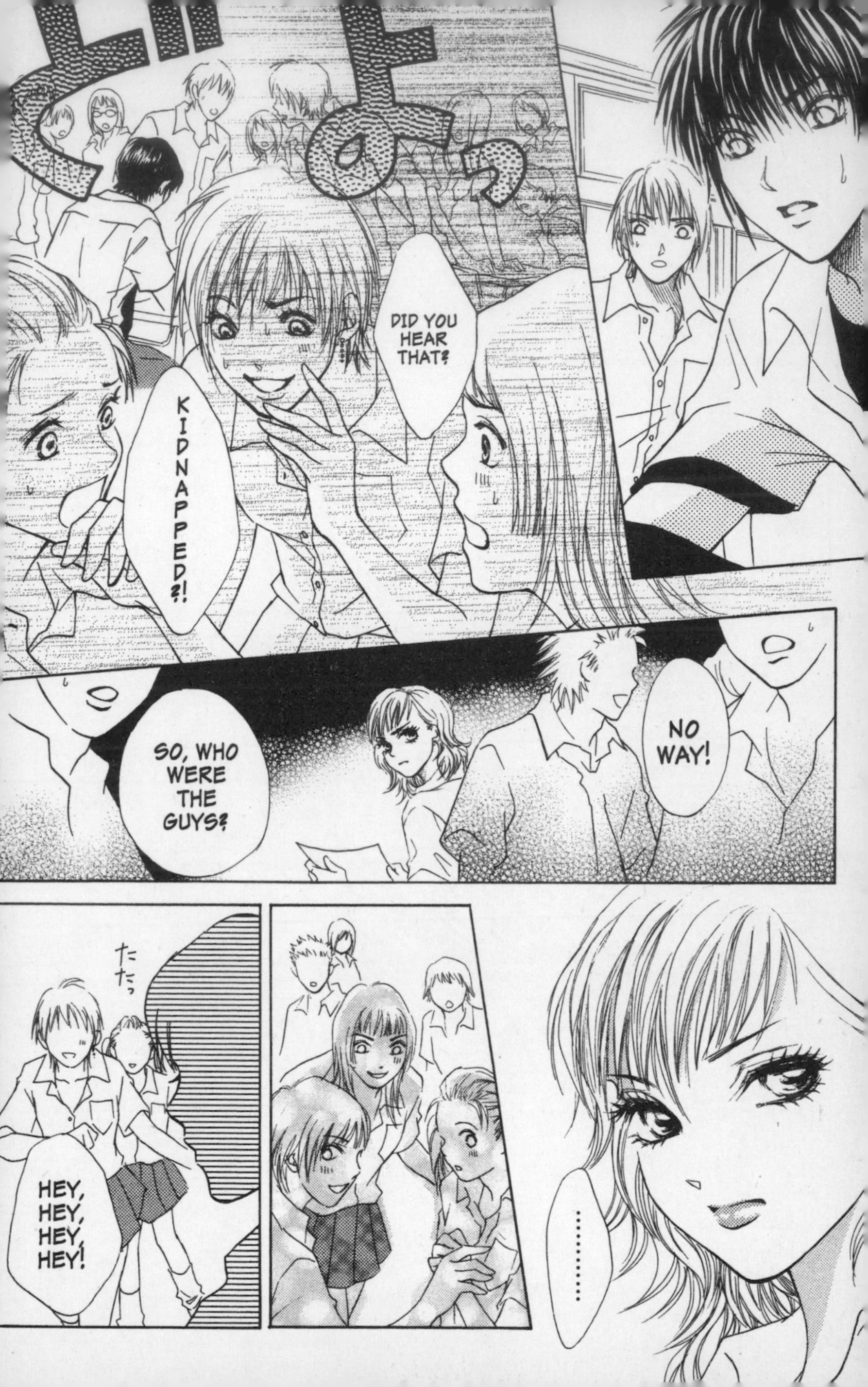
どよっ
DID YOU HEAR THAT?
KIDNAPPED?!
NO WAY!
SO, WHO WERE THE GUYS?
……
たたっ
HEY, HEY, HEY, HEY!

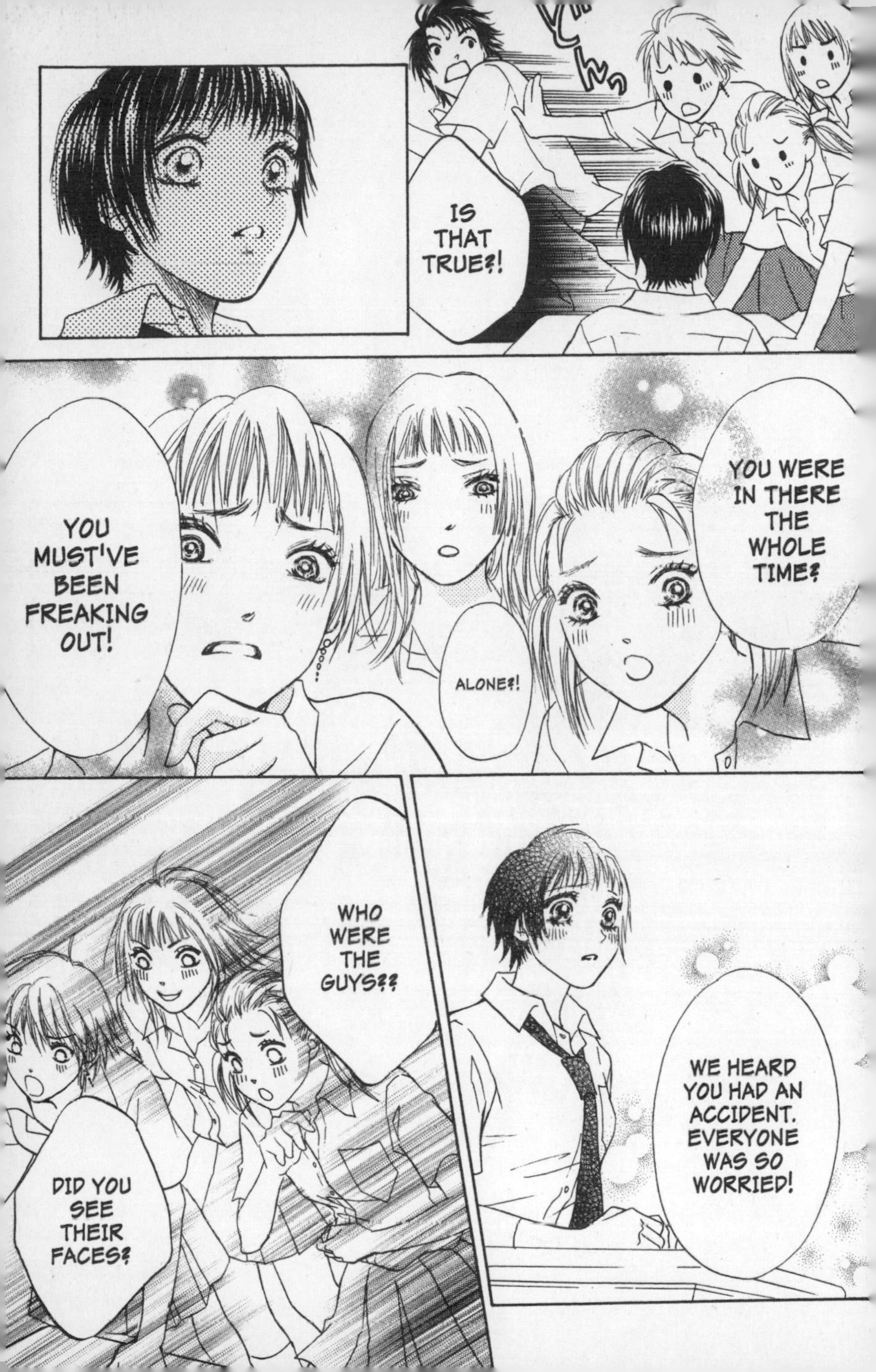
IS THAT TRUE?!
YOU WERE IN THERE THE WHOLE TIME?
ALONE?!
YOU MUST'VE BEEN FREAKING OUT!
WE HEARD YOU HAD AN ACCIDENT. EVERYONE WAS SO WORRIED!
WHO WERE THE GUYS??
DID YOU SEE THEIR FACES?

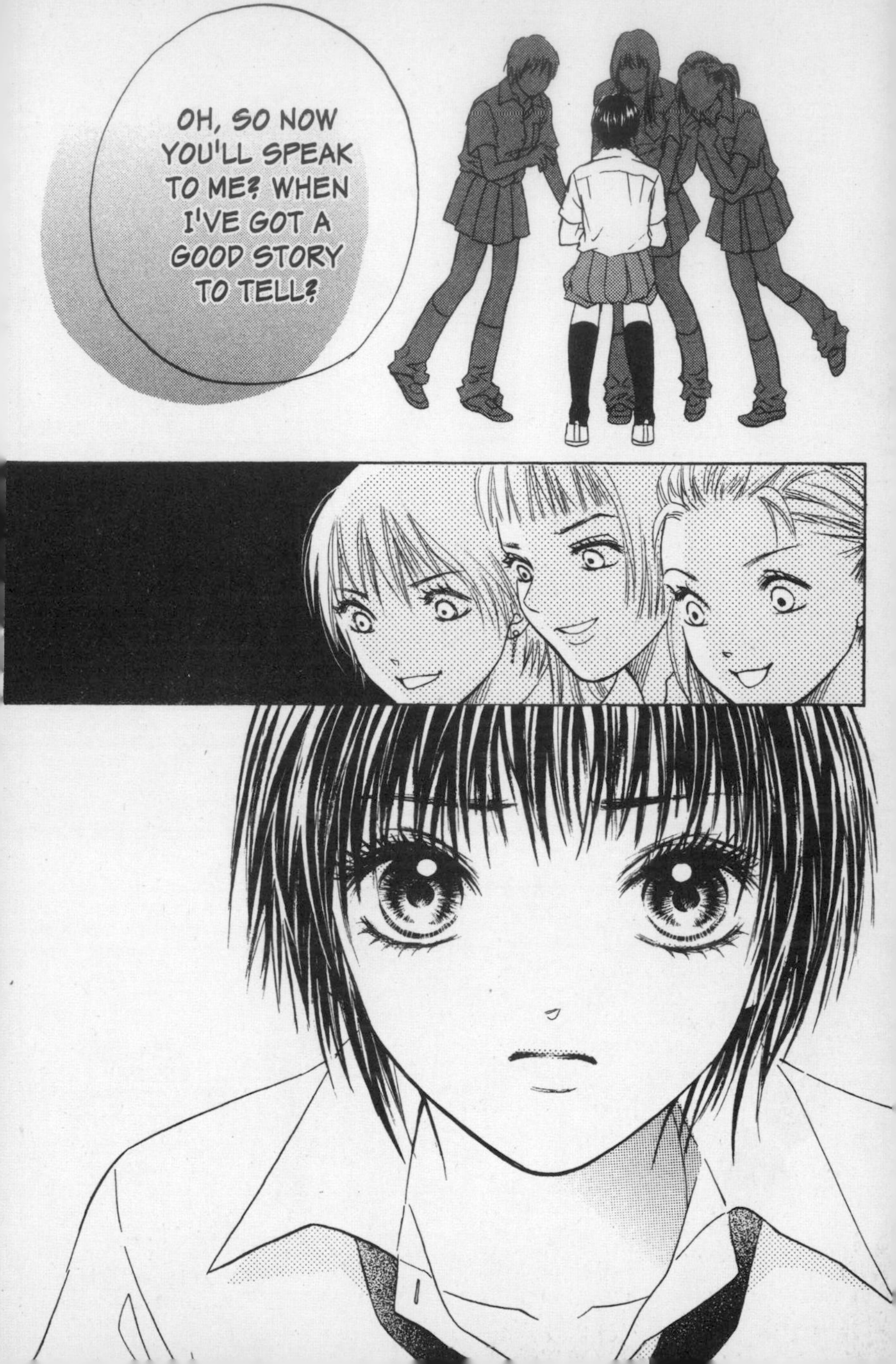
OH, SO NOW YOU'LL SPEAK TO ME? WHEN I'VE GOT A GOOD STORY TO TELL?

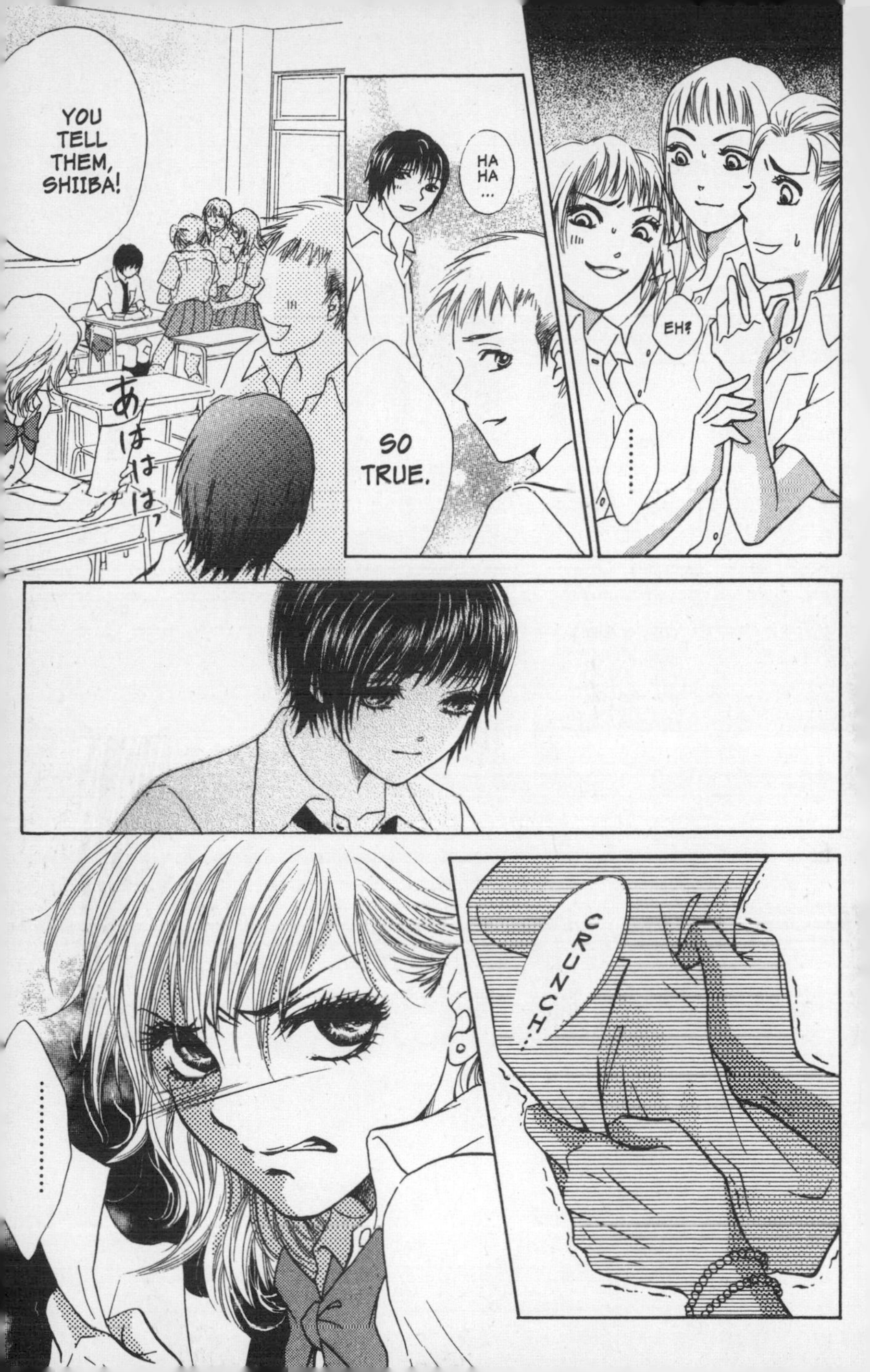
EH?
......
HA HA ...
SO TRUE.
YOU TELL THEM, SHIIBA!
あははは,
CRUNCH...
....

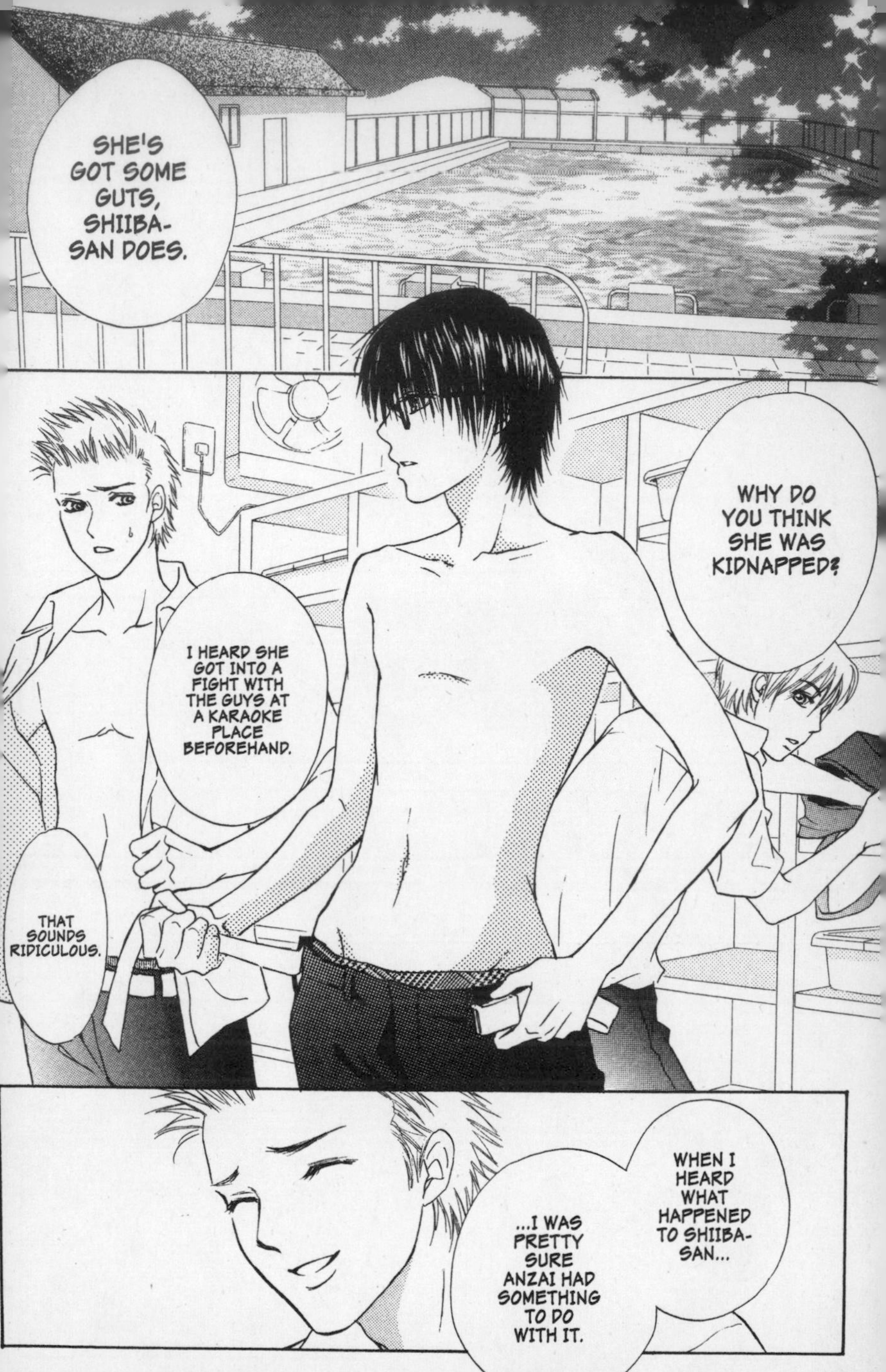
SHE'S GOT SOME GUTS, SHIIBA-SAN DOES.
WHY DO YOU THINK SHE WAS KIDNAPPED?
I HEARD SHE GOT INTO A FIGHT WITH THE GUYS AT A KARAOKE PLACE BEFOREHAND.
THAT SOUNDS RIDICULOUS.
WHEN I HEARD WHAT HAPPENED TO SHIIBA-SAN...
...I WAS PRETTY SURE ANZAI HAD SOMETHING TO DO WITH IT.

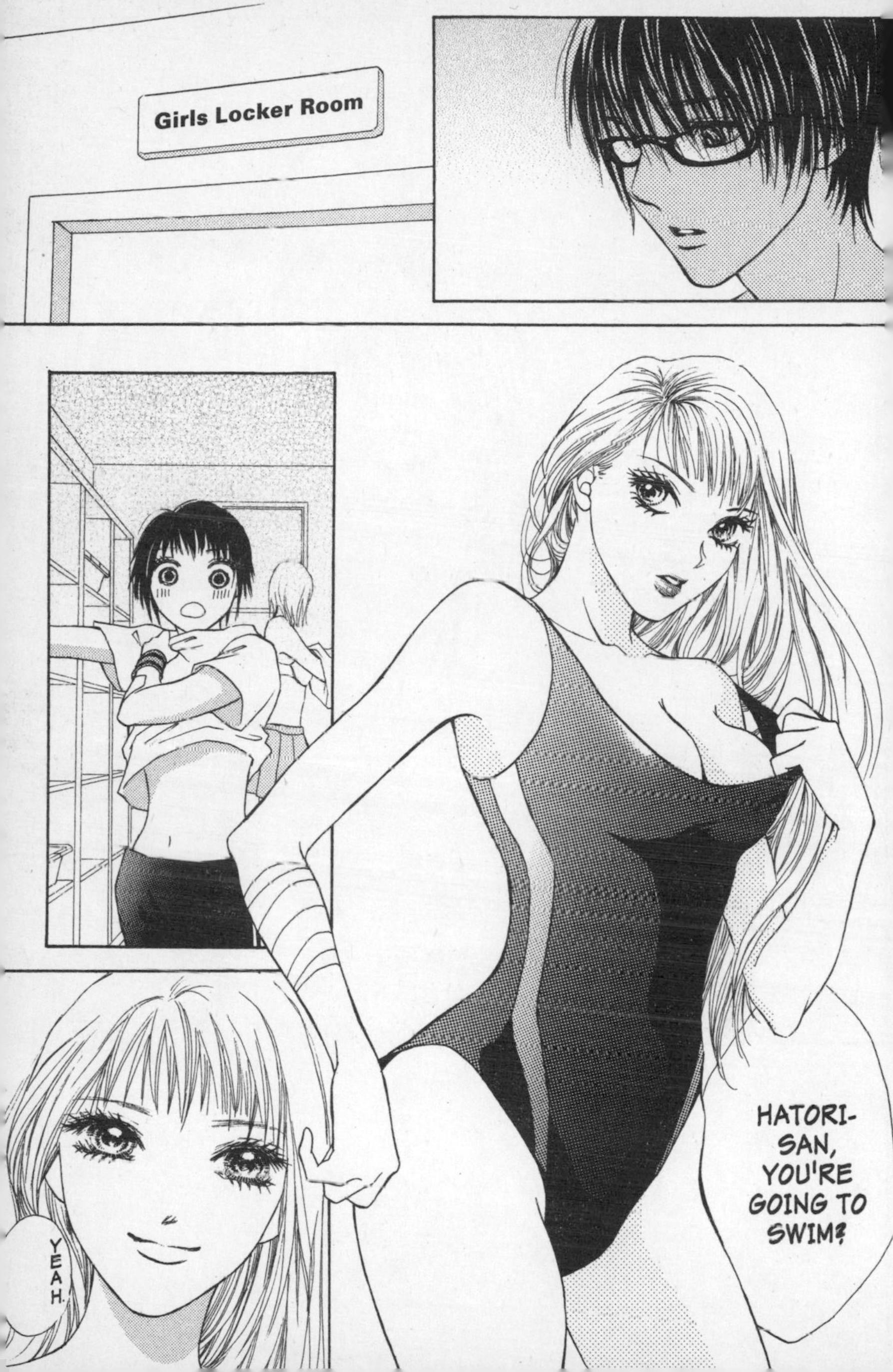
Girls Locker Room
HATORI-SAN, YOU'RE GOING TO SWIM?
YEAH.

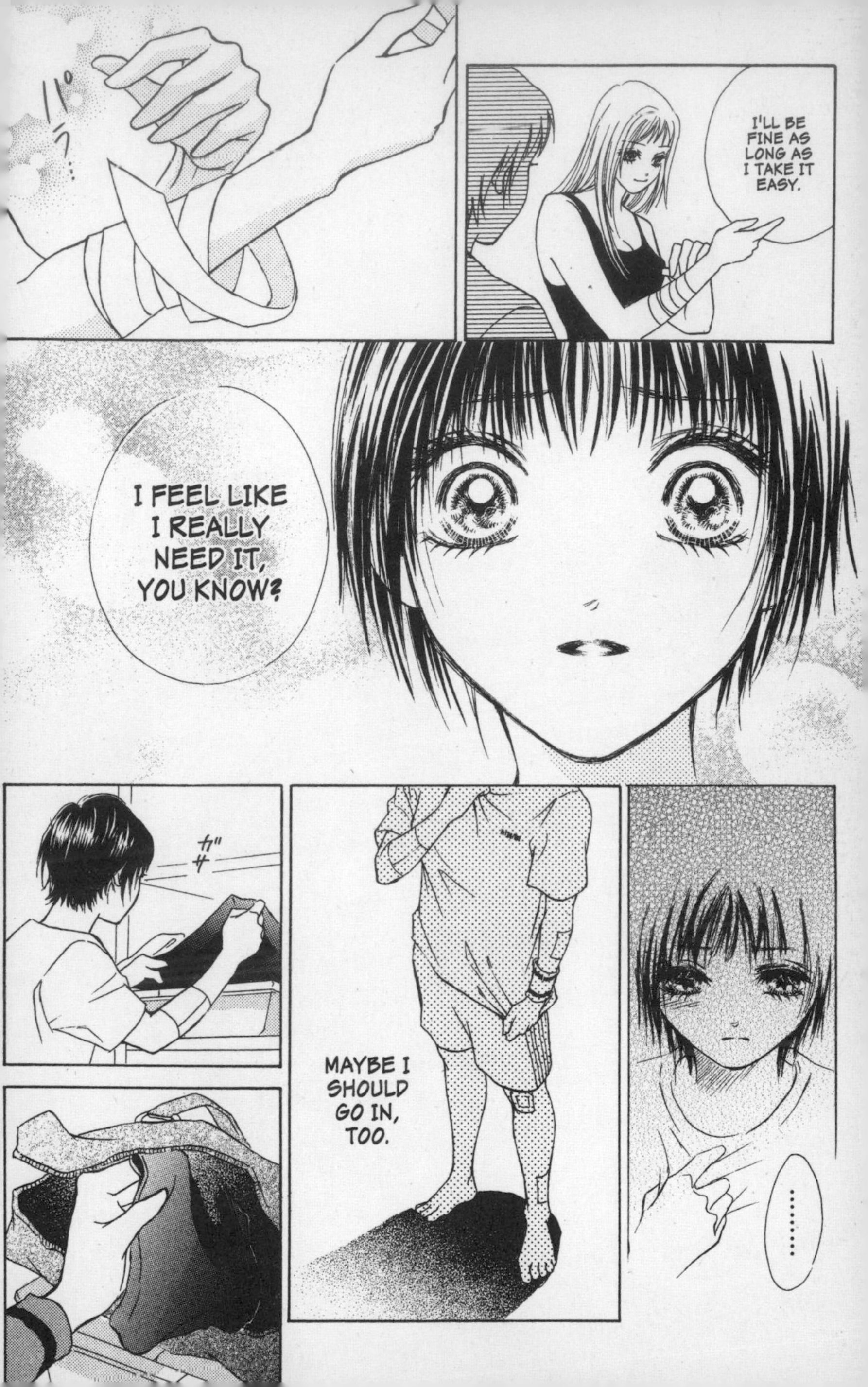
I'LL BE FINE AS LONG AS I TAKE IT EASY.
パラ…
I FEEL LIKE I REALLY NEED IT, YOU KNOW?
....
MAYBE I SHOULD GO IN, TOO.
ガサ

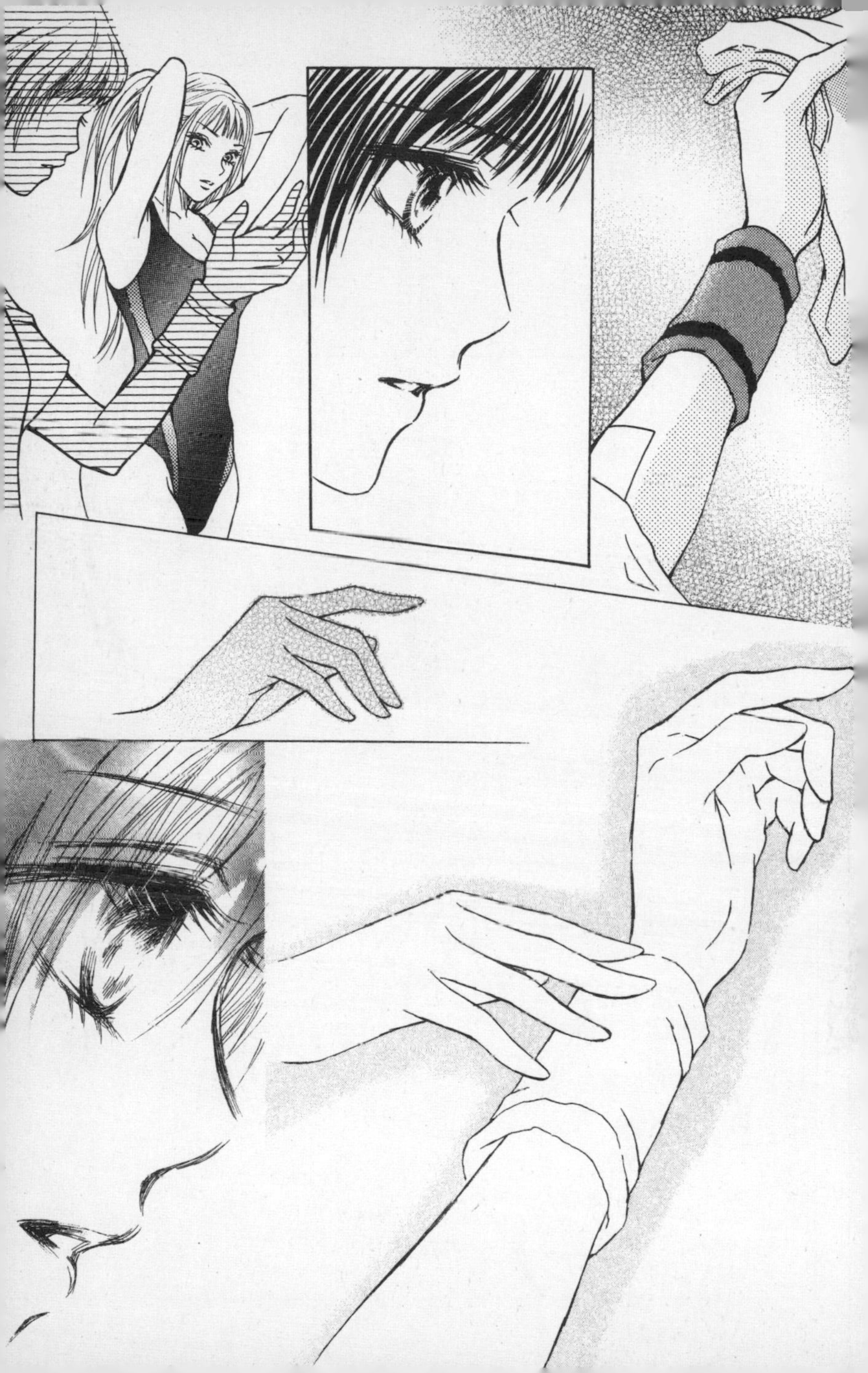

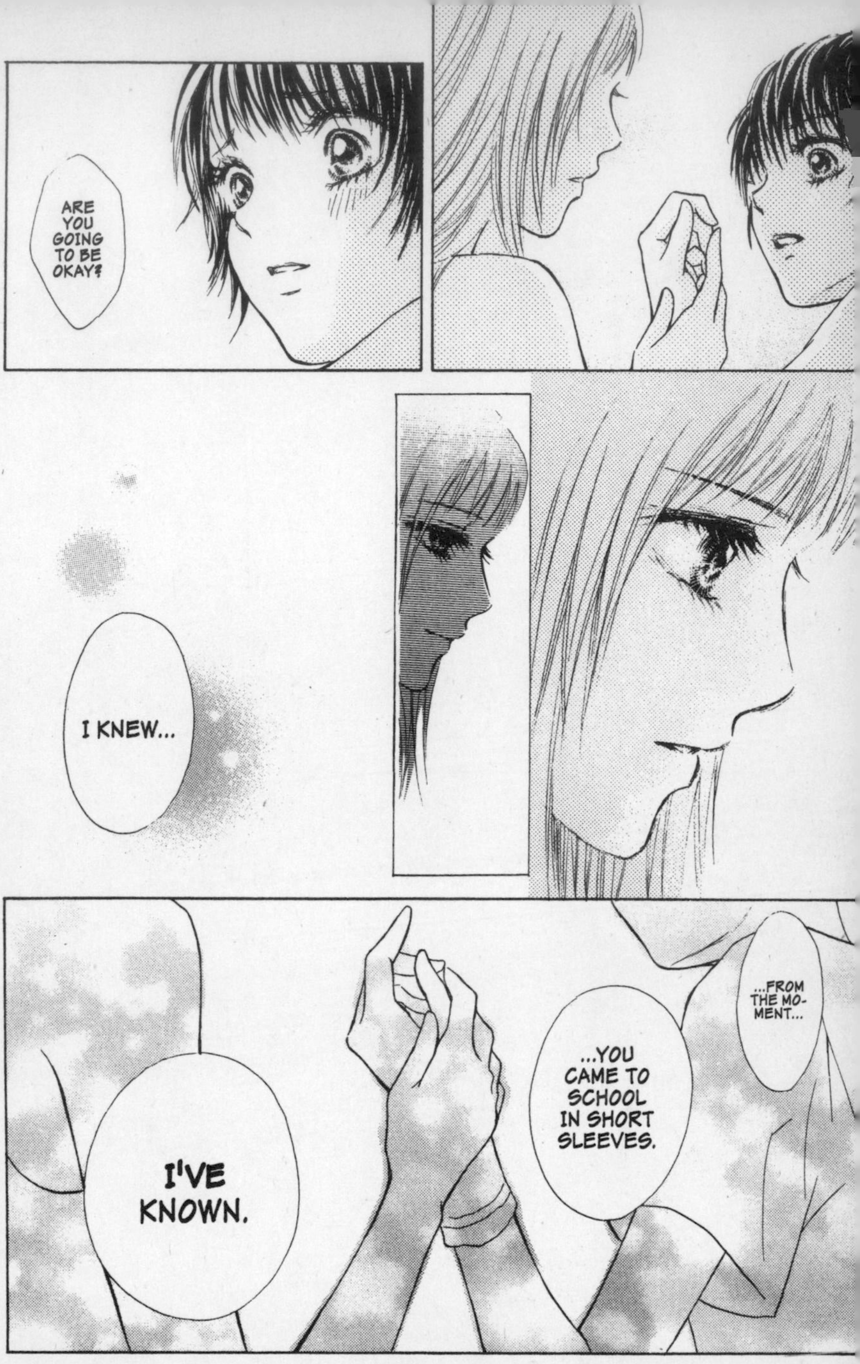
ARE YOU GOING TO BE OKAY?
I KNEW...
...FROM THE MO- MENT...
...YOU CAME TO SCHOOL IN SHORT SLEEVES.
I'VE KNOWN.

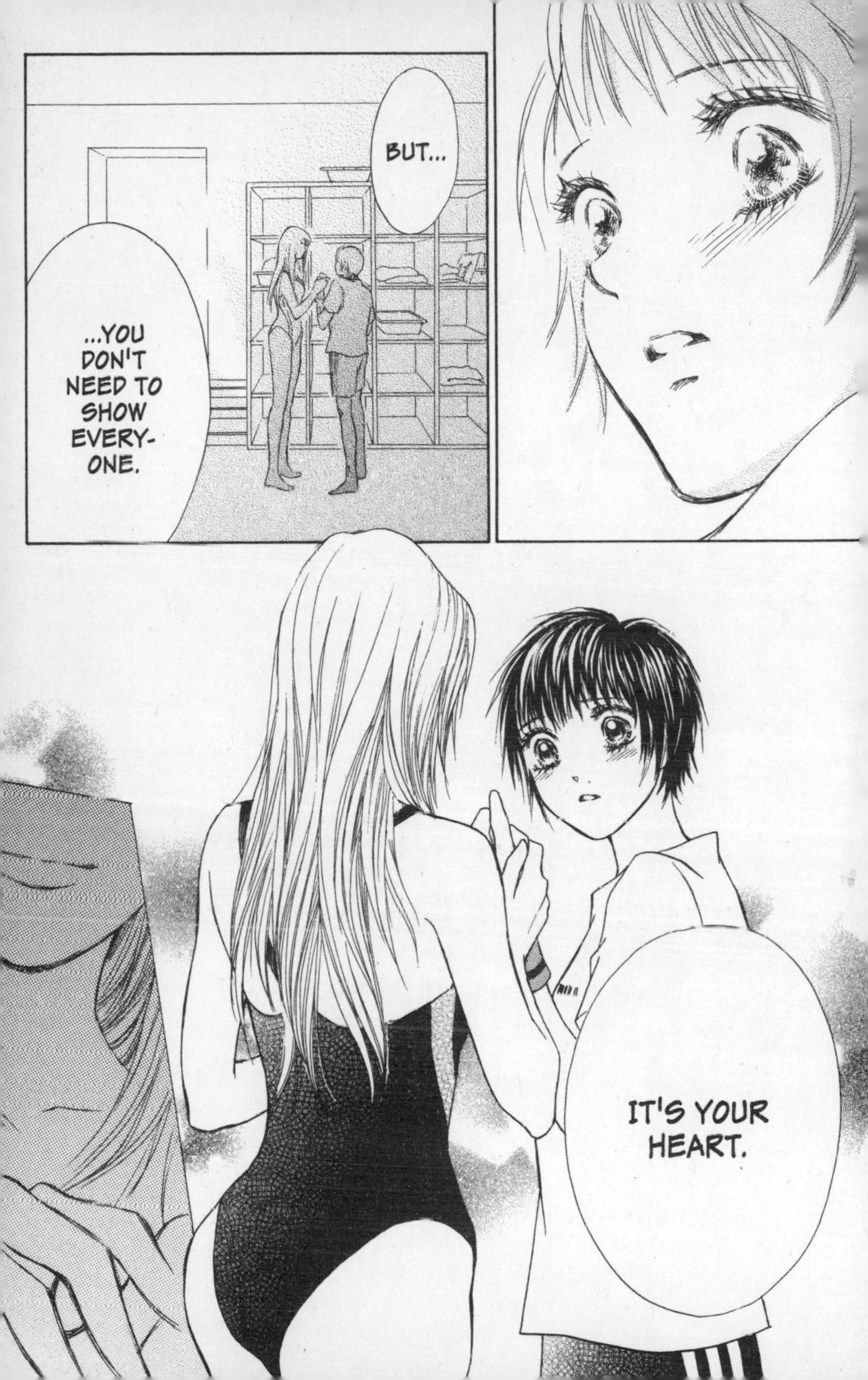
BUT...
...YOU DON'T NEED TO SHOW EVERY-ONE.
IT'S YOUR HEART.

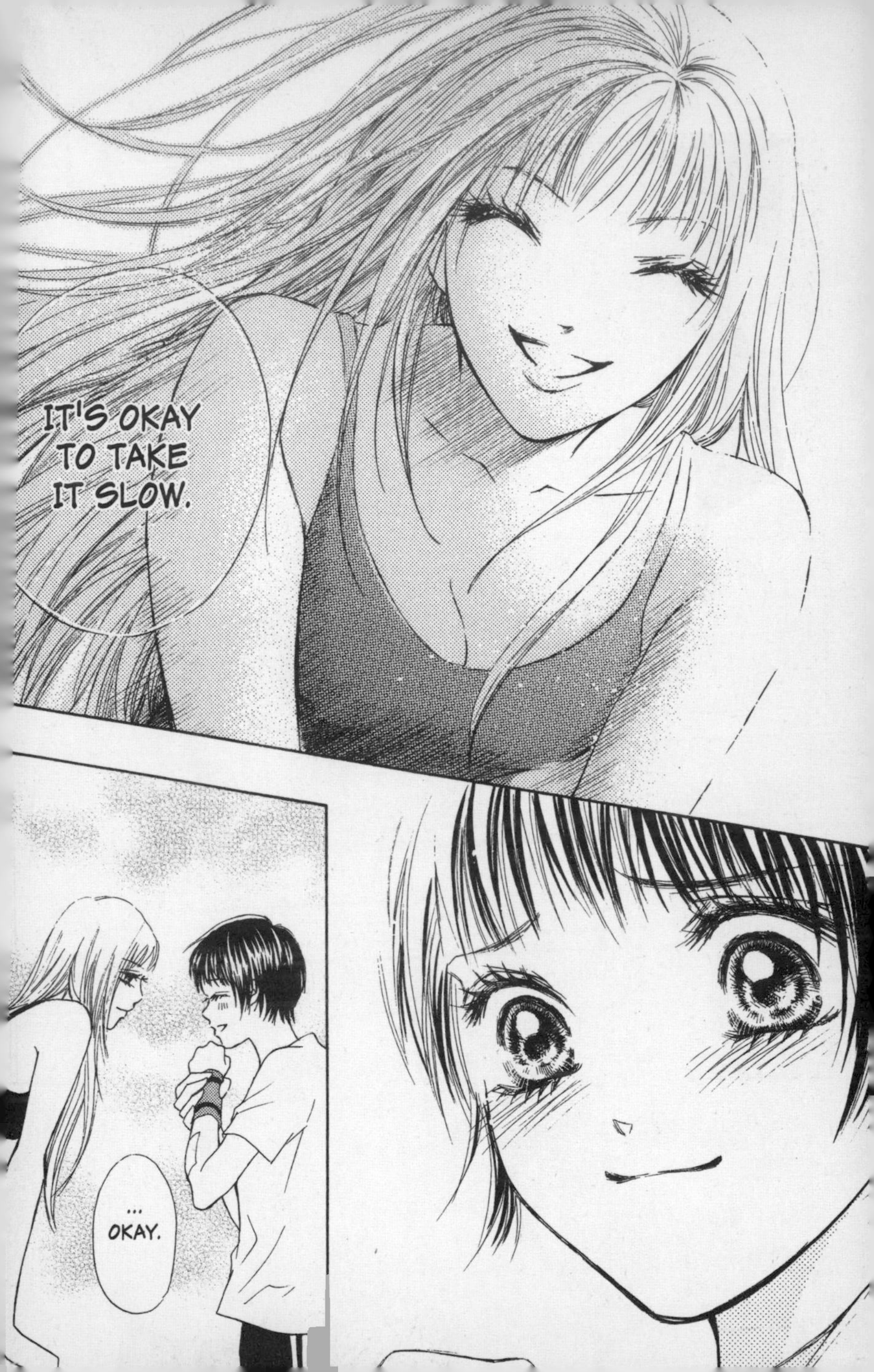
IT'S OKAY TO TAKE IT SLOW.
... OKAY.

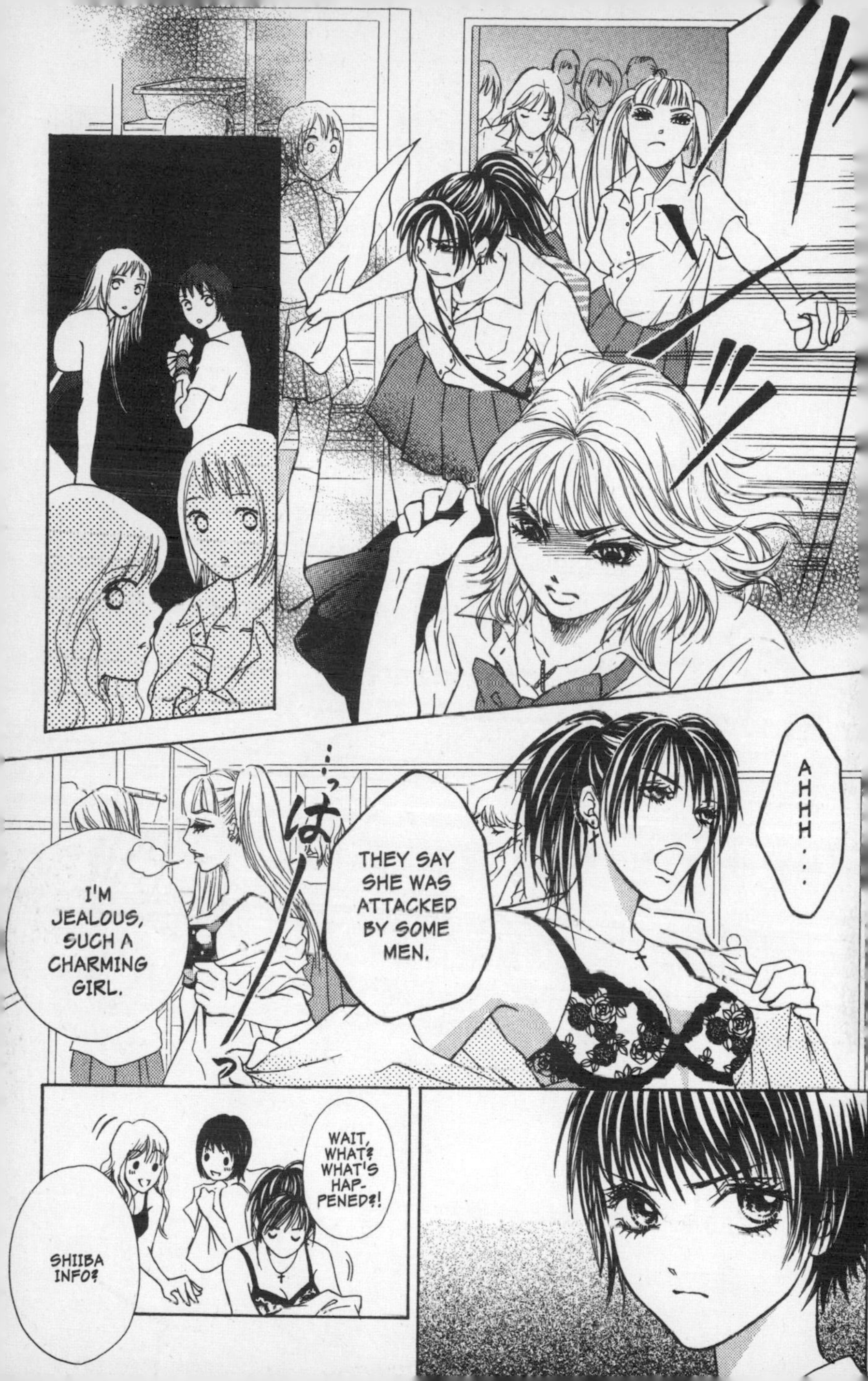
AHHH...
THEY SAY SHE WAS ATTACKED BY SOME MEN.
は
I'M JEALOUS, SUCH A CHARMING GIRL.
WAIT, WHAT?! WHAT'S HAP-PENED?!
SHIIBA INFO?

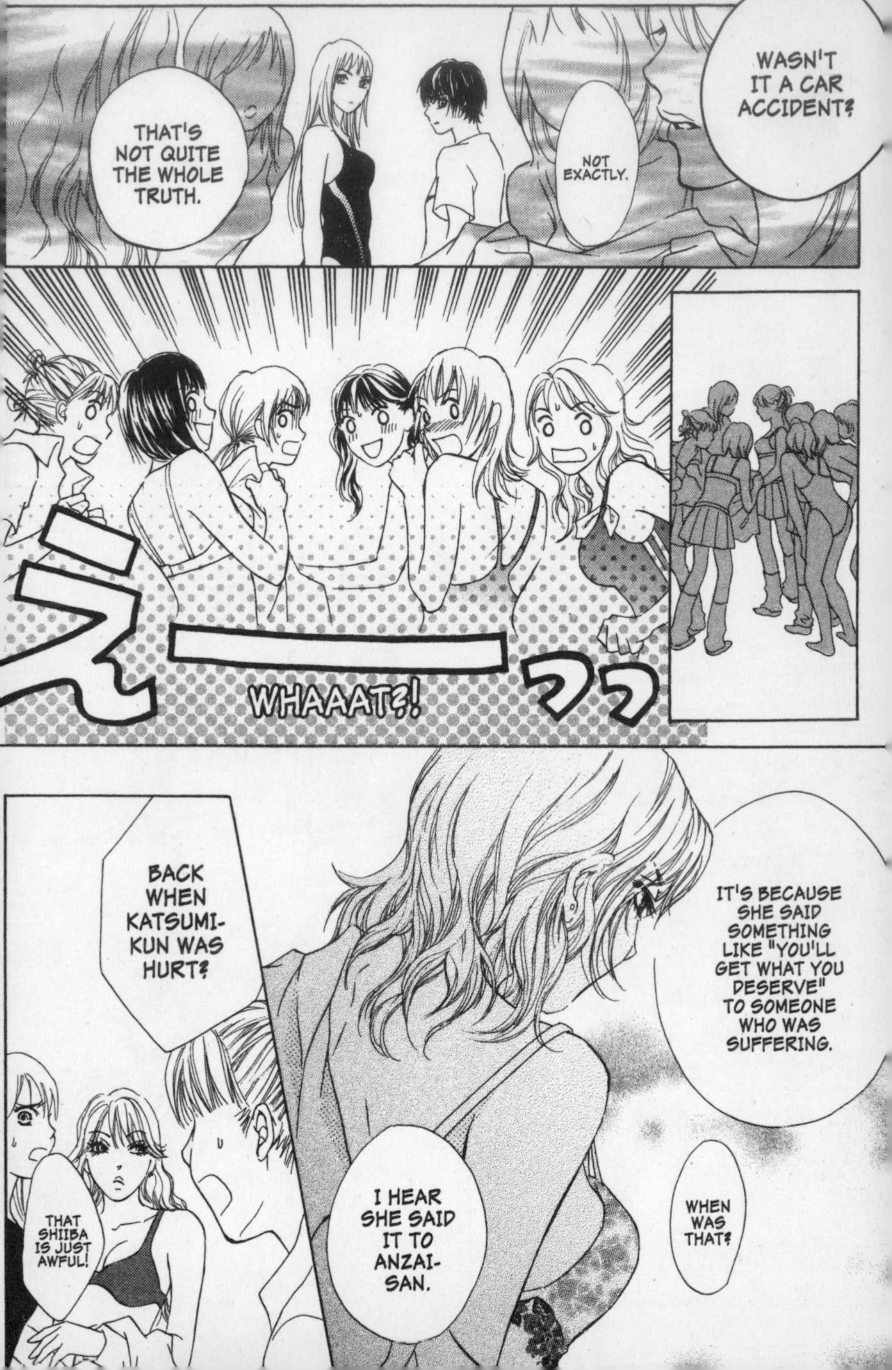
WASN'T IT A CAR ACCIDENT?
NOT EXACTLY.
THAT'S NOT QUITE THE WHOLE TRUTH.
えーっっ
WHAAAT?!
IT'S BECAUSE SHE SAID SOMETHING LIKE "YOU'LL GET WHAT YOU DESERVE" TO SOMEONE WHO WAS SUFFERING.
WHEN WAS THAT?
I HEAR SHE SAID IT TO ANZAI-SAN.
BACK WHEN KATSUMI-KUN WAS HURT?
THAT SHIIBA IS JUST AWFUL!

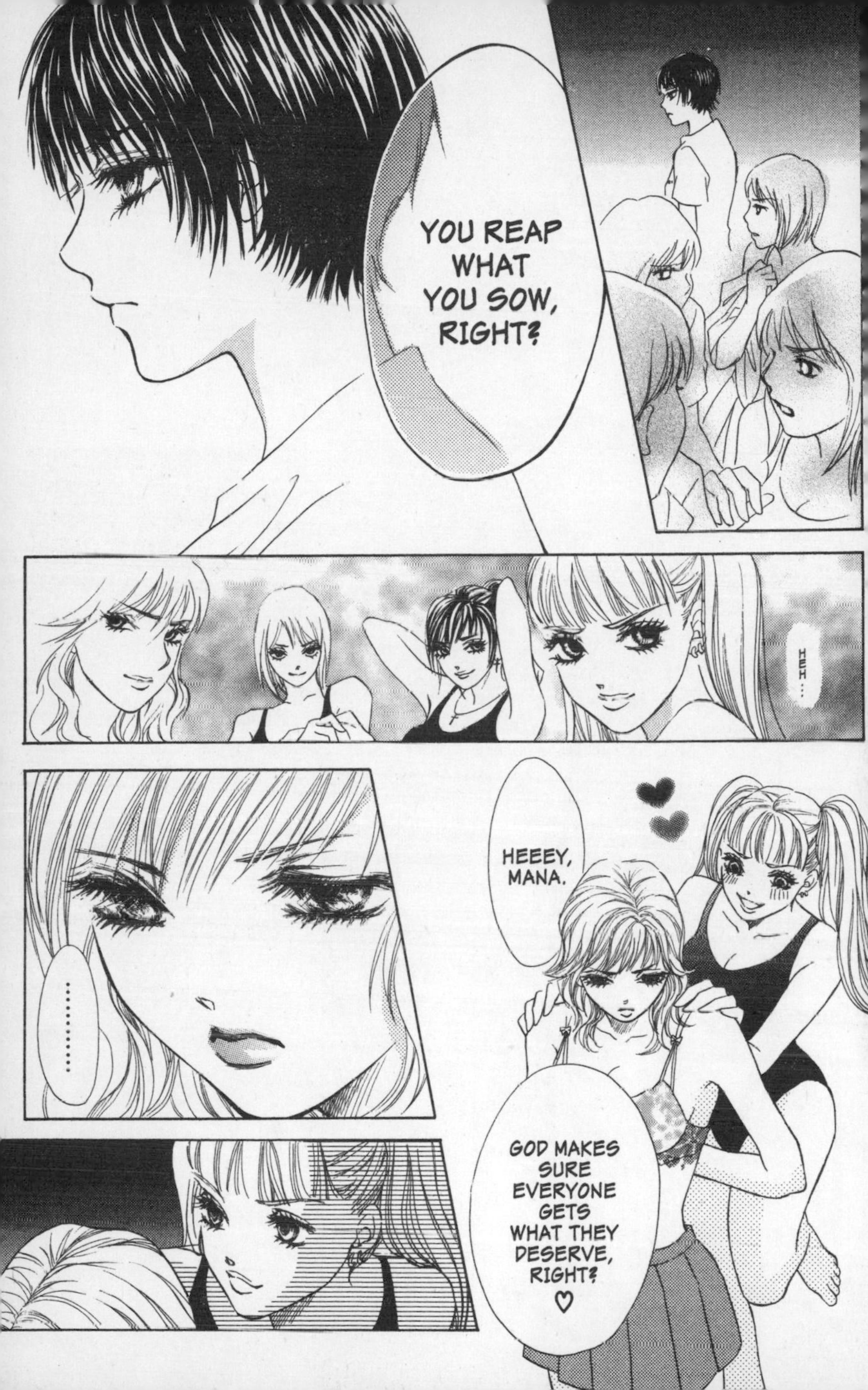
YOU REAP WHAT YOU SOW, RIGHT?
HEH...
HEEEY, MANA.
GOD MAKES SURE EVERYONE GETS WHAT THEY DESERVE, RIGHT? ♡
......

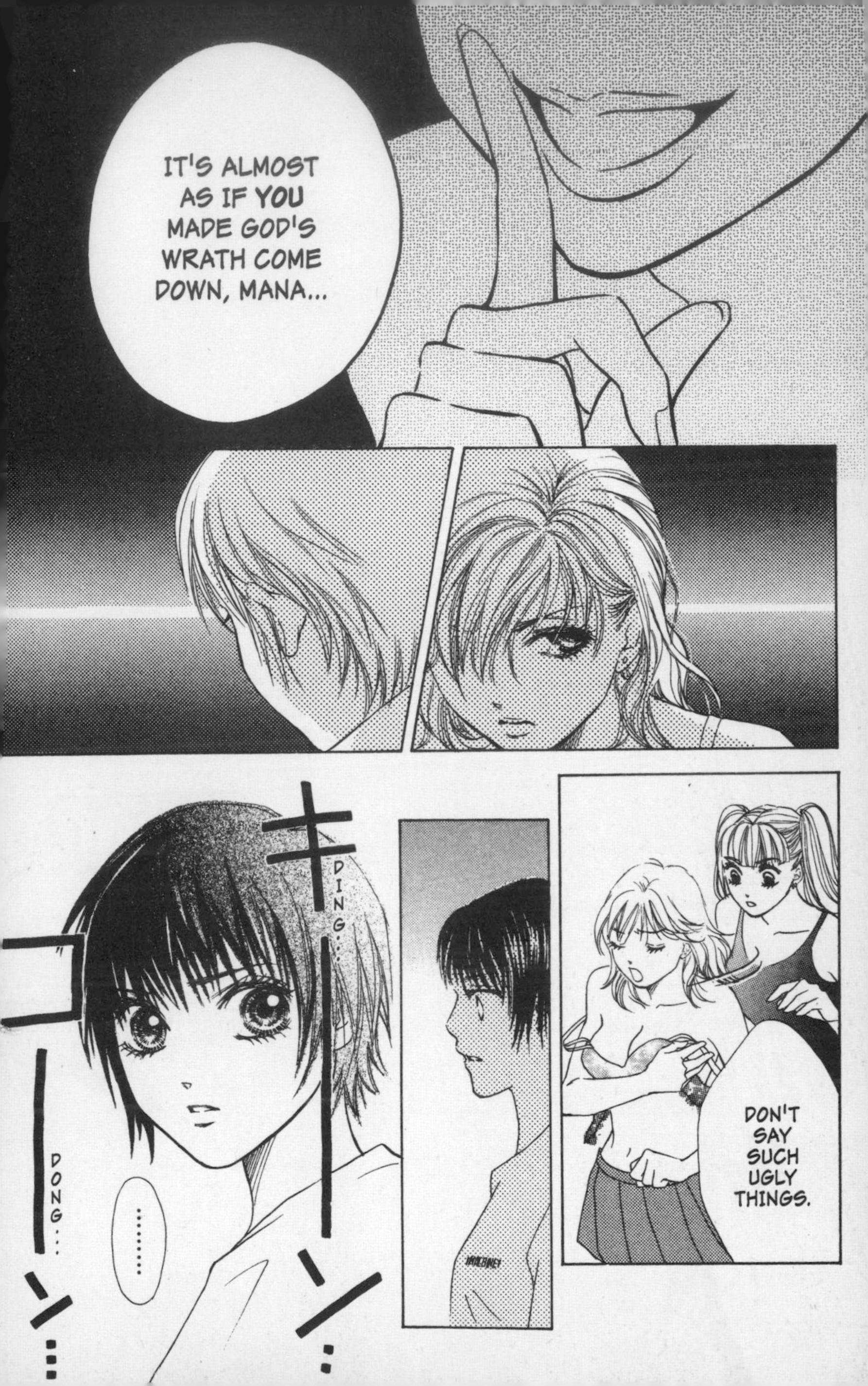
IT'S ALMOST AS IF YOU MADE GOD'S WRATH COME DOWN, MANA...
DON'T SAY SUCH UGLY THINGS.
DING...
DONG...
....

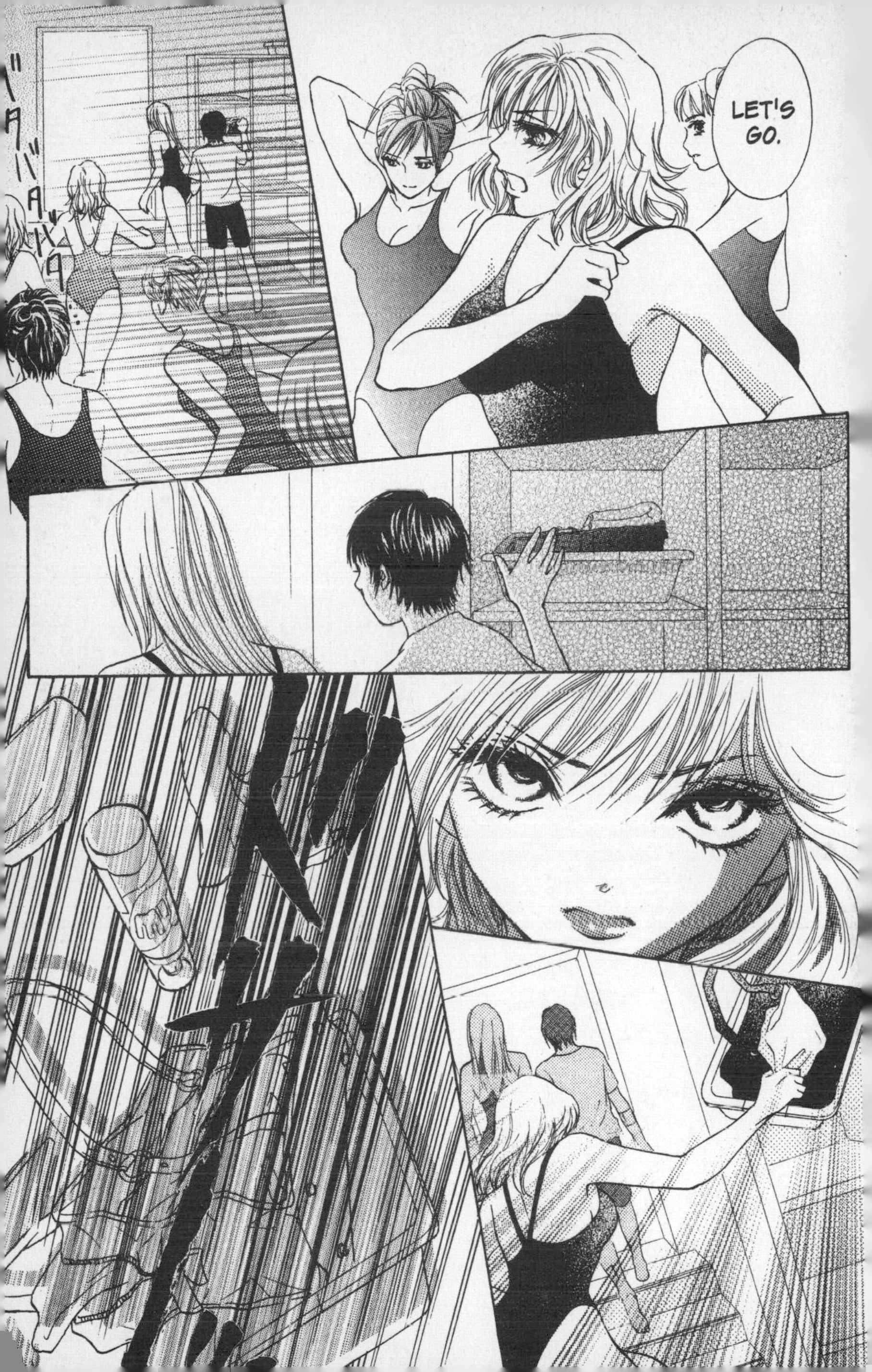
LET'S GO.
バタバタバタ
ドサ

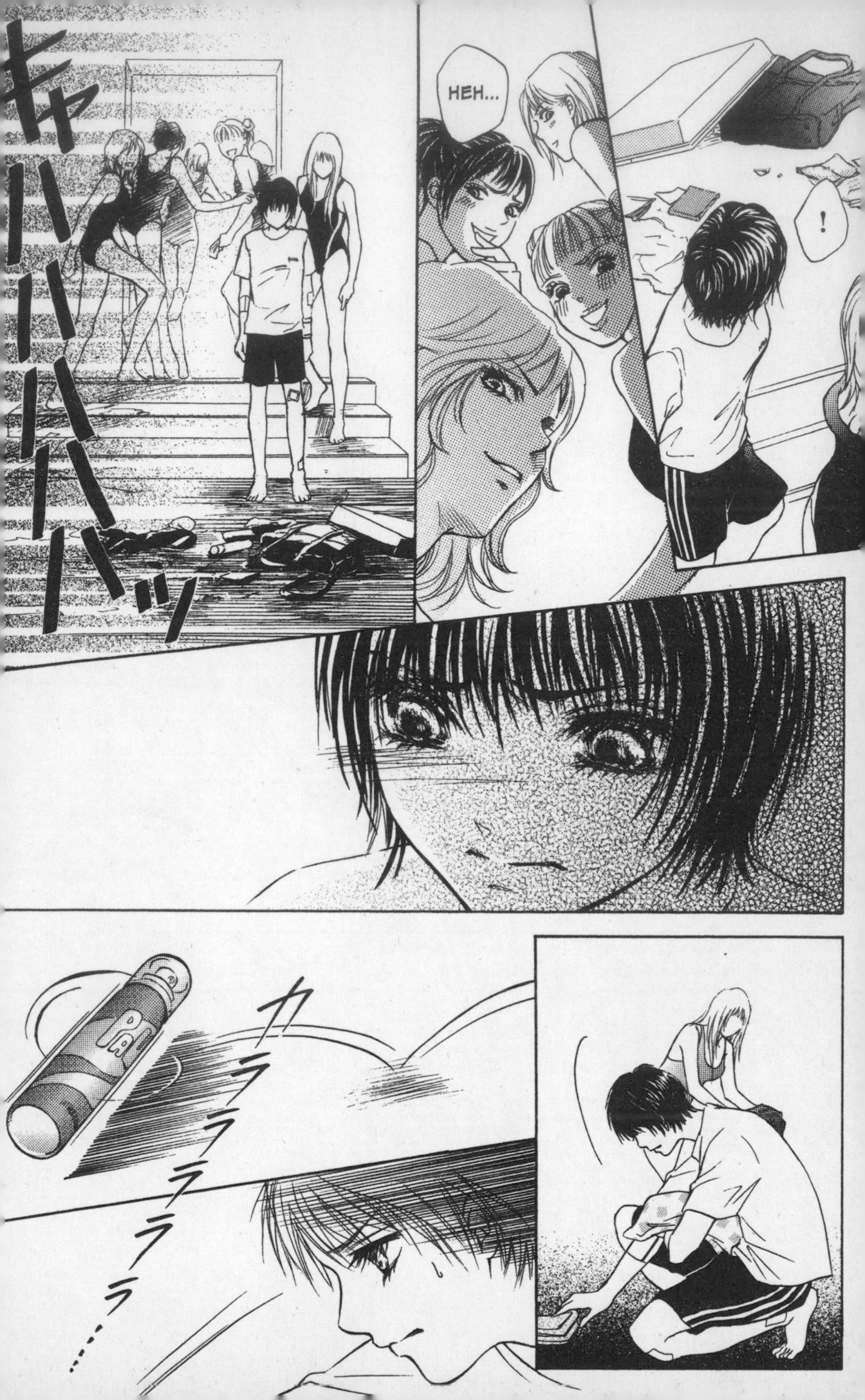
!
HEH...
キャハハハハバッ
カラララララ…

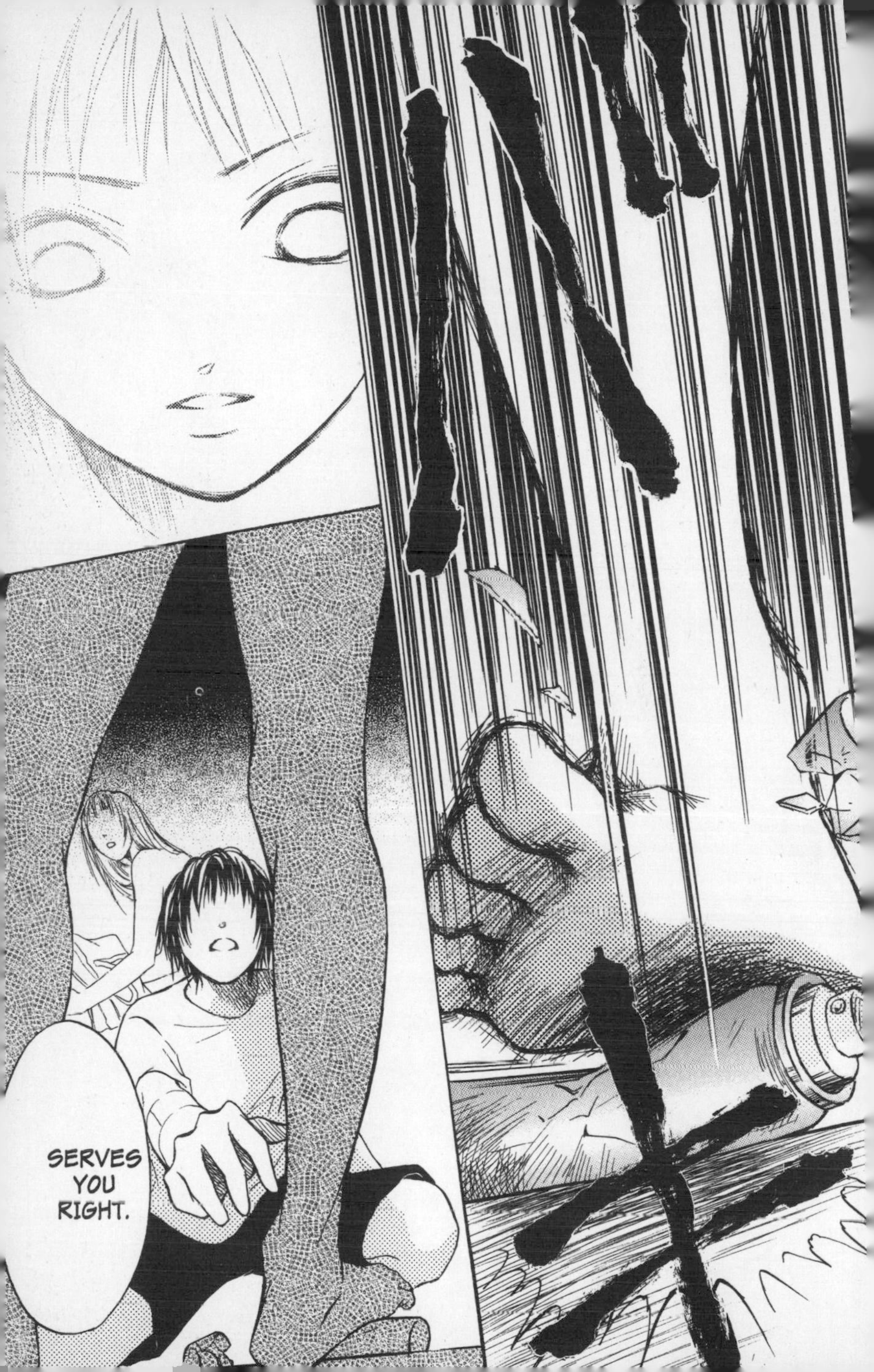
SERVES YOU RIGHT.

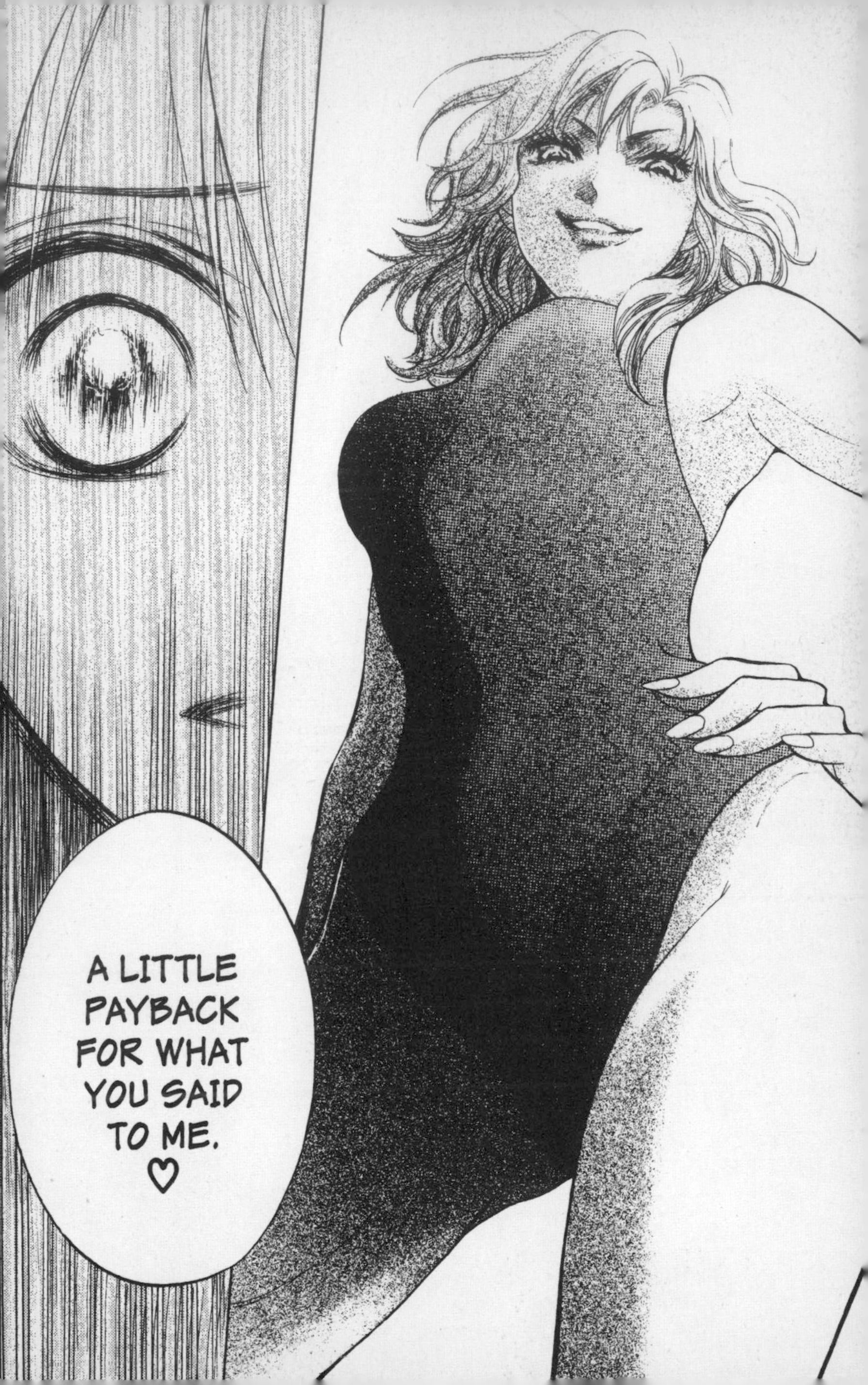
A LITTLE PAYBACK FOR WHAT YOU SAID TO ME. ♡

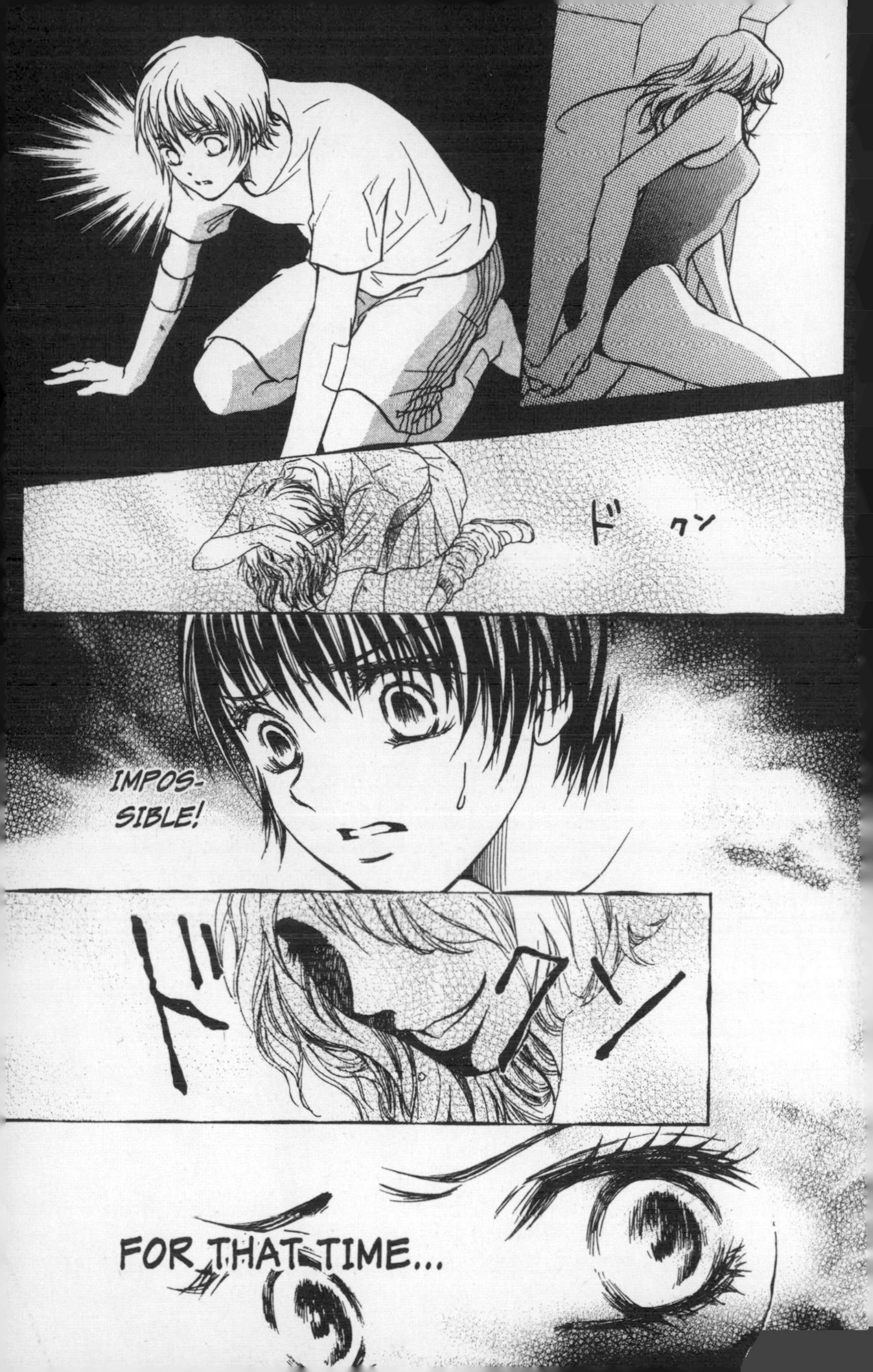
ドクン
IMPOS-
SIBLE!
ドクン
FOR THAT TIME...

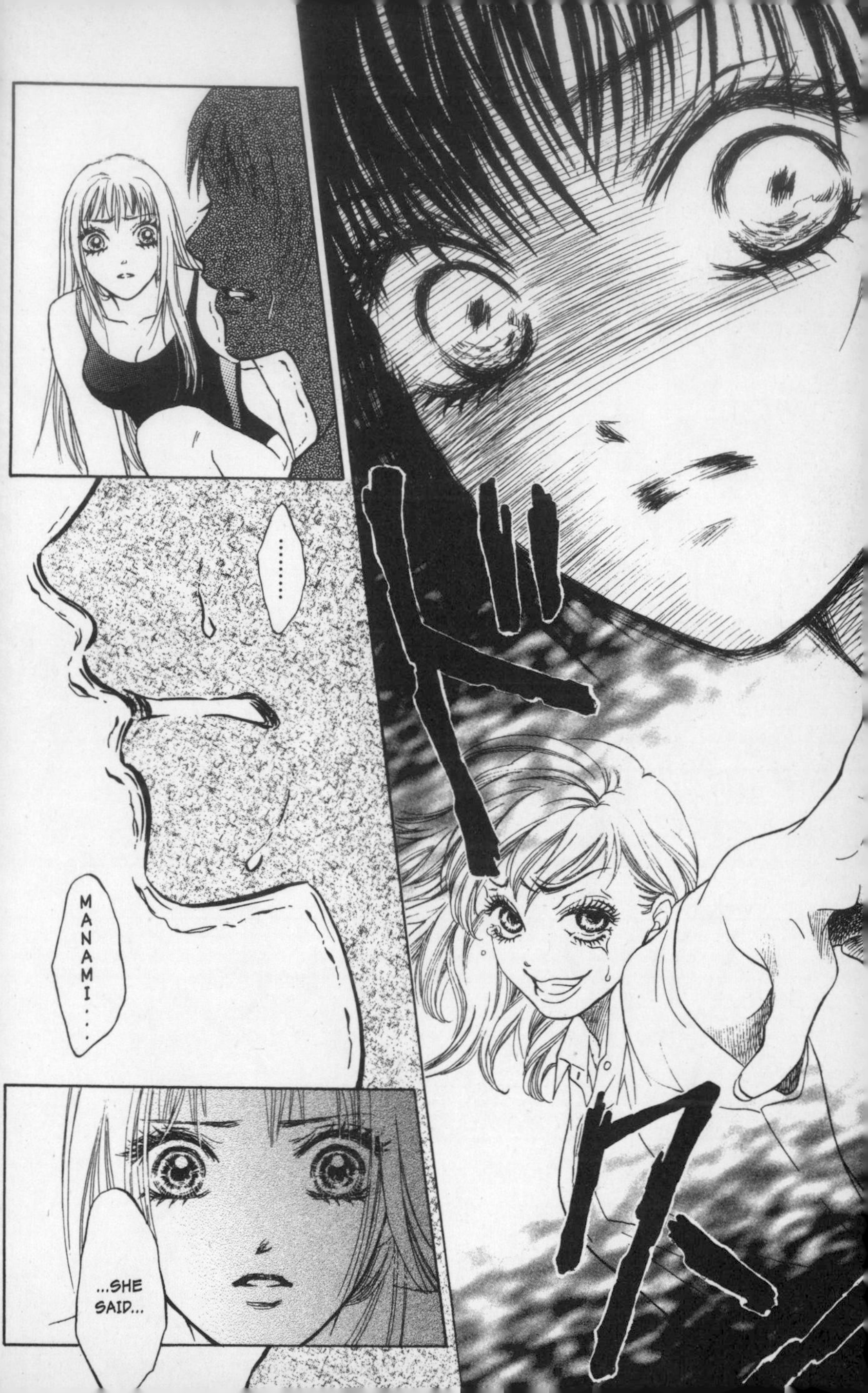
......
MANAMI...
...SHE SAID...

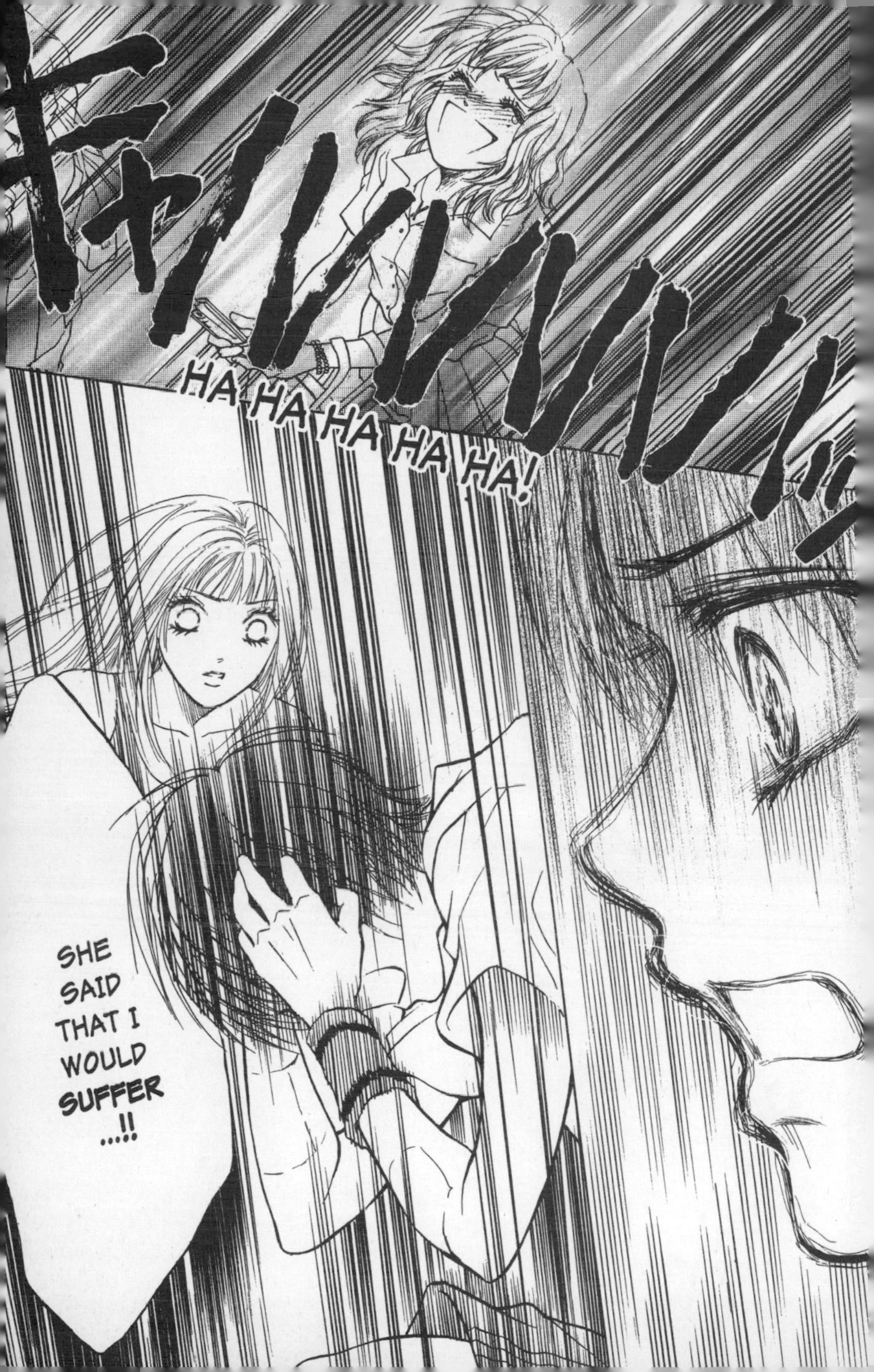
HA HA HA HA HA!
SHE SAID THAT I WOULD SUFFER ...!!

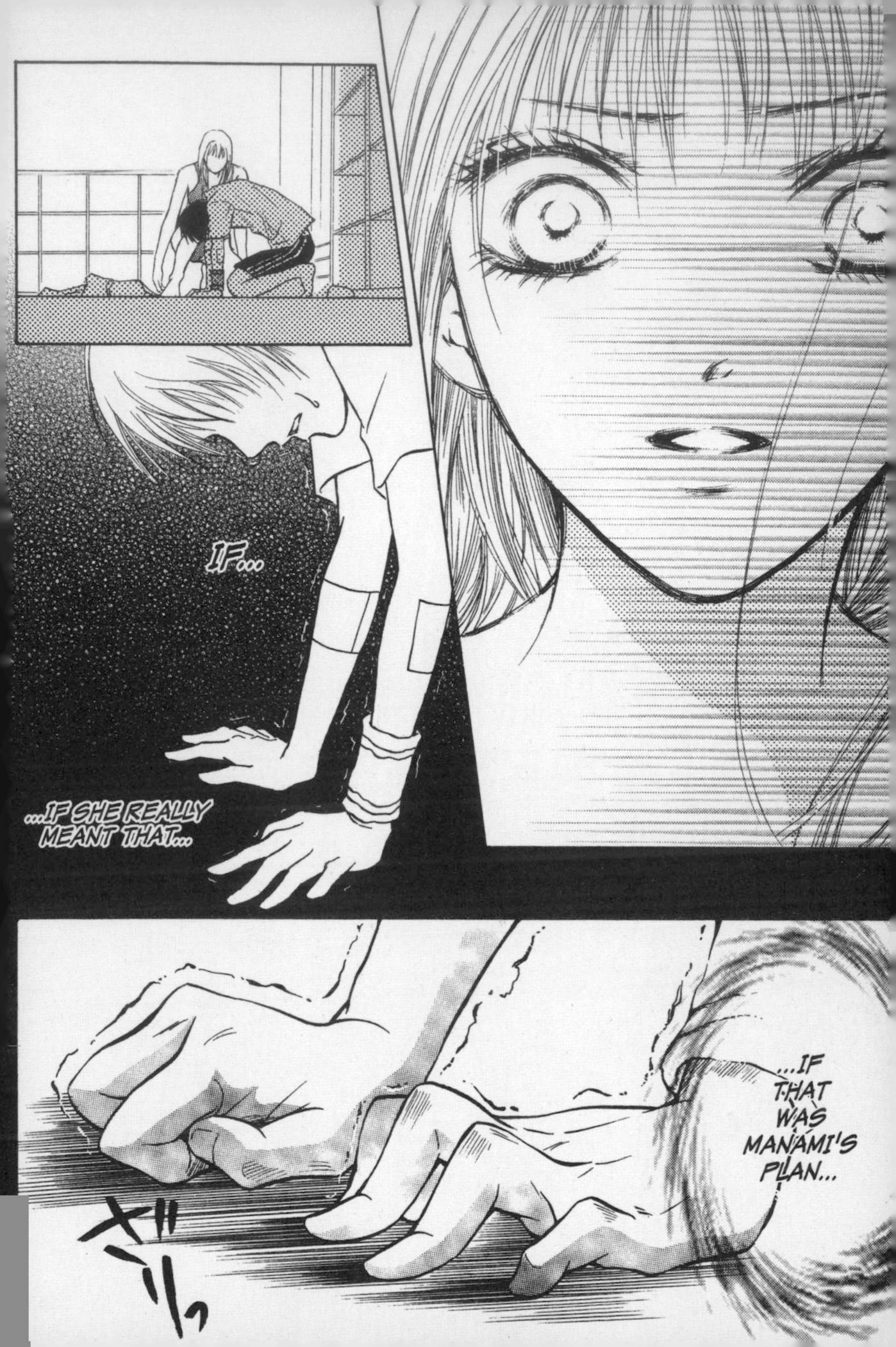
IF...
...IF SHE REALLY MEANT THAT...
...IF THAT WAS MANAMI'S PLAN...

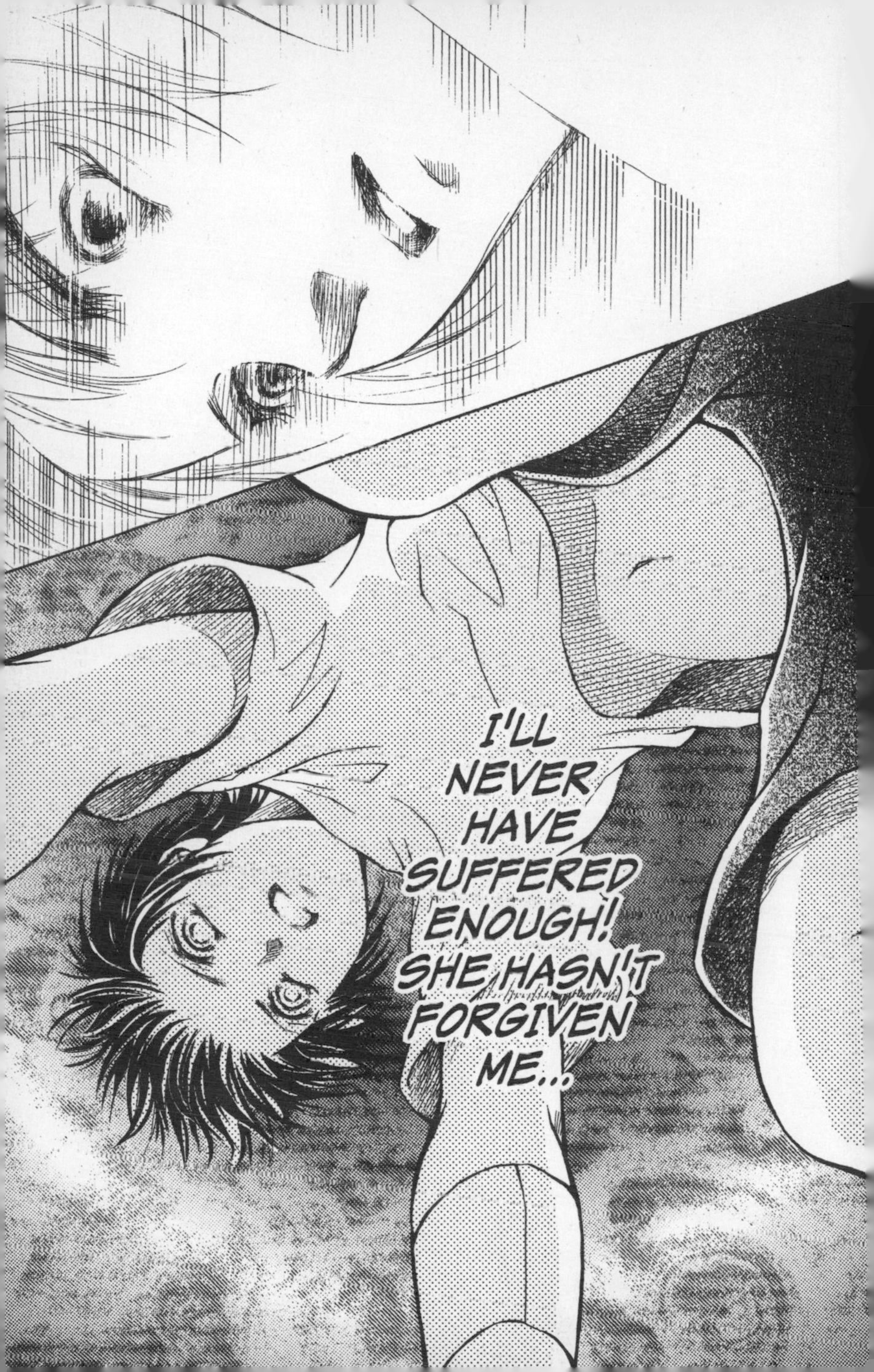
I'LL NEVER HAVE SUFFERED ENOUGH! SHE HASN'T FORGIVEN ME...

ライフ
Life

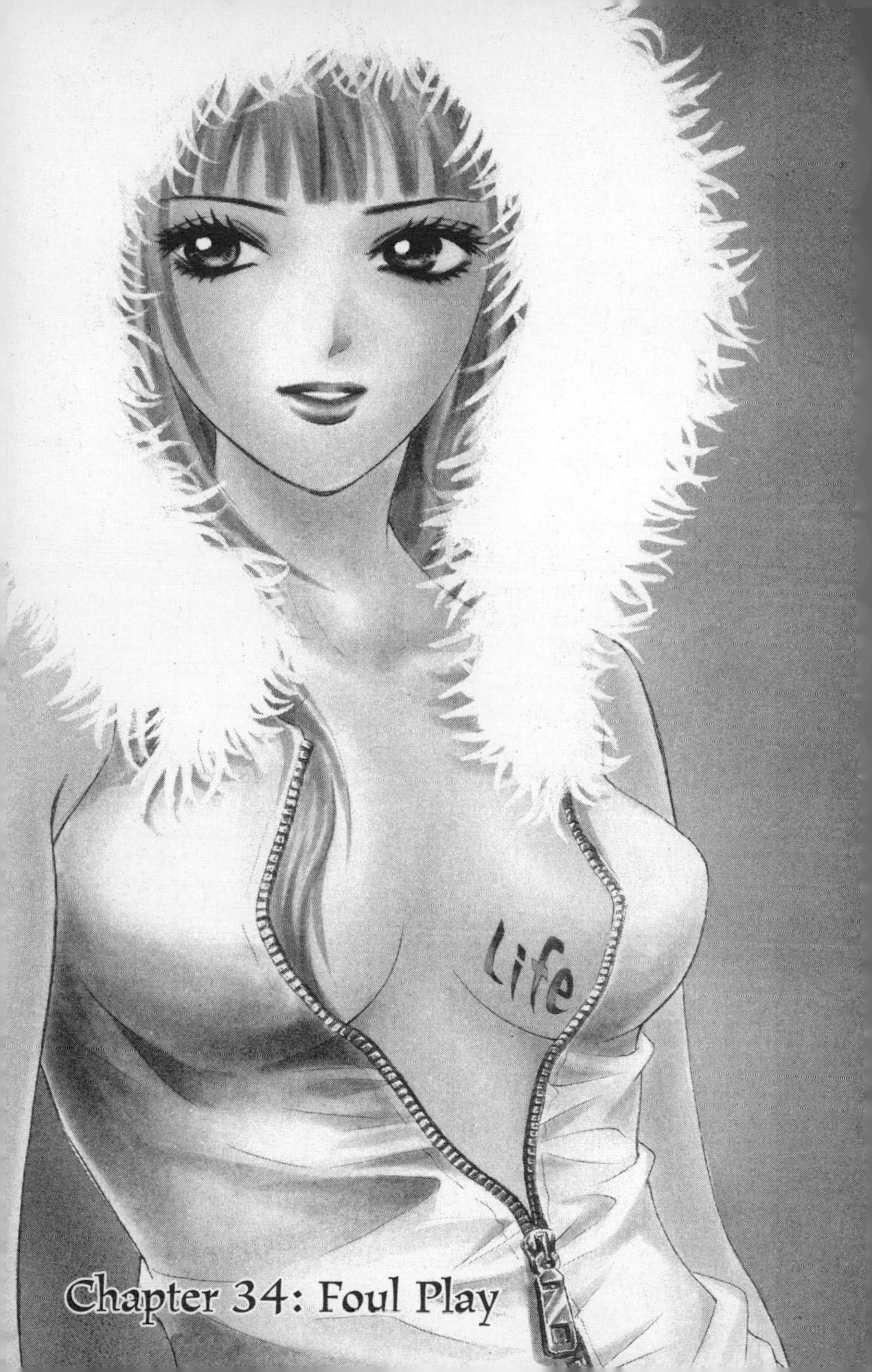
Life

Chapter 34: Foul Play

ライフ Life

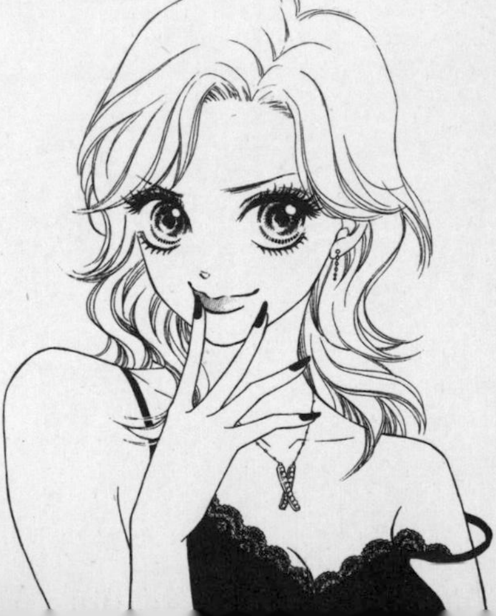

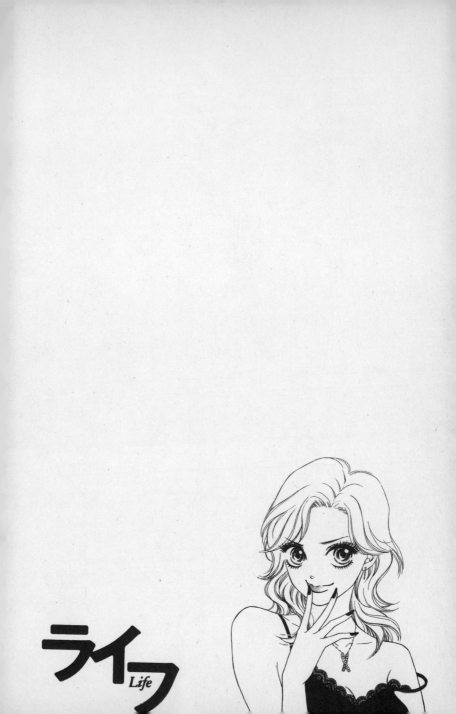

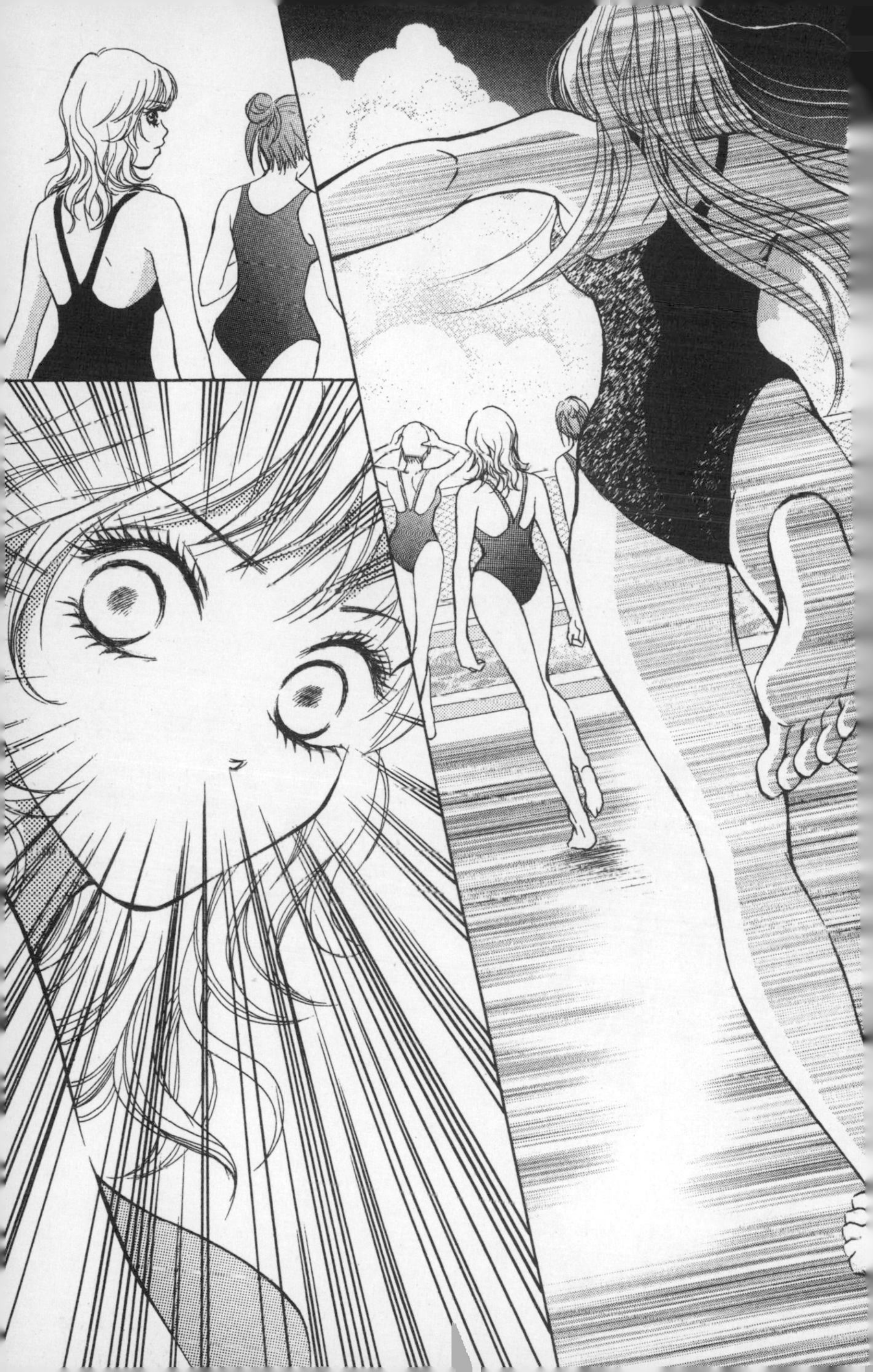

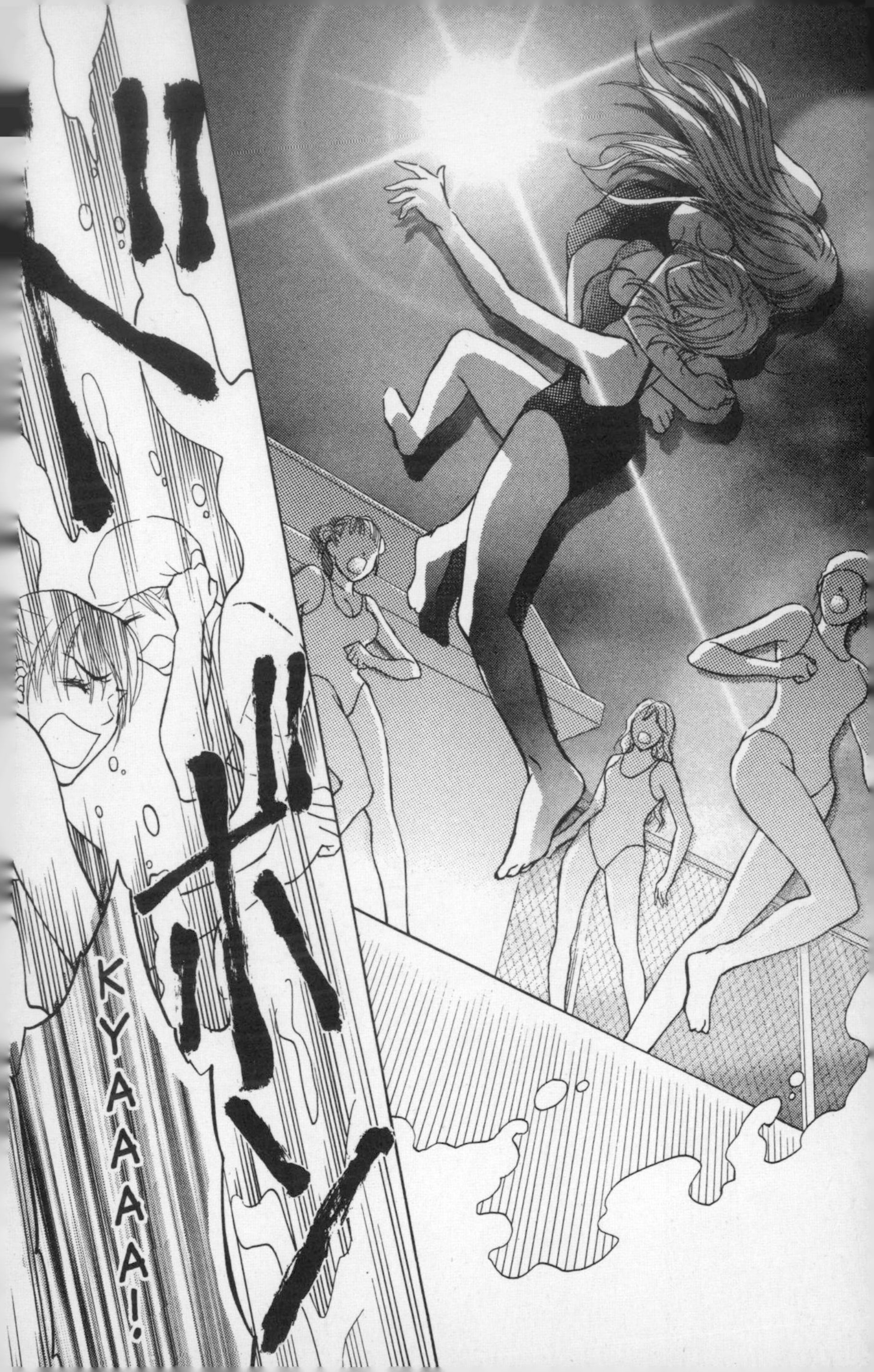
KYAAAA!

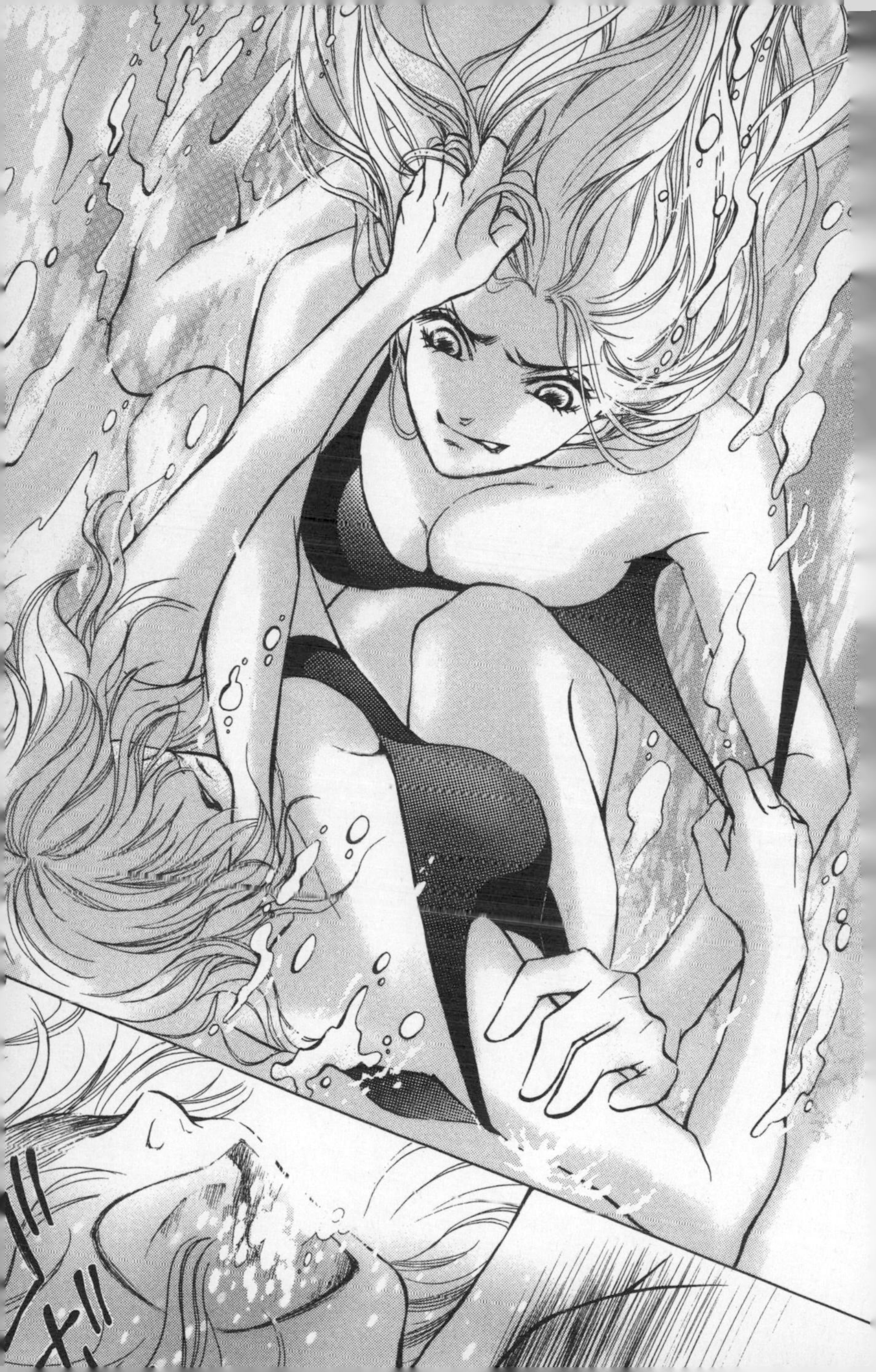

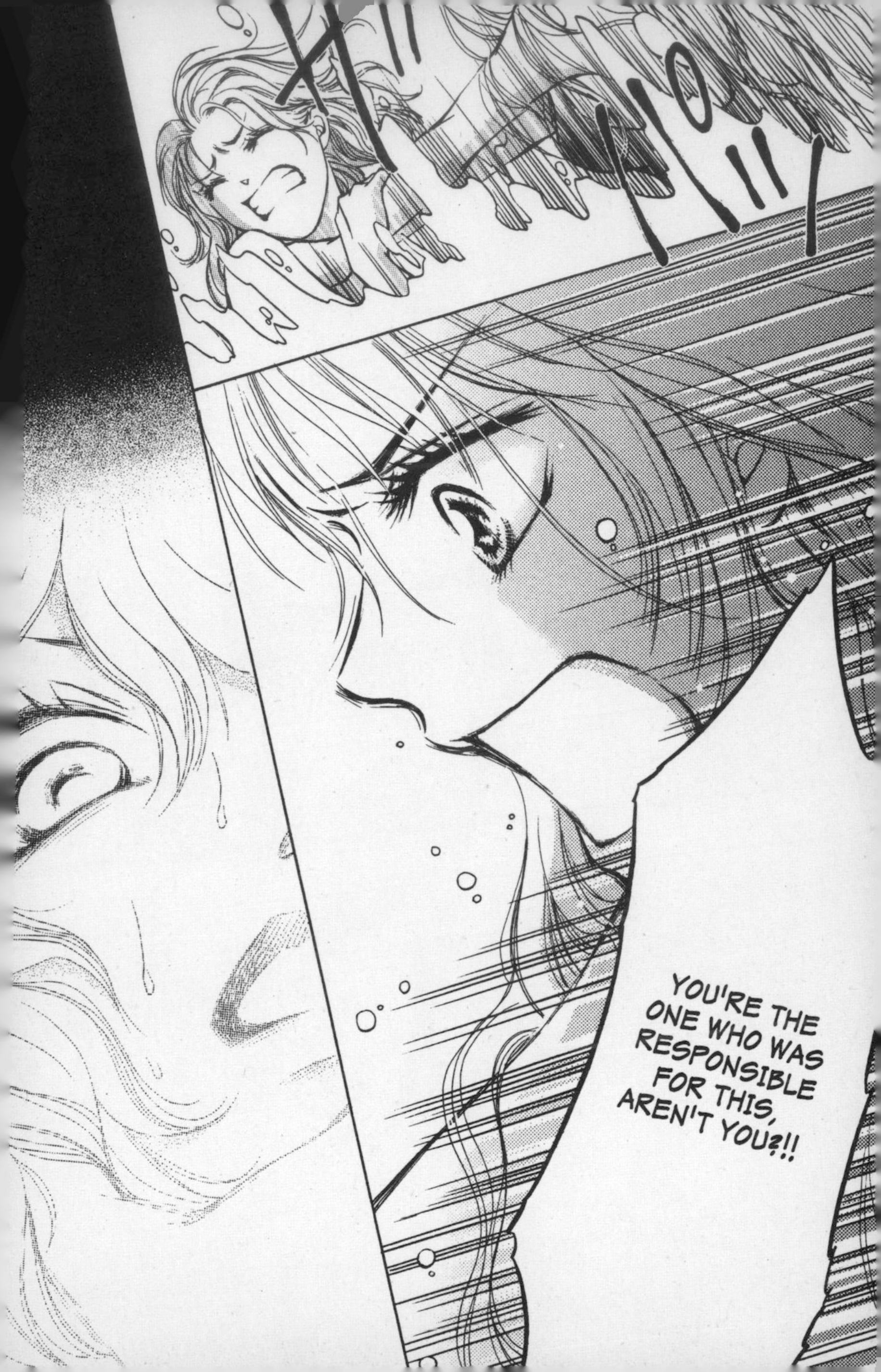
YOU'RE THE ONE WHO WAS RESPONSIBLE FOR THIS, AREN'T YOU?!!

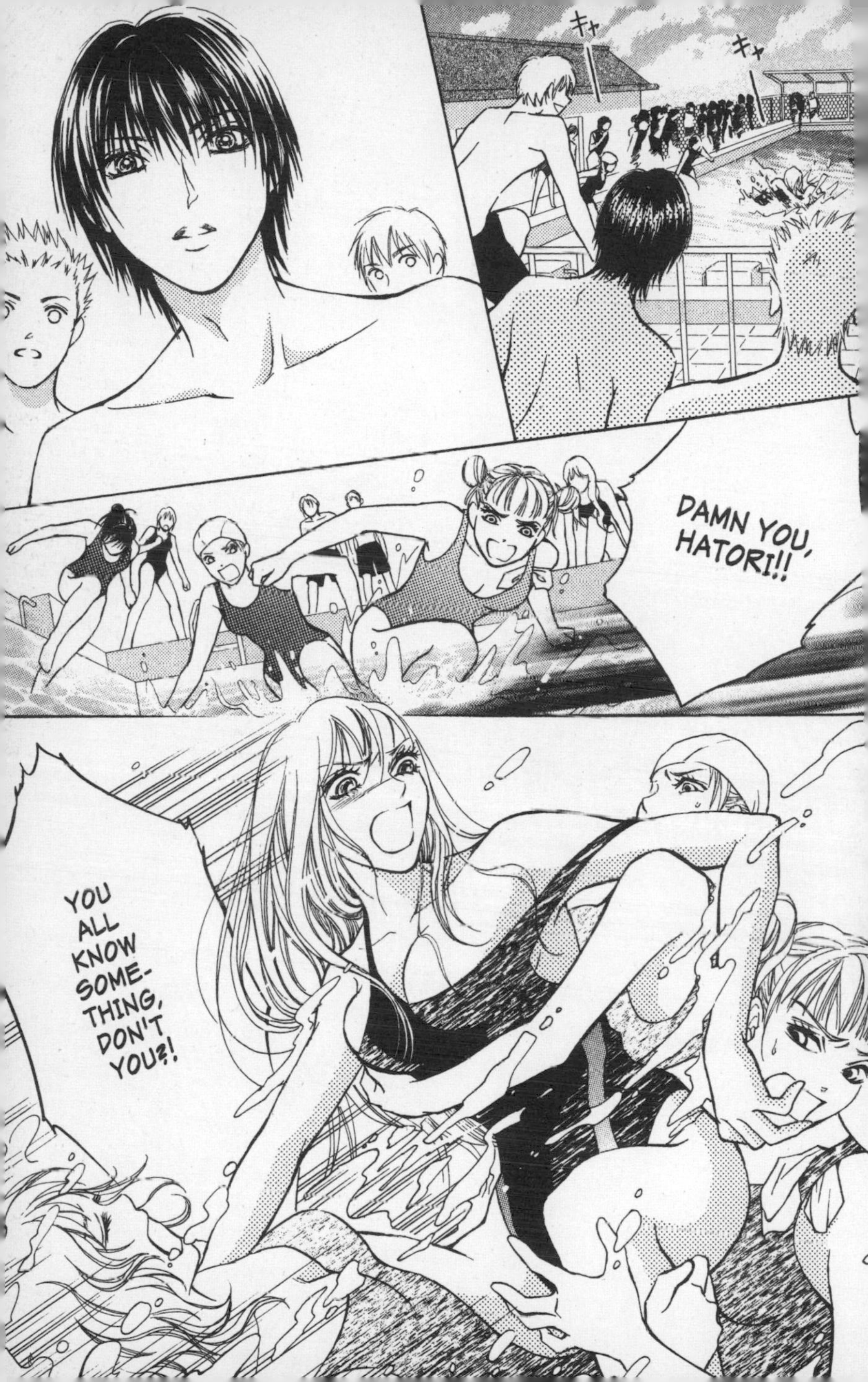
キャ
キャ
DAMN YOU, HATORI!!
YOU ALL KNOW SOME-THING, DON'T YOU?!

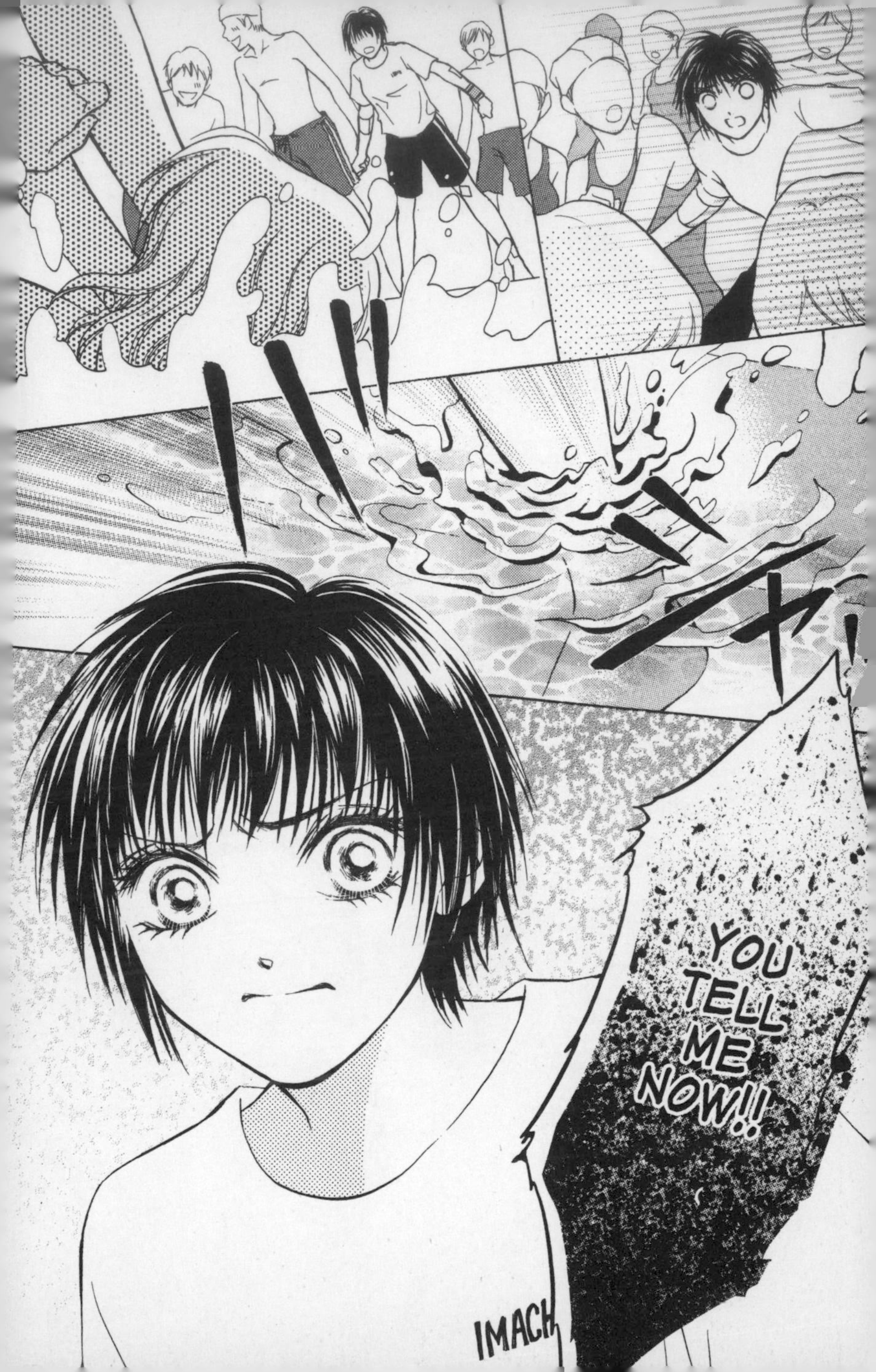
YOU TELL ME NOW!!
IMACH

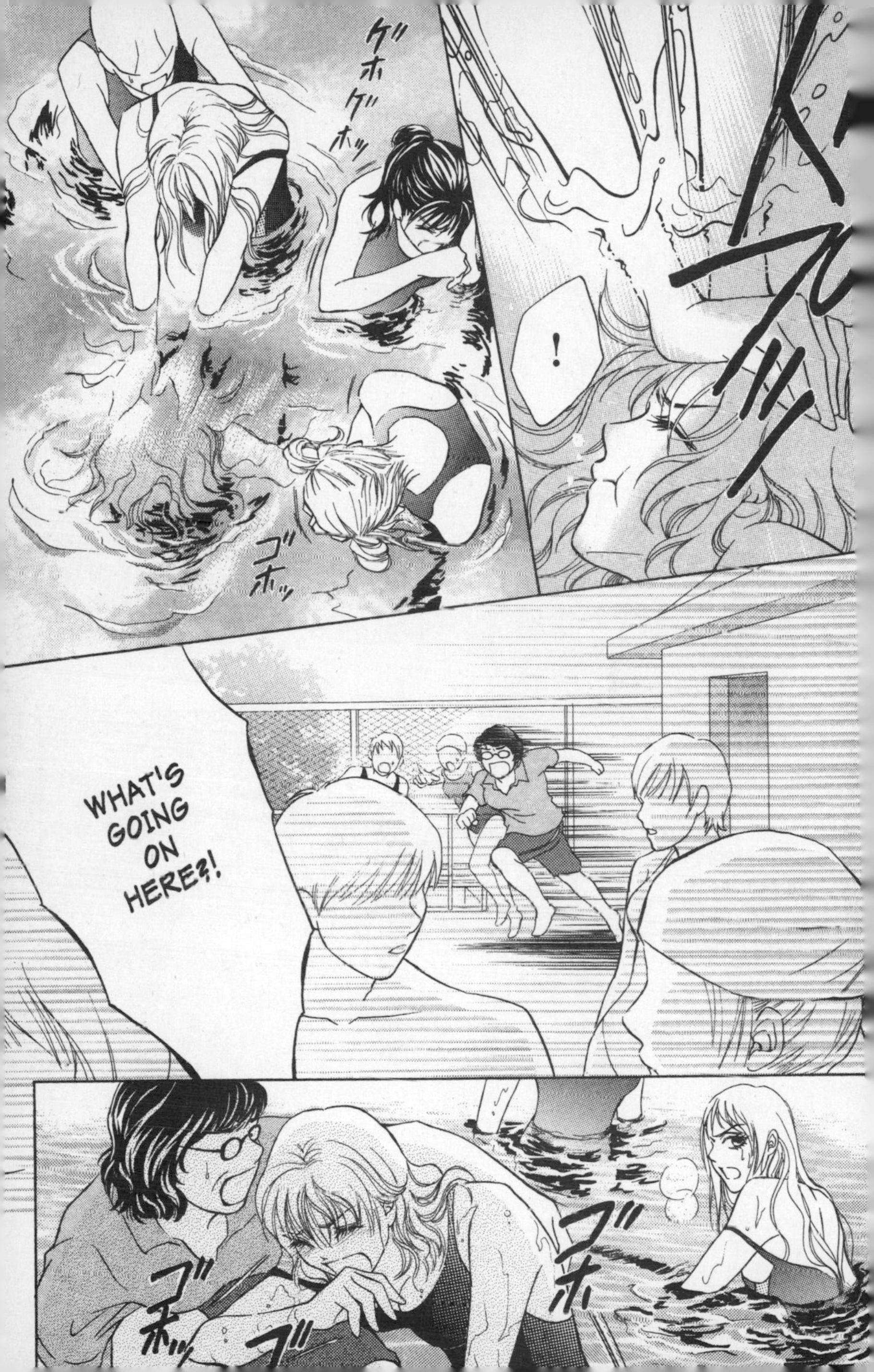
!
ゲホゲホッ
ゴホッ
WHAT'S GOING ON HERE?!
ゴボ
ゴホッ
ゴ

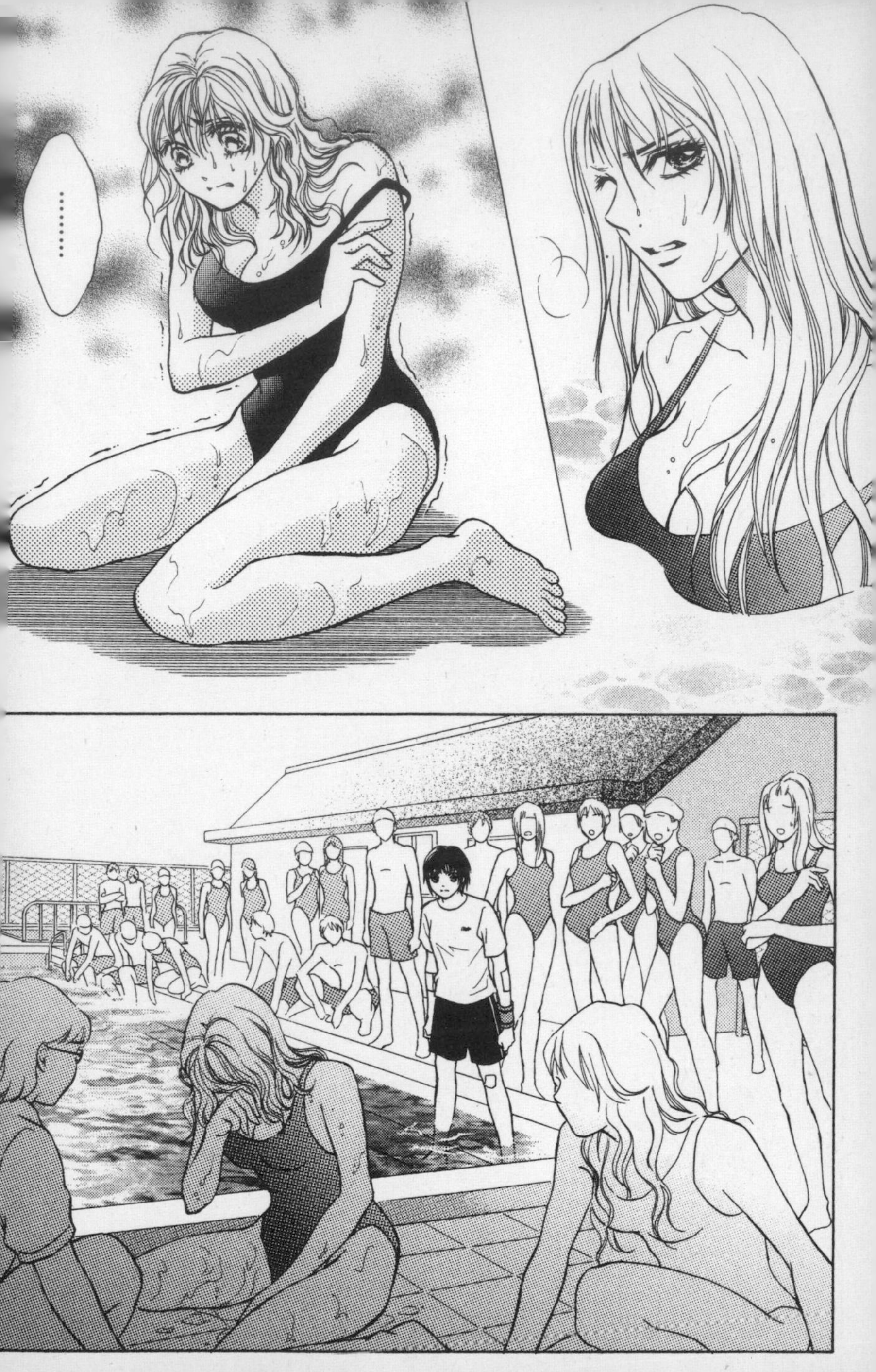
……

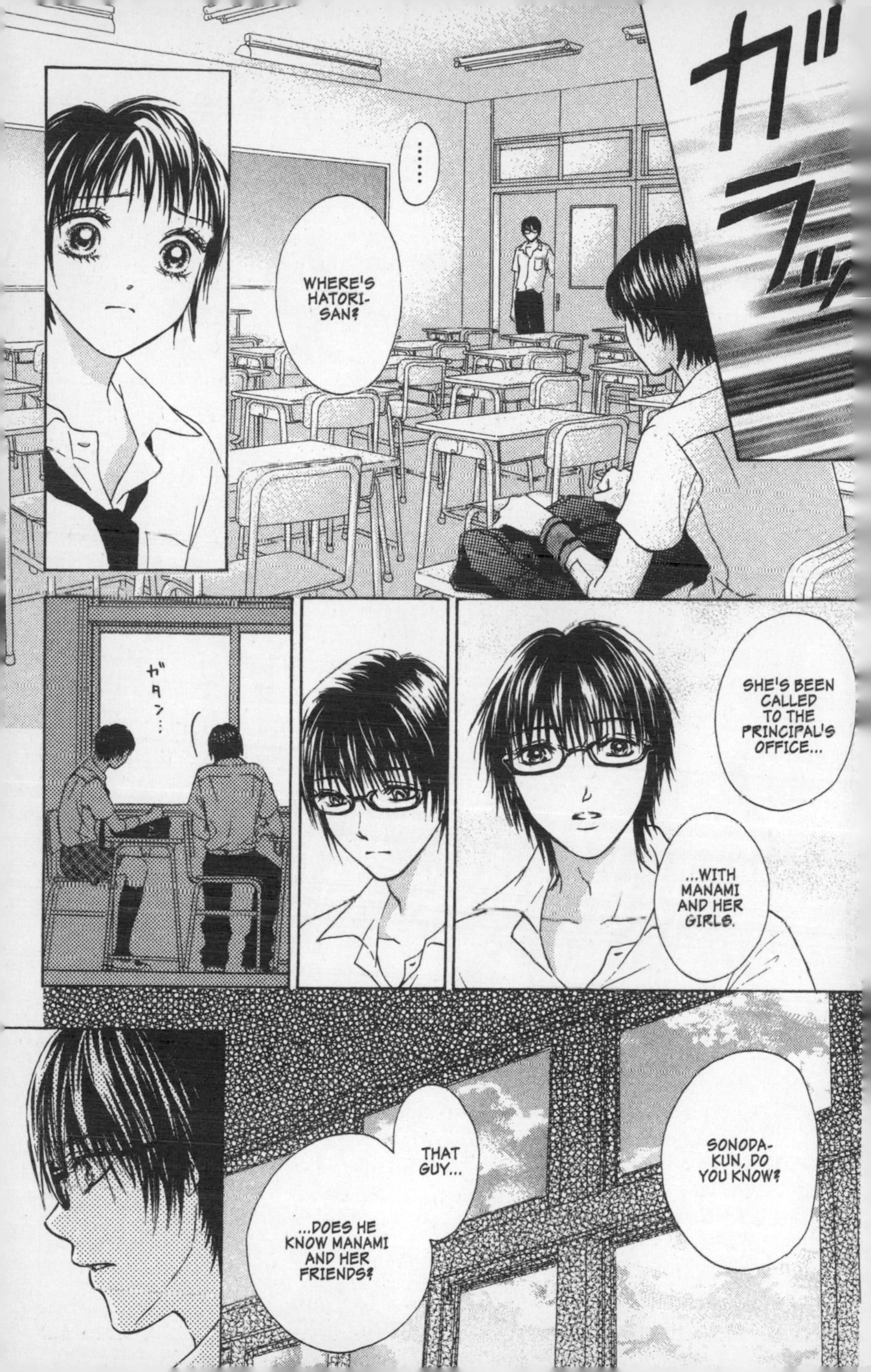
ガラッ
WHERE'S HATORI-SAN?
……
SHE'S BEEN CALLED TO THE PRINCIPAL'S OFFICE...
...WITH MANAMI AND HER GIRLS.
ガタン…
SONODA-KUN, DO YOU KNOW?
THAT GUY...
...DOES HE KNOW MANAMI AND HER FRIENDS?

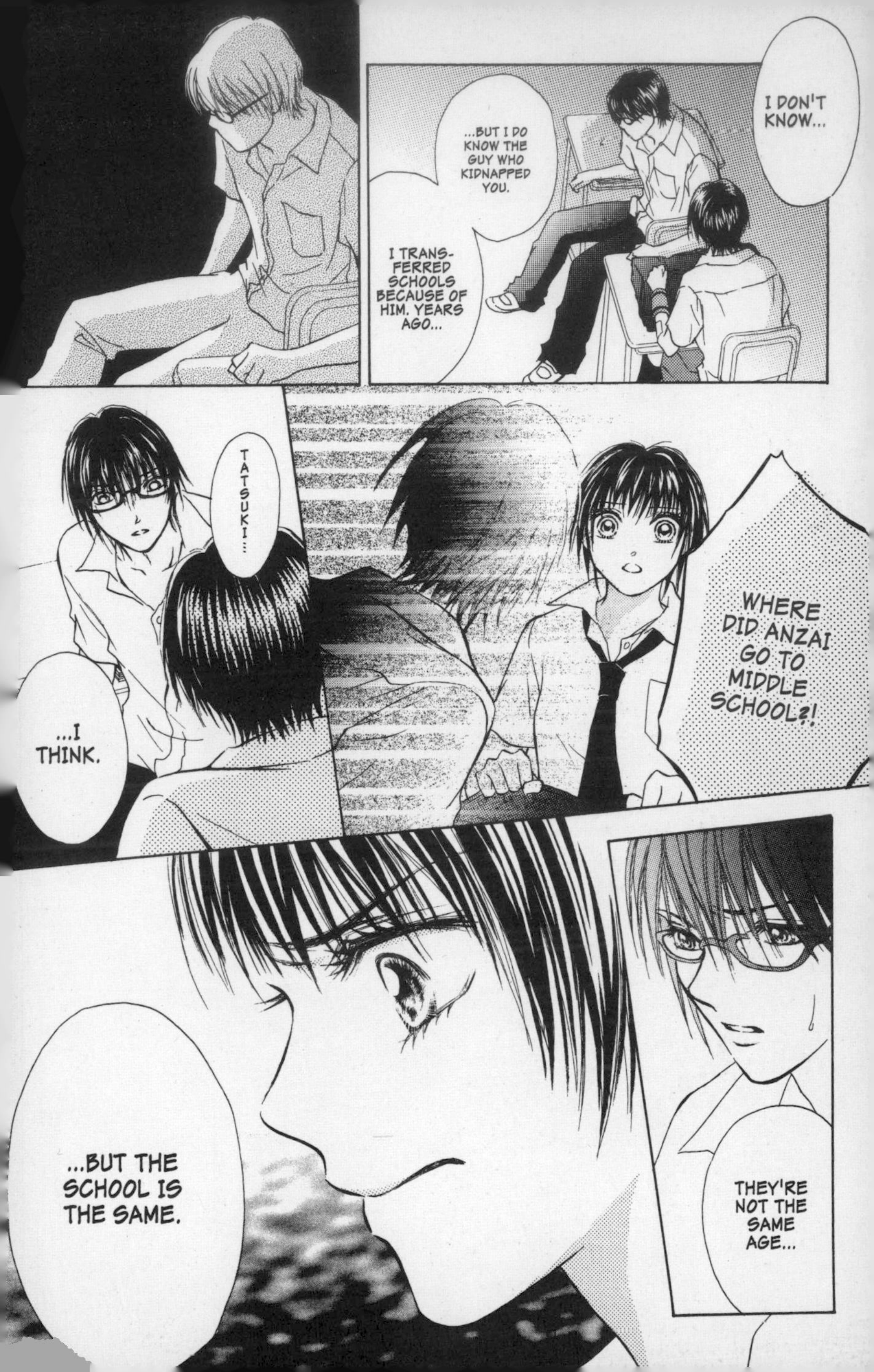
I DON'T KNOW...
...BUT I DO KNOW THE GUY WHO KIDNAPPED YOU.
I TRANS-FERRED SCHOOLS BECAUSE OF HIM. YEARS AGO...
WHERE DID ANZAI GO TO MIDDLE SCHOOL?!
TATSUKI...
...I THINK.
THEY'RE NOT THE SAME AGE...
...BUT THE SCHOOL IS THE SAME.

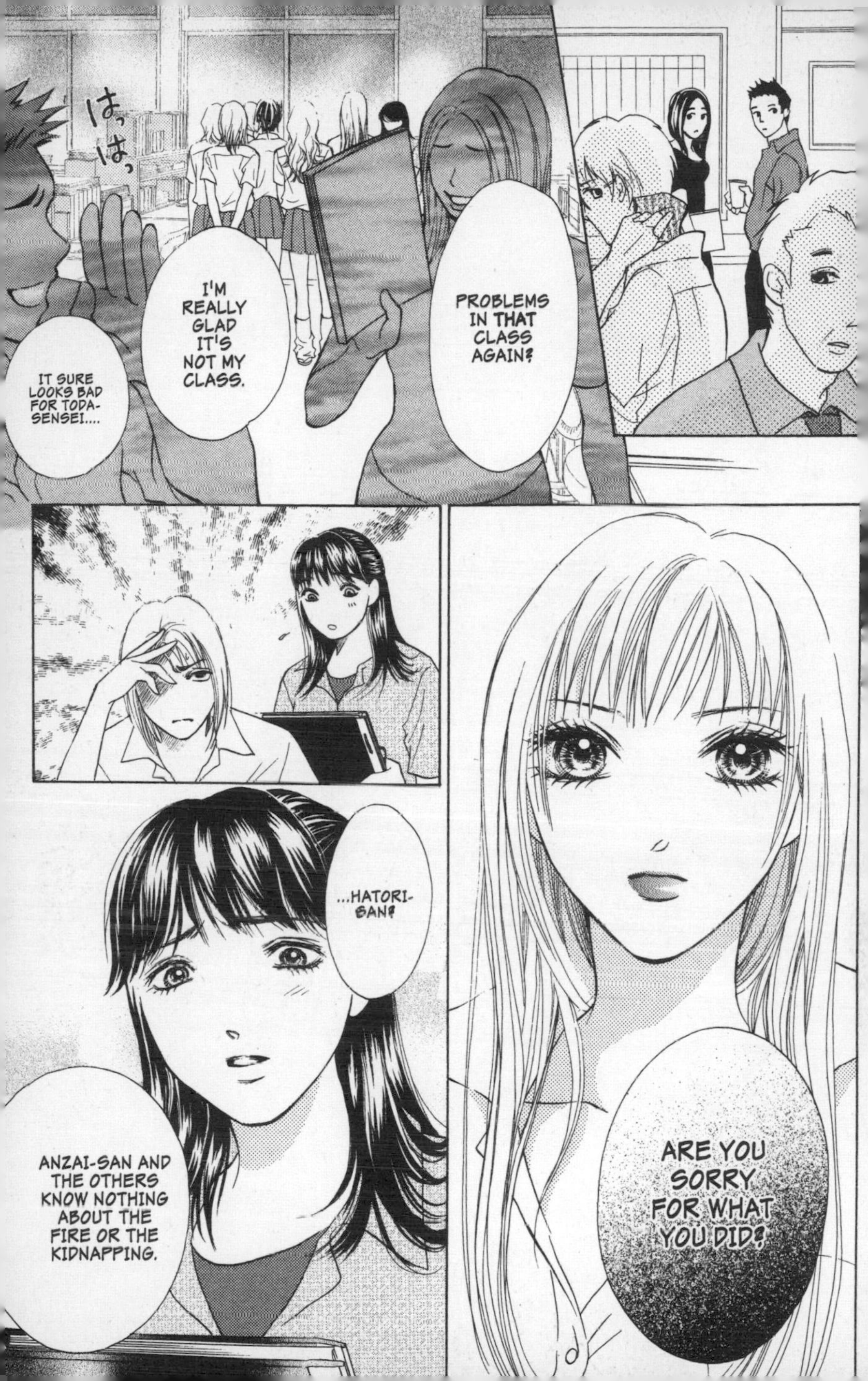
PROBLEMS IN THAT CLASS AGAIN?
I'M REALLY GLAD IT'S NOT MY CLASS.
はっはっ
IT SURE LOOKS BAD FOR TODA-SENSEI....
ARE YOU SORRY FOR WHAT YOU DID?
...HATORI-SAN?
ANZAI-SAN AND THE OTHERS KNOW NOTHING ABOUT THE FIRE OR THE KIDNAPPING.

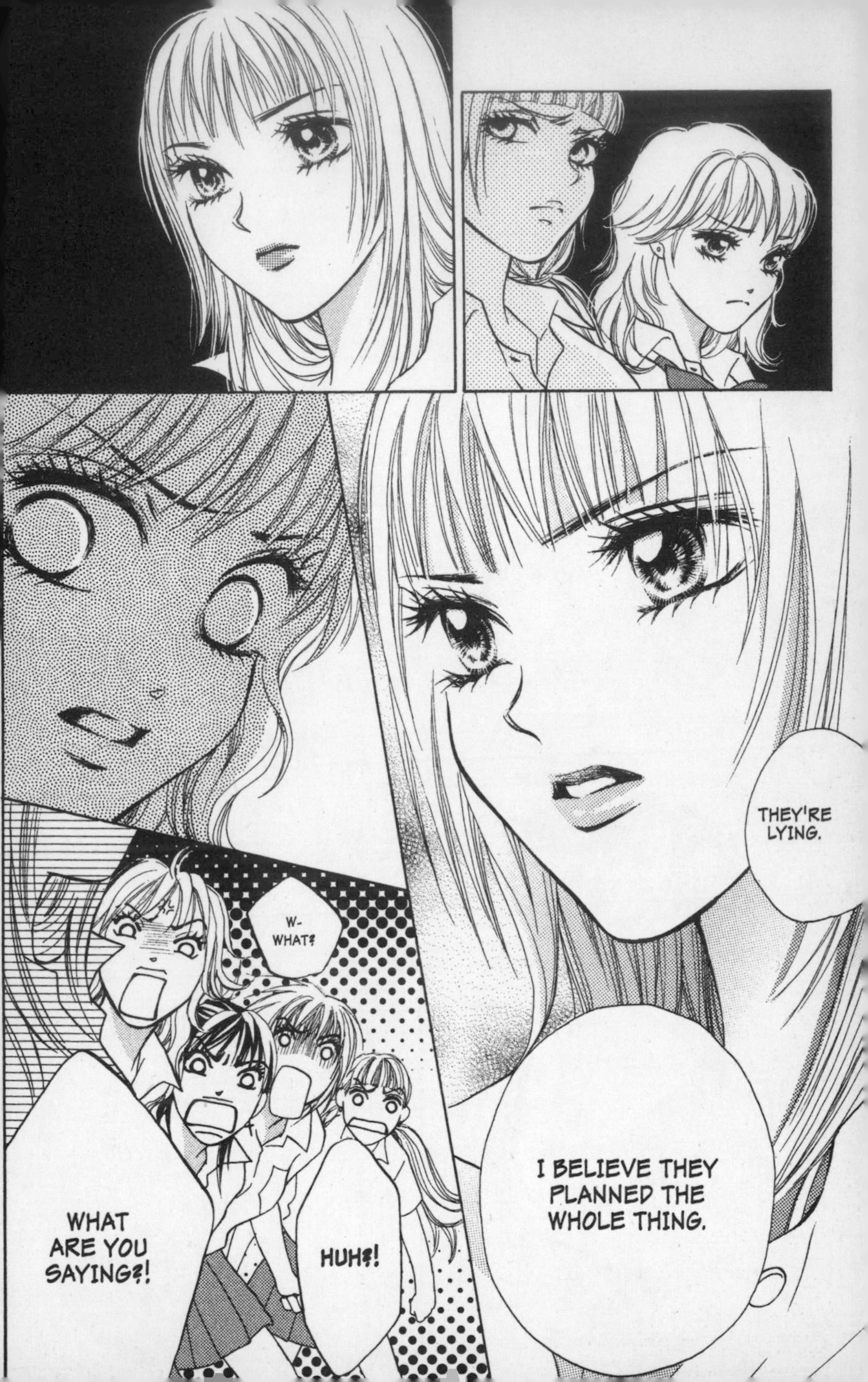
THEY'RE LYING.
I BELIEVE THEY PLANNED THE WHOLE THING.
W-WHAT?
HUH?!
WHAT ARE YOU SAYING?!

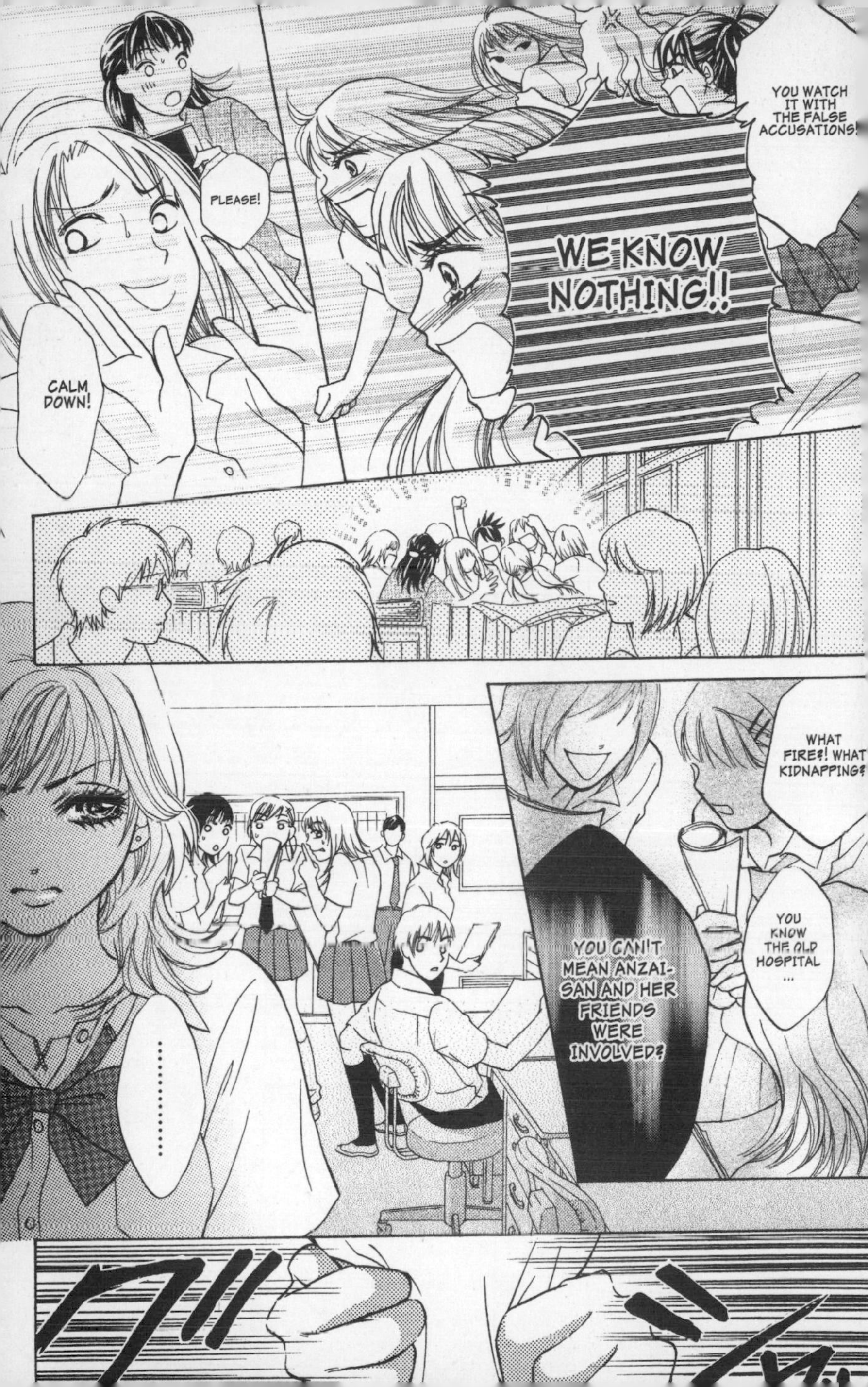
YOU WATCH IT WITH THE FALSE ACCUSATIONS!
WE KNOW NOTHING!!
PLEASE!
CALM DOWN!
WHAT FIRE?! WHAT KIDNAPPING?
YOU KNOW THE OLD HOSPITAL ...
YOU CAN'T MEAN ANZAI-SAN AND HER FRIENDS WERE INVOLVED?
......

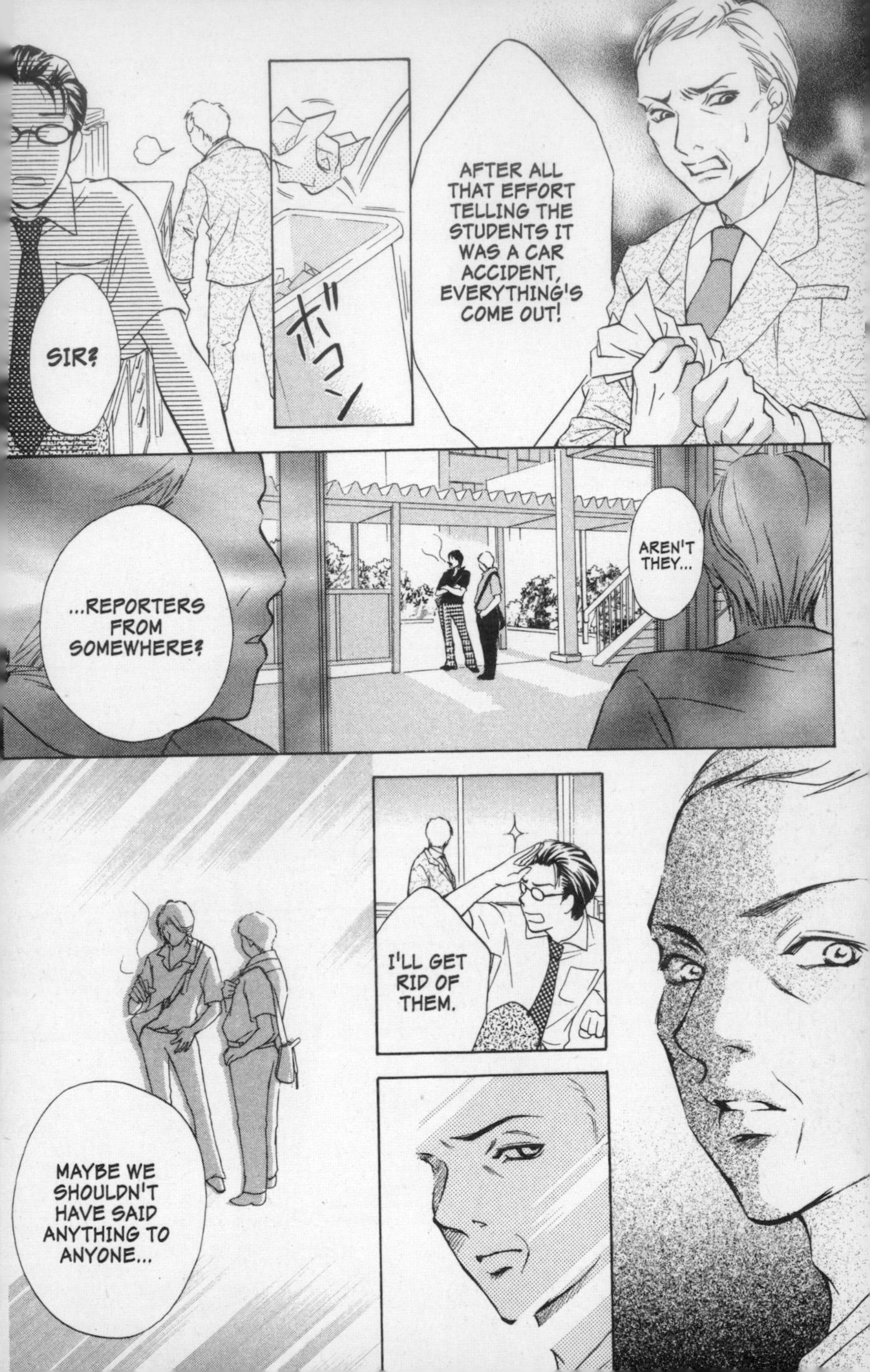
AFTER ALL THAT EFFORT TELLING THE STUDENTS IT WAS A CAR ACCIDENT, EVERYTHING'S COME OUT!
ボコン
SIR?
AREN'T THEY...
...REPORTERS FROM SOMEWHERE?
I'LL GET RID OF THEM.
MAYBE WE SHOULDN'T HAVE SAID ANYTHING TO ANYONE...

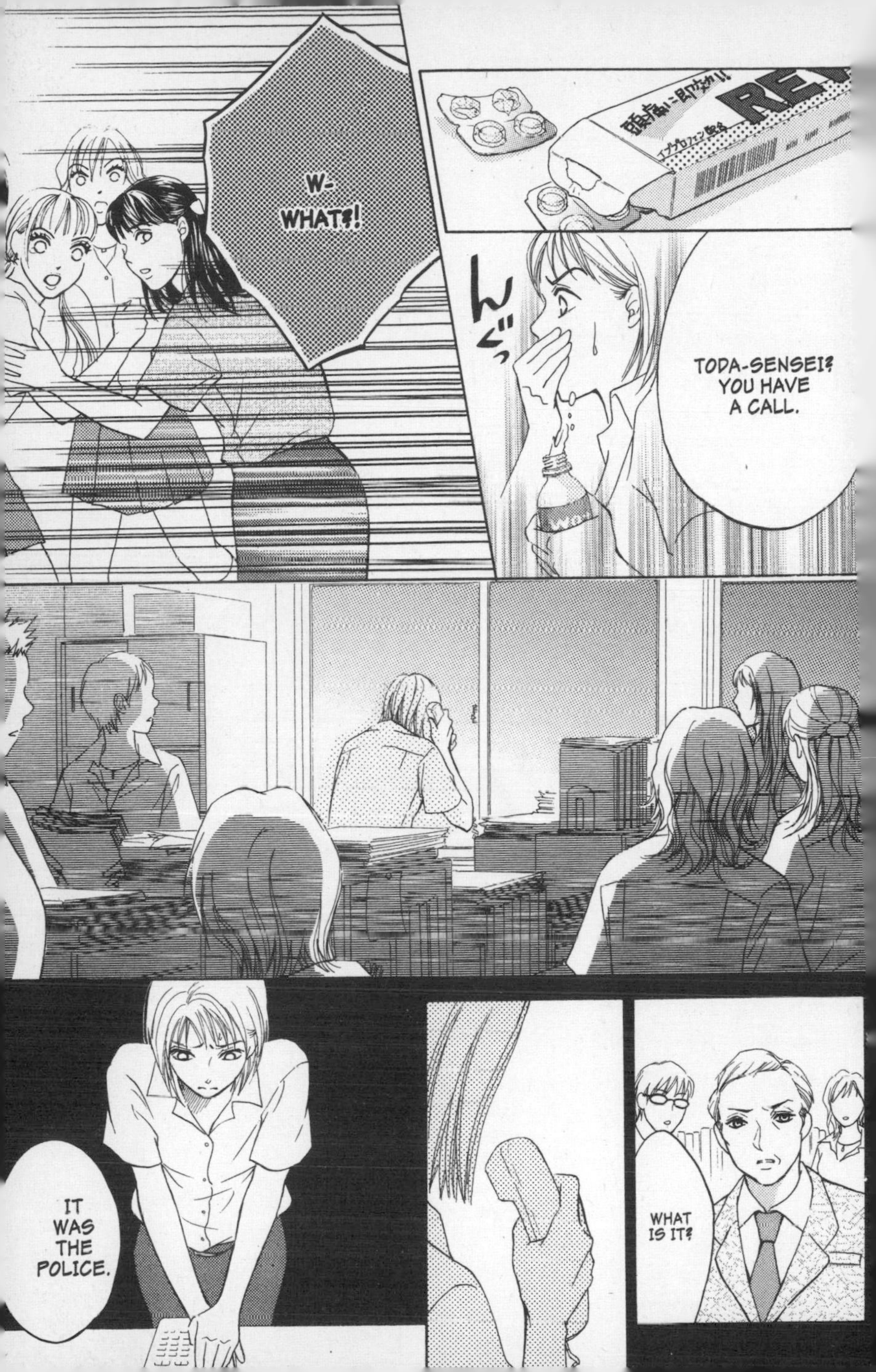
んぐっ
TODA-SENSEI? YOU HAVE A CALL.
W- WHAT?!
WHAT IS IT?
IT WAS THE POLICE.

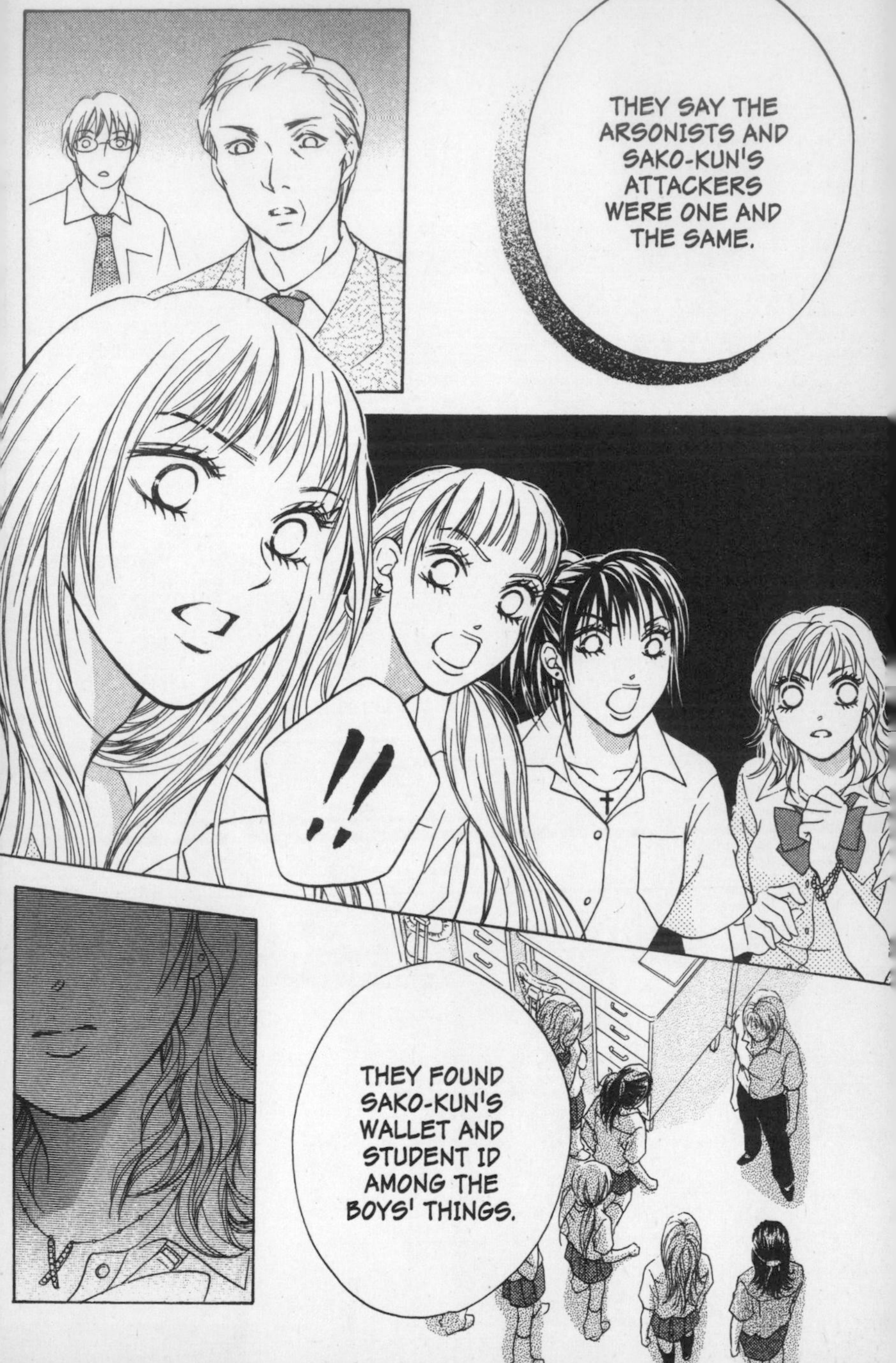
THEY SAY THE ARSONISTS AND SAKO-KUN'S ATTACKERS WERE ONE AND THE SAME.
!!
THEY FOUND SAKO-KUN'S WALLET AND STUDENT ID AMONG THE BOYS' THINGS.

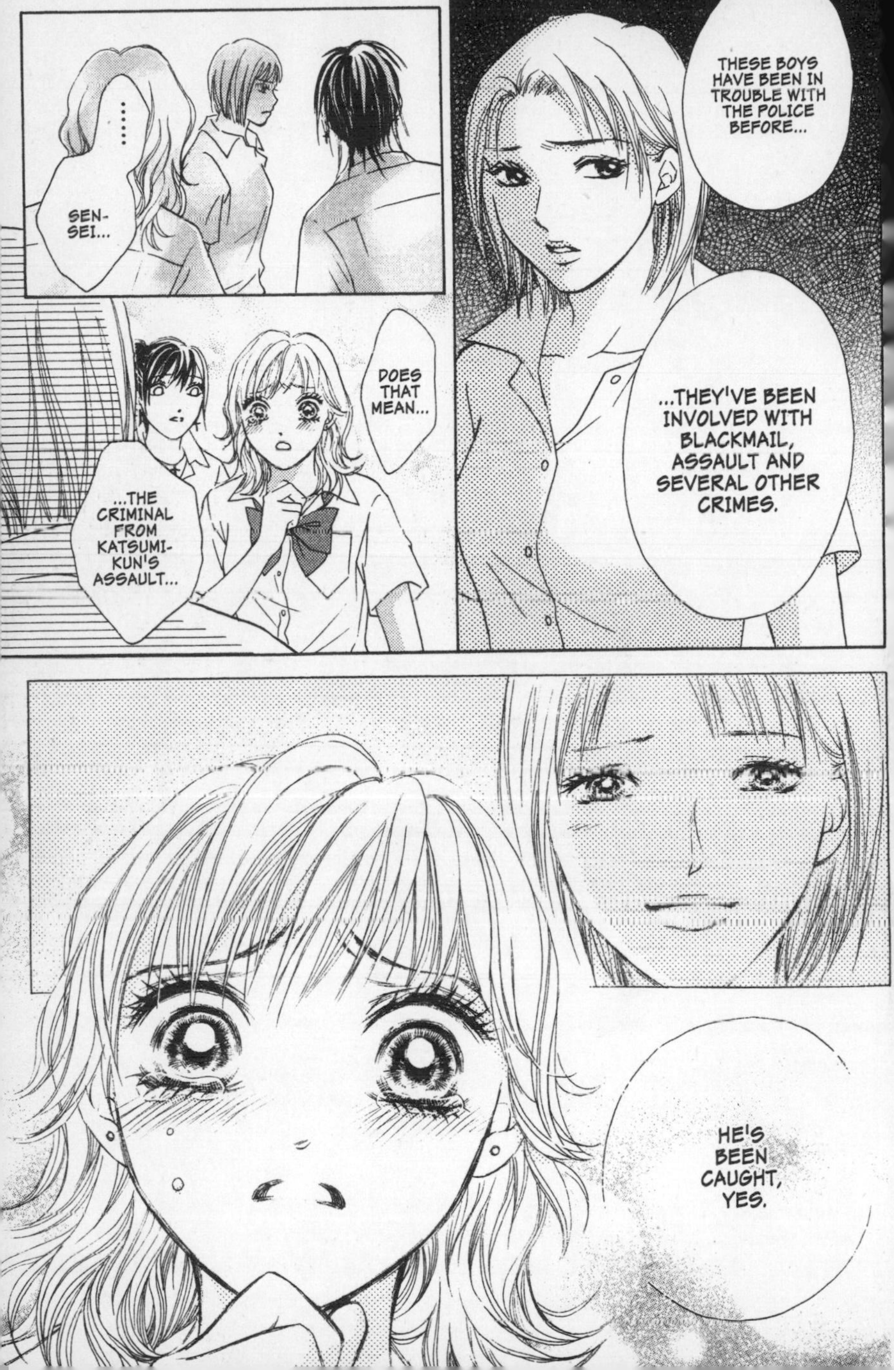
THESE BOYS HAVE BEEN IN TROUBLE WITH THE POLICE BEFORE...
...THEY'VE BEEN INVOLVED WITH BLACKMAIL, ASSAULT AND SEVERAL OTHER CRIMES.
......
SEN-SEI...
DOES THAT MEAN...
...THE CRIMINAL FROM KATSUMI-KUN'S ASSAULT...
HE'S BEEN CAUGHT, YES.

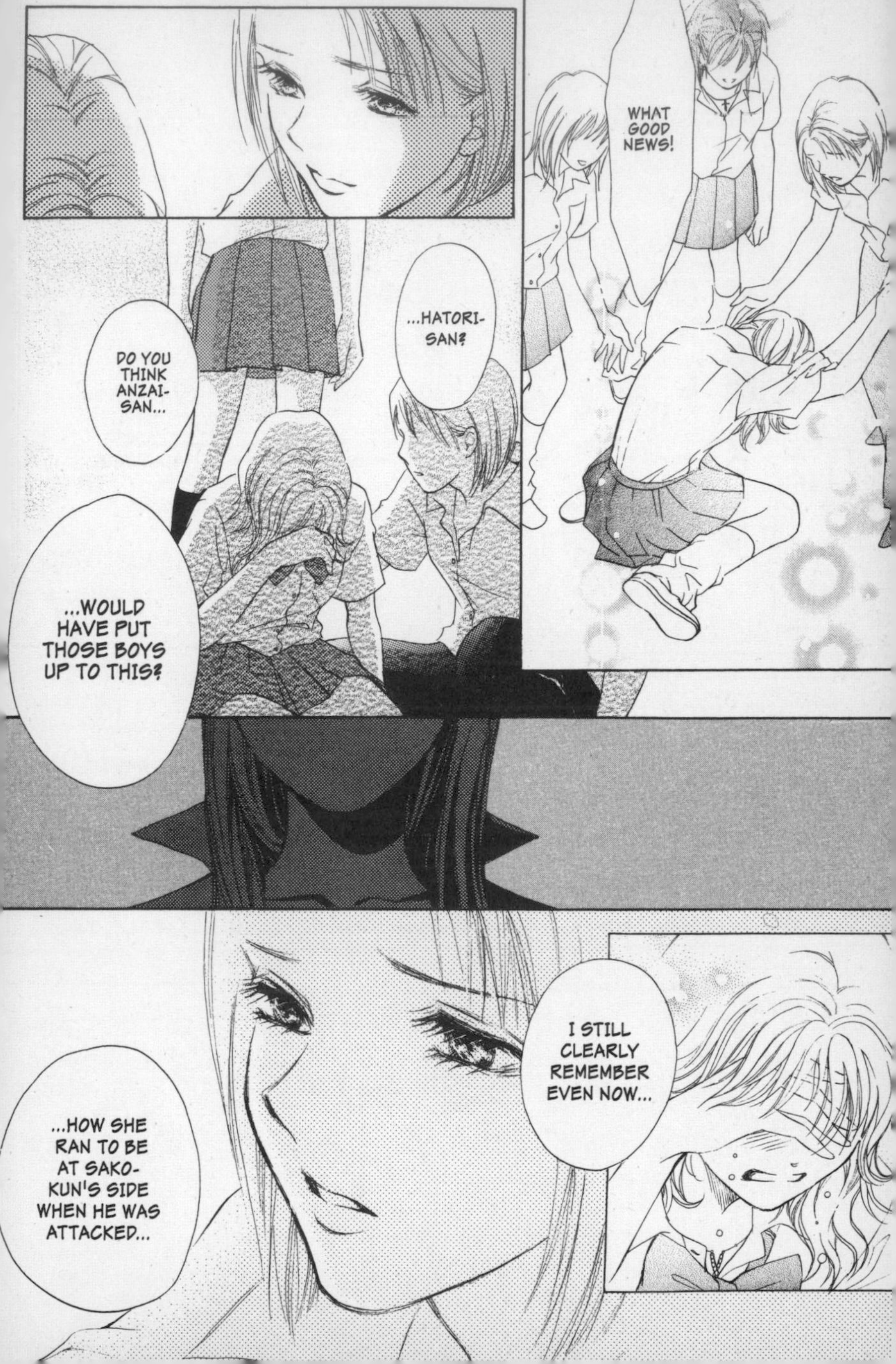
WHAT GOOD NEWS!
...HATORI-SAN?
DO YOU THINK ANZAI-SAN...
...WOULD HAVE PUT THOSE BOYS UP TO THIS?
I STILL CLEARLY REMEMBER EVEN NOW...
...HOW SHE RAN TO BE AT SAKO-KUN'S SIDE WHEN HE WAS ATTACKED...

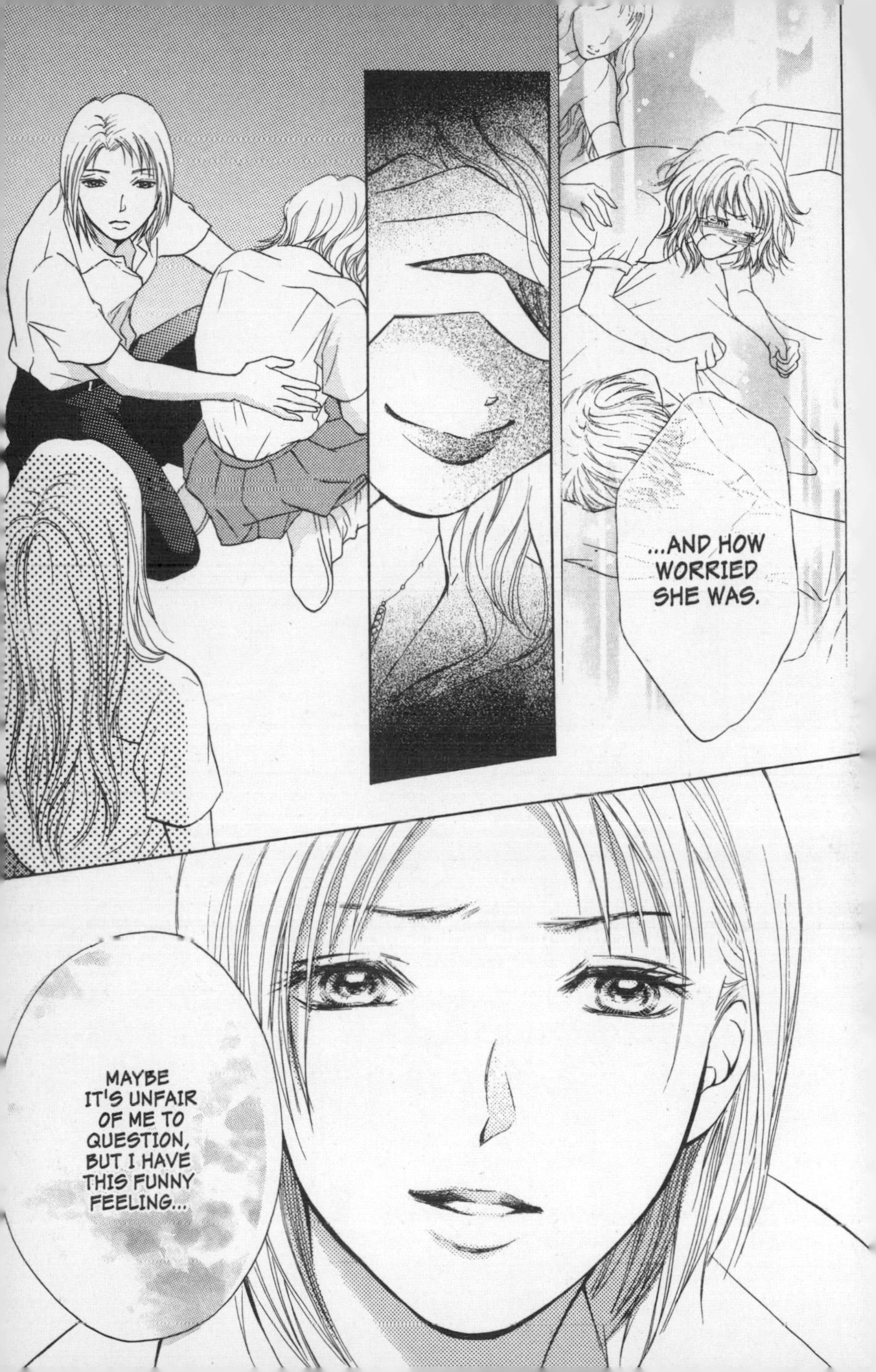
...AND HOW WORRIED SHE WAS.
MAYBE IT'S UNFAIR OF ME TO QUESTION, BUT I HAVE THIS FUNNY FEELING...

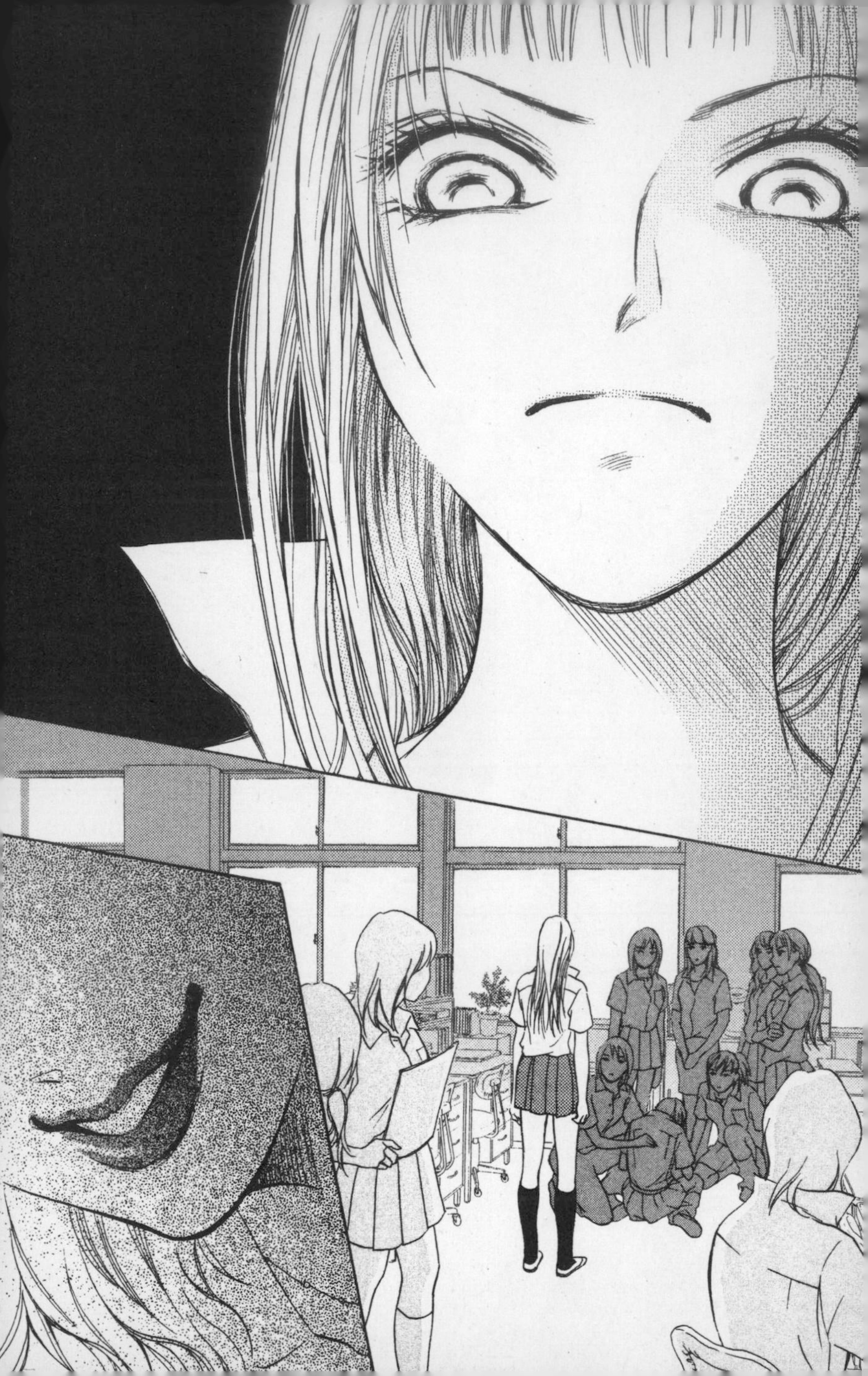

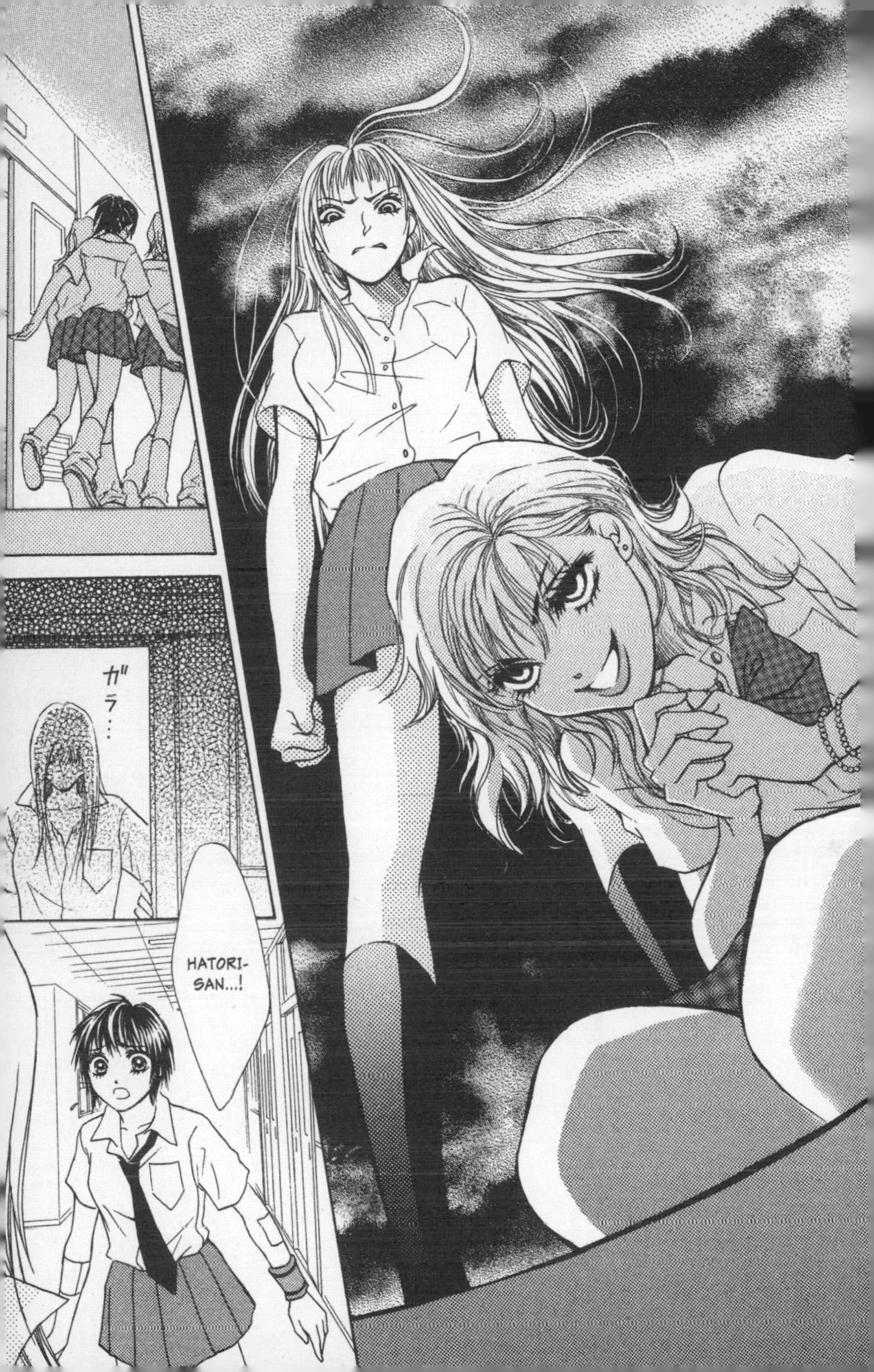
ガラ…
HATORI-SAN...!

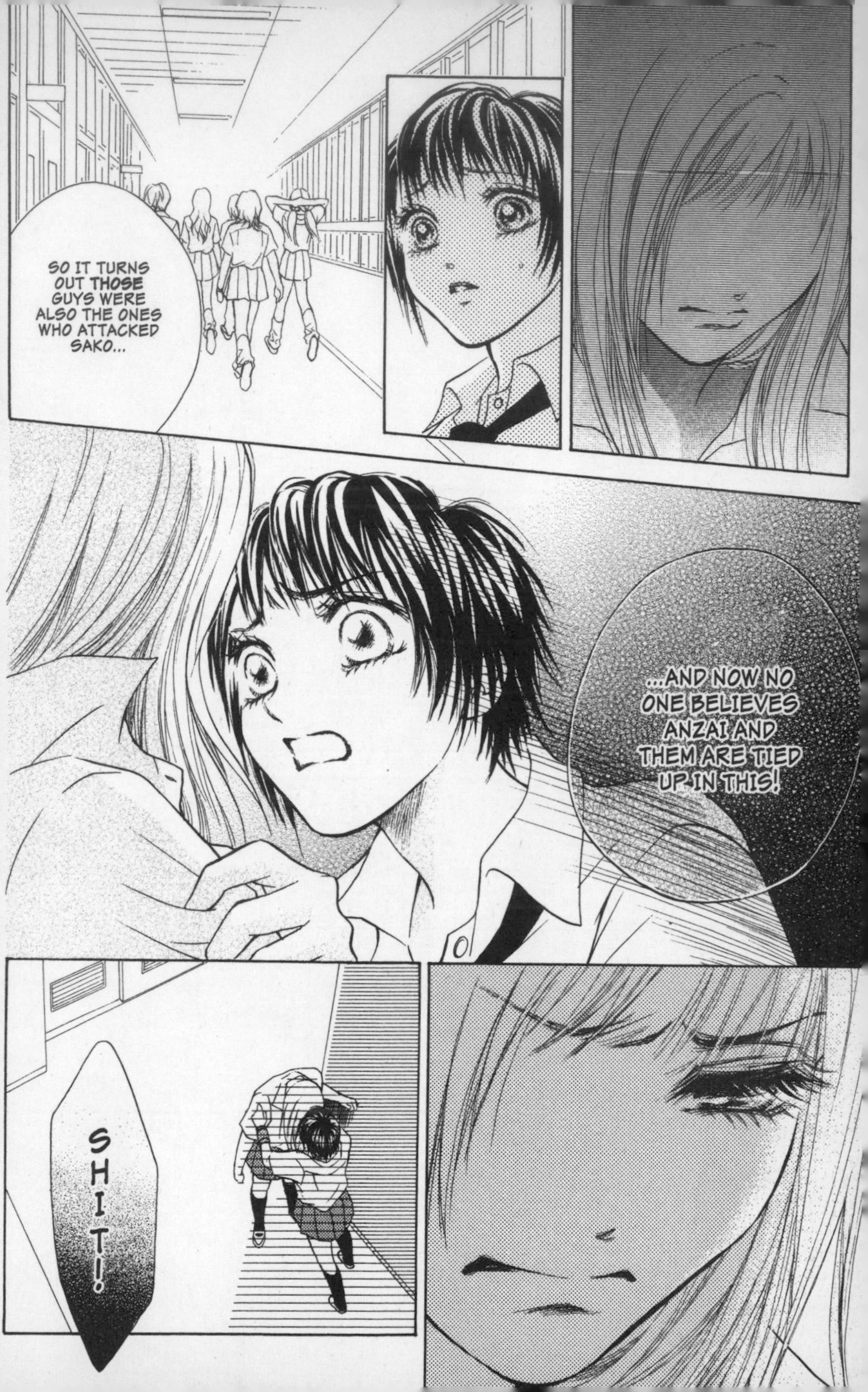
SO IT TURNS OUT THOSE GUYS WERE ALSO THE ONES WHO ATTACKED SAKO...
...AND NOW NO ONE BELIEVES ANZAI AND THEM ARE TIED UP IN THIS!
SHIT!

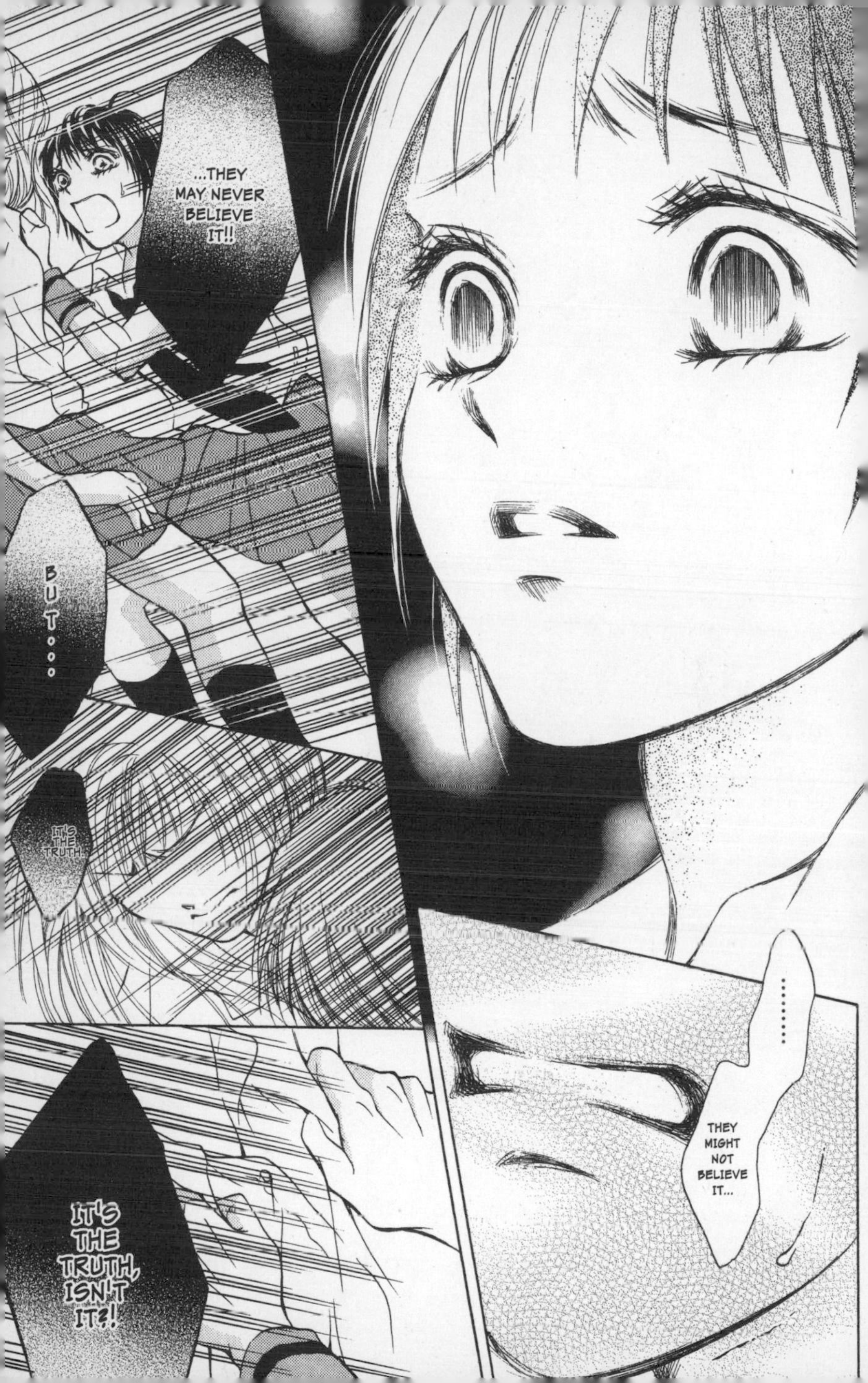
...THEY MAY NEVER BELIEVE IT!!
BUT...
IT'S THE TRUTH.
......
THEY MIGHT NOT BELIEVE IT...
IT'S THE TRUTH, ISN'T IT?!

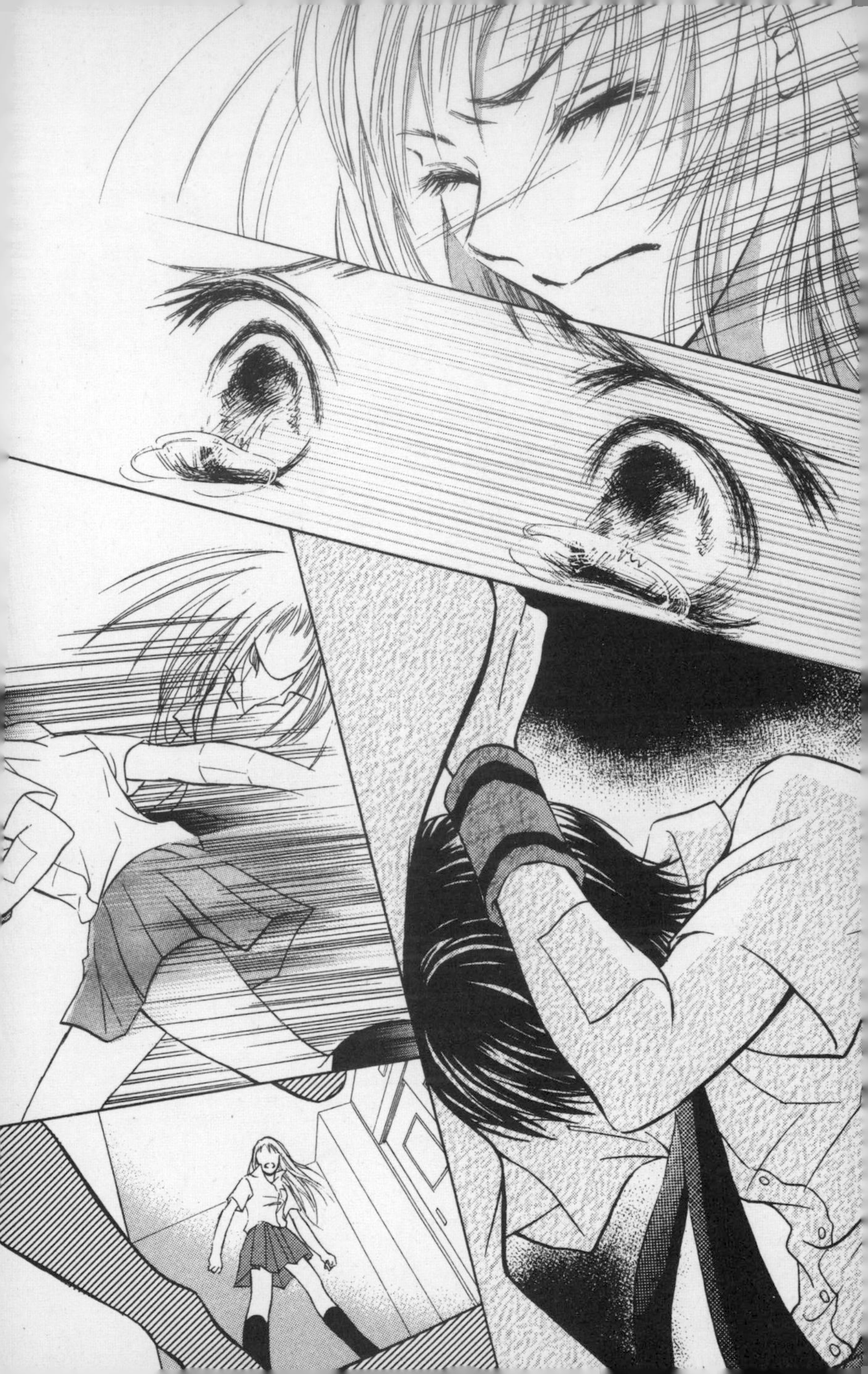

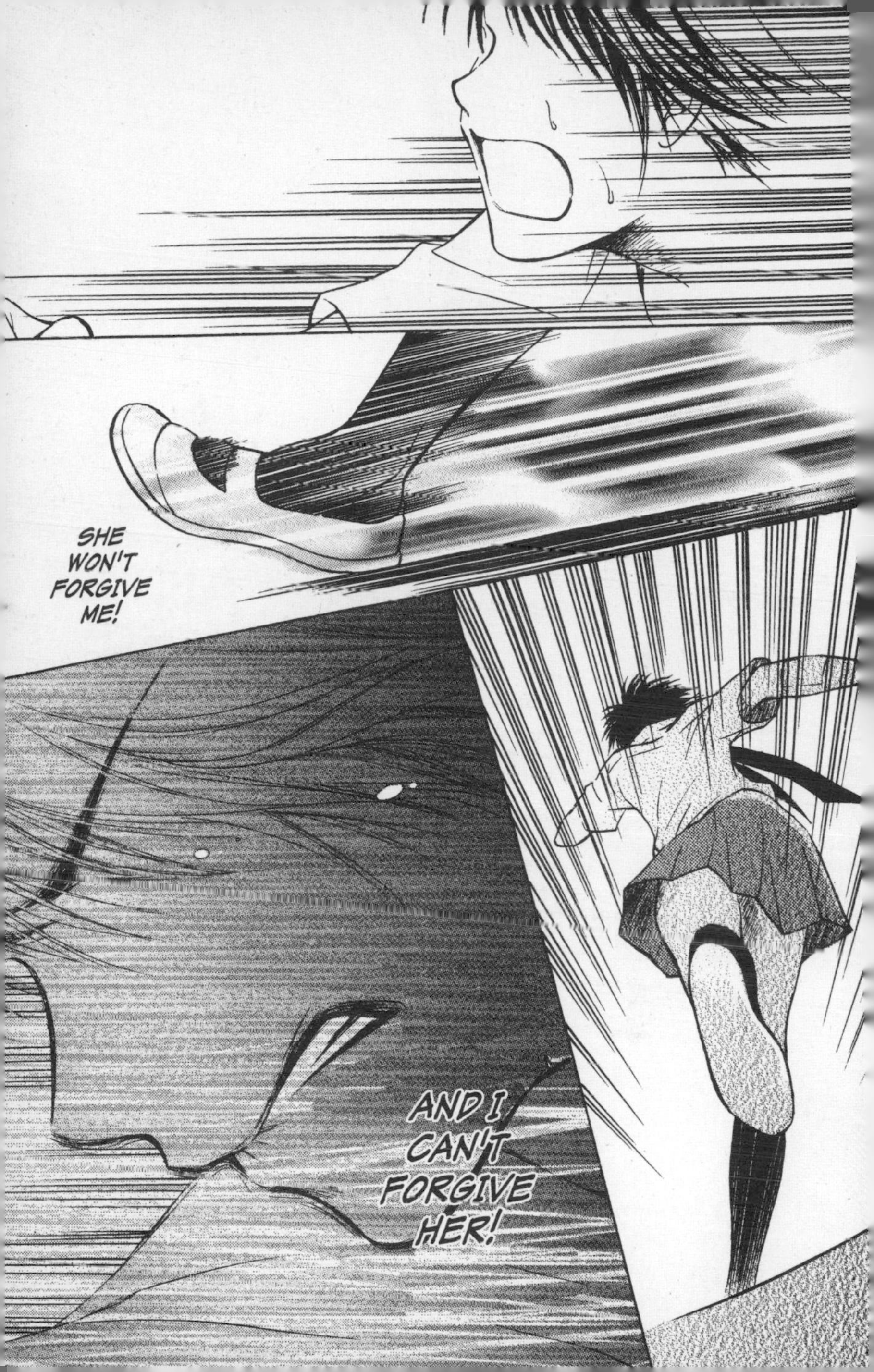
SHE WON'T FORGIVE ME!
AND I CAN'T FORGIVE HER!

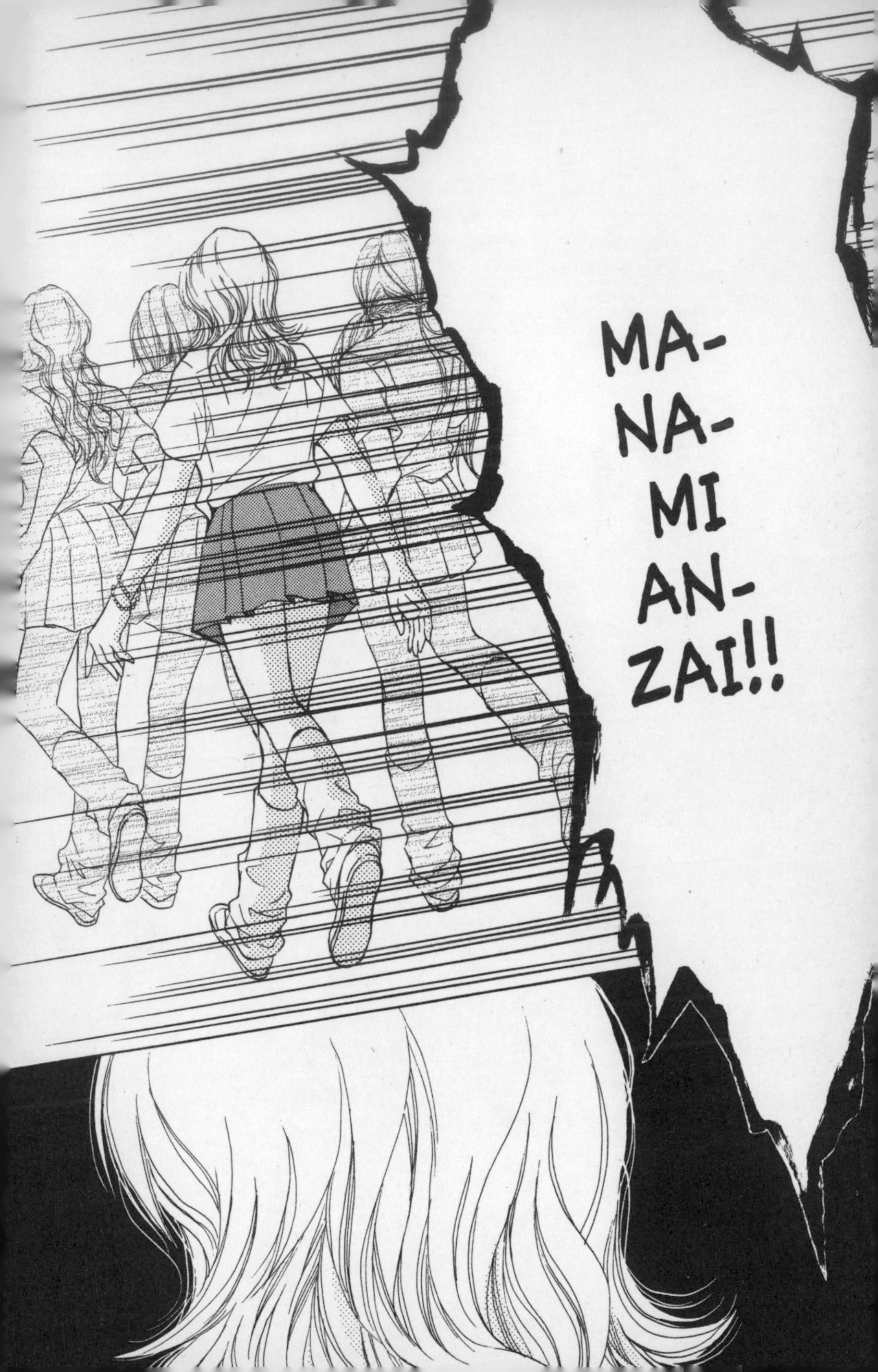
MA-
NA-
MI
AN-
ZAI!!

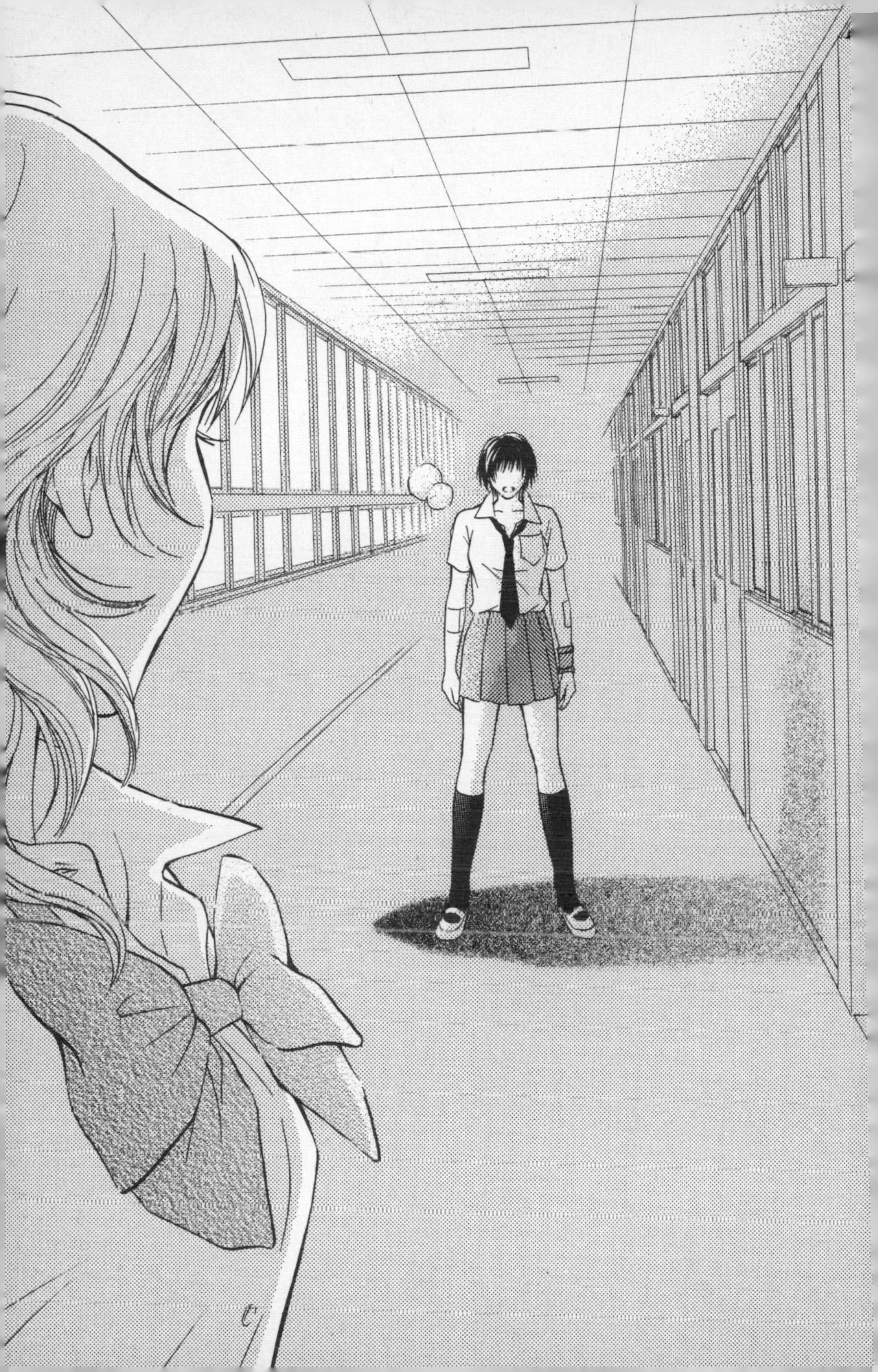

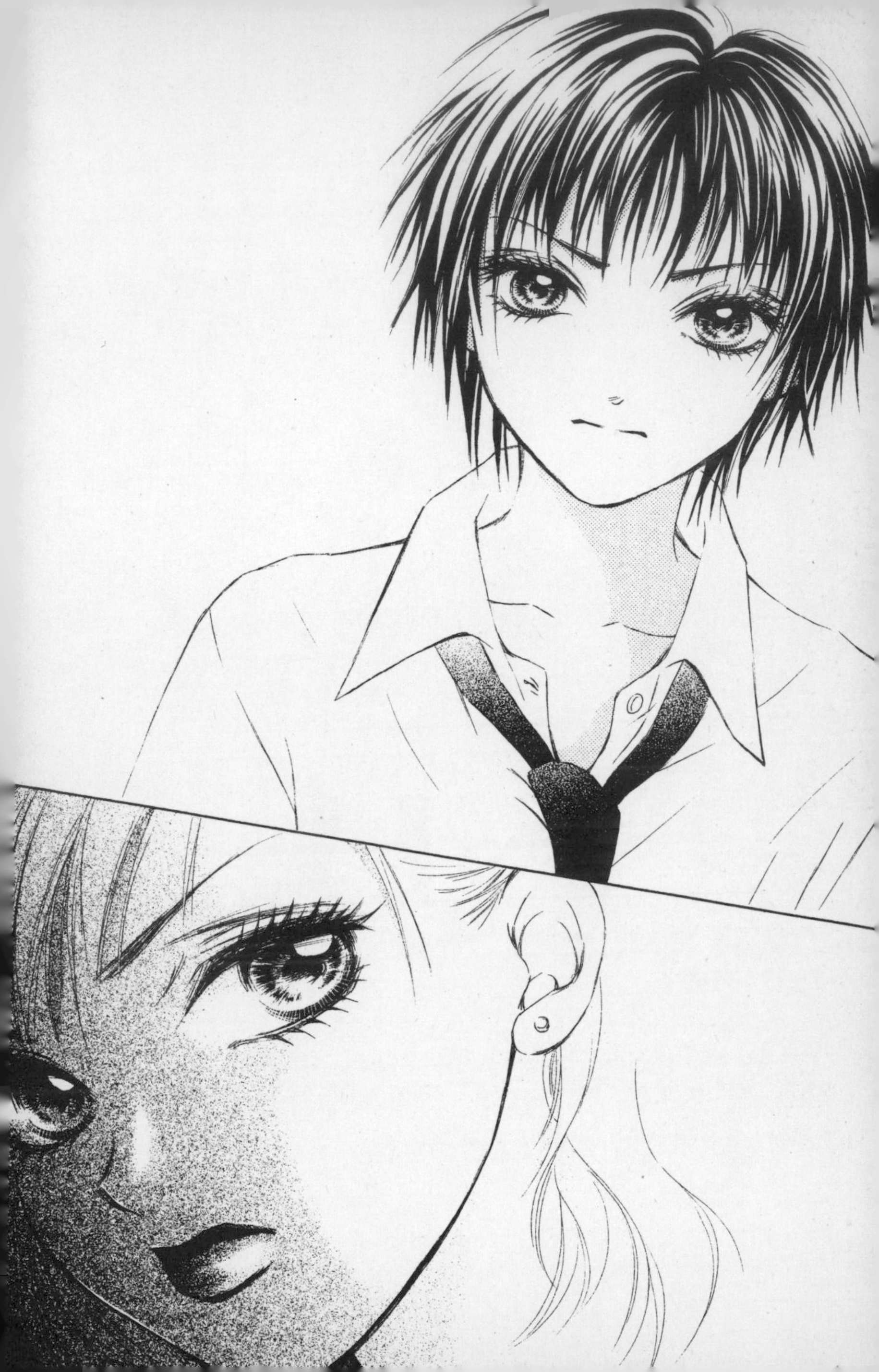

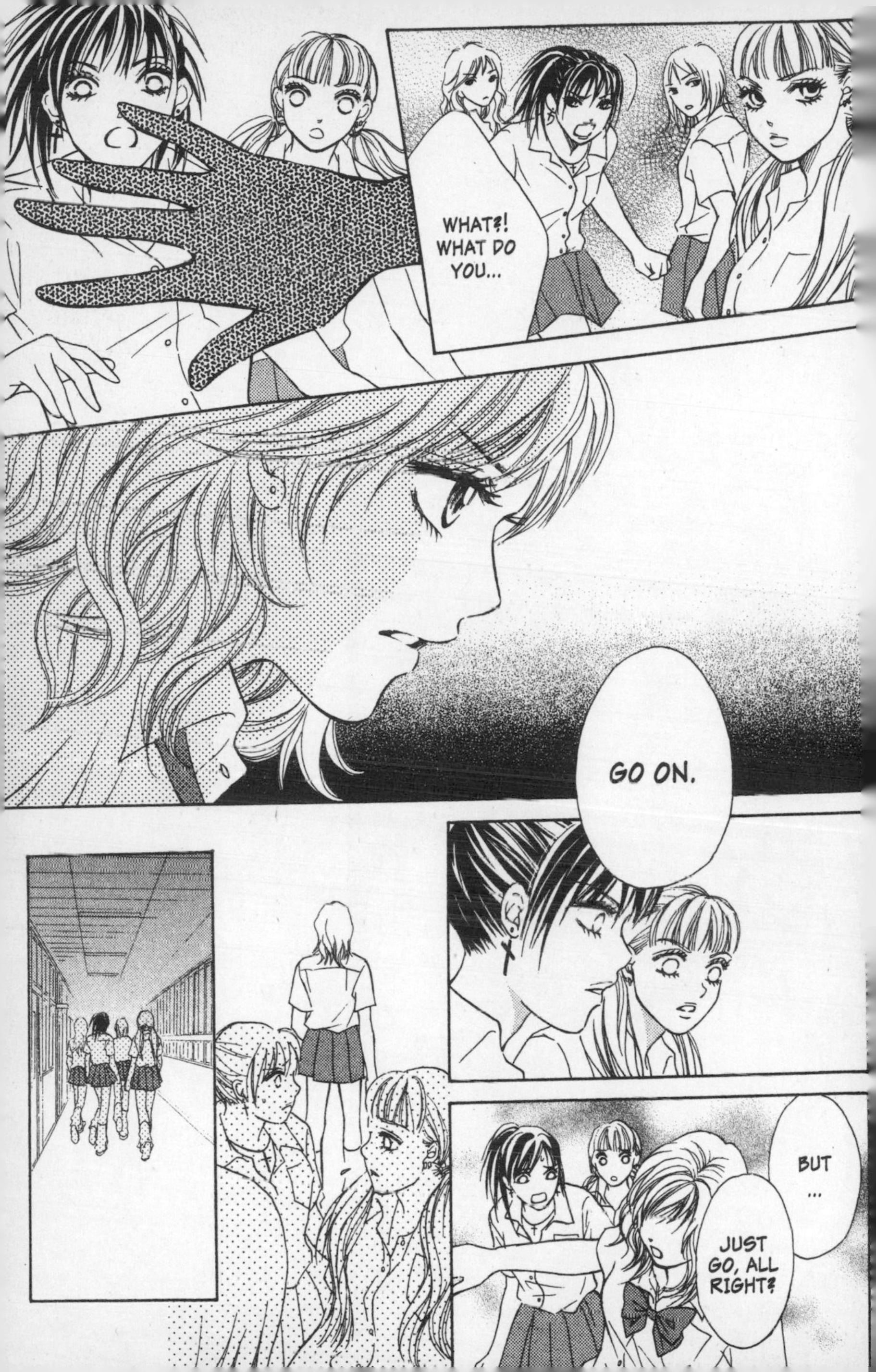
WHAT?! WHAT DO YOU...
GO ON.
BUT ...
JUST GO, ALL RIGHT?

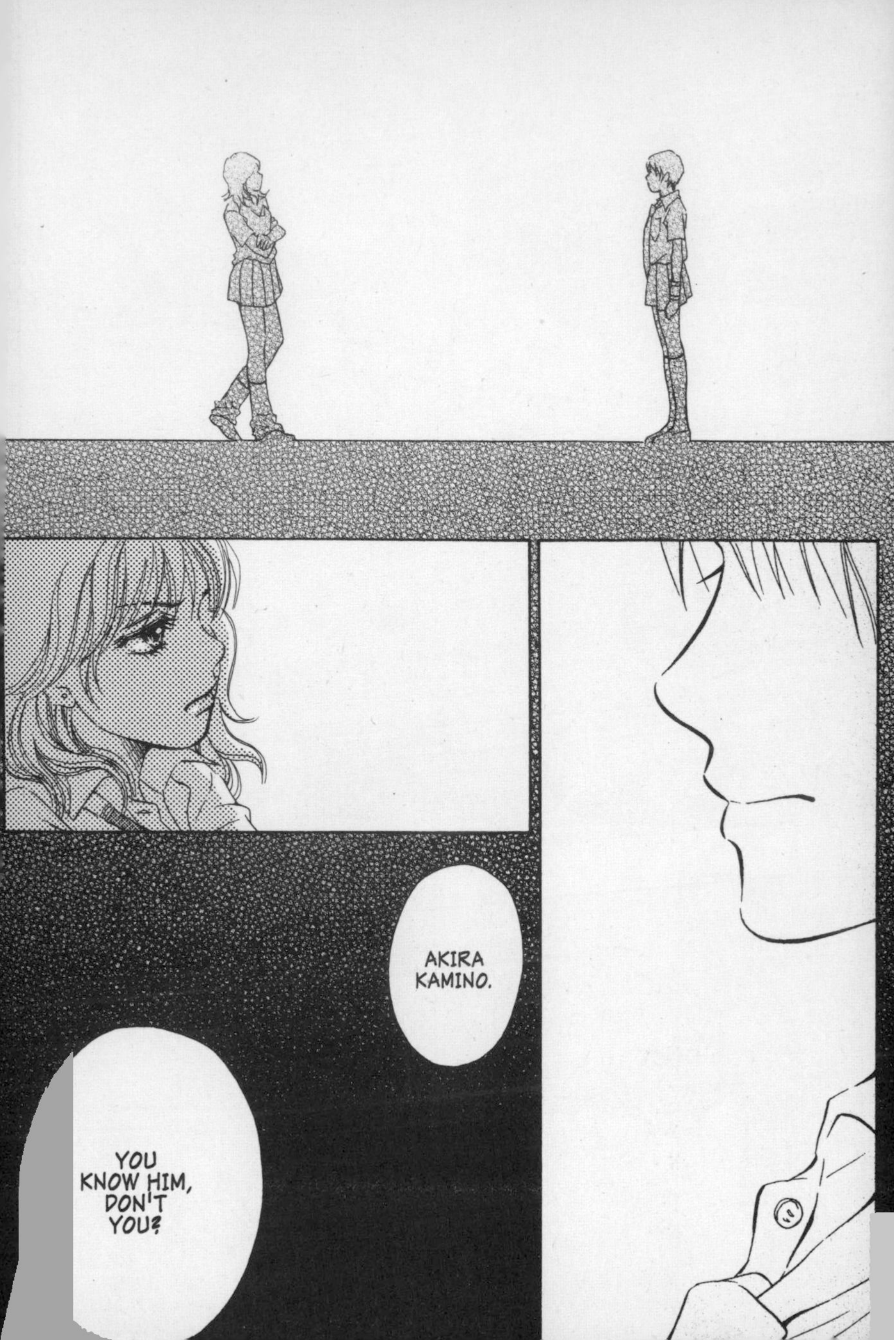
AKIRA KAMINO.
YOU KNOW HIM, DON'T YOU?

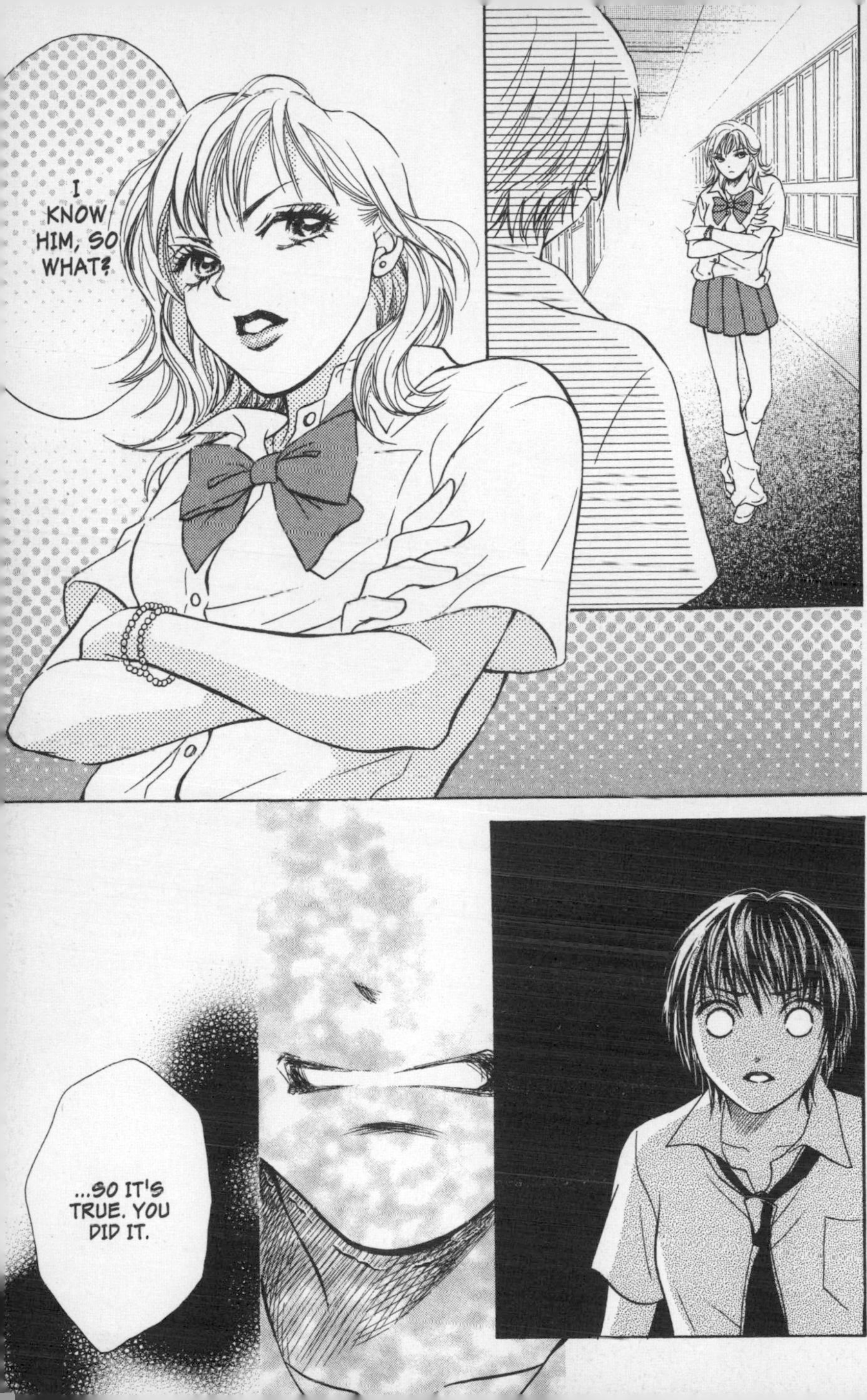
I KNOW HIM, SO WHAT?
...SO IT'S TRUE. YOU DID IT.

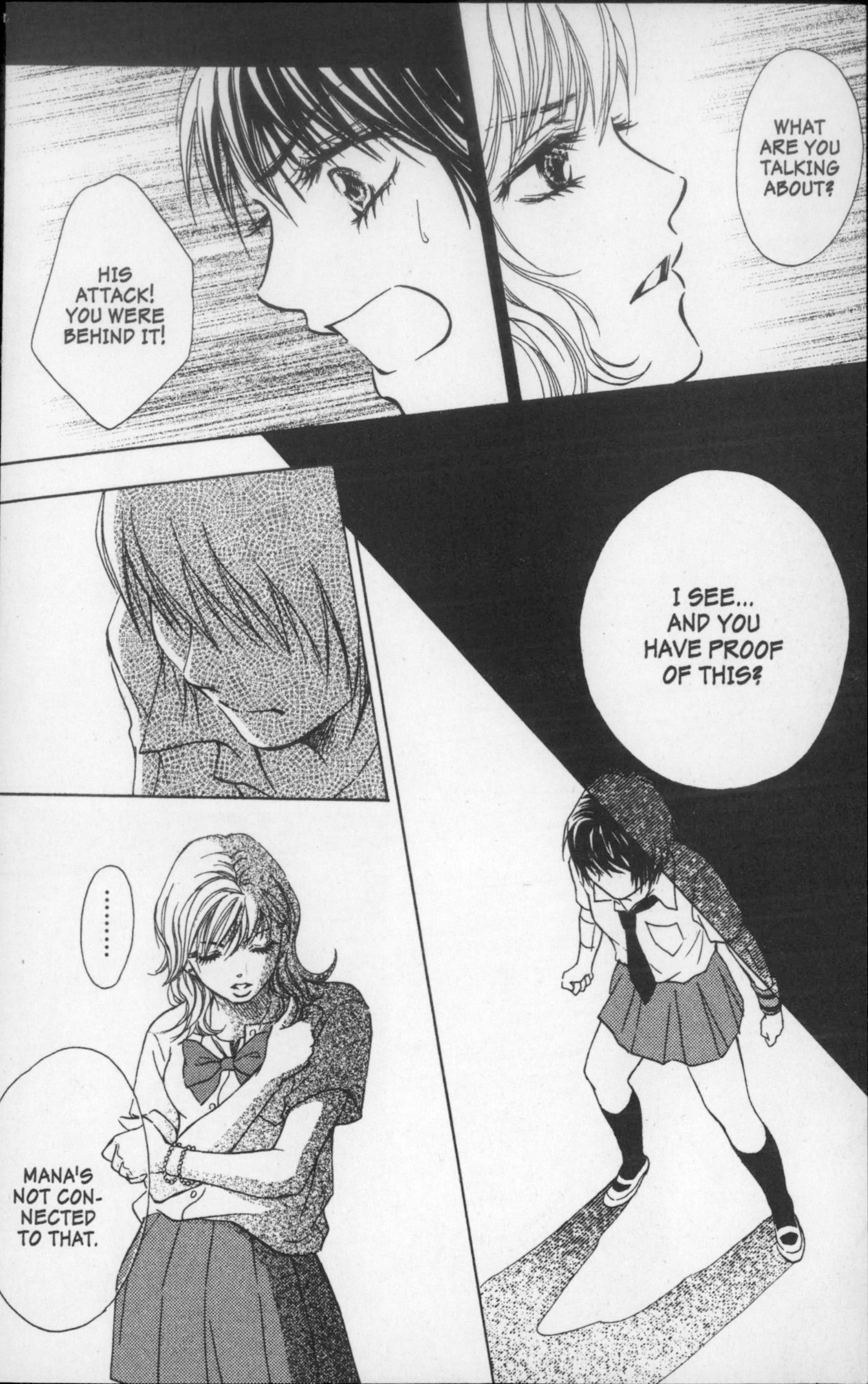
WHAT ARE YOU TALKING ABOUT?
HIS ATTACK! YOU WERE BEHIND IT!
I SEE... AND YOU HAVE PROOF OF THIS?
......
MANA'S NOT CONNECTED TO THAT.

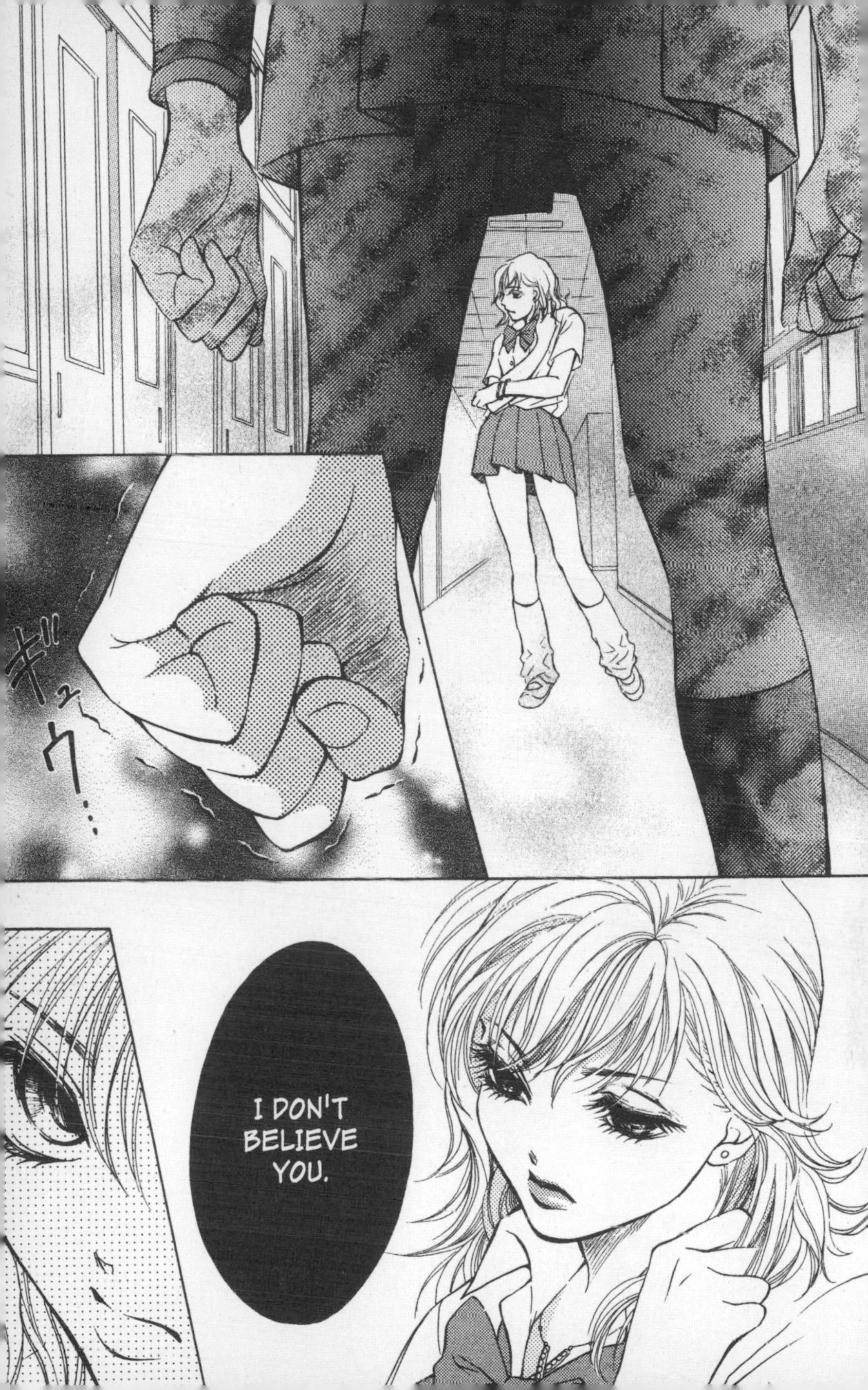
ギュウ…
I DON'T BELIEVE YOU.

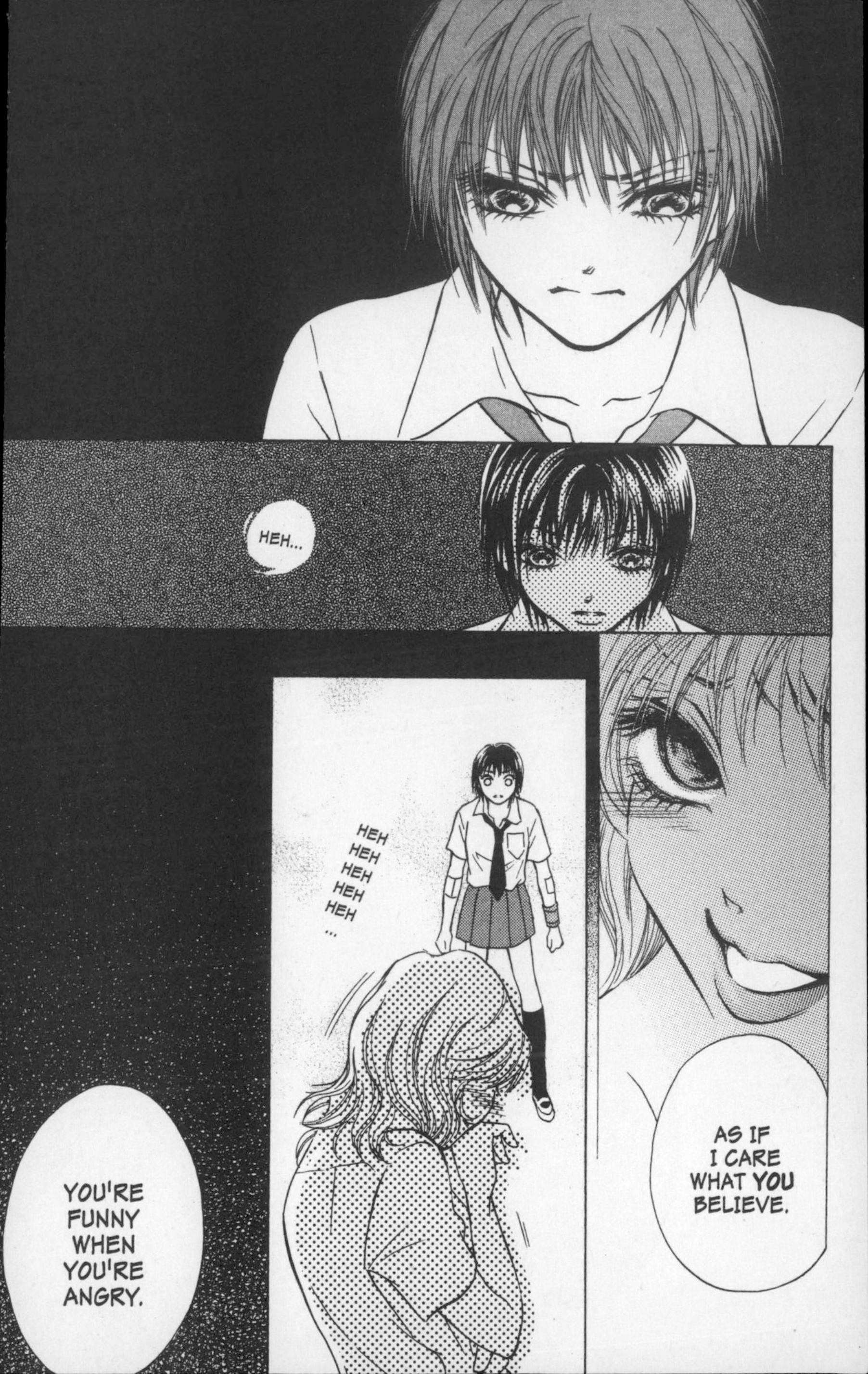
HEH...
AS IF I CARE WHAT **YOU** BELIEVE.
HEH HEH HEH HEH HEH ...
YOU'RE FUNNY WHEN YOU'RE ANGRY.

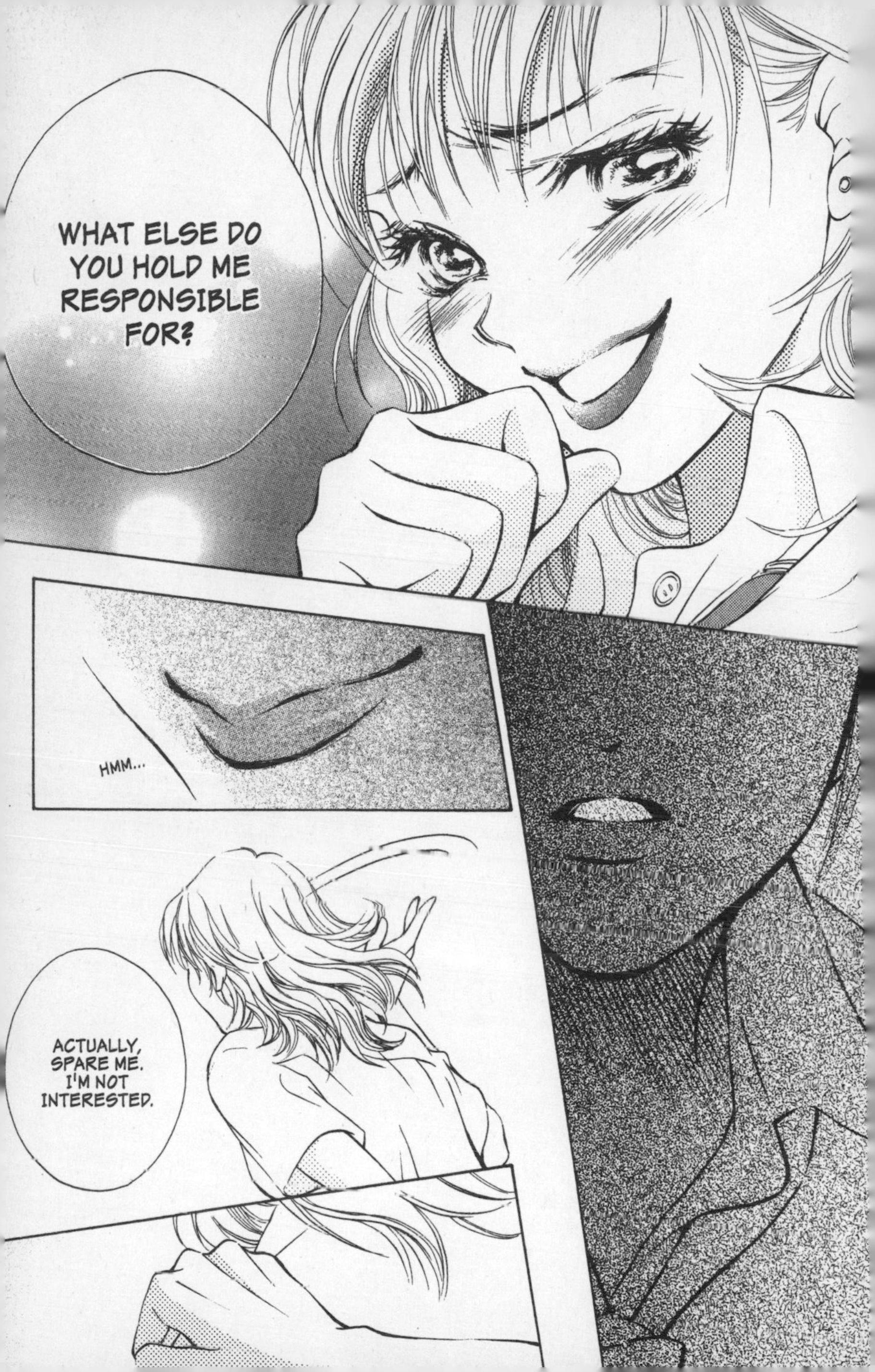
WHAT ELSE DO YOU HOLD ME RESPONSIBLE FOR?
HMM...
ACTUALLY, SPARE ME. I'M NOT INTERESTED.

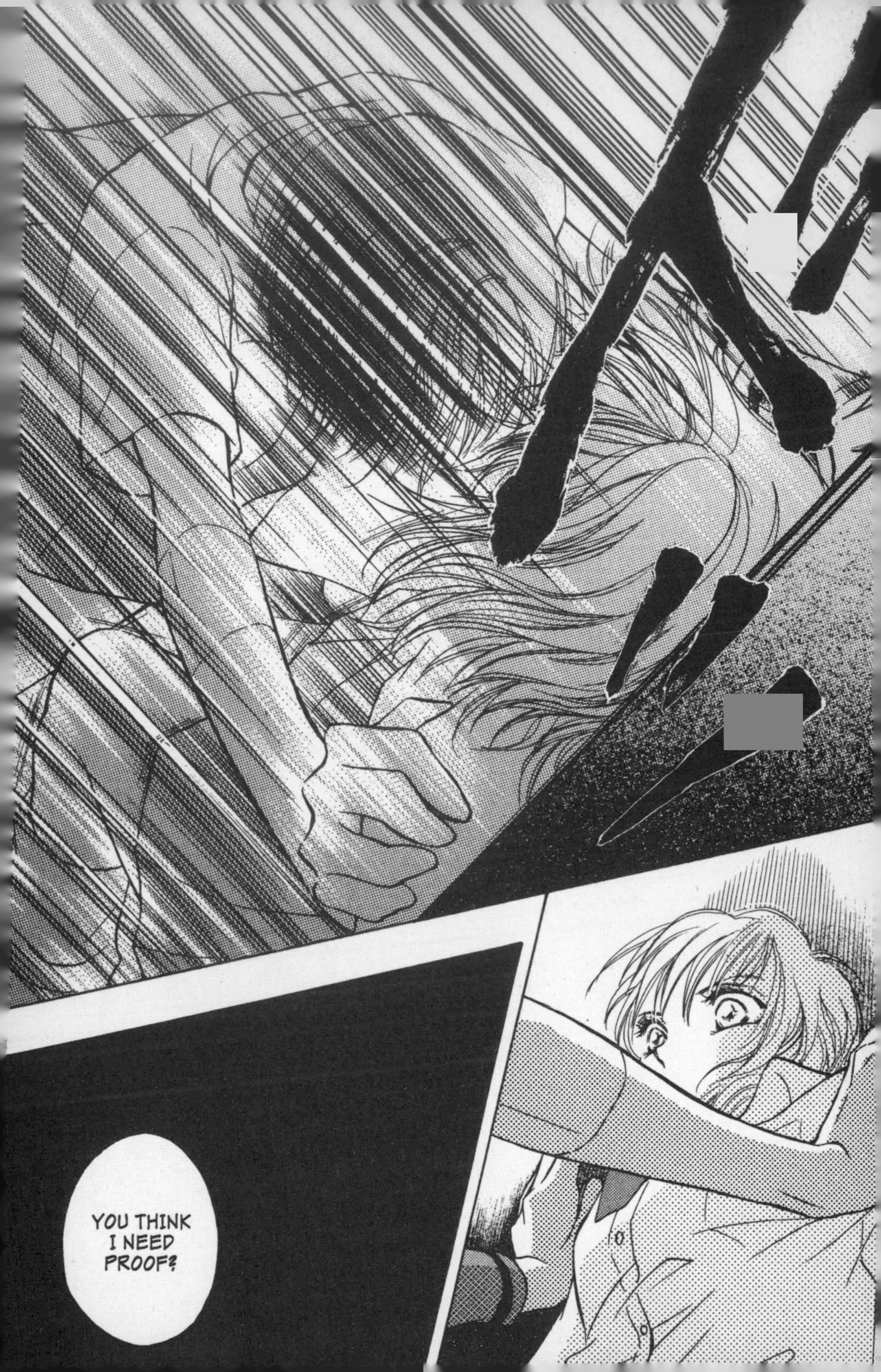
YOU THINK I NEED PROOF?

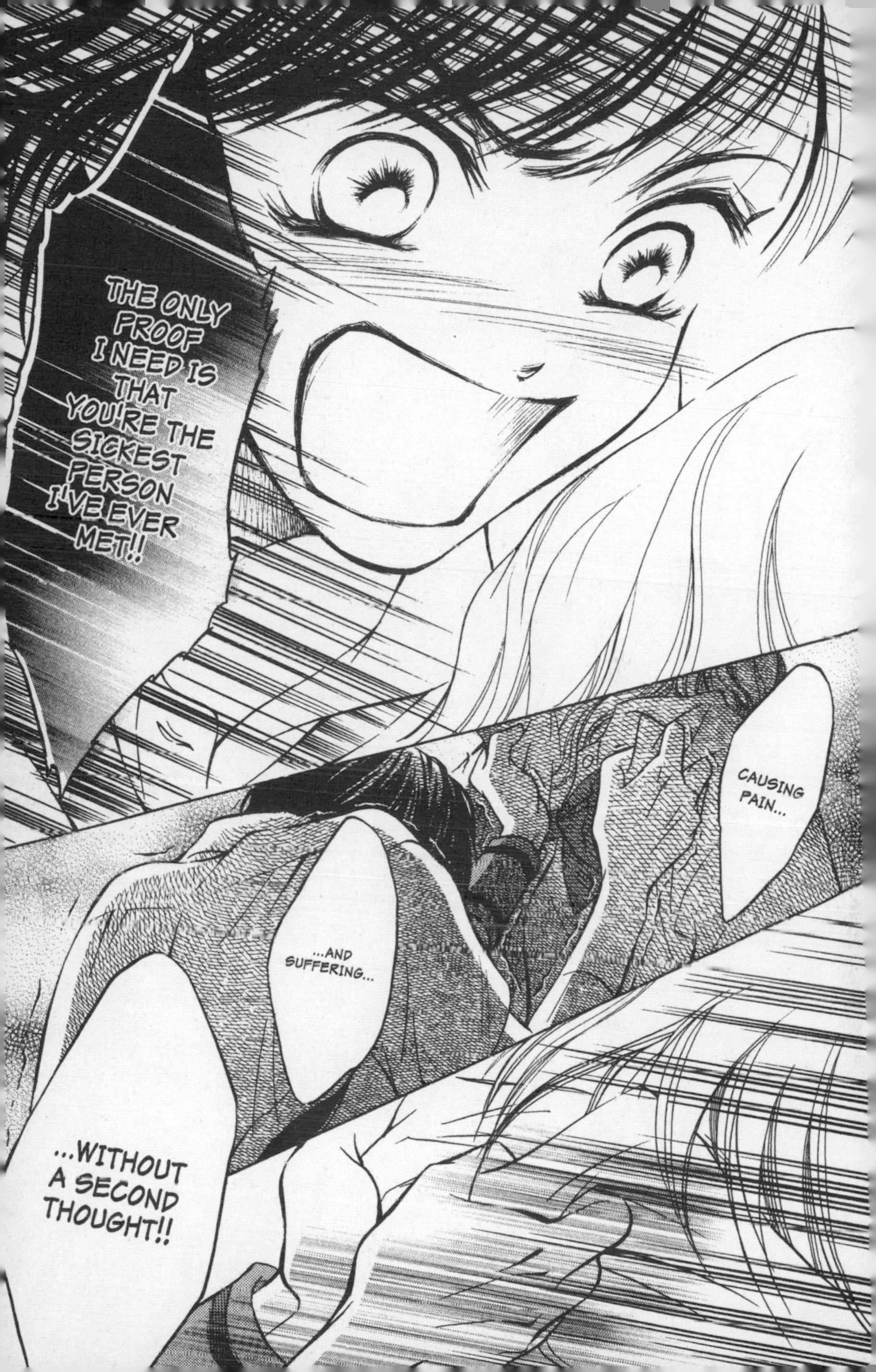
THE ONLY PROOF I NEED IS THAT YOU'RE THE SICKEST PERSON I'VE EVER MET!!
CAUSING PAIN...
...AND SUFFERING...
...WITHOUT A SECOND THOUGHT!!

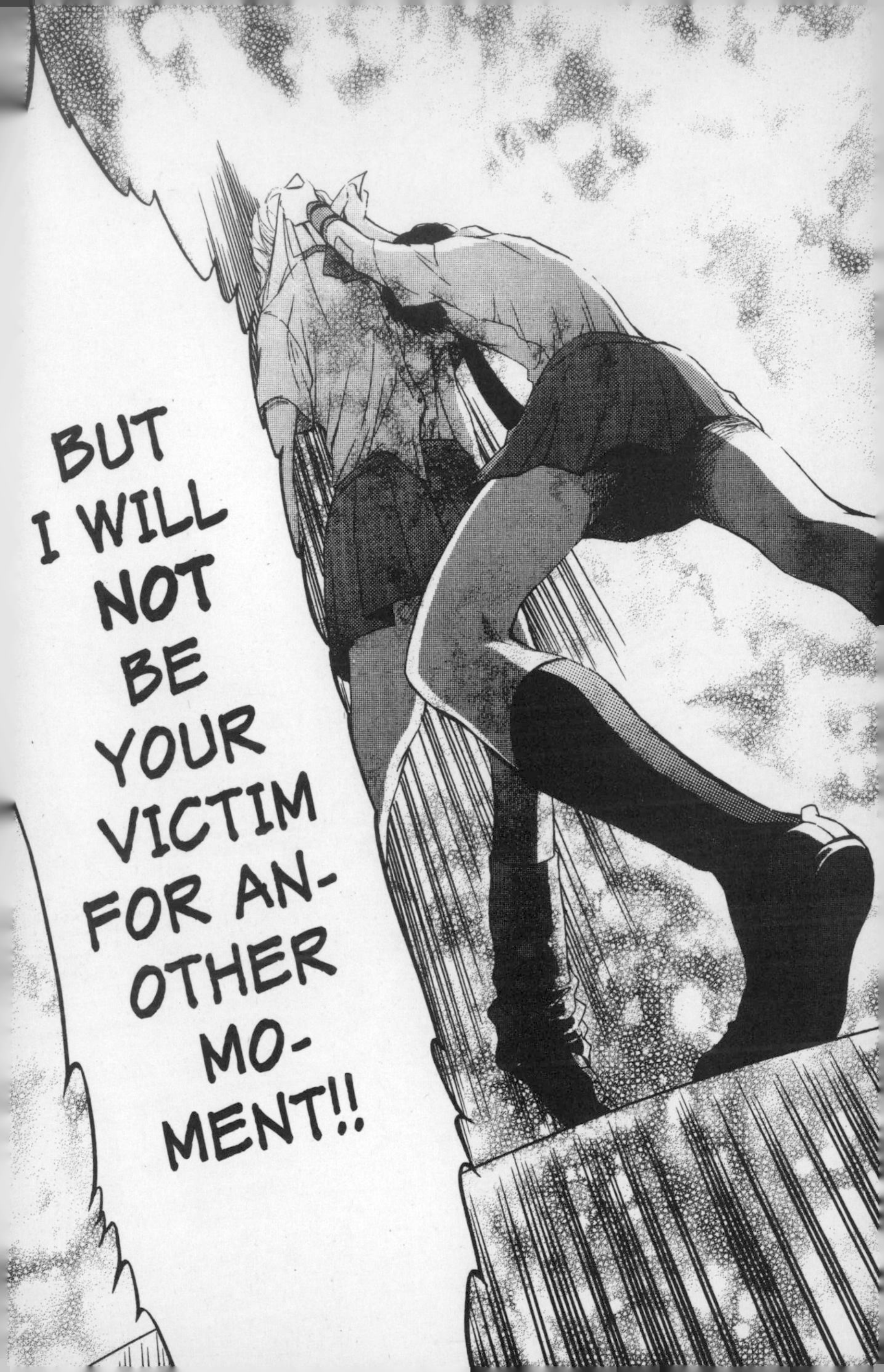
BUT I WILL NOT BE YOUR VICTIM FOR AN-OTHER MO-MENT!!

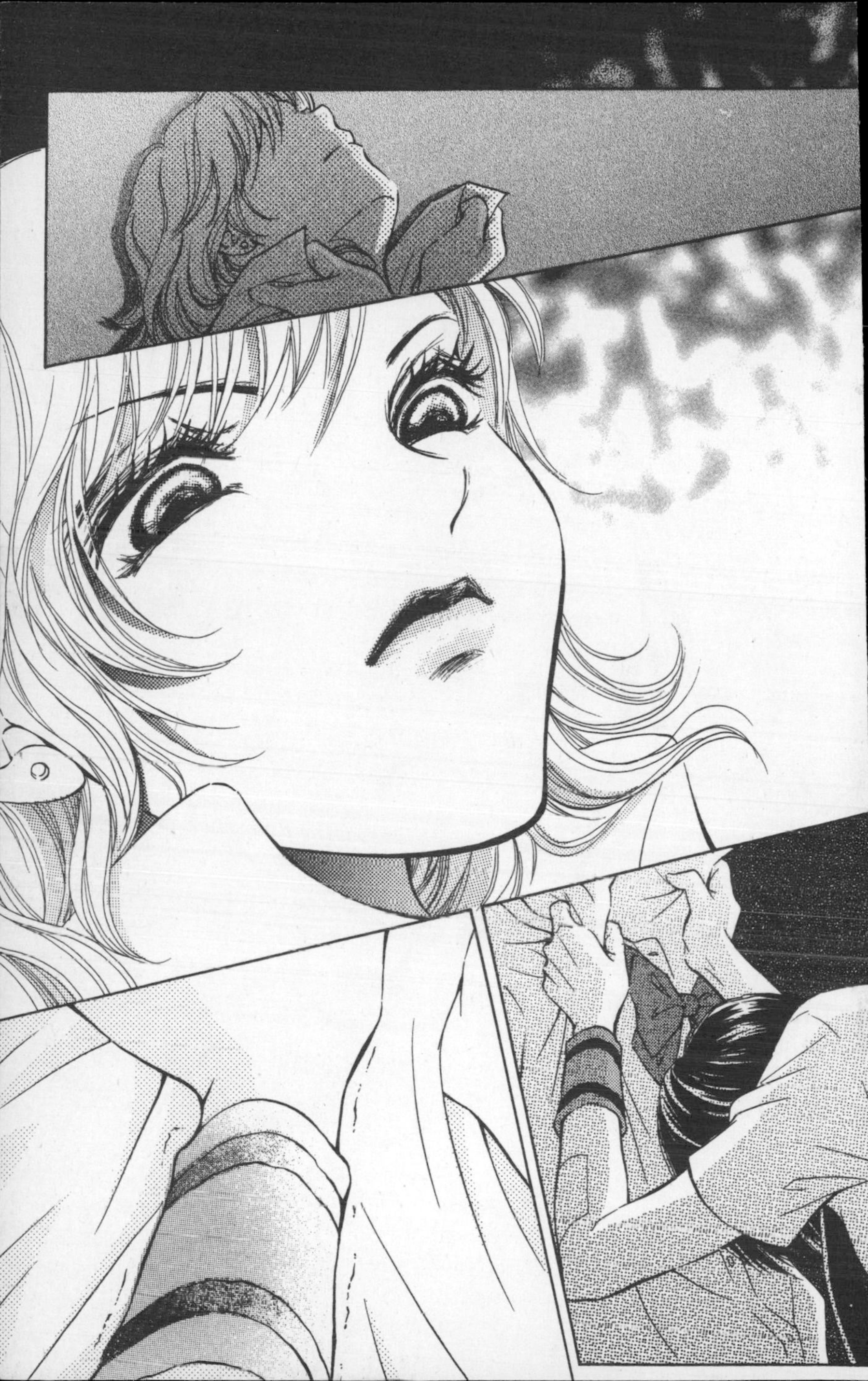

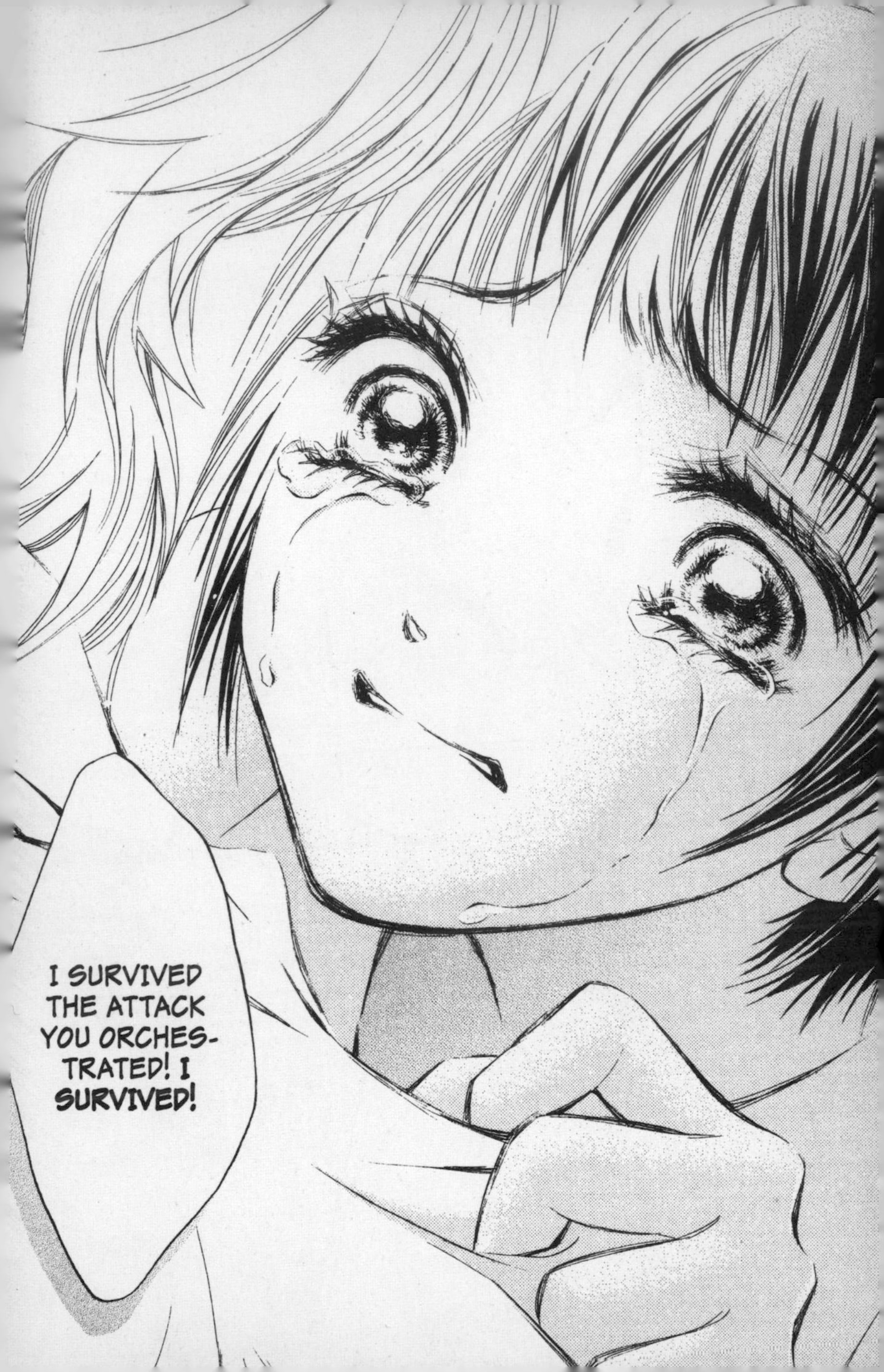
I SURVIVED THE ATTACK YOU ORCHES-TRATED! I SURVIVED!

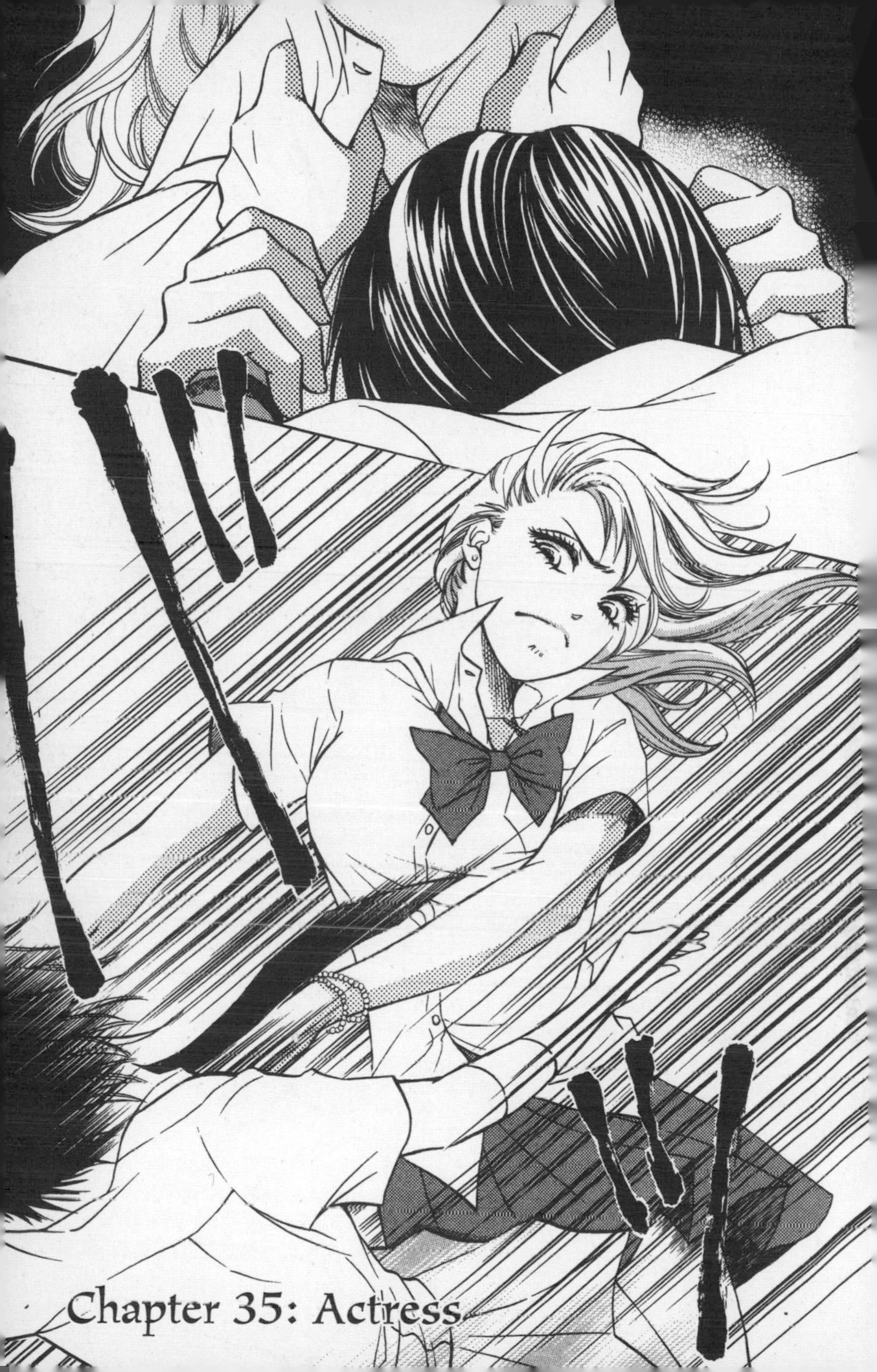

Chapter 35: Actress

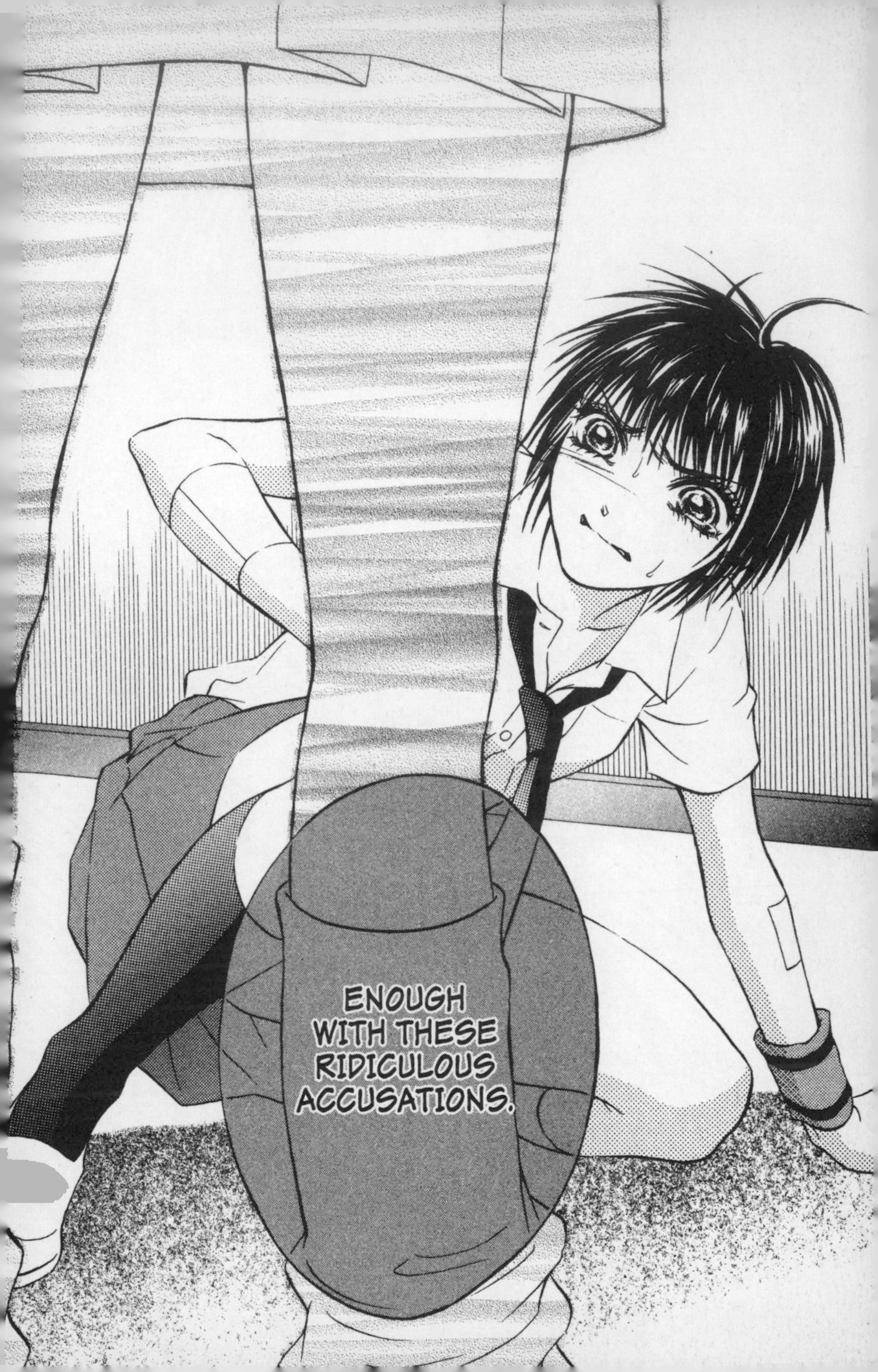
ENOUGH WITH THESE RIDICULOUS ACCUSATIONS.

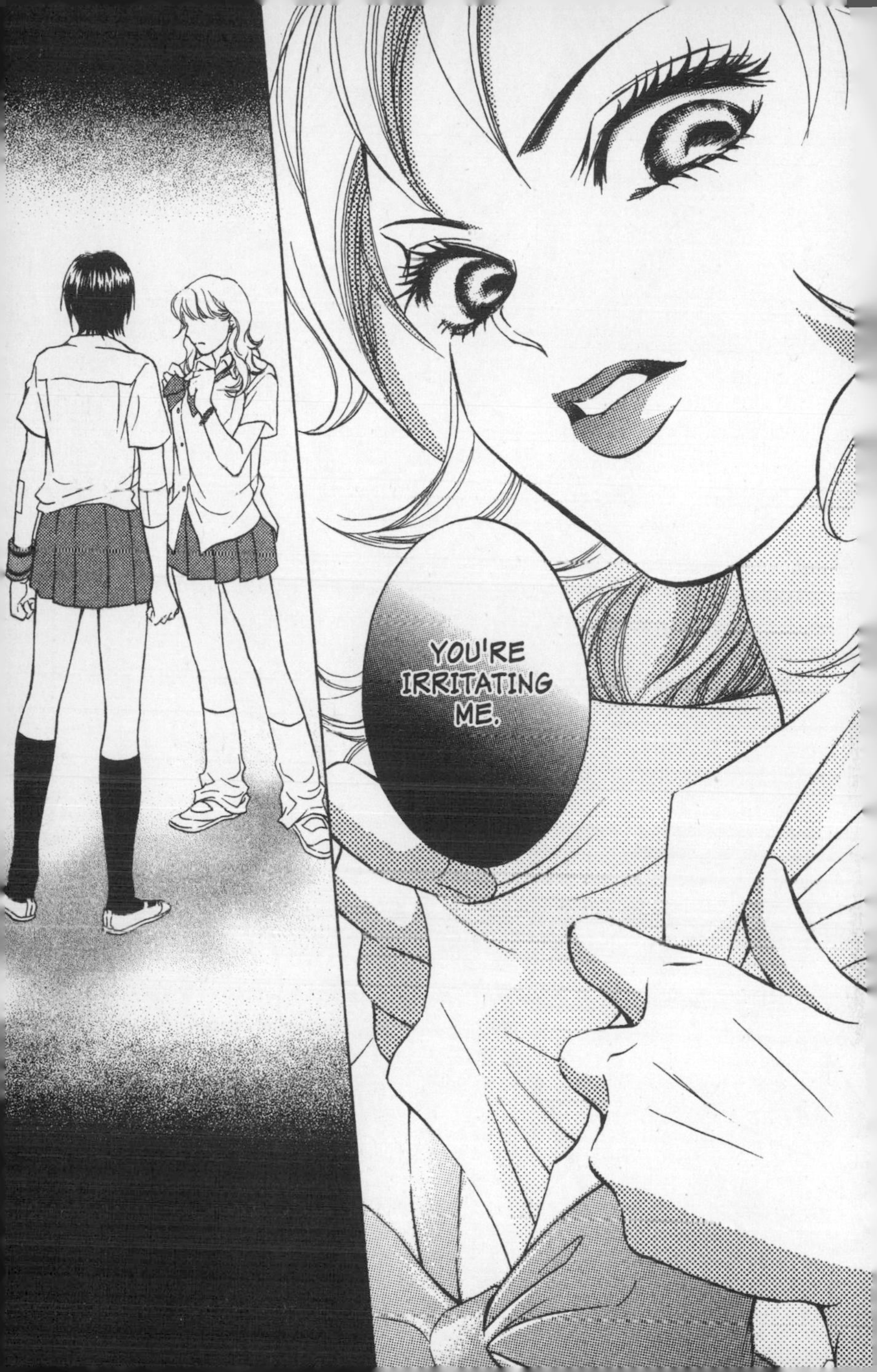
YOU'RE IRRITATING ME.

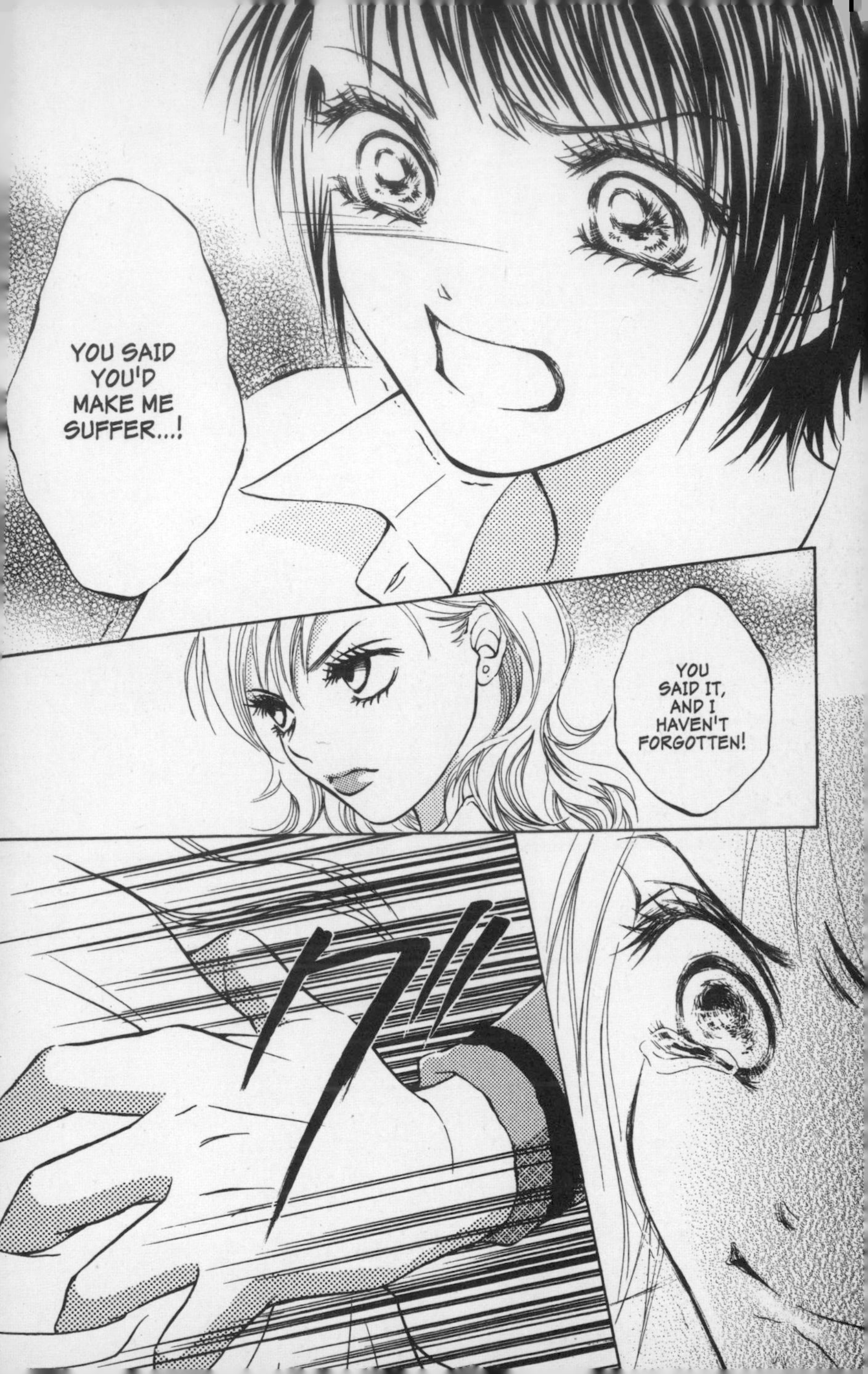
YOU SAID YOU'D MAKE ME SUFFER...!
YOU SAID IT, AND I HAVEN'T FORGOTTEN!

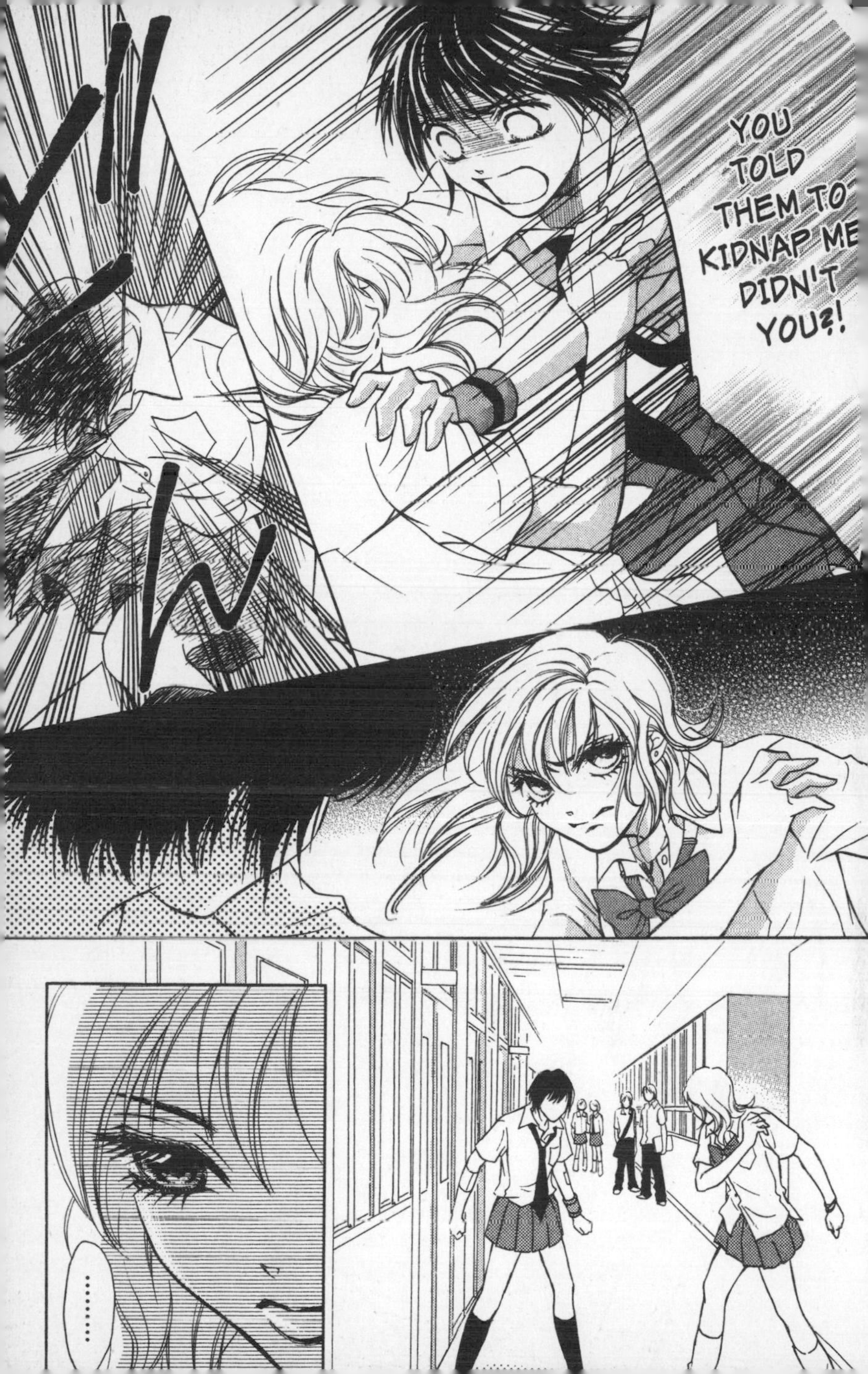
YOU TOLD THEM TO KIDNAP ME DIDN'T YOU?!
....

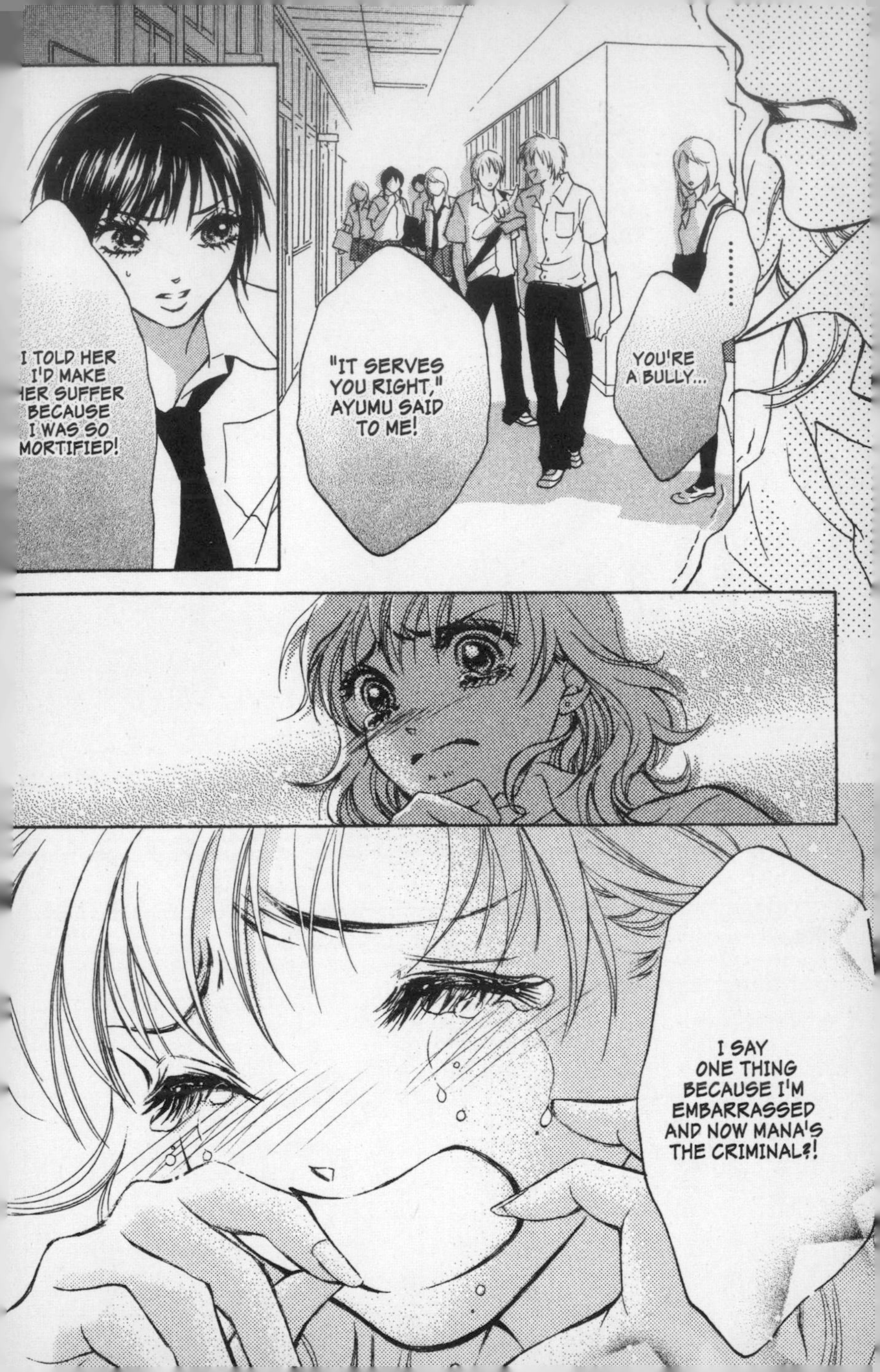
......
YOU'RE A BULLY...
"IT SERVES YOU RIGHT," AYUMU SAID TO ME!
I TOLD HER I'D MAKE HER SUFFER BECAUSE I WAS SO MORTIFIED!
I SAY ONE THING BECAUSE I'M EMBARRASSED AND NOW MANA'S THE CRIMINAL?!

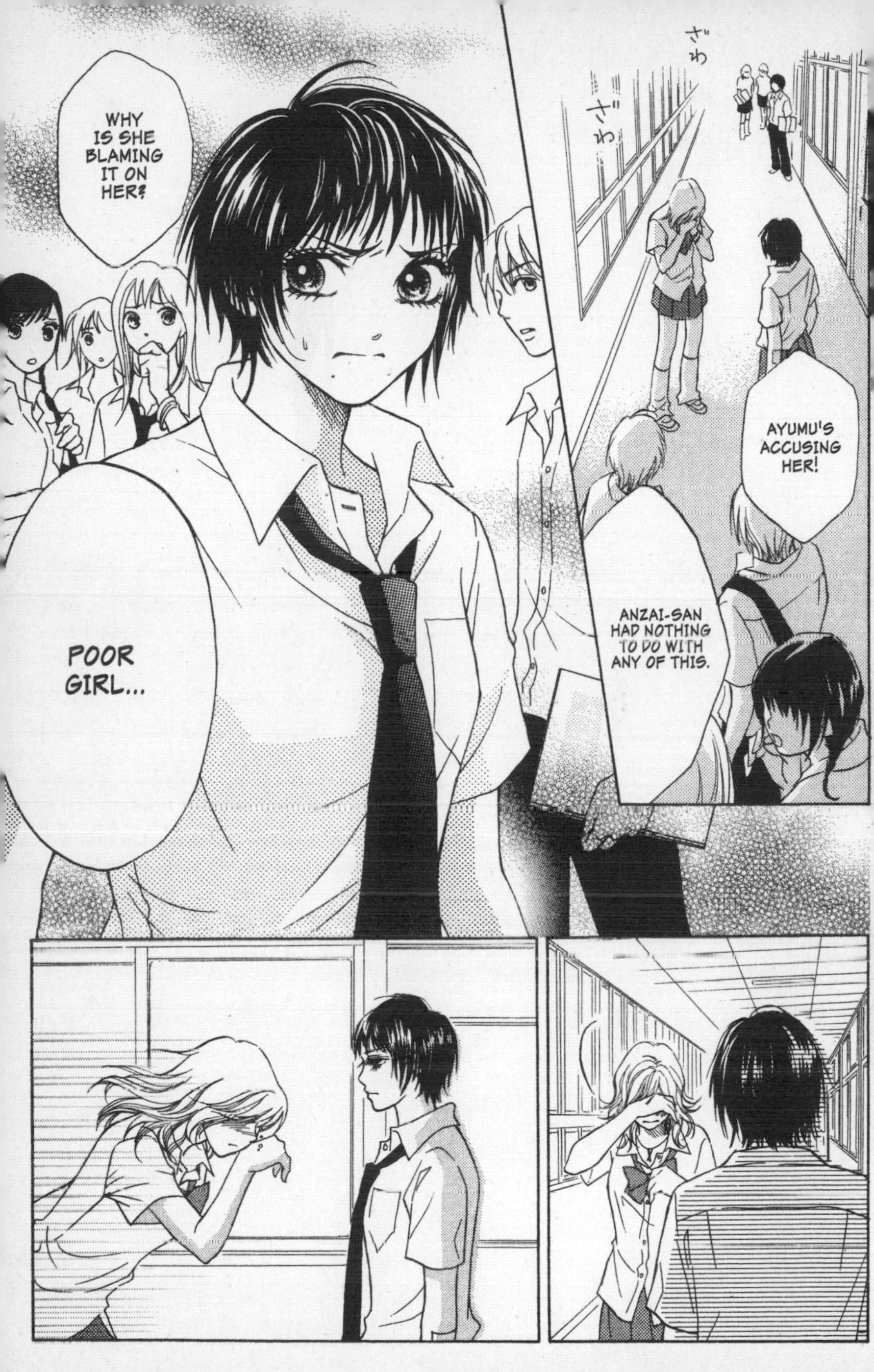
ざわ
ざわ
AYUMU'S ACCUSING HER!
ANZAI-SAN HAD NOTHING TO DO WITH ANY OF THIS.
WHY IS SHE BLAMING IT ON HER?
POOR GIRL...

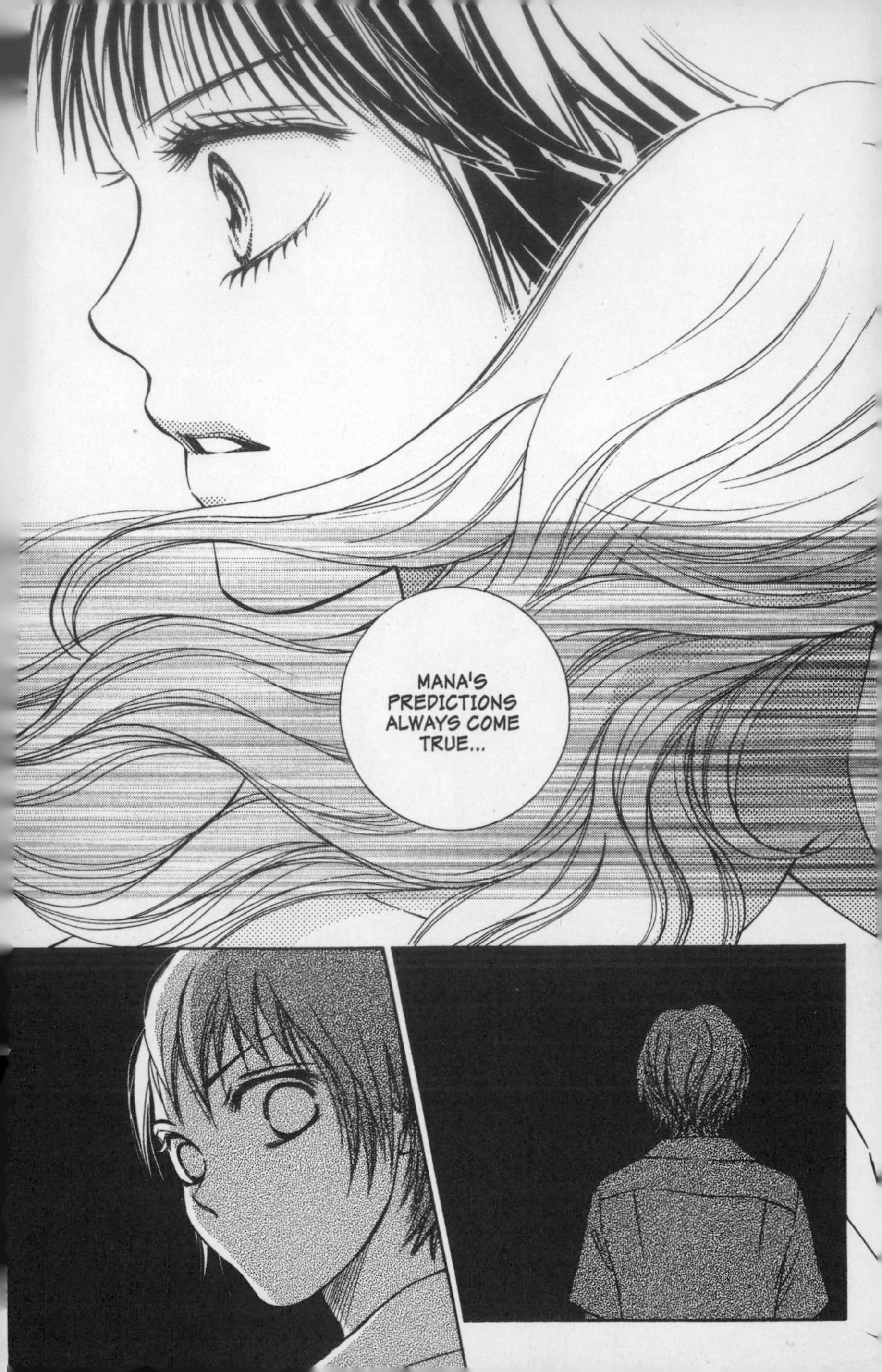
MANA'S PREDICTIONS ALWAYS COME TRUE...

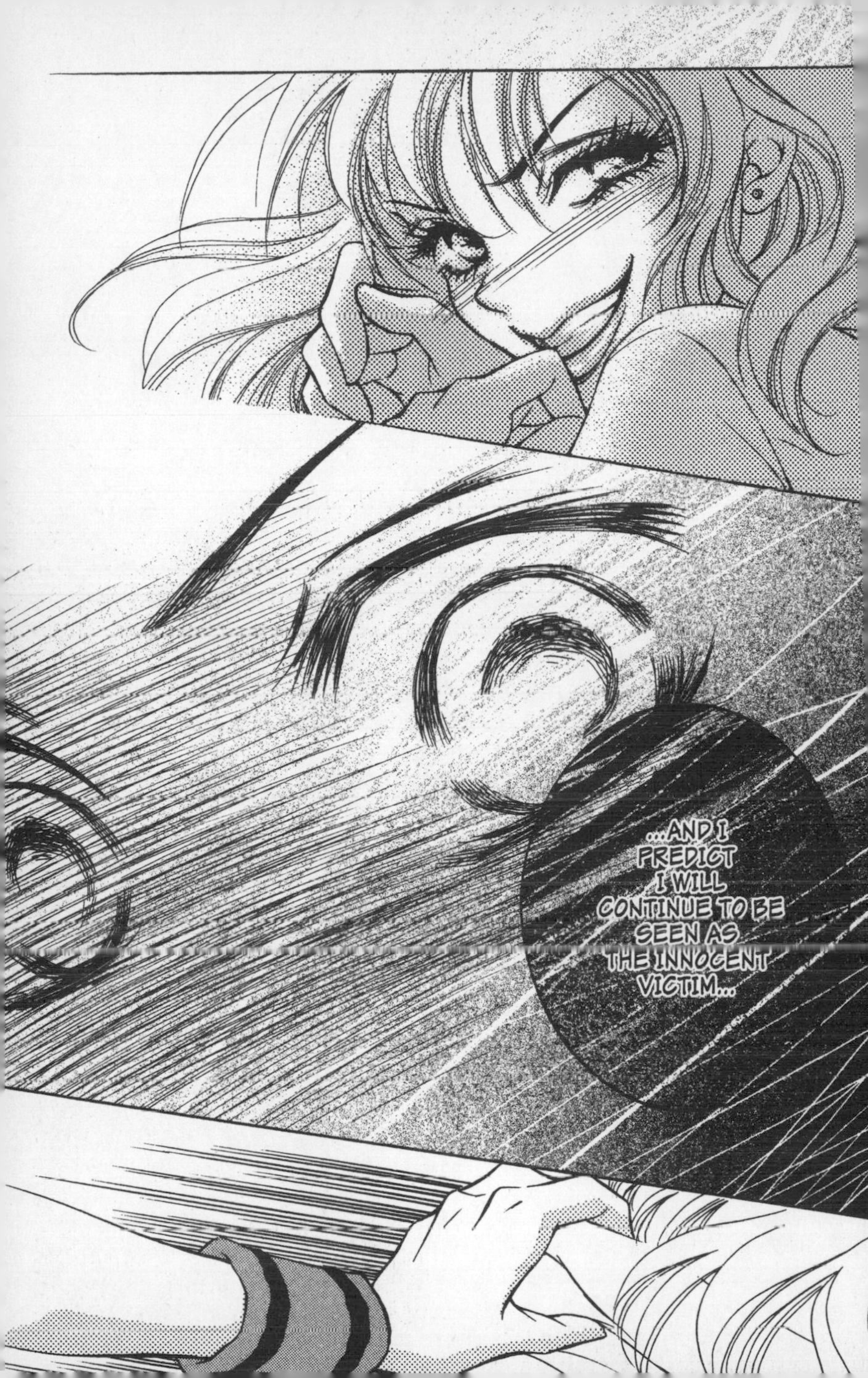
...AND I PREDICT I WILL CONTINUE TO BE SEEN AS THE INNOCENT VICTIM...

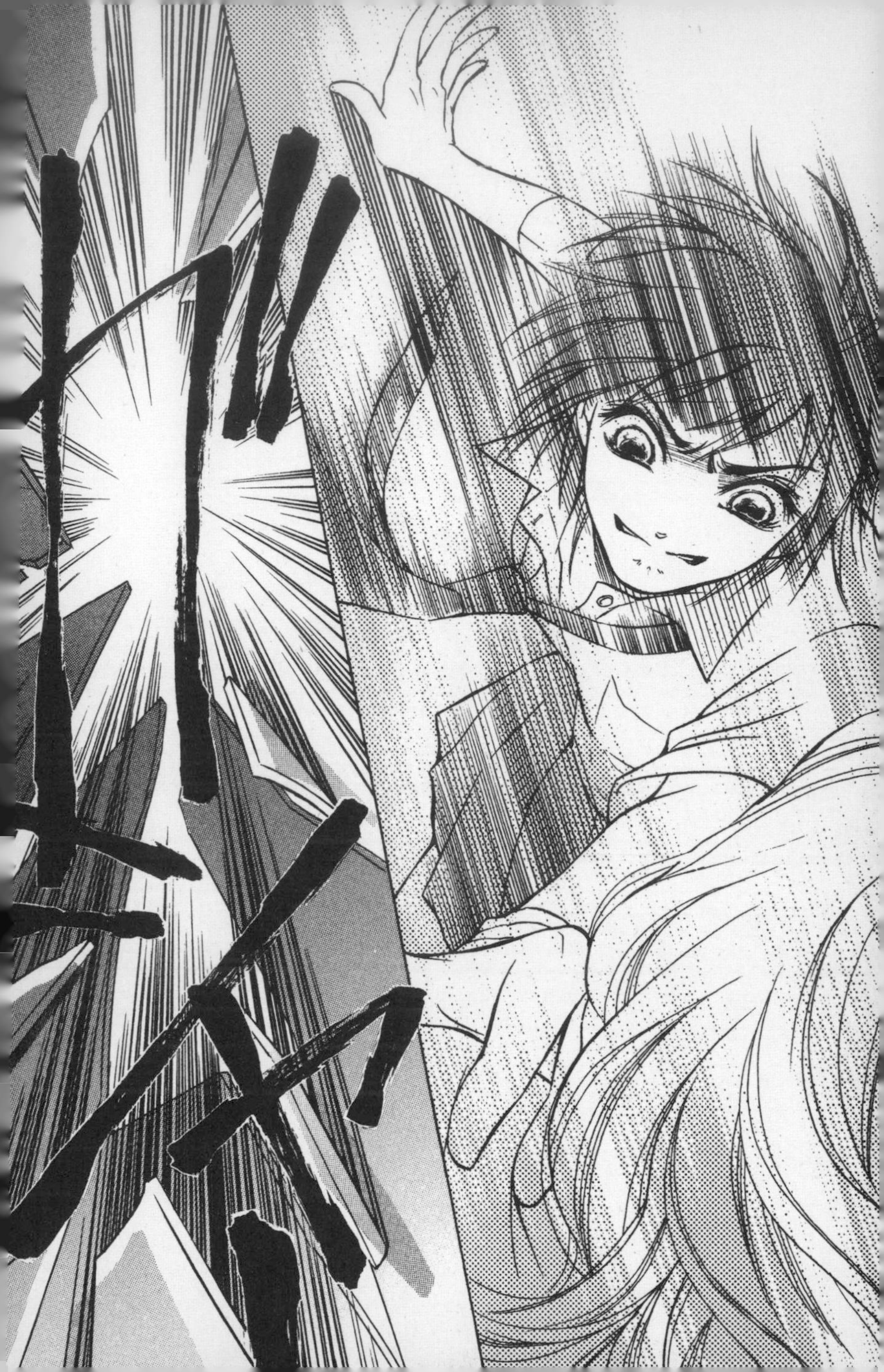

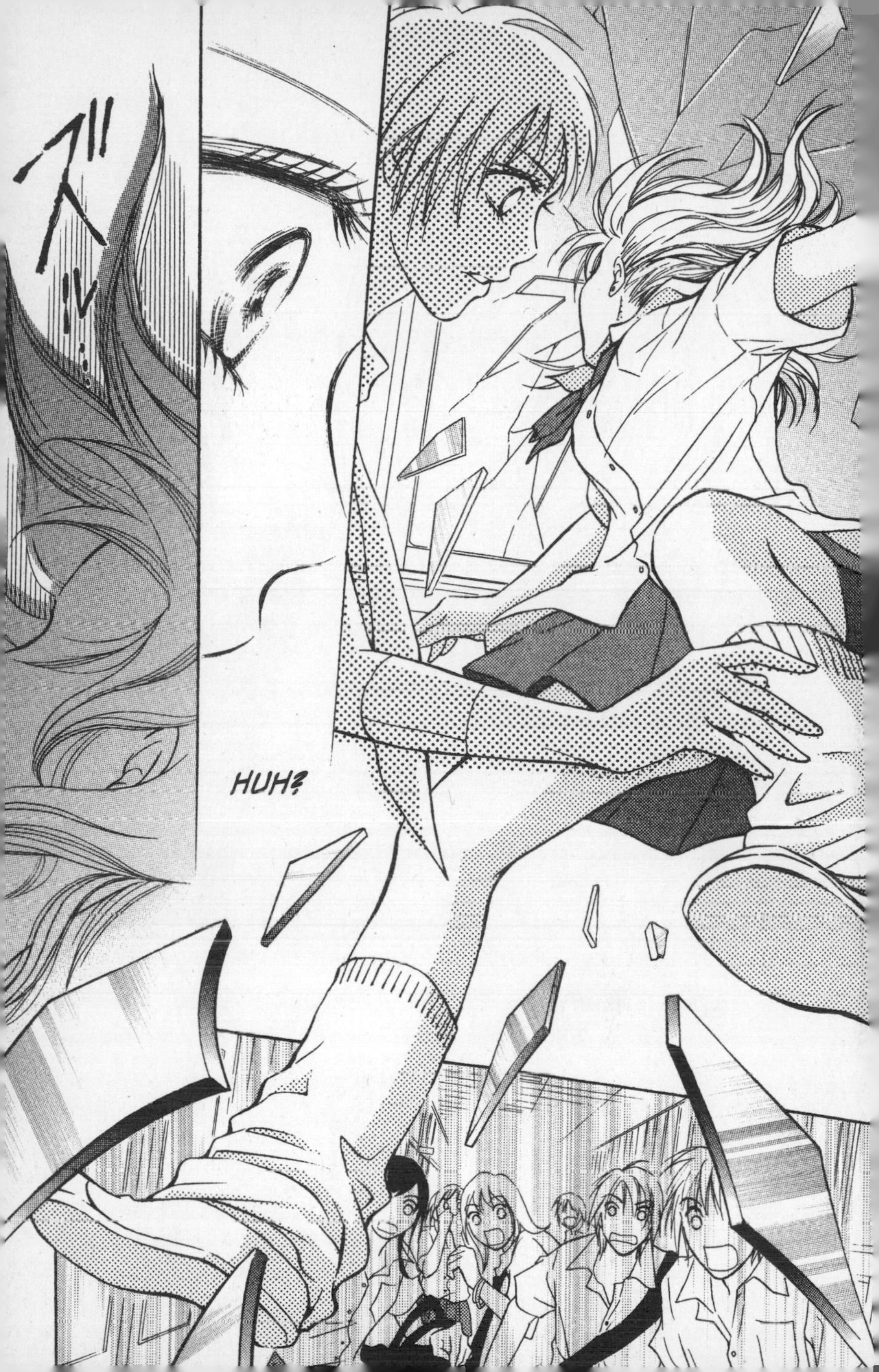

ズル…
HUH?

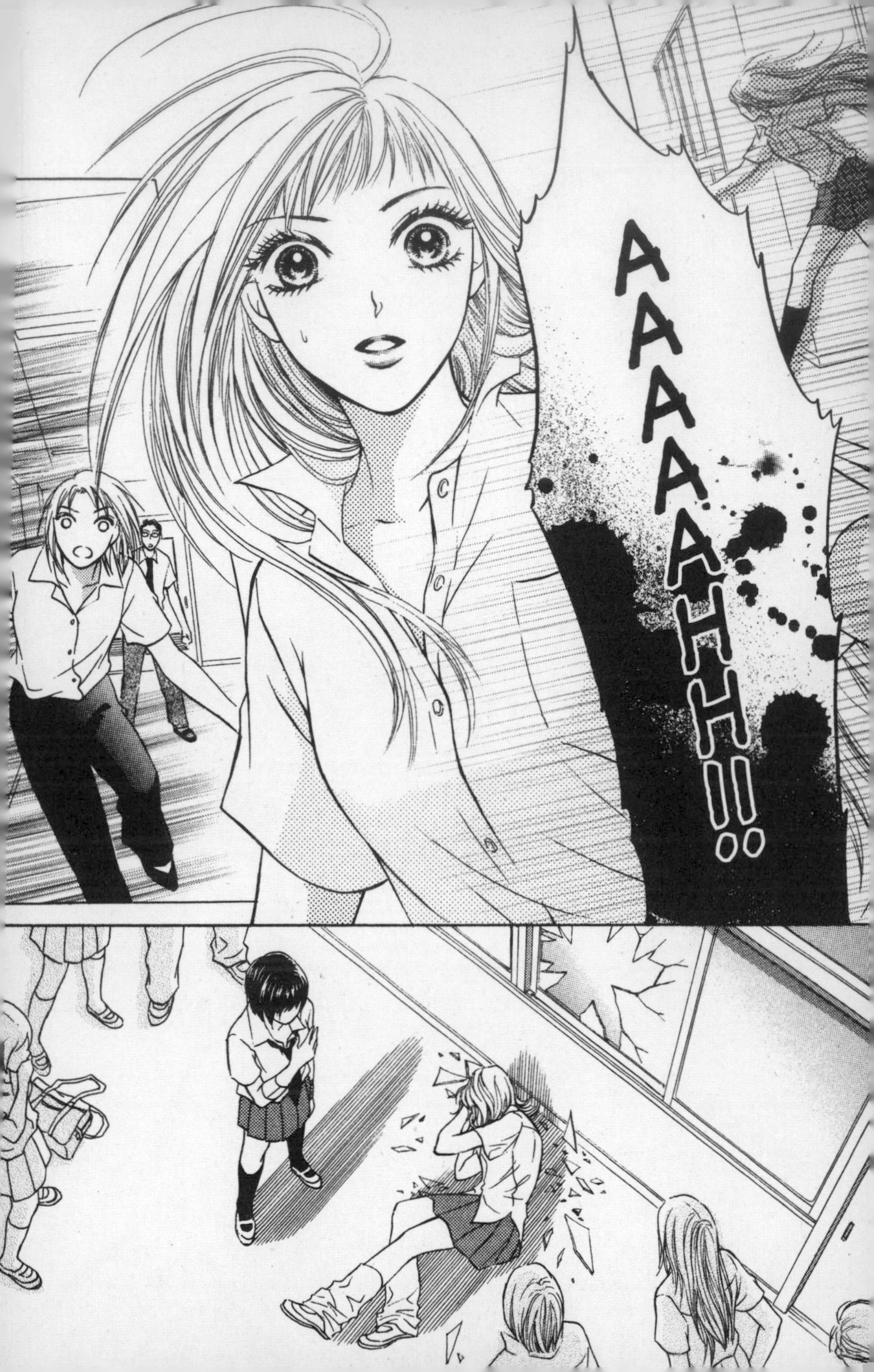
AAAAAAHH!!

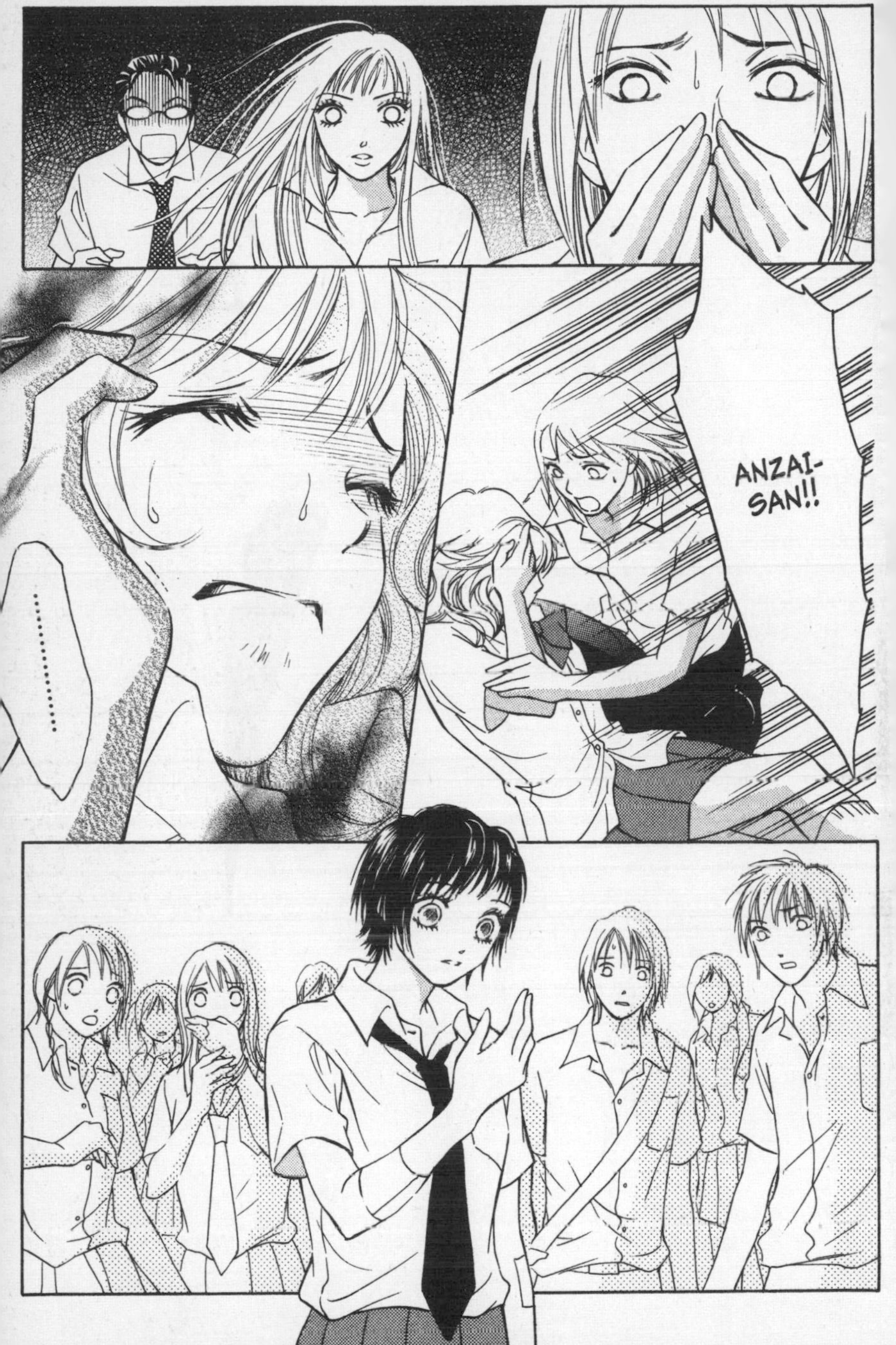
ANZAI-SAN!!
......

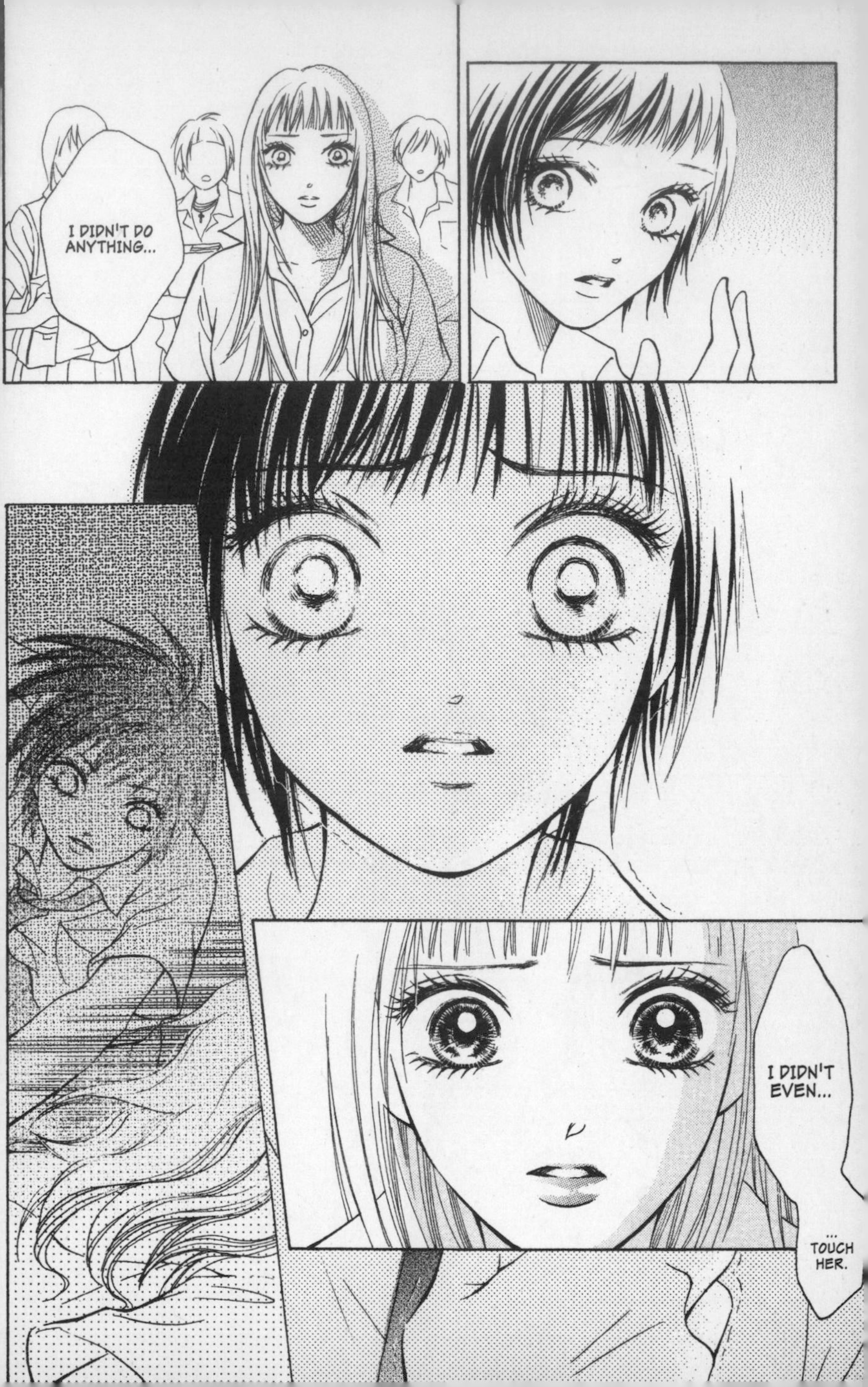
I DIDN'T DO ANYTHING...
I DIDN'T EVEN...
... TOUCH HER.

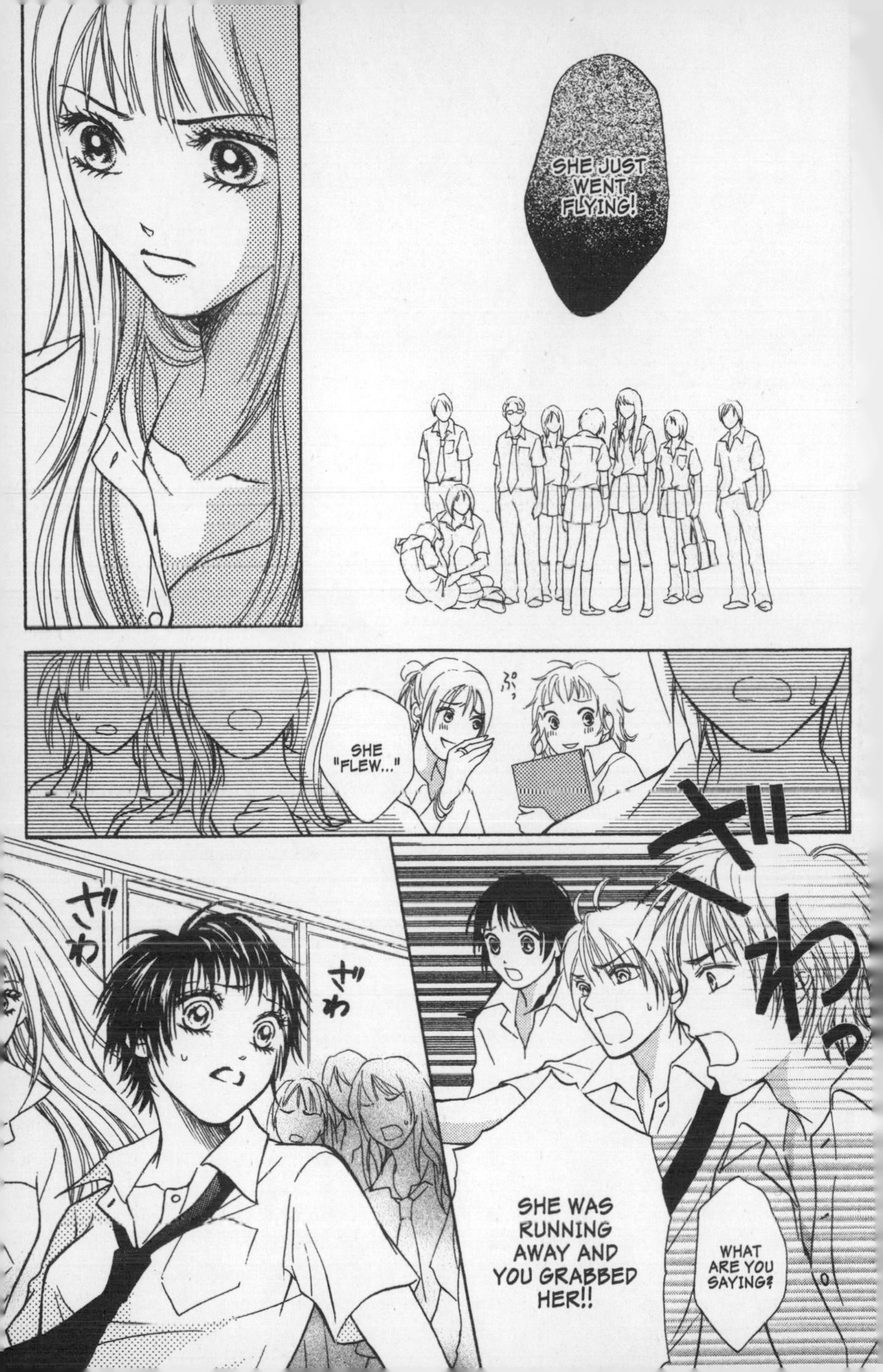
SHE JUST WENT FLYING!
ぷっ
SHE "FLEW..."
ざわっ
WHAT ARE YOU SAYING?
SHE WAS RUNNING AWAY AND YOU GRABBED HER!!
ざわ
ざわ

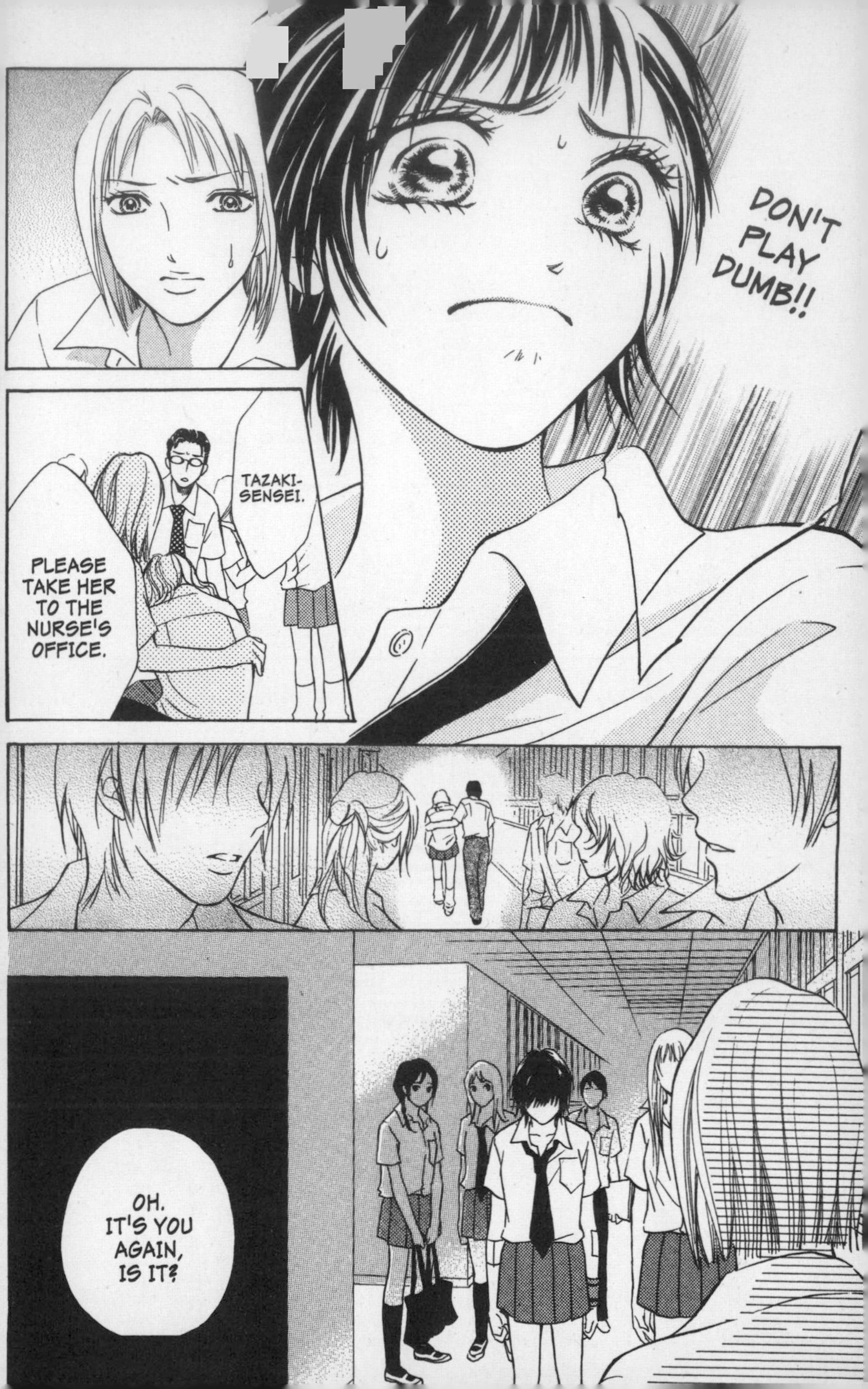
DON'T PLAY DUMB!!
TAZAKI-SENSEI.
PLEASE TAKE HER TO THE NURSE'S OFFICE.
OH. IT'S YOU AGAIN, IS IT?

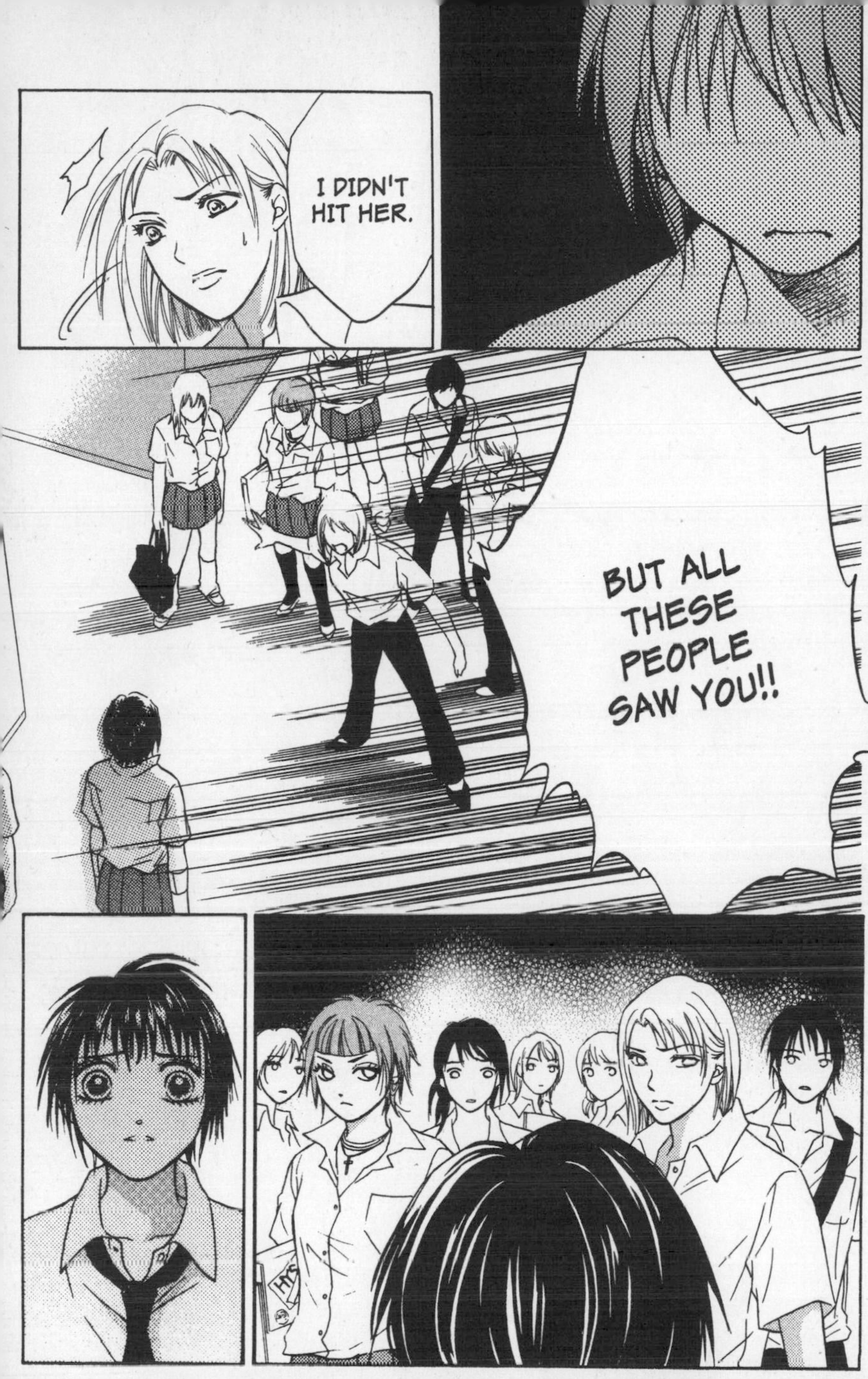
I DIDN'T HIT HER.
BUT ALL THESE PEOPLE SAW YOU!!

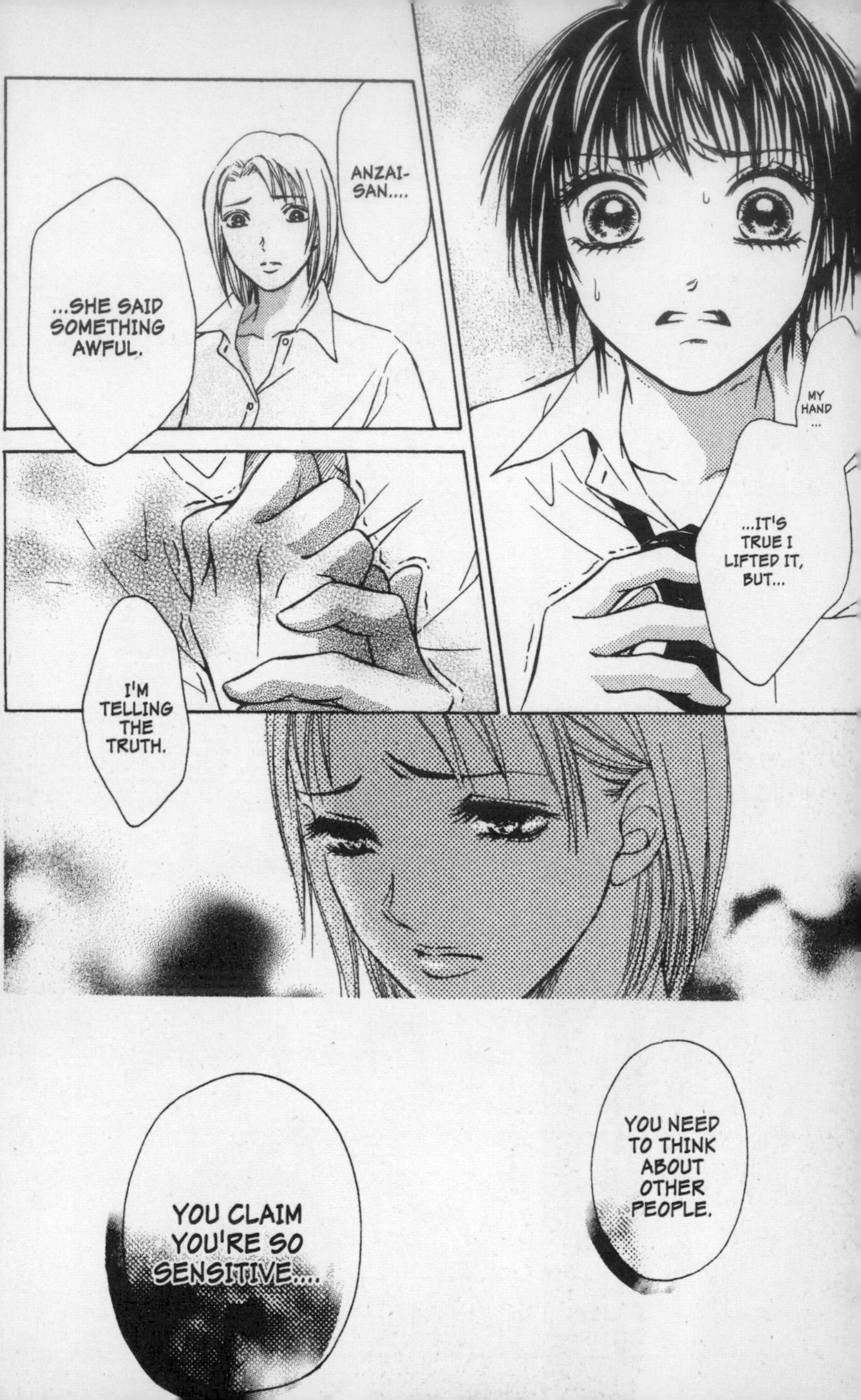
MY HAND ...
...IT'S TRUE I LIFTED IT, BUT...
ANZAI-SAN....
...SHE SAID SOMETHING AWFUL.
I'M TELLING THE TRUTH.
YOU NEED TO THINK ABOUT OTHER PEOPLE.
YOU CLAIM YOU'RE SO SENSITIVE....

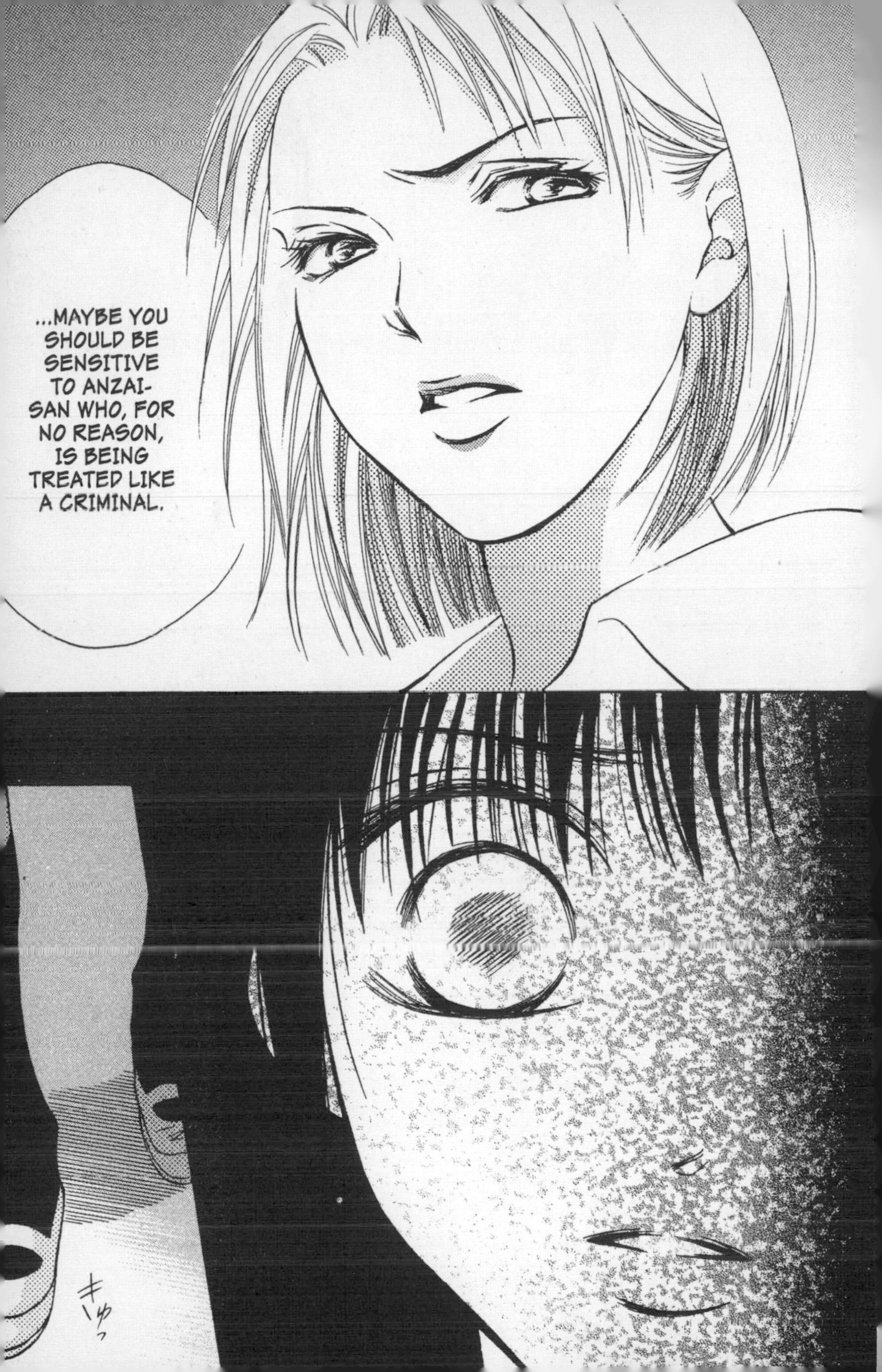
...MAYBE YOU SHOULD BE SENSITIVE TO ANZAI-SAN WHO, FOR NO REASON, IS BEING TREATED LIKE A CRIMINAL.
キゅっ

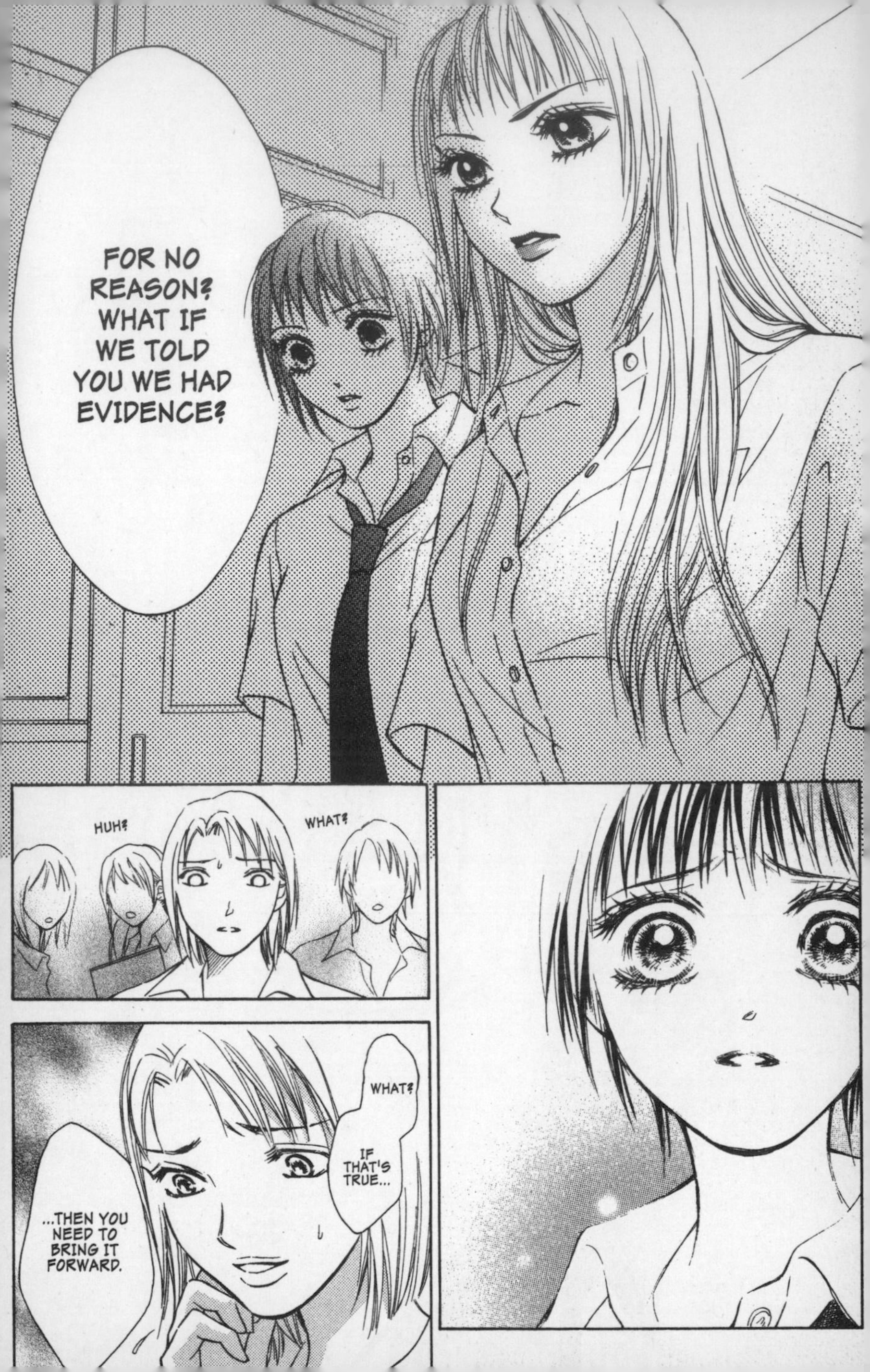
FOR NO REASON? WHAT IF WE TOLD YOU WE HAD EVIDENCE?
WHAT?
HUH?
WHAT?
IF THAT'S TRUE...
...THEN YOU NEED TO BRING IT FORWARD.

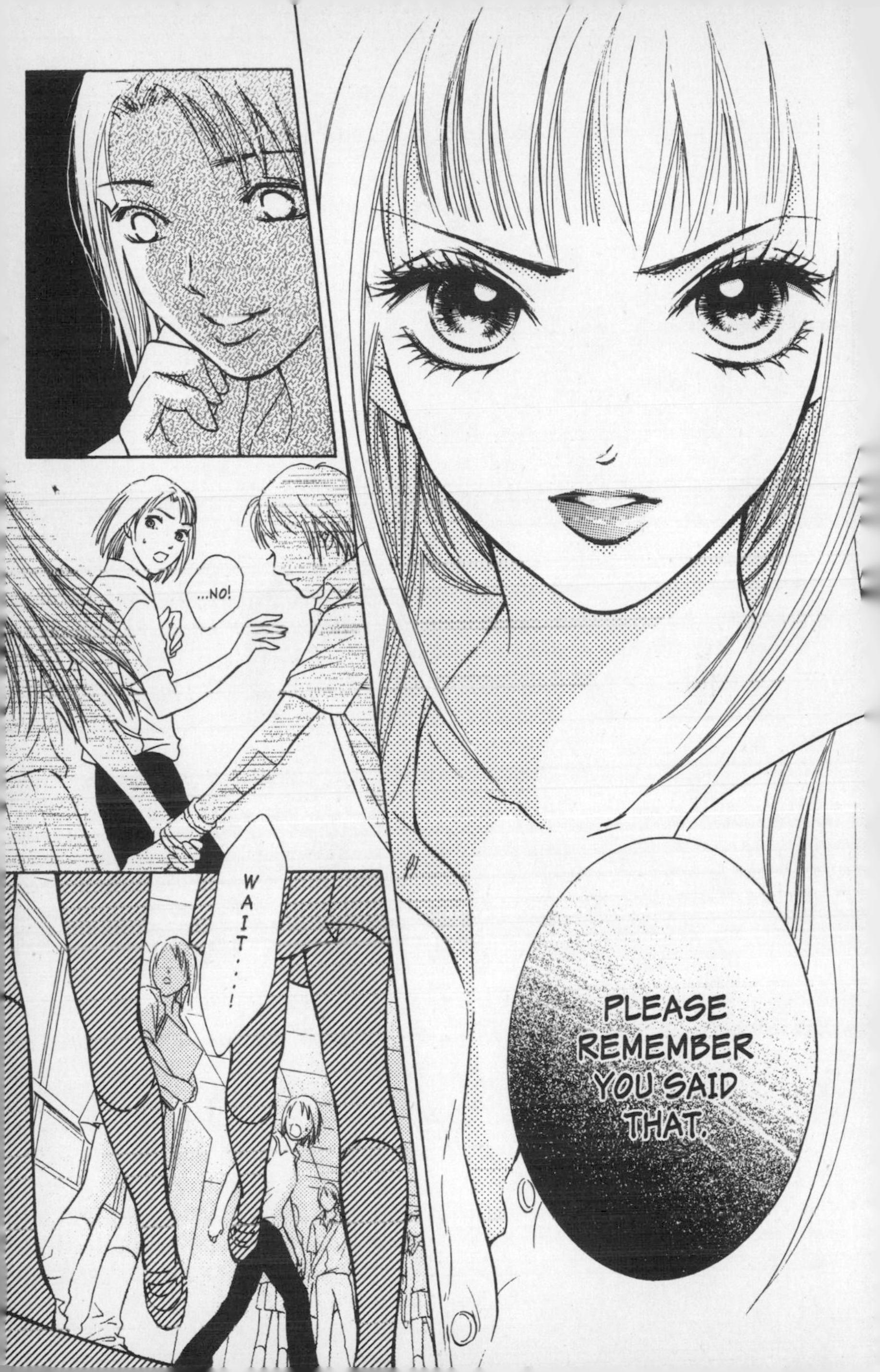
PLEASE REMEMBER YOU SAID THAT.
...NO!
WAIT...!

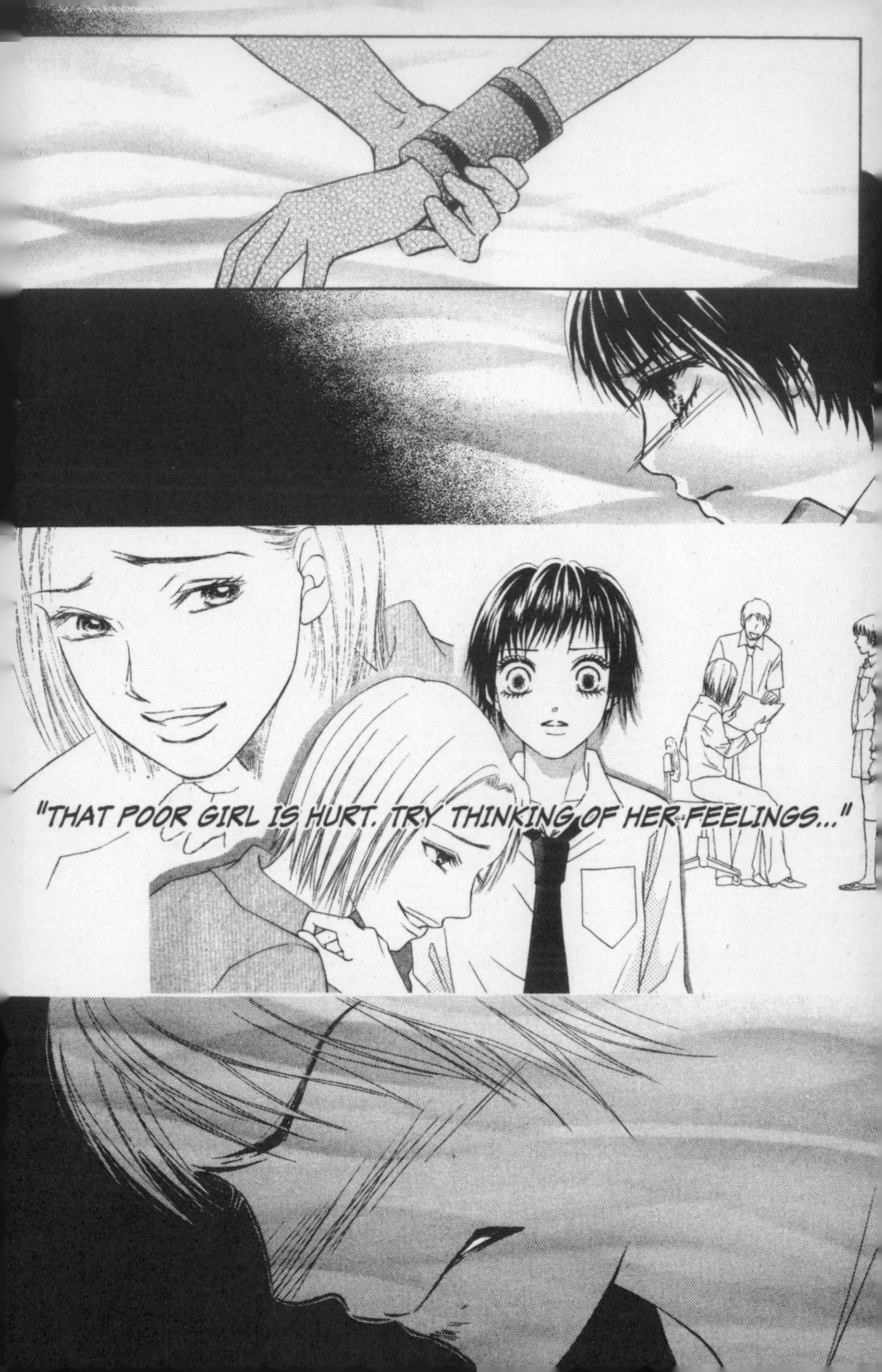
"THAT POOR GIRL IS HURT. TRY THINKING OF HER FEELINGS..."

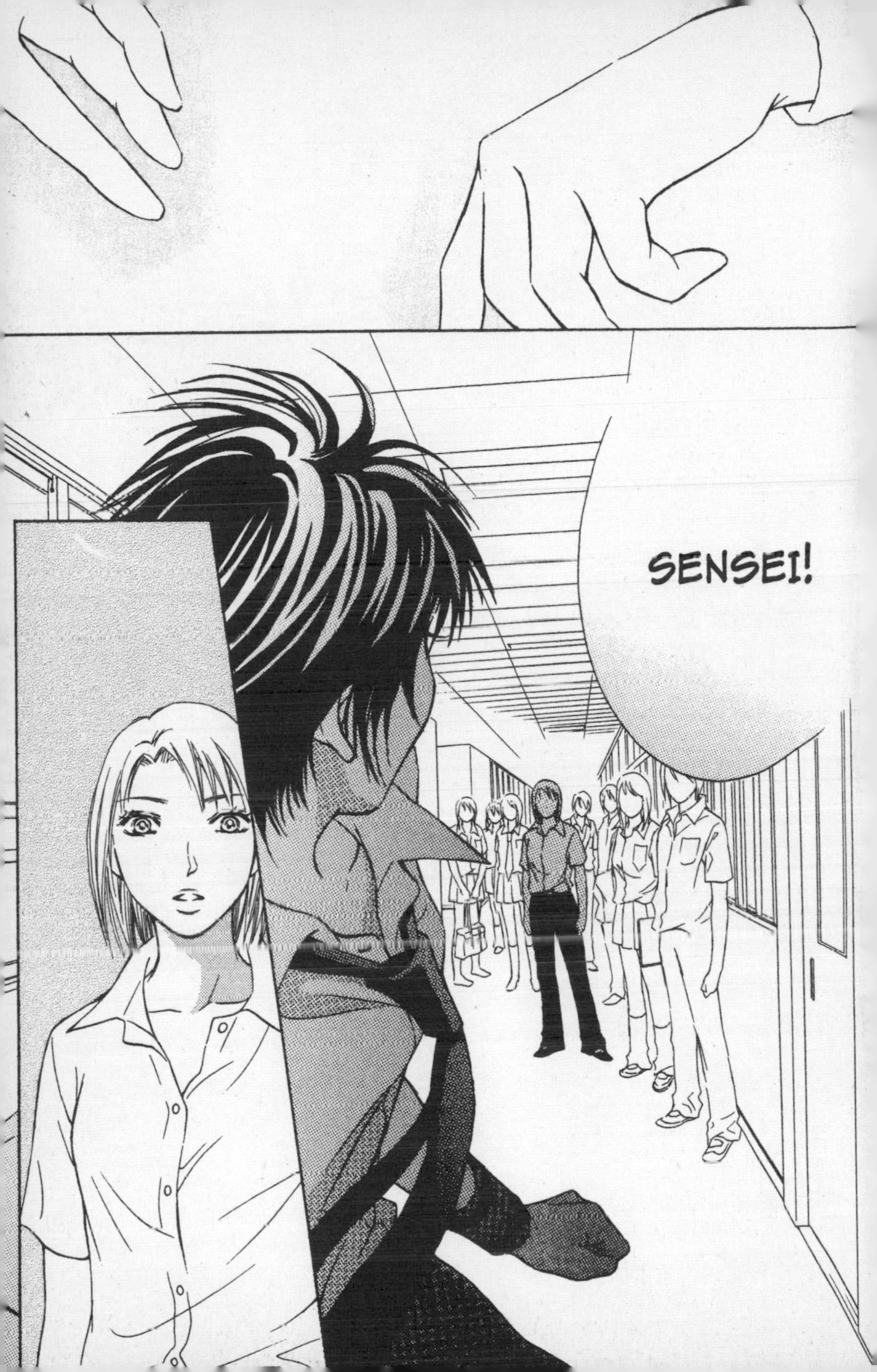
SENSEI!

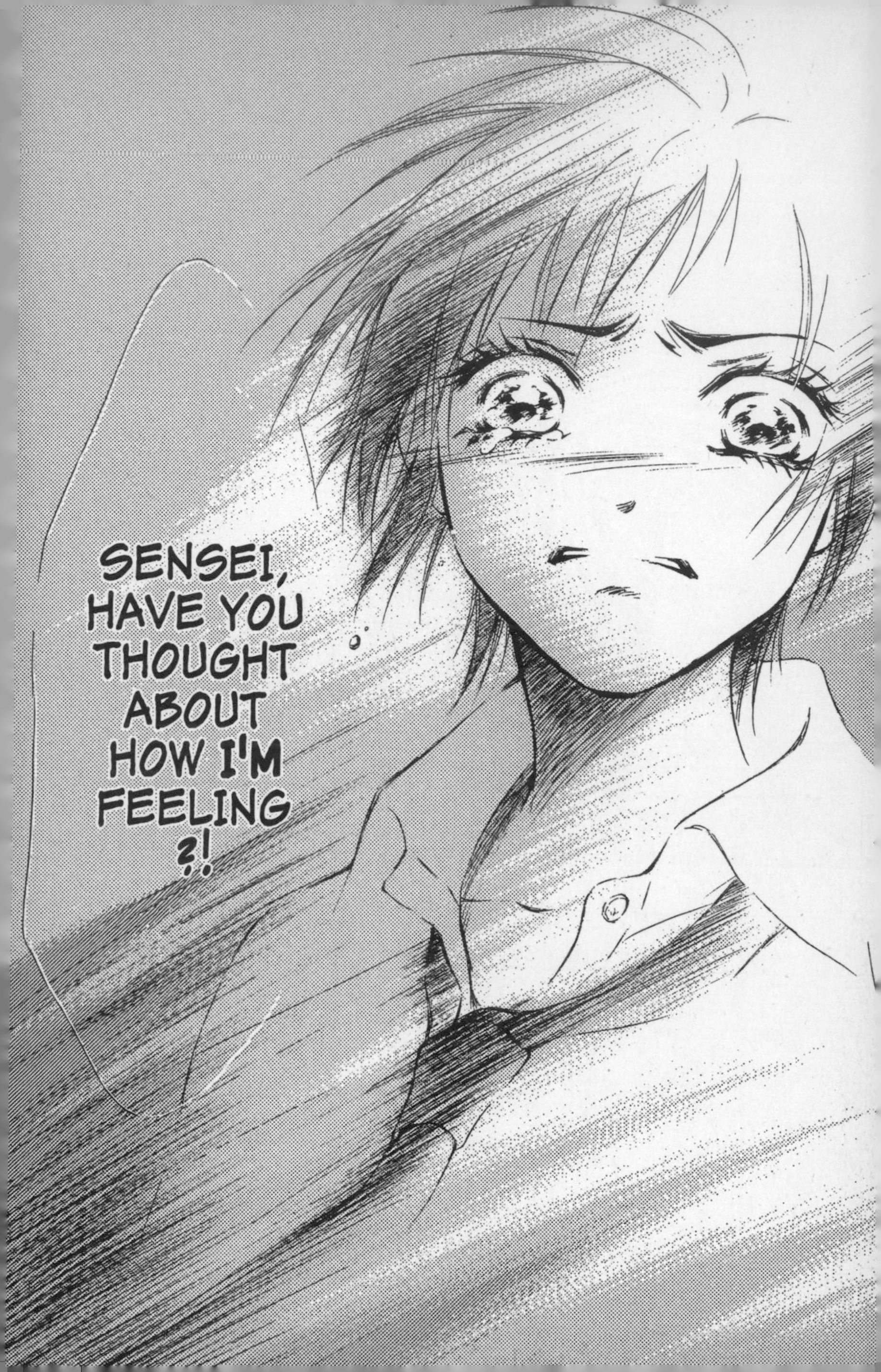
SENSEI, HAVE YOU THOUGHT ABOUT HOW I'M FEELING ?!

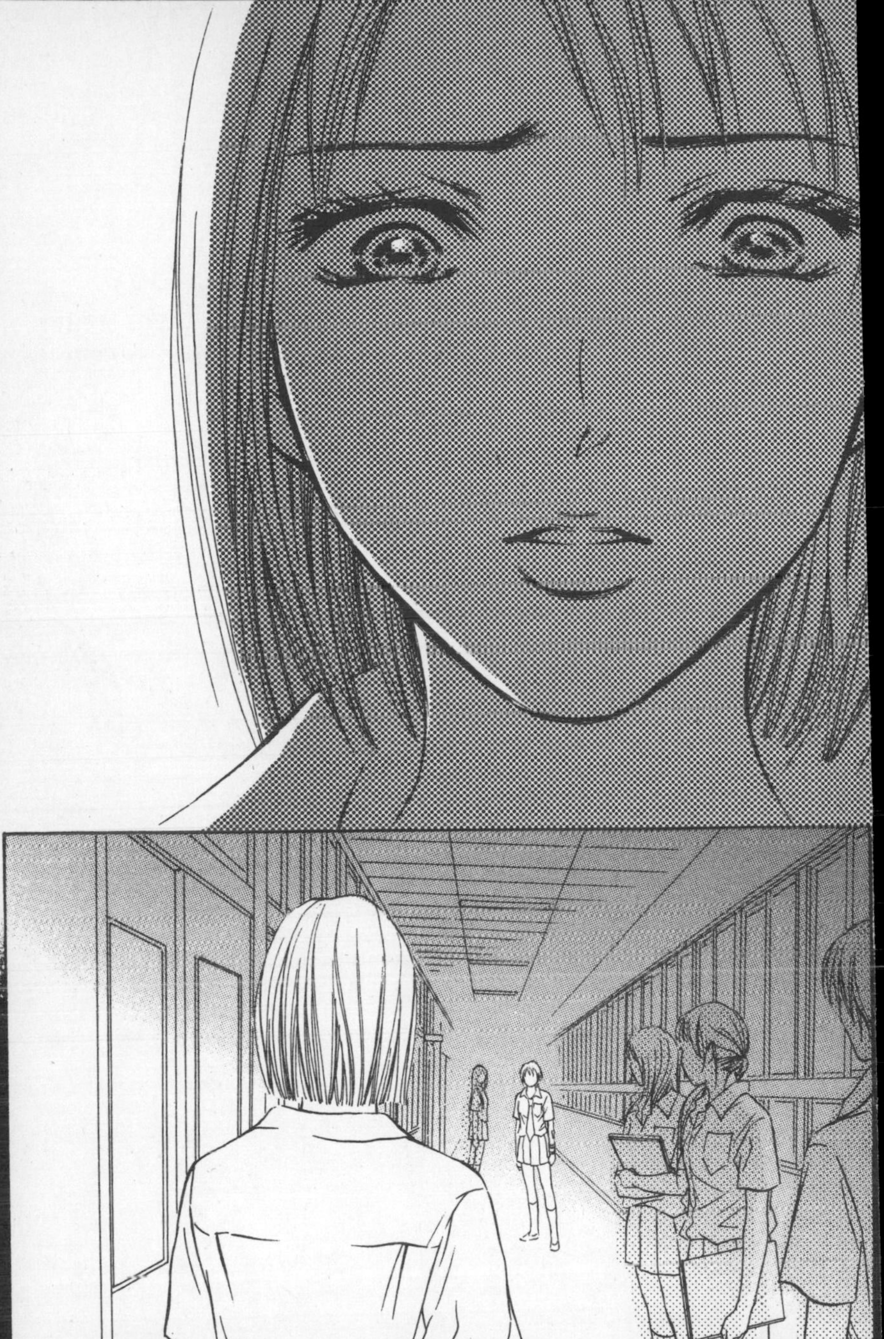

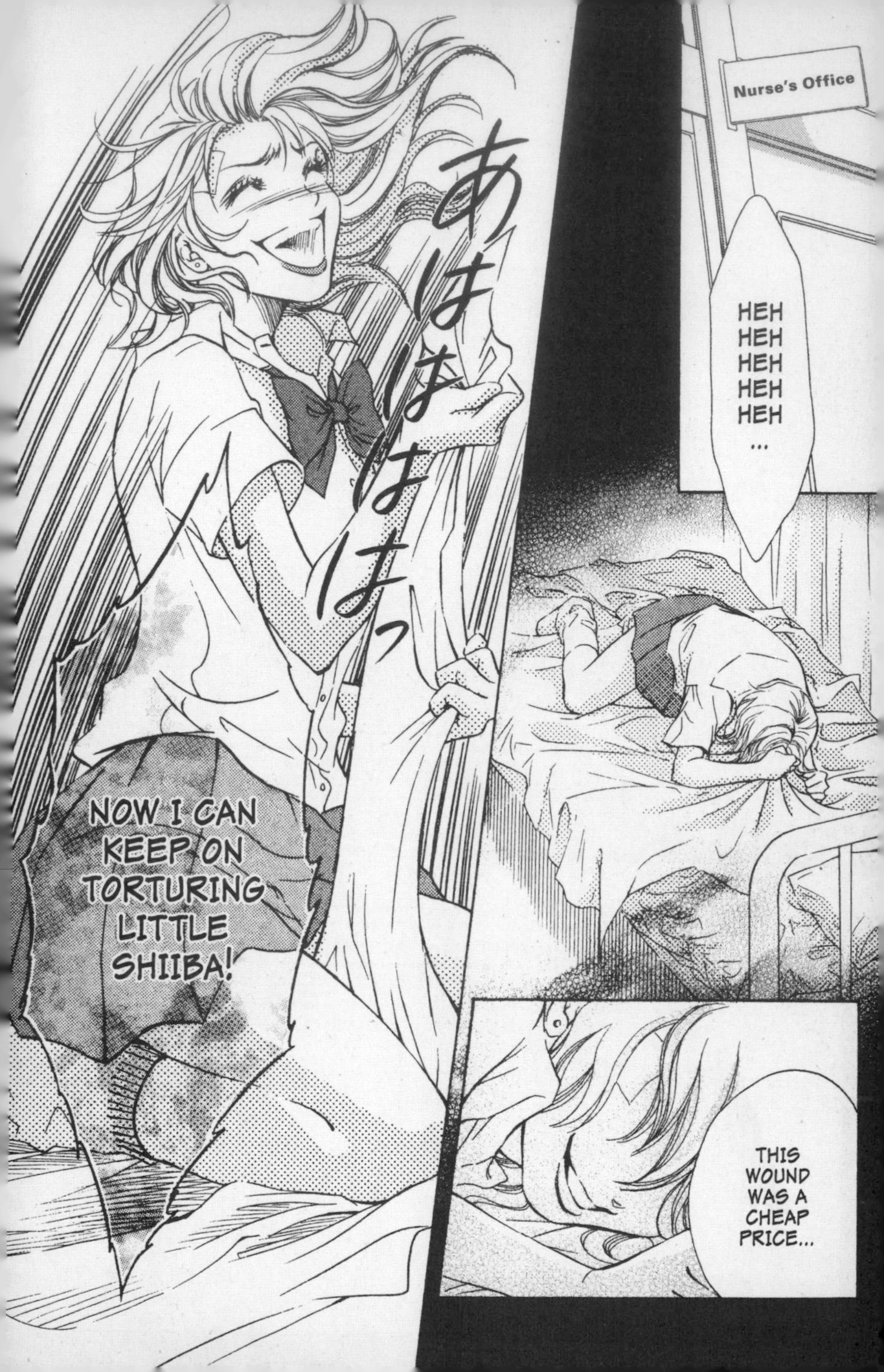
Nurse's Office
HEH HEH HEH HEH HEH ...
THIS WOUND WAS A CHEAP PRICE...
あははははっ
NOW I CAN KEEP ON TORTURING LITTLE SHIIBA!

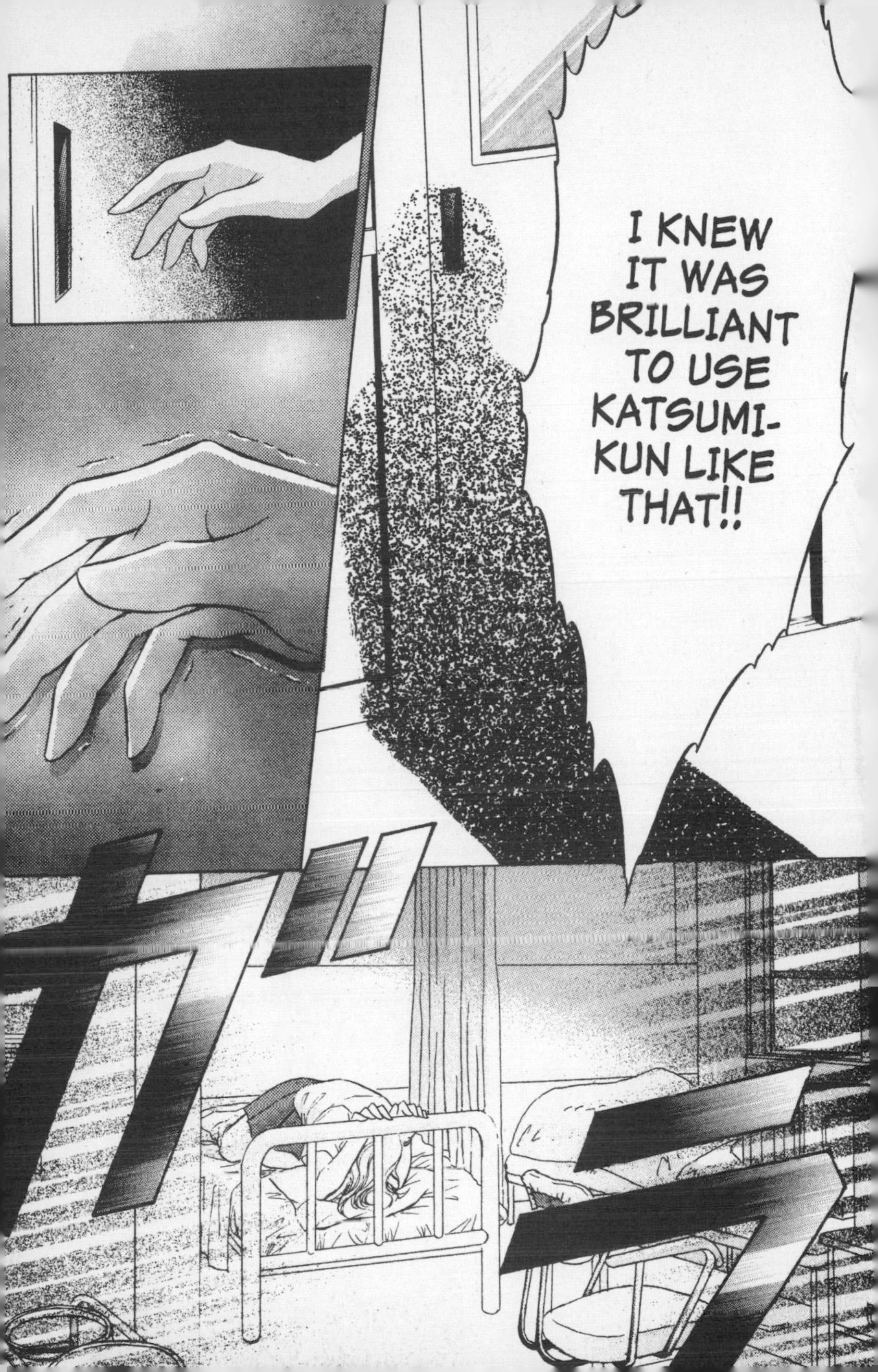
I KNEW IT WAS BRILLIANT TO USE KATSUMI-KUN LIKE THAT!!

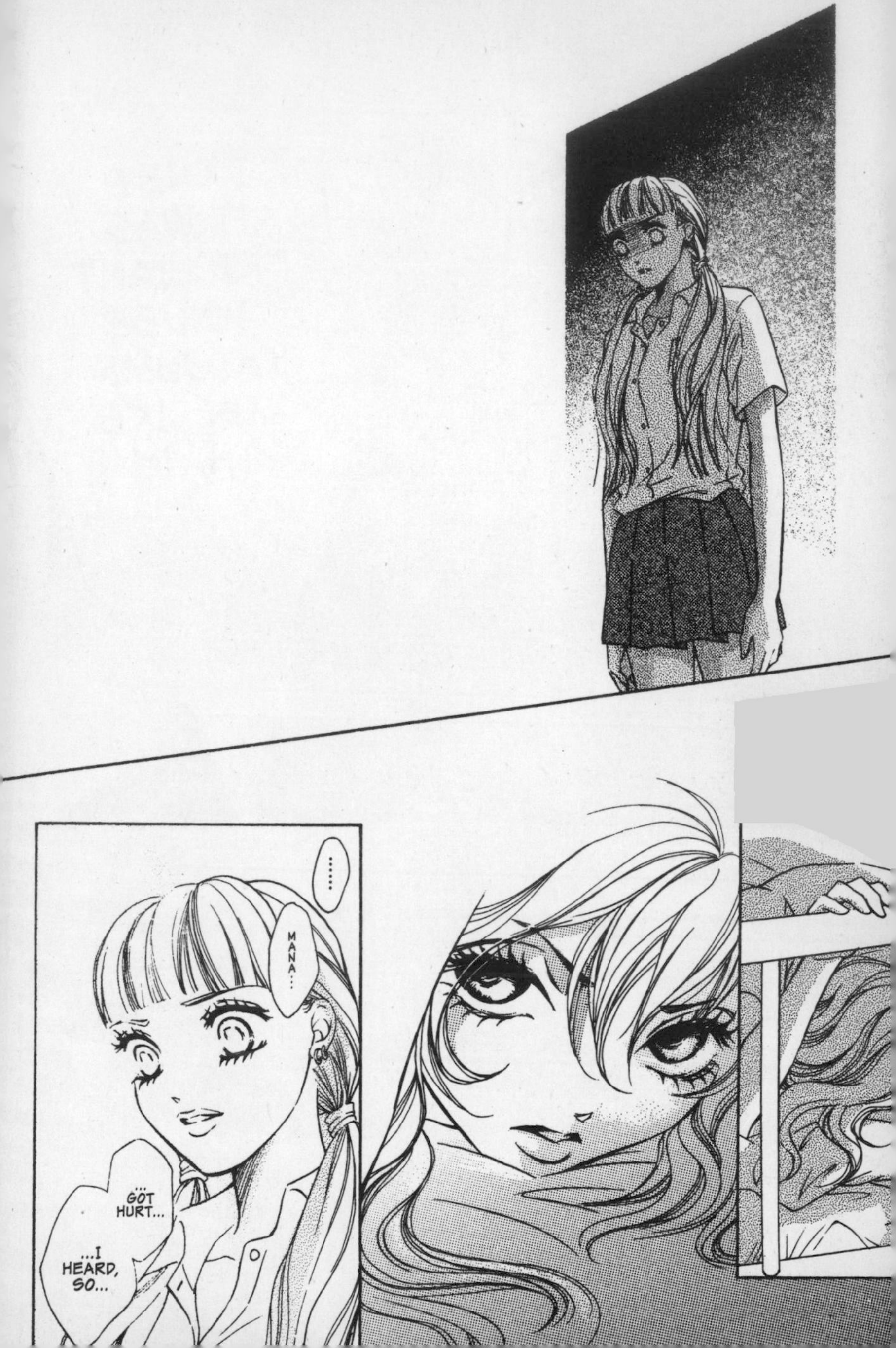
......
MANA...
...GOT HURT...
...I HEARD, SO...

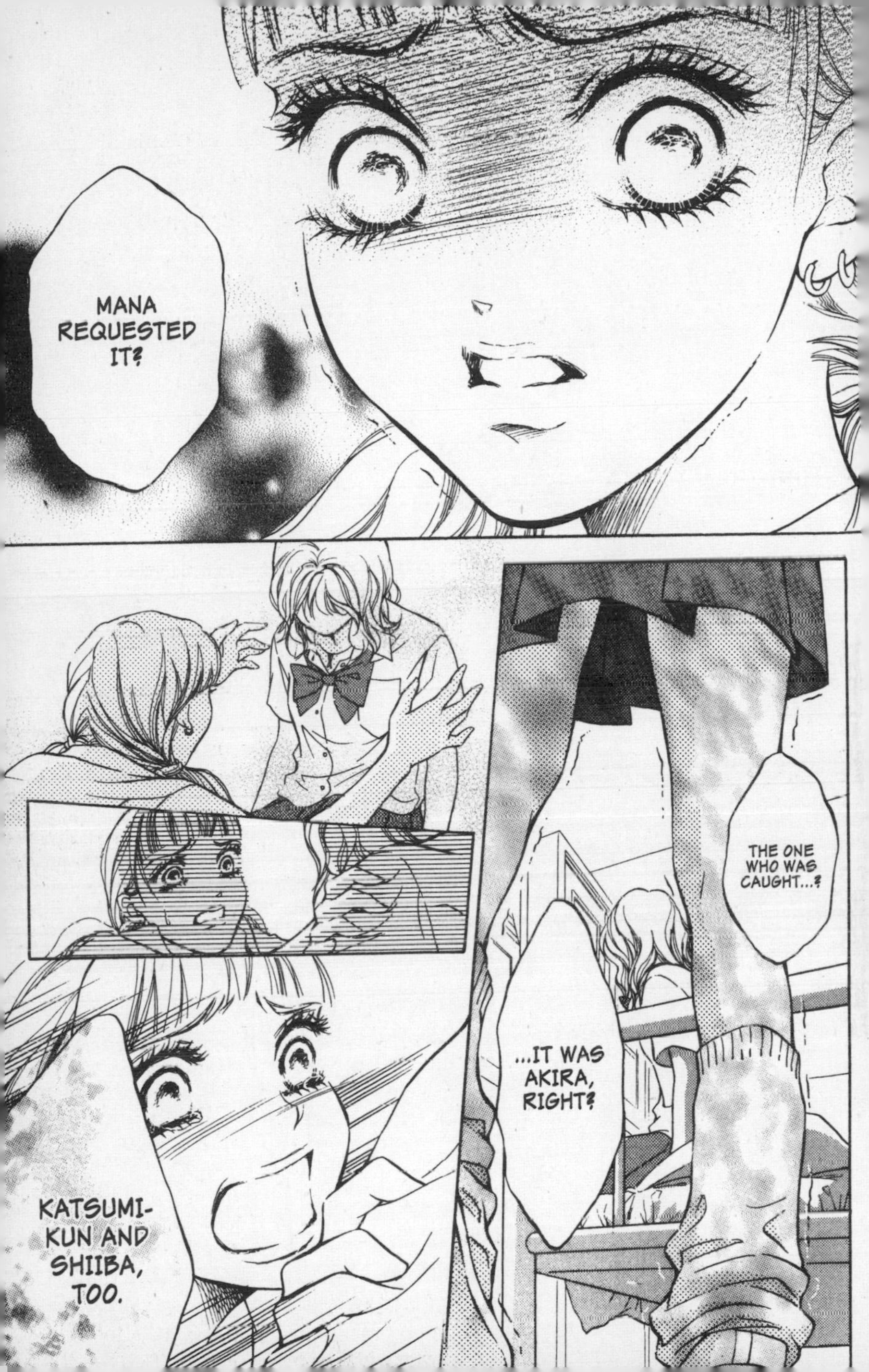
MANA REQUESTED IT?
THE ONE WHO WAS CAUGHT...?
...IT WAS AKIRA, RIGHT?
KATSUMI-KUN AND SHIIBA, TOO.

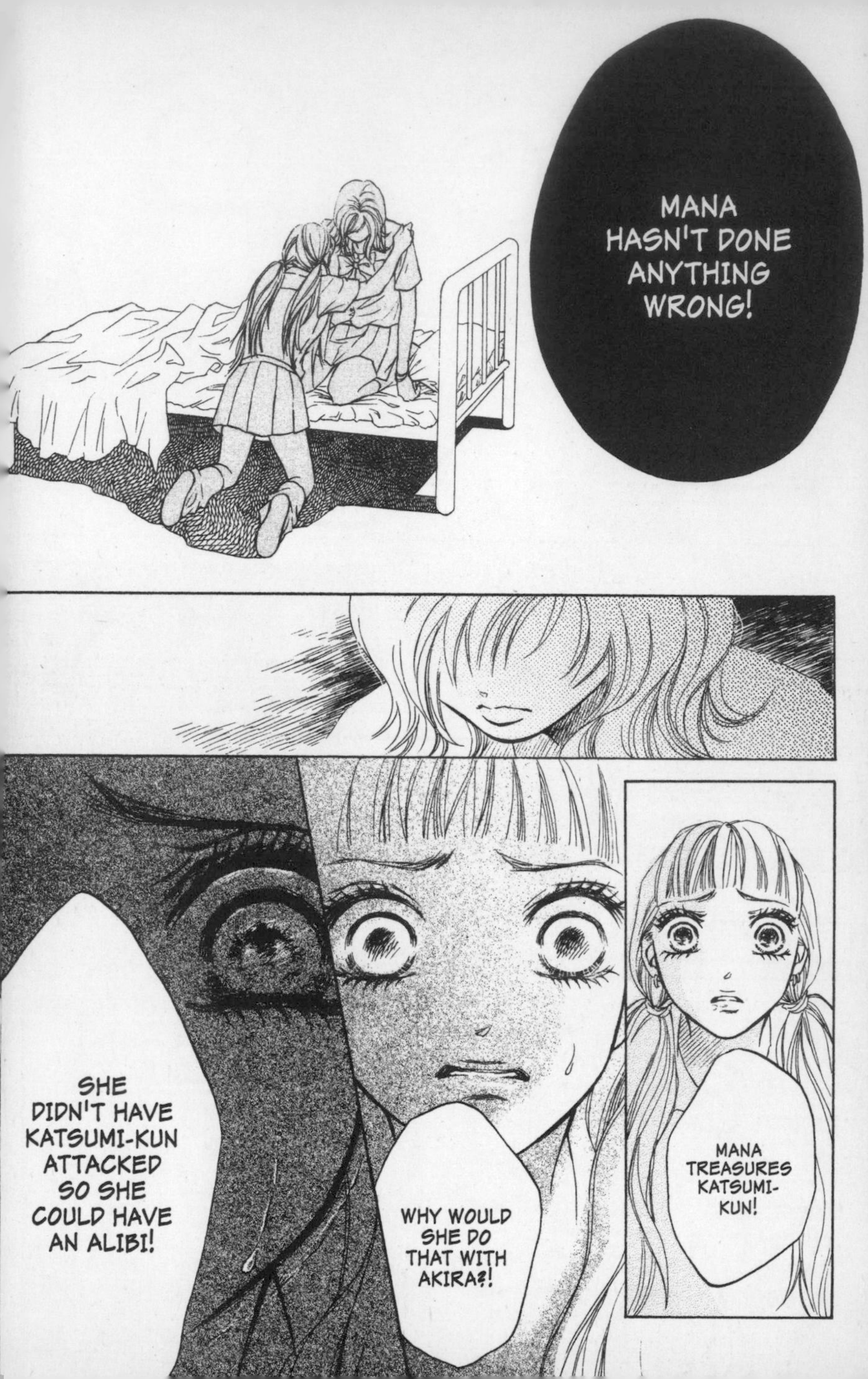
MANA HASN'T DONE ANYTHING WRONG!
MANA TREASURES KATSUMI-KUN!
WHY WOULD SHE DO THAT WITH AKIRA?!
SHE DIDN'T HAVE KATSUMI-KUN ATTACKED SO SHE COULD HAVE AN ALIBI!

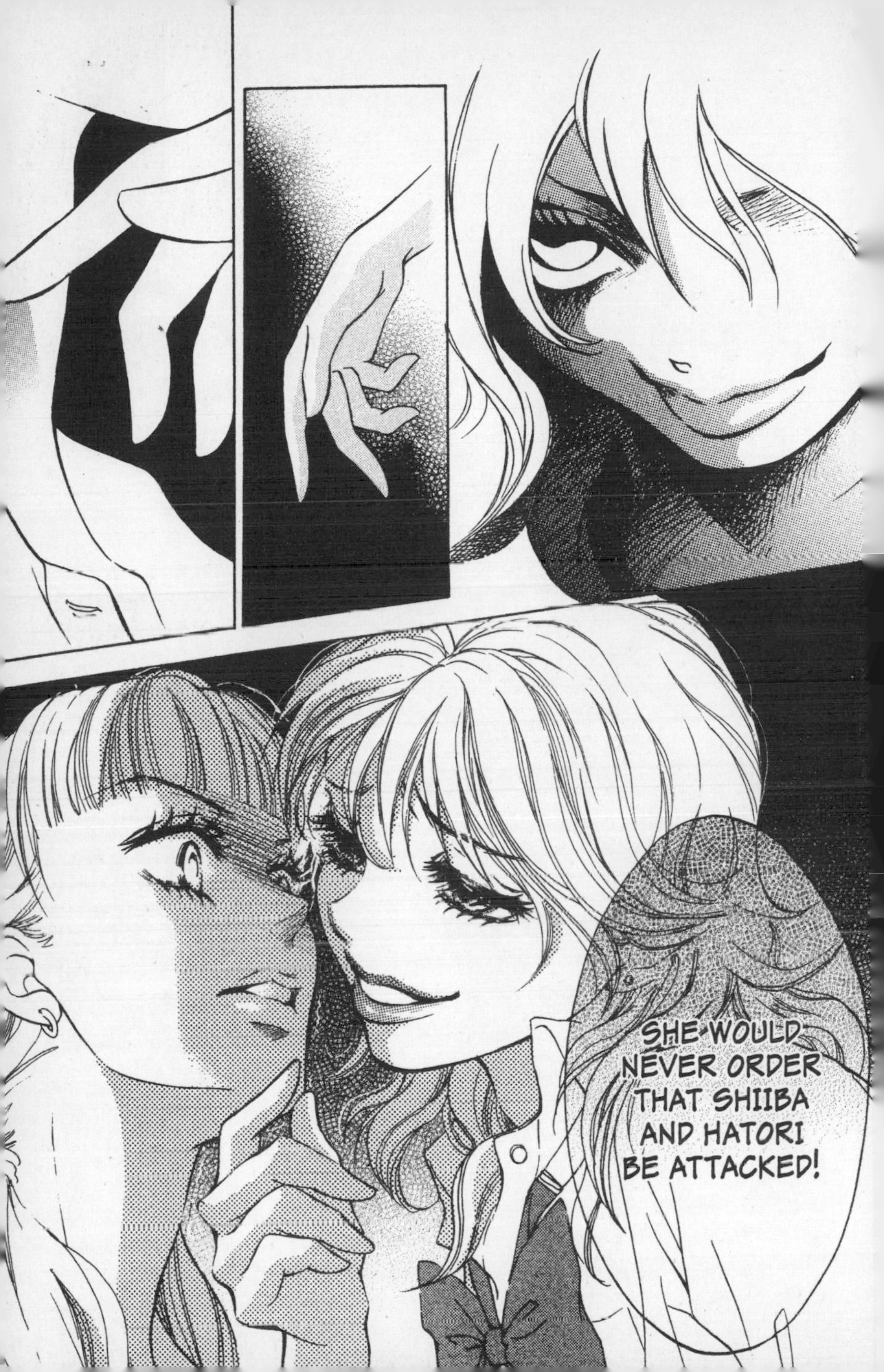
SHE WOULD NEVER ORDER THAT SHIIBA AND HATORI BE ATTACKED!

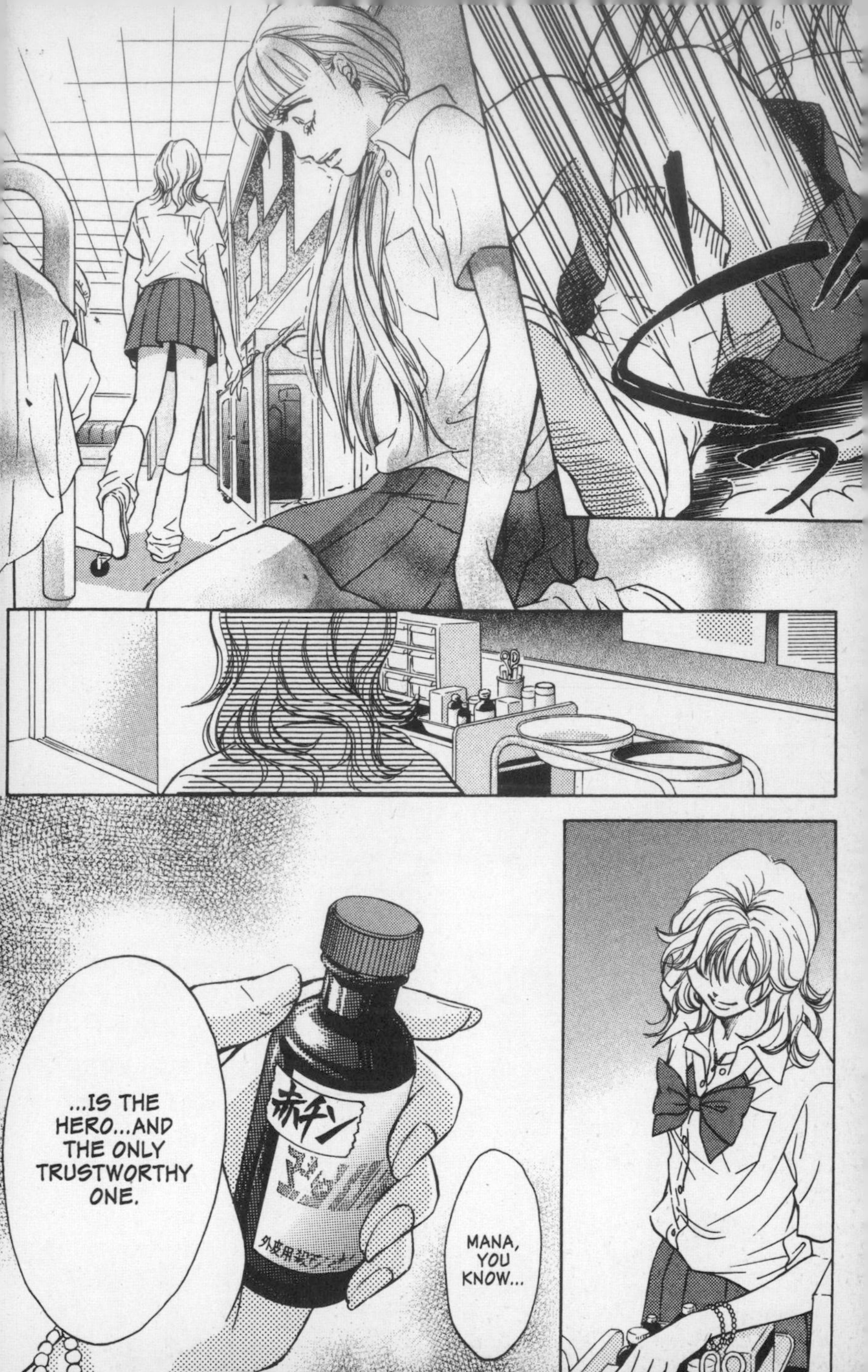
MANA, YOU KNOW...
...IS THE HERO...AND THE ONLY TRUSTWORTHY ONE.
赤チン

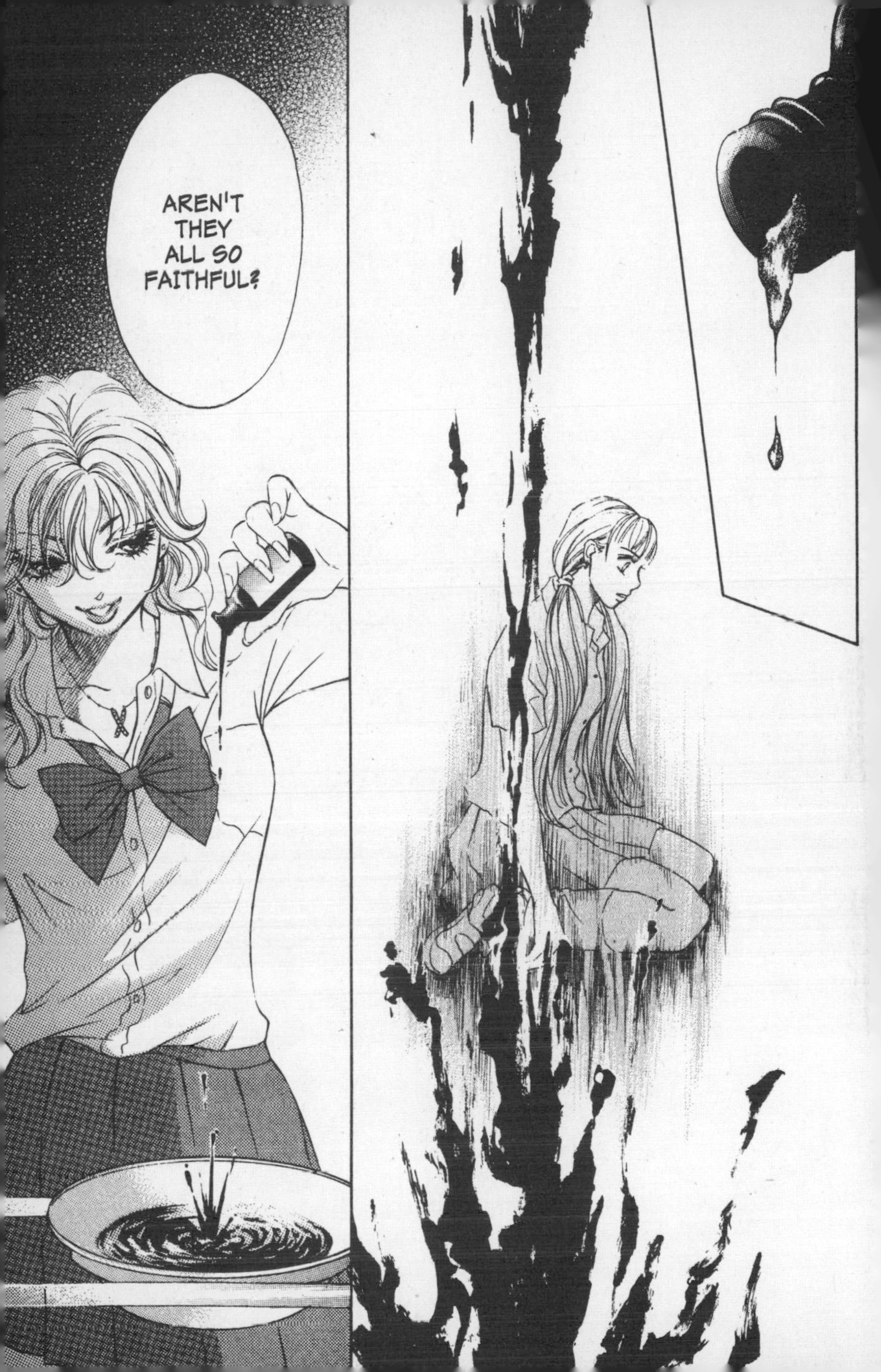
ARE'N'T THEY ALL SO FAITHFUL?

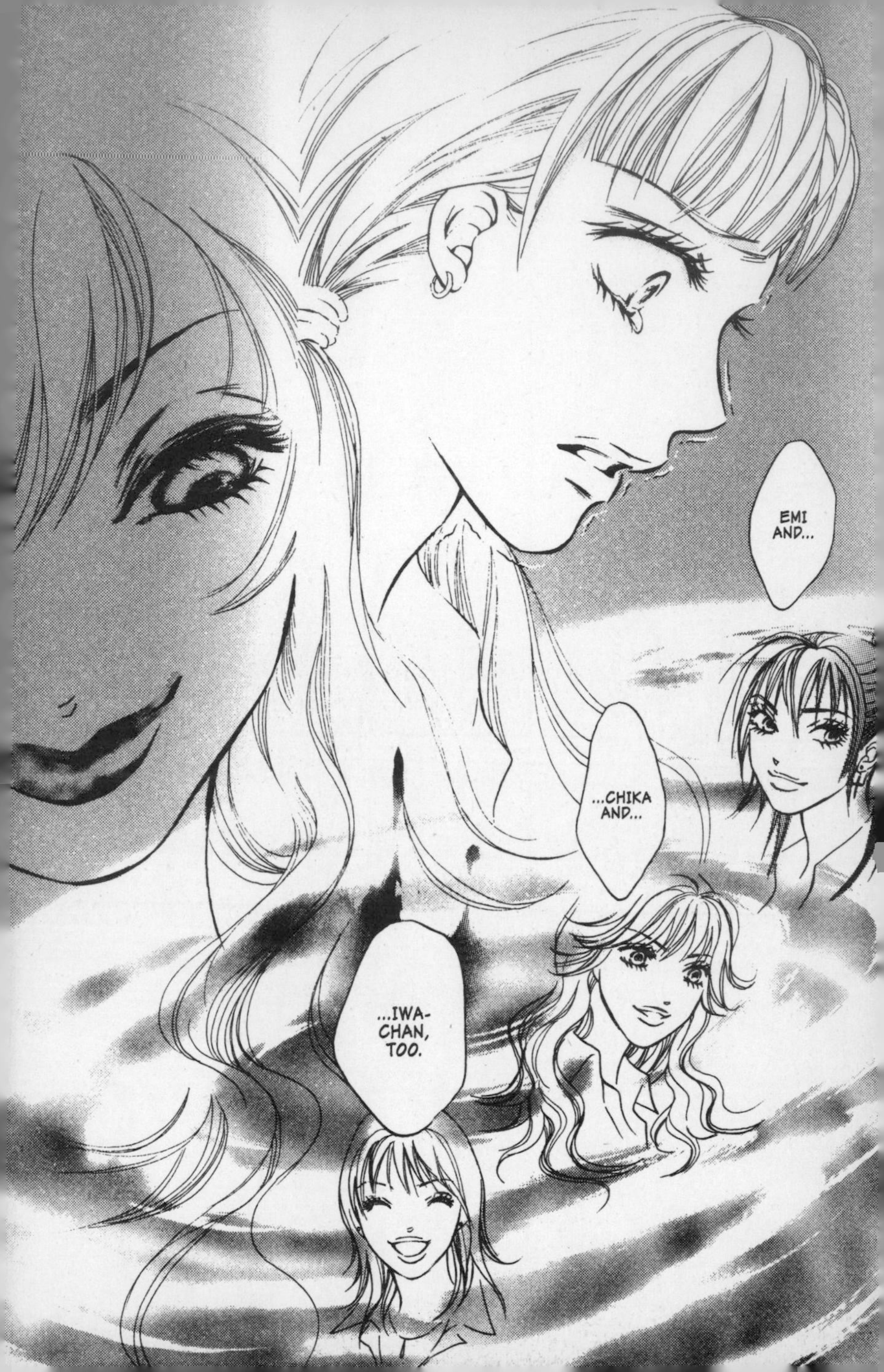
EMI AND...
...CHIKA AND...
...IWA-CHAN, TOO.

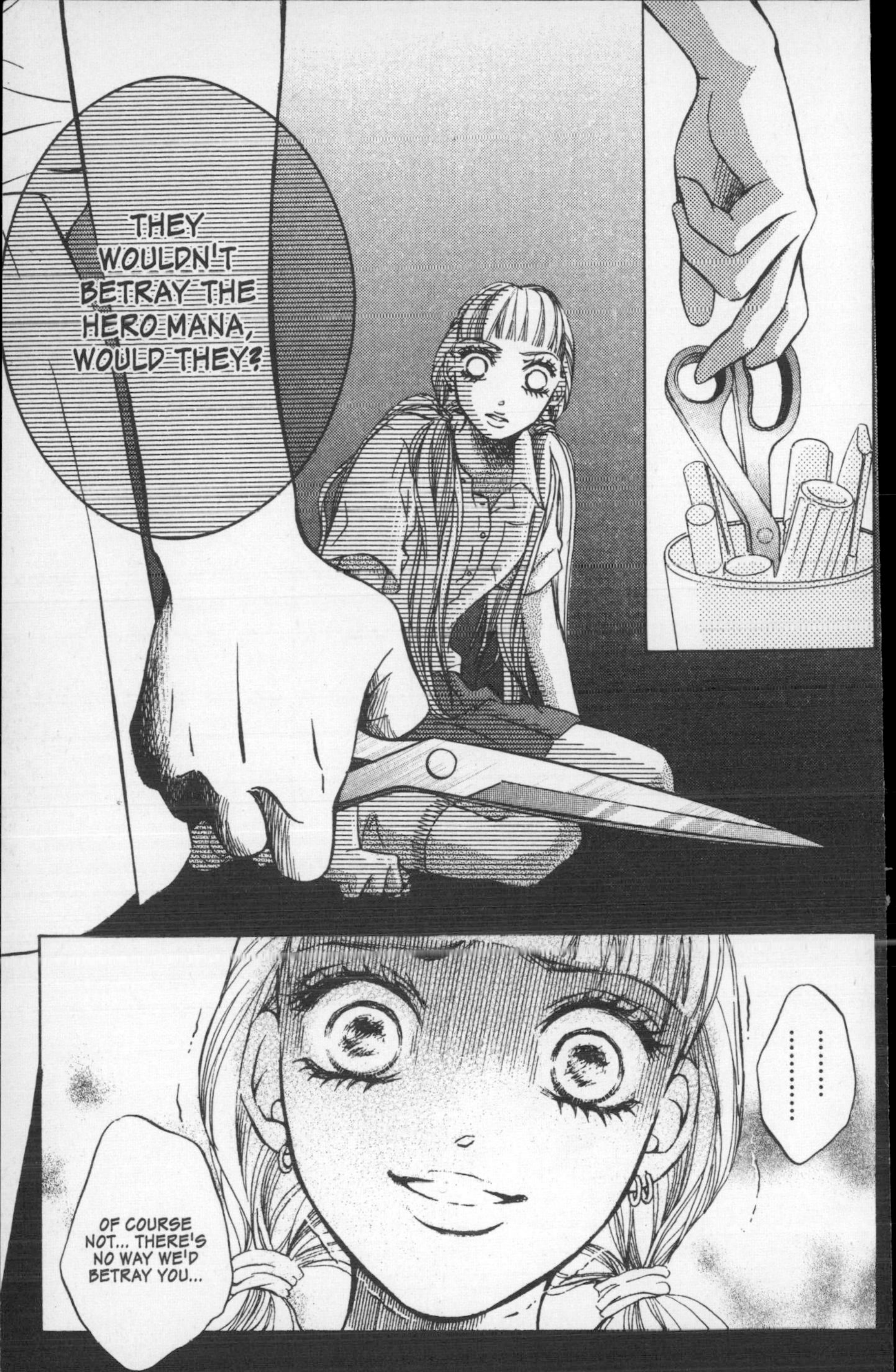
THEY WOULDN'T BETRAY THE HERO MANA, WOULD THEY?
......
OF COURSE NOT... THERE'S NO WAY WE'D BETRAY YOU...

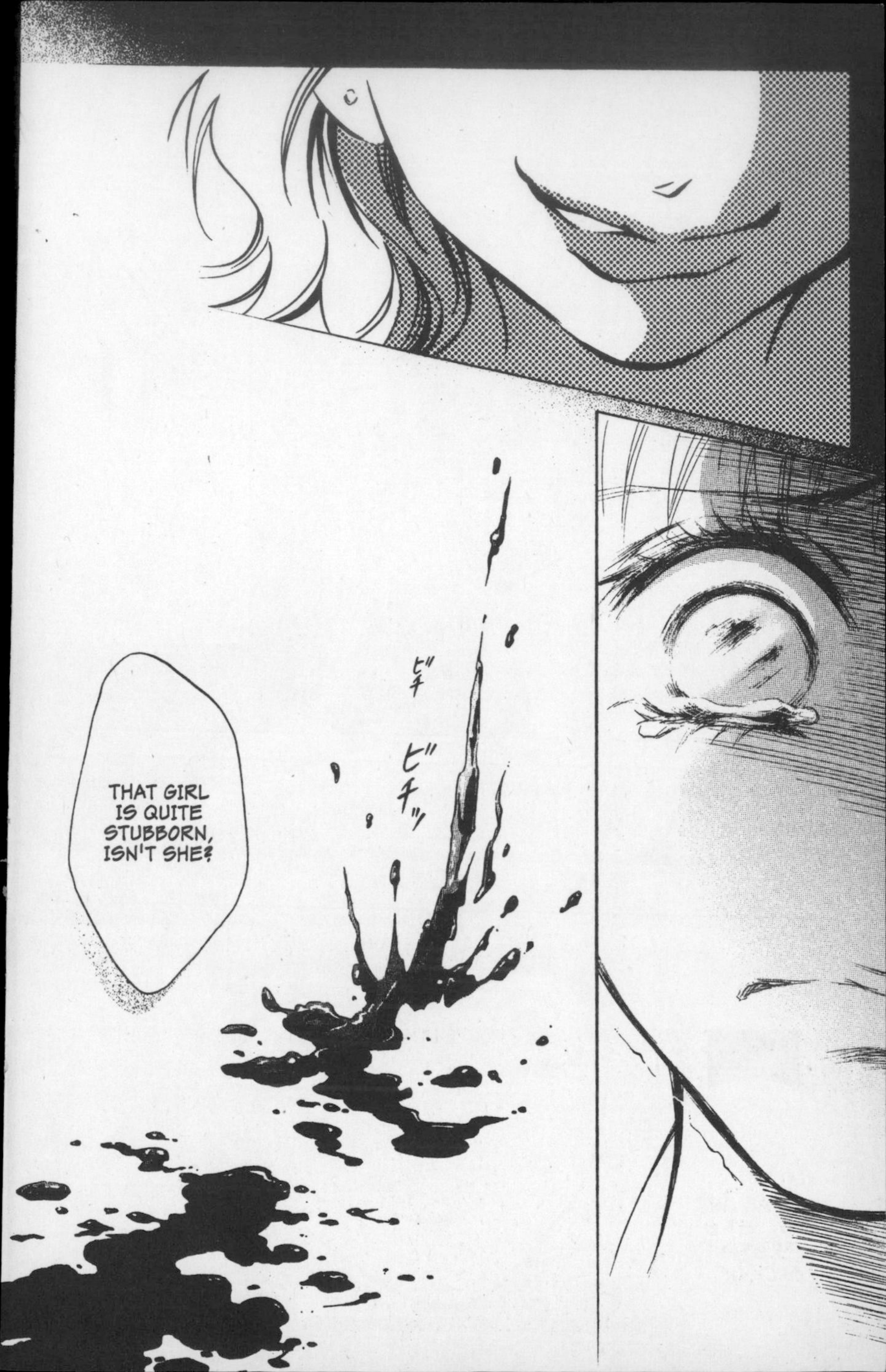
ビチ
ビチッ
THAT GIRL IS QUITE STUBBORN, ISN'T SHE?

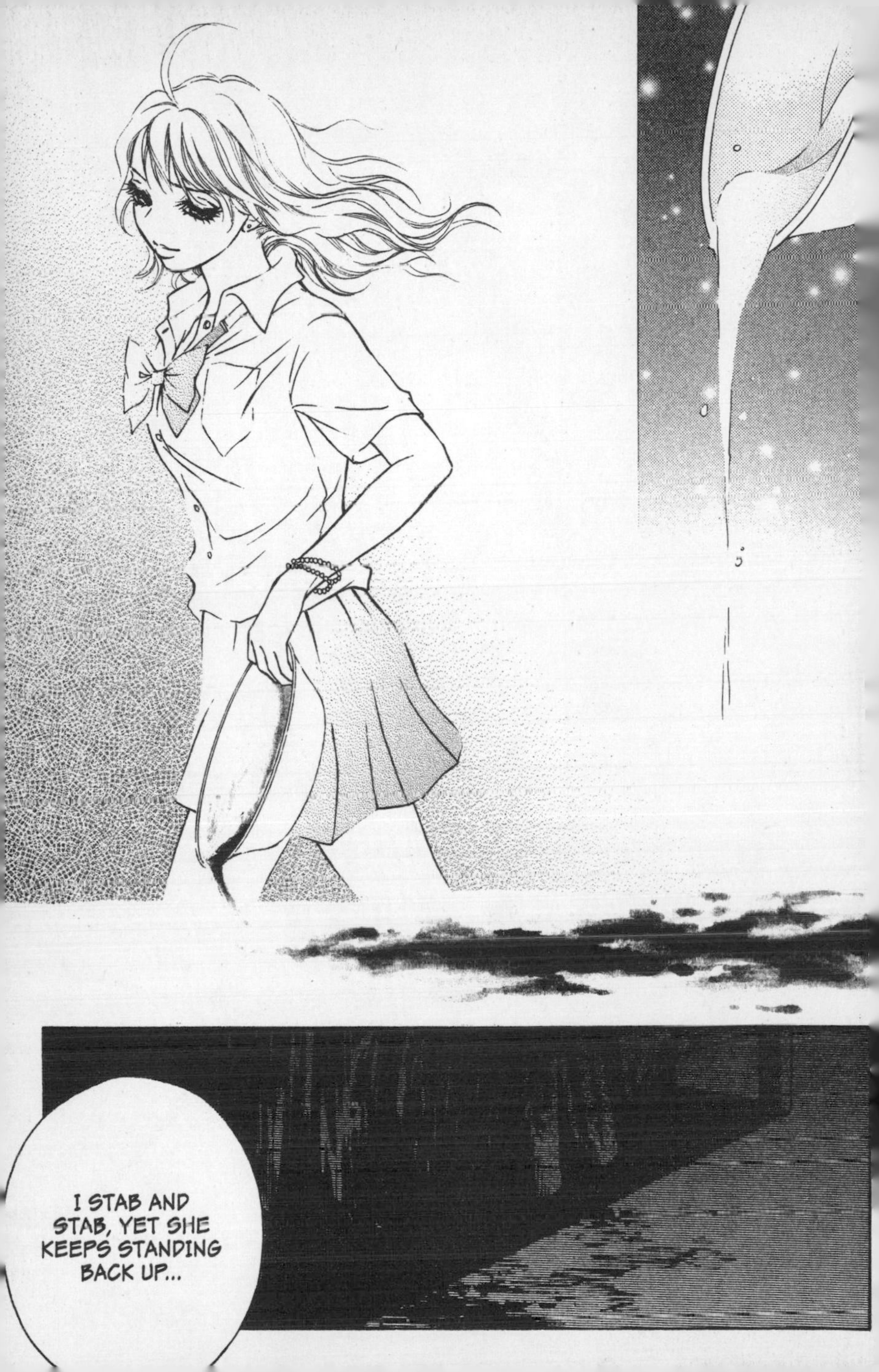
I STAB AND STAB, YET SHE KEEPS STANDING BACK UP...

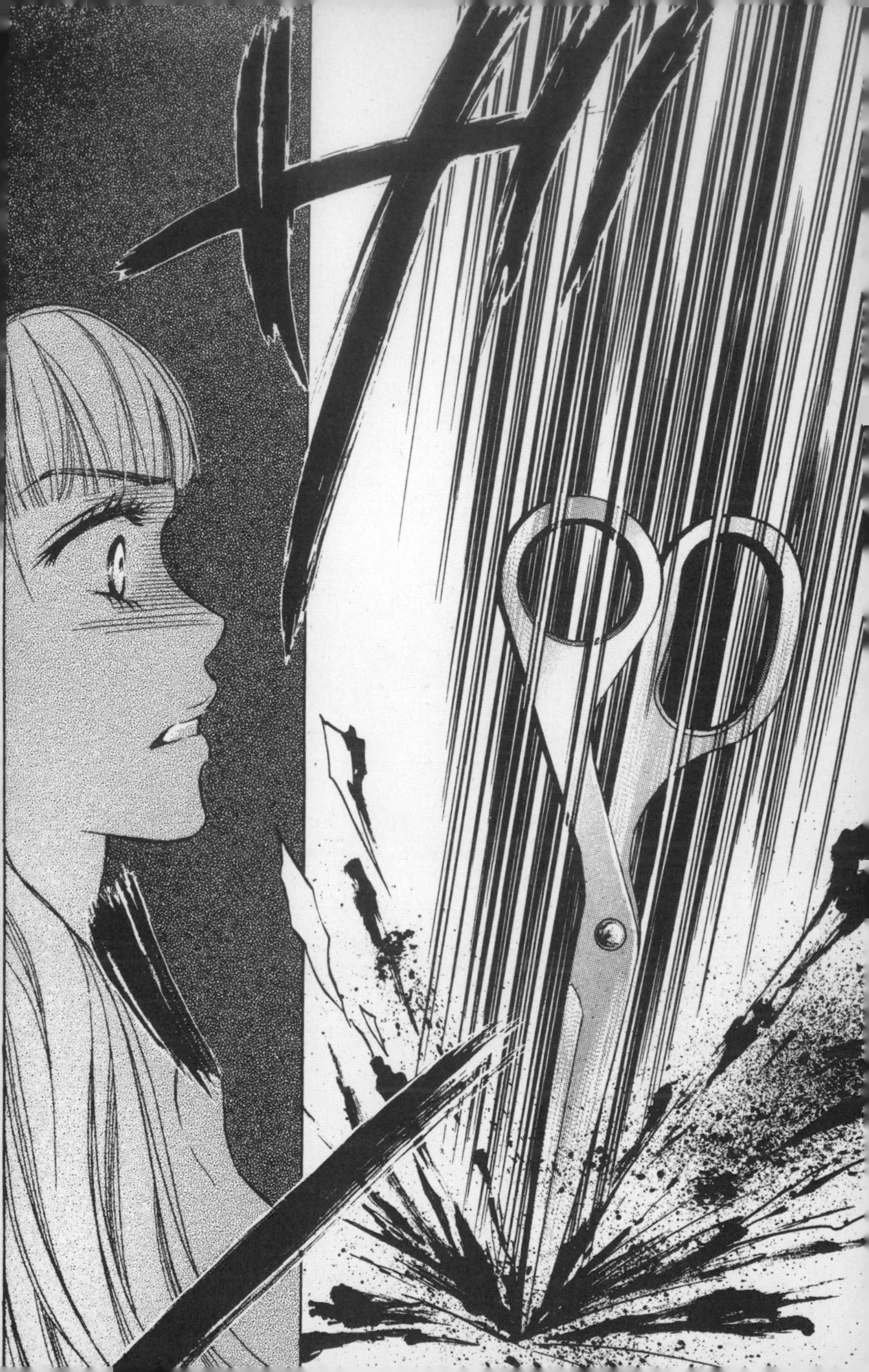

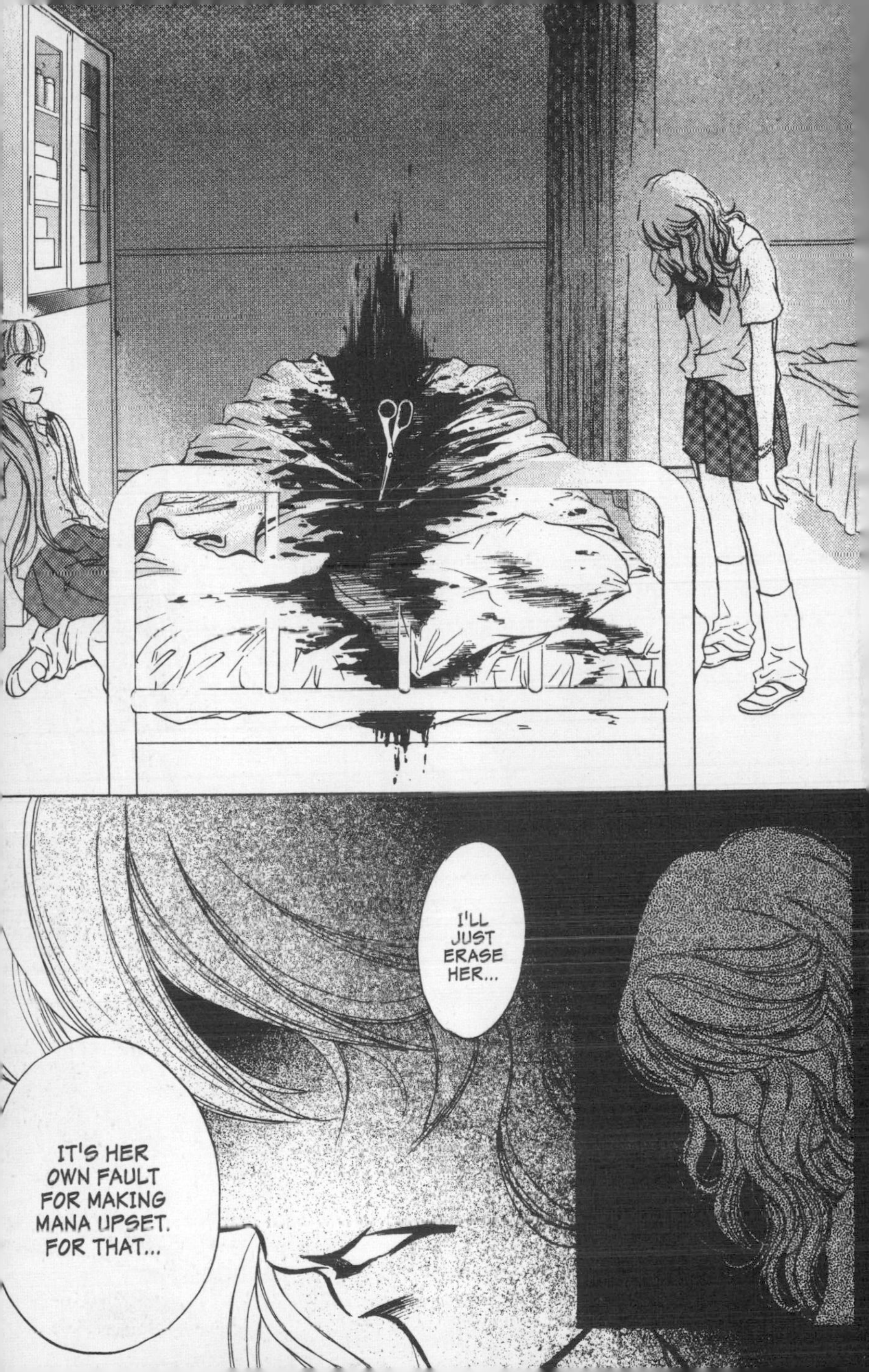
I'LL JUST ERASE HER...
IT'S HER OWN FAULT FOR MAKING MANA UPSET. FOR THAT...

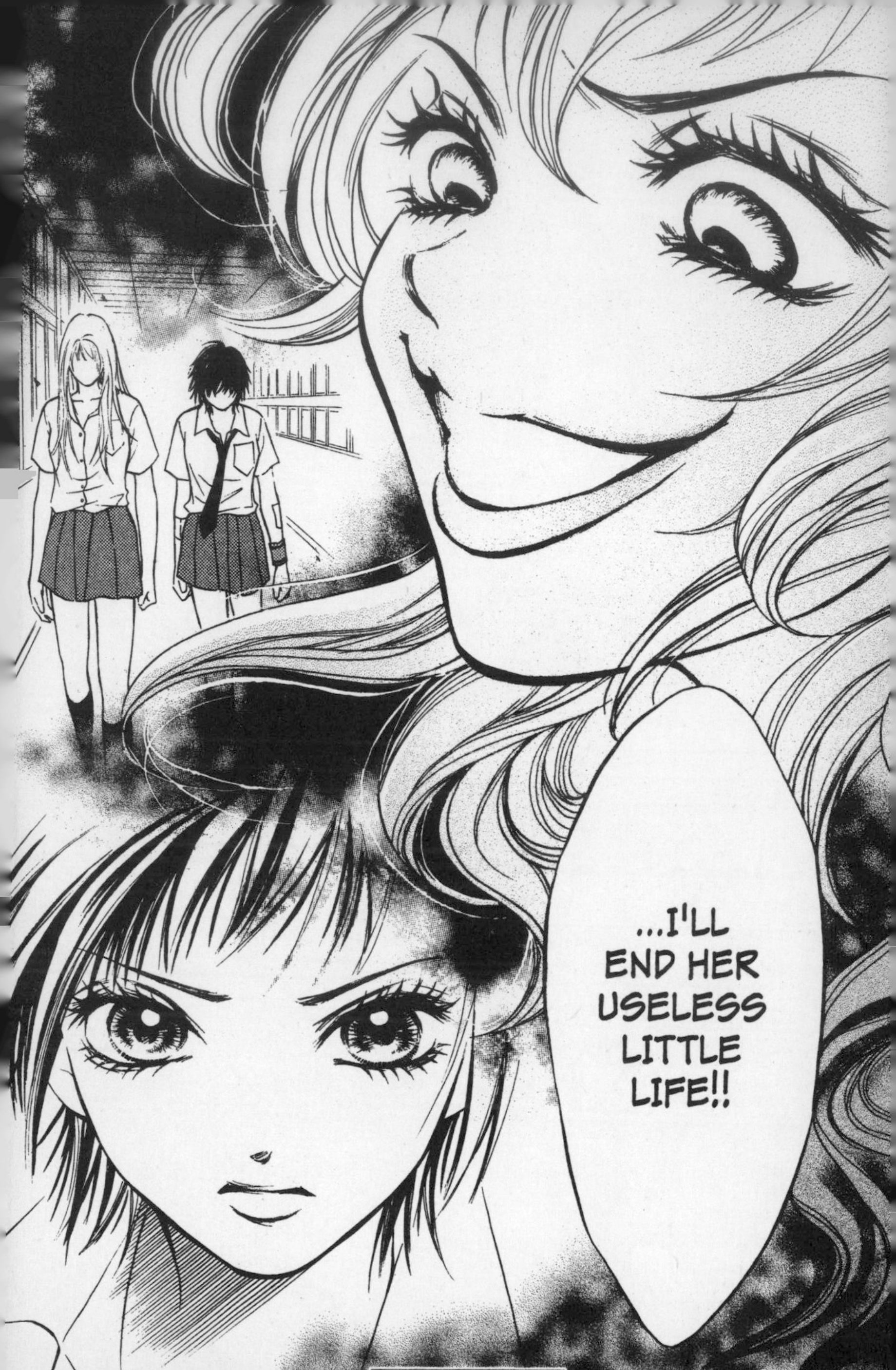
...I'LL END HER USELESS LITTLE LIFE!!

Continued in Life 10

What does LIFE have in store...

Manami's father, a president of a huge company, arrives at the school, the staff is put between a rock and a hard place. And when Ayumu finally admits to what has been going on behind their backs, they are forced to deal with an even more awkward situation...

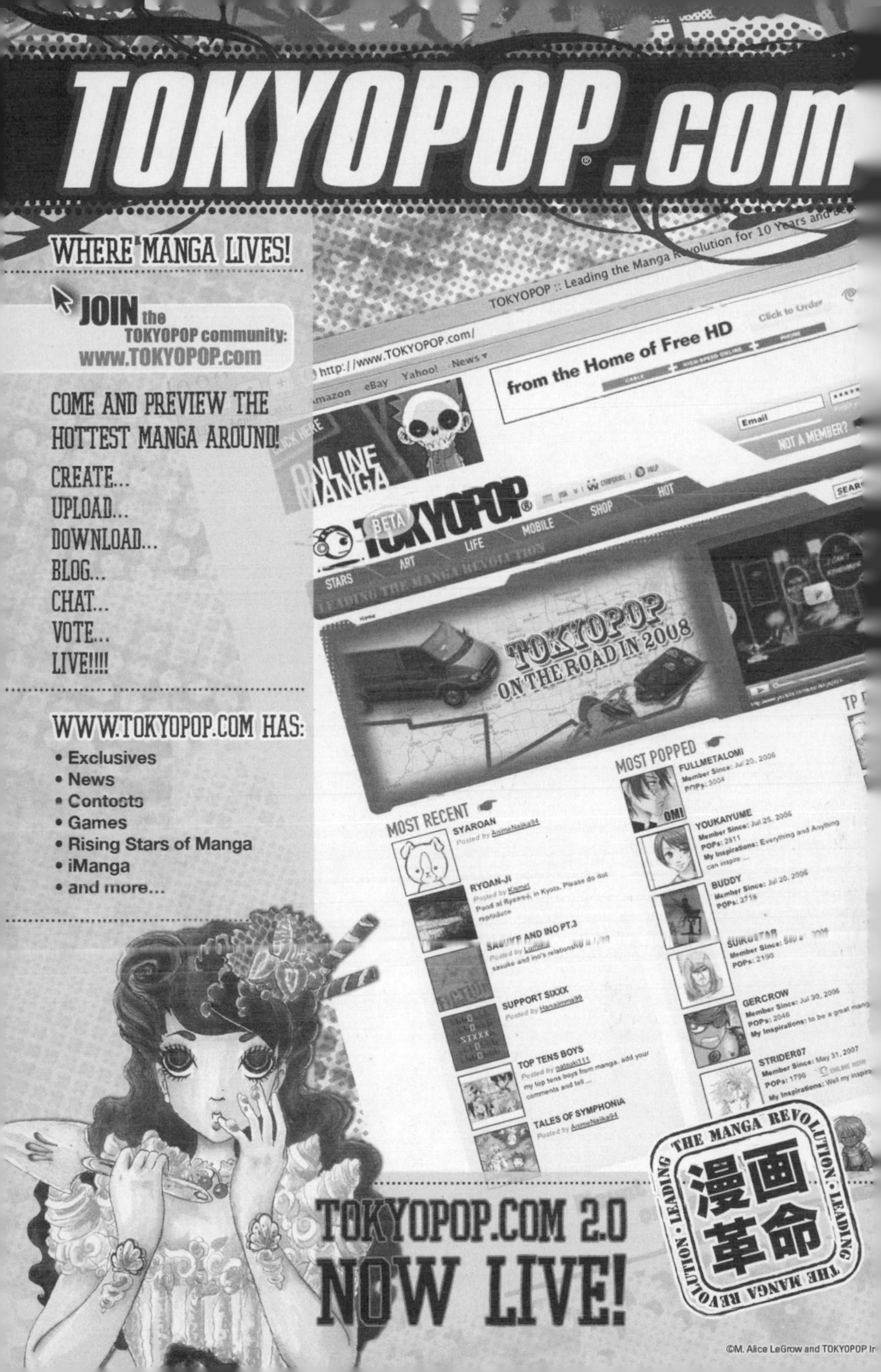
TOKYOPOP.com
WHERE MANGA LIVES!
JOIN the TOKYOPOP community: www.TOKYOPOP.com
COME AND PREVIEW THE HOTTEST MANGA AROUND!
CREATE...
UPLOAD...
DOWNLOAD...
BLOG...
CHAT...
VOTE...
LIVE!!!!
WWW.TOKYOPOP.COM HAS:
• Exclusives
• News
• Contests
• Games
• Rising Stars of Manga
• iManga
• and more...
TOKYOPOP :: Leading the Manga Revolution for 10 Years and Be
http://www.TOKYOPOP.com/
from the Home of Free HD
ONLINE MANGA
TOKYOPOP ON THE ROAD IN 2008
MOST RECENT
MOST POPPED
THE MANGA REVOLUTION · LEADING
漫画革命
TOKYOPOP.COM 2.0
NOW LIVE!
©M. Alice LeGrow and TOKYOPOP In

STOP!

This is the back of the book.
You wouldn't want to spoil a great ending!

This book is printed "manga-style," in the authentic Japanese right-to-left format. Since none of the artwork has been flipped or altered, readers get to experience the story just as the creator intended. You've been asking for it, so TOKYOPOP® delivered: authentic, hot-off-the-press, and far more fun!

DIRECTIONS

If this is your first time reading manga-style, here's a quick guide to help you understand how it works.

It's easy... just start in the top right panel and follow the numbers. Have fun, and look for more 100% authentic manga from TOKYOPOP®!